The MILITARY EXPERIENCE
in the AGE of REASON
1715-1789

The MILITARY EXPERIENCE
in the AGE OF REASON
1715-1789

CHRISTOPHER DUFFY

BARNES
&NOBLE
BOOKS
NEW YORK

1997 Barnes & Noble Books

ISBN 0-7607-0441-4

Printed and bound in the United States of America

97 98 99 00 01 M 9 8 7 6 5 4 3 2 1

QF

Contents

Preface

Anybody who has a serious interest in history must have asked himself whether his experiences in his own time offer him a direct insight into the life which people led in the past. Is it, in fact, really true that the distance is so great that 'the past is another country'?

The present book applies this question to the military world of the eighteenth century. Although it is a period which has long exercised a fascination for me, I have become increasingly conscious of some formidable obstacles in the way of our understanding of what went on in the powdered and bewigged heads of those old-time soldiers. I believe that we must look for something more penetrating and analytical than yet another study of kings and battles, a compendium of eyewitness accounts, or a book with a title like *Daily Life in George Washington's Army*.

Nothing could be more tedious than to impose a mechanical formula on historical writing, but I have borne three considerations constantly in mind throughout the study: first, what was it about the eighteenth-century military profession that was peculiar to individual nations? Second, what was common to the military experience in all times? Third, what, by process of elimination, was characteristic of eighteenth-century armies in general?

The source material must be approached with great caution. Often, when we think we are moving over firm ground, it sinks beneath our feet. When countries like Prussia and Russia resorted to conscription, it was not to summon up the resources of the nation, as in the Napoleonic period, but to limit and control the demands which the army made on the useful and hardworking civilian population. Again in 1759 Dr Carl Friedrich Pauli sent forth what sounds at first hearing like a nationalistic clarion call, demanding recognition for genuine German military heroes. His understanding of 'German' must represent something very different from ours, for we note that his pantheon contains Maximilian Ulysses Browne, who hailed from County Limerick, and Octavio Piccolomini, the son of a line of Sienese *condottieri*.

When, finally, we take the books or documents in our hands, we have to bear in mind that we are dealing with the testimony of survivors, and survivors who for the most part presented experiences in a way that was acceptable to themselves and posterity. Ulrich Bräker is one of the few soldiers who writes frankly about having deserted, just as Garrett Watts of the North Carolina Militia appears to be the one individual who owns up to having fled in action, and yet we know in a general way that desertion and flight were at least as common in the eighteenth century as in other periods of history.

Such contamination of the sources does not necessarily originate in anything as simple as lying. On this point the German general Verdy du Vernois wrote about his campaign in 1866 thirty years after the event:

> One must not forget that in the course of the years we tend to confuse the explanations and accounts we receive from other parties with the recollection of our own impressions at the time. We come to believe that we have thought, or even experienced such and such a thing, when it actually became lodged in our minds by some other means, and perhaps in a totally misleading way.

Another characteristic failing of the tribe of military historians is that we are inclined to jump from one 'famous name' to another, and parade extracts from the writings of great men without due regard for the context. The *Rêveries* of Maurice de Saxe were dashed off in the course of thirteen sleepless nights in 1732, in other words long before the marshal's fulminating campaigns in the Netherlands in the 1740s, and they no more represent a considered military testament than do the *Principes Généraux* (1748) of Frederick the Great, which were composed well before the Seven Years War. We can retrieve the military thought of Saxe, Frederick and the rest only by the laborious business of retracing their campaigns (a deeply unfashionable exercise among practitioners of the New Military History), and by reading correspondence and other forms of evidence that were totally unknown to most of their contemporaries.

French authors are plentiful, but when they are not dogmatic or geometrical in tone they tend toward the self-centred and the bombastic. Russian accounts are the most vivid, and they speak the most directly from the heart without respect to conventions. The Prussian writers are the most reflective, and their ranks embrace individuals like the hussar officer Lojewsky, to whom we owe unique insights into mounted combat, or the *Feldprediger* Carl Daniel Küster, who posed the kind of questions which military psychologists like to ask today. The Spaniards as a whole have the least to say, but they are redeemed by the singularly informative tomes of the Marqués de Santa Cruz.

We accompany our warriors on some sea voyages (see pp. 157–9), but we otherwise stay rooted on *terra firma*. Much information on naval life in this period will be found in Rodger, N. A. (1986), *The Wooden World. An Anatomy of the Georgian Navy*, London. I owe a great deal to years of association with Paddy Griffith, Richard Holmes and John Keegan, who have striven to show that the details of the military experience are worth taking seriously, and whose work commands respect well beyond the shores of the United Kingdom. Dr Jeremy Black has kindly supplied me with manuscript material relating to the period of the War of the Polish Succession. My final salute is to the officers and men of the eighteenth century, who have proved to be such entertaining companions, and have given us, on balance, much more to like and esteem than to condemn.

Part I

The armies of the Enlightenment

1

Military Europe

The character and importance of the eighteenth century

The time has long passed since it was fashionable to dismiss the eighteenth century as a decorative interval, suspended between the glooms and dooms of the Wars of Religion and the grinding industrialisation of the nineteenth century. Just as the works of Haydn and Mozart now make up part of 'our' music, so their contemporaries among the statesmen and soldiers addressed themselves to questions of major historical import. It still matters today that Russia secured the domination of eastern Europe, that Prussia became the most vital power in Germany, and that the Americans wrested control of their future from British hands.

Perhaps we should not attempt to define too closely what is meant by the eighteenth century, other than the span of years extending from 1701 to 1800. Three, four or five generations were alive during this time. Few of the people who made them up were conscious of living through a particular period of history, and many of them never escaped from a physical and mental environment which had changed little since the Middle Ages.

If, however, we define a period in terms of public affairs, fashion and the other concerns of the literate minority, then the eighteenth century has a number of recognisable characteristics, and most of them have to do with the age's feeling for style and restraint. The eighteenth century seemed to be incapable of creating anything which looked or sounded ugly – to the extent that the graffiti of the tourists were carved with the utmost elegance. No less impressively, men of the eighteenth century, although much given to fighting wars,

3

conducted them with much less of the inhumanity which has stained the records of the ages.

The middle of the century, and more specifically the years between 1748 and 1763, was a peculiarly vital and innovatory time, and may be seen as the epitome of the so-called 'Age of Reason', which is generally taken to be the period between the death of Louis XIV in 1715 and the outbreak of the French Revolution in 1789.

The year 1748 saw both the beginning of the transformation of the Austrian state by Maria Theresa, and the publication of David Hume's *Philosophical Essays Concerning Human Understanding*. The first volume of Denis Diderot's *Encyclopédie* appeared in 1751; the *Species Plantarum* of Carl Linnaeus was published in 1752, and three years later Samuel Johnson's *Dictionary* represented a further significant step in categorising knowledge and making it more accessible. Burke, Bishop Butler, Benjamin Franklin, Kant, Adam Smith and Voltaire were all scribbling significant texts at the same time. In the sphere of the arts Frederick of Prussia continued to champion the decorative and elegant rococo style in architecture and painting, while the Elector Palatine's orchestra at Mannheim set standards in expression and ensemble which hastened the coming of the Classical age of music. Gluck's *Orfeo*, the first of the 'reform' operas, received its première in 1762.

The period from 1748 to 1763 also corresponds very closely with the 'Diplomatic Revolution' in European politics, and the ensuing Seven Years War, which was a genuine global conflict: 'This wide geographical spread; this involvement of the major Powers; this loss of life and outpouring of treasure; marked the greatest upheaval the world had yet seen' (Savory, 1966, vii).

The transforming impetus was sustained beyond 1789 and into the new century. Something of the old unities and the old lightness of heart was admittedly lost in the process. The rococo age and its artefacts came to seem ridiculous and doll-like to those scholars and gentlemen who embraced the neo-classical style in the visual arts, which was a self-conscious product of study and principle. The cult of Sensibility was the expression of a different impulse – a turning to what seemed direct and natural. There was a detectable *Sturm und Drang* period in German literature, whose energy and emotion spilled over into some of the symphonies of Haydn and Mozart. Landscapes of 'useless woods and forests', which to members of the older generation owned 'a barbaric and savage appearance' (Burney, 1775, 69) now entranced the eye and improved the soul of the younger folk. Among leaders of society in the rococo period it had not been considered 'fashionable to be a good father or a good husband' (Ligne, 1928, I, 7), but now family life and conjugal love became matters of celebration.

In things material, the last decades of the century witnessed some changes that reached down to the lower orders of society. The Industrial Revolution gathered force in Britain in the 1780s, and in Europe generally a decline in mortality from infectious diseases contributed to the beginning of a significant rise in population. From about 118 million in 1700 the total reached 187 million by the end of the century, and it continued to rise without check for more than 150 years. It is difficult to determine whether standards of living improved correspondingly. From about 1740 there was a deterioration in diet in Leipzig and other cities of Central Europe, and in the second half of the century a decline was observed in the height of groups as various as Swedish recruits, London pauper boys, American negro slaves, and the peoples of Bohemia and Lower Austria (Komlos, 1985, 1, 155–9).

General ideas on statecraft and war

ENLIGHTENED ABSOLUTISM

The most common generalisations about the eighteenth century have been enshrined in the school textbooks for many years, and, as long as they are regarded as no more than average truths, they have stood up pretty well to the test of time. The 'Enlightenment', properly speaking, refers more particularly to some of the ideas promoted by some German writers from the middle of the eighteenth century, but the idea of rational enquiry, and how it could be used for the physical and moral betterment of humankind, was one which had a wider application. A Dutch colonel summed it up as a 'philosophical spirit', which he defined as 'the engrained habit of reducing our ideas to order, and of examining, observing, judging and relating everything to its true principles before we are prepared to believe, accept, decide and act' (Nockhern de Schorn, 1783, xi). On the continent of Europe it helped to inspire a kind of controlled revolution from above, for the central bureaucracy grew in size and power, and the sovereigns mounted an assault on local or private

5

interests which obstructed the public good. In several countries a genuine attempt was made to improve the condition of the serfs, and Austria witnessed the beginnings of general primary education.

Order and harmony were preserved as far as possible in this process, and most of the princely courts remained or became magnificent establishments which defined standards of taste and etiquette. This was something which Europe inherited from the later seventeenth century and which strongly influenced the conduct of public and private affairs: 'Ceremonial has reached a peak of development in our period; warfare itself has a very large share therein'. Etiquette determined what you ought to do when you received recruits, presented new officers to their regiment, mounted the guard, exchanged prisoners, or arranged the surrender of a fortress. The study of military ceremonial was not only a pleasing diversion for a young officer, 'but also, when you talk to others, it helps to create the impression that you have served in a large number of foreign armies' (Fleming, 1726, I, 94, 188).

While they discover so much to admire in the public life of the eighteenth century, commentators have long been aware that the reforming drive lacked continuity and depth. There was little motivation to carry on the good work, once the enlightened prince had died or his trusted minister had fallen from grace. Damaging compromises were all too often made with established centres of power, and in many states the underlings were able to offer a muted but effective opposition to the process of change. A civil servant from Baden wrote in 1786, 'What use are the finest directives, when they are not carried out?' (Hartung, 1955, 34). Frederick of Prussia regarded superstition as the daughter of timidity, weakness and ignorance, and he rejoiced with Voltaire that this 'vast empire of fanaticism' had retreated to the peripheries of Europe (8 January 1766, Frederick, 1846–57, XXIII, 96). The fact remains that religion and custom continued to offer the guiding principles for most of the peoples of Europe.

The gap between what was ordained and what was actually carried out inevitably places the historian of military affairs in some embarrassment. Unless he is on his guard, he will assume that central direction was effective as it is in the much more tightly controlled world of the twentieth century. It is easy enough to write about such and such a regulation or practice being ordained by Frederick the Great, Maria Theresa or the Duc de Choiseul: it is difficult, and sometimes impossible, to find how far their armies responded to the messages which came from above.

PATRIOTISM

When we look back at the eighteenth century from the present day, we recognise patriotism in its most readily identifiable form in two countries which stood on the fringes of Europe, namely Britain and Russia. Here it was encouraged by physical isolation and the racial and religious differences which separated their peoples from their nearest neighbours. More admirable in its way was the patriotism associated with republics like the Netherlands and Switzerland, where it was linked with a form of government which also promoted toleration and equality. Frederick of Prussia had much private sympathy with republican ideals, though he doubted whether the republics could long survive in co-existence with the great monarchies.

Elsewhere patriotism wore some curious guises. Germany, for example, was a notorious paradox, forming at once a cultural nation in the linguistic sense, but divided into a multitude of sovereign states. The political and military fragmentation was intensified by the experience of the Seven Years War (1756–63), which brought French and Russian armies onto German soil. On the one side there can be no doubt that many of the Hanoverians, Brunswickers, Hessians and native Prussians believed that the welfare of their homes and families, and the survival of the Protestant religion, were now at stake. The Protestant Germans had long resented the pretensions of France, and many of them responded with enthusiasm in the spiritual leadership which they thought they had found in Frederick the Great. In such an interest the poet Gleim took issue with his cosmopolitan friend Lessing, and Thomas Abbt came from Ulm to sing the praises of Prussia's hero-king, all covered in sweat and dust (*Vom Tode fürs Vaterland*, 1761).

On the other side the soldiers of Saxony, equally German, and for the most part equally Protestant, rejected Frederick and everything Prussian out of loyalty to their own sovereign prince. The Saxon army of 18,000 men was captured intact by Old Fritz at Pirna in 1756, and the wretched troops were dragooned into the Prussian service. Frederick was ready to cope with individual deserters from among these unwilling recruits, but he was powerless to stop the mass breakouts which actually took place. A French officer saw the Saxons who came over to the French army, and he could find nothing but admiration for heroic figures like Sergeant Kinabe of the battalion of Prinz Xaver and

> many others of the same stamp who have given such convincing proofs of their fidelity. Out of all the Saxon officers, and even all the Saxon soldiers we have with us here, there is not a single one who has not spurned tempting offers from the enemy, or braved manifold dangers in order to expend his blood in the service of his fatherland and his sovereign. (Mopinot de la Chapotte, 1905, 226–7).

The hostilities were sometimes powered by grudges and blood feuds, like the one which the Prussian army harboured against the Russians after Frederick's soldiers had seen the devastation at Cüstrin and in the Neumark in 1758. The peculiar bitterness between the Prussian and Saxon forces went back to the battle of Hohenfriedeberg (1745), when Frederick's cavalry had massacred the Saxon infantry, and the quarrel flared up again whenever one party had the other at its mercy during the Seven Years War.

The spirit of faction had its counterpart in civilian society, where close relations sometimes found themselves bitterly divided, like Goethe's father and grandfather at Frankfurt. Life was no less uncomfortable in the princely household at Dessau, as a result of the bad blood which existed between the princes Dietrich and Eugen: 'Dietrich is an out-and-out Prussian, while Eugen is a dyed-in-the-wool Saxon. These two brothers therefore live on a constant war footing' (Lehndorff, 1910–13, I, 231). Among the ordinary people, the enthusiasms had much in common with the emotional support which twentieth-century crowds show for sporting teams. There can be no other explanation for the violent confrontations between the *Teresiani* and *Prussiani* among the Venetian monks and gondoliers in the Seven Years War.

The manifestations of faction, as here described, stood at an important remove from political commitment. Zeal for the cause of Frederick outside Prussia had nothing to do with a desire to become his subjects (God forbid!). Goethe and his young friends were first and foremost 'Fritzians', and not proto-Prussians. In wartime only a minority of Europeans were motivated by anything which at all approached modern definitions of patriotism, and in time of peace such individuals were still more difficult to find. What were the reasons?

In the first place, life for many of the countryfolk was bounded by narrow horizons, arising from the spirit of *campanilismo* and the social divisions as outlined by the Spanish general Santa Cruz:

> It is rare to find a country where the people are not at daggers drawn with the aristocracy, or the nobles are not divided among themselves . . . The inhabitants of two neighbouring localities will usually be on bad terms. Their hostility derives from the endless disputes over rights to water, woodland or pasture along their borders; each village wishes to extend its borders at the expense of the other. (Santa Cruz, 1735–40, IV, 224)

On occasion foreign invaders were faced with total passive opposition from the people, such as the Prussians encountered in the 'Austrian' provinces of Bohemia and Moravia. In other theatres the arrival of the newcomers was frequently welcomed by the local underdogs, who now had the opportunity to declare themselves against their masters. Thus, when the Austrians invaded the republic of Genoa in 1746, they were well received by the peasants just outside Genoa city, who tried to warn them against the dangers of camping on the dried bed of the Polceverra river. Again, in North America in the War of Independence, the passage of the rival armies left a smouldering trail of civil strife and miniature revolutions.

The concept of honour, which was a very complicated idea in its own right (see p. 74), corresponded only indirectly, if at all, with a patriotic cause. Count Wilhelm Friedrich Ernst von Schaumburg-Lippe wrote sarcastically about

> the custom which exists by common consent among almost all the peoples of Europe, but especially those of Germany, namely that of earning your daily bread by pursuing the military profession as you would embrace any other trade. You sell yourself to the highest bidder, and you kill and destroy while remaining totally indifferent to the motives and objectives behind the war. (Schaumburg-Lippe, 1977–83, III, 158–9).

Cosmopolitanism was an actively hostile agent. It scorned the monoglot stay-at-homes, and in the same degree it promoted personal mobility and universal values. A knowledge of French was a prerequisite for a man who wished to be at home in European society, and Prince Henry of Prussia advised a young officer to master this language 'lest one should be considered some kind of Germanic beast' (Berenhorst, 1845–7, I, xiv).

The very supporters of patriotism defined it in cool and distant terms. Carl Abraham Zedlitz explained it to the Berlin *Académie Royale* in 1776: 'What we call "patriotism" is a lively attachment to the laws, customs, institutions, advantages and glory of the society in which we live. The sentiment is a subdivision of love in general – in other words it is a passion.' This not particularly passionate declaration was delivered in French (Zedlitz, 1776, 5. See also Sonnenfels, 1783–7; Ligne, 1795–1811, X, 10–11). Even the celebrated Jacques de Guibert, who looked forward to a truly national army, elevated a kind of patriotism that would be ennobled by reason, and rise above unworthy sentiments of fanaticism and hate (Guibert [1772], 1804, I, 2).

The word 'advantages', as mentioned by Zedlitz, came from a sense of mutual obligation and benefit which probably derived from feudal society. This idea is a very important one for our understanding of the mentality of the military aristocracy in the eighteenth century, and it was developed at greater length by Carl Gottfried Wolff in the same year as the Zedlitz address. Wolff's definition of patriotism was almost identical with that of Zedlitz, and he deduced that the Fatherland had a call on one's loyalty only as long as the subject was allowed freedom of conscience and a share in the common prosperity. When these benefits ceased, the individual was at liberty to seek 'another Fatherland' (Wolff, 1776, 60).

Other authorities were willing to maintain that patriotism scarcely existed at all. Voltaire found that 'the concept of fatherland is variable and contradictory. Most of the inhabitants of a country like France do not know what it means' (entry 'Patrie' in his *Dictionnaire philosophique*). Many military men would have found themselves in agreement with the Austrian officer Cogniazzo, who claimed that for contemporary armies 'patriotism' was the equivalent of a spare wheel on a vehicle, to be put into use when the others had worn out (Cogniazzo, 1779, 103).

THE LIMITATION OF WAR

The Seven Years War, as the culminating military effort of old Europe, was fought for important objectives, and on the whole with a great deal of energy: soldiers carried out the same mindless vandalisms they have worked in all times and places; public opinion took a lively interest in the progress of the campaigns, and bellicose religious enthusiasm underwent something of a revival, at least in Central Europe, which gave the war an emotional charge roughly comparable with that provided by the issue of slavery in the American Civil War. However the observers and historians were surely in the right when they looked on the eighteenth century as a period of remarkable restraint in the conduct of warfare.

Physical constraints

The involuntary limitations were of two kinds, resulting from the excruciating difficulty of moving and supplying armies, and the heavy investment that was made in training the professional soldiers, who therefore became a valuable commodity.

As a general rule the regular formations remained totally inactive in winter quarters from about October until the month of May, which was when the grass began to grow and the armies' huge complement of horses (required for cavalry, and drawing guns and carts) could graze in the open fields. The campaigning season was therefore confined to about five months of the year, and even then the armies moved so ponderously that it was difficult to bring an unwilling enemy to fight. When, at last, the forces did meet in battle, it was common to lose up to one-third of your men in a few hours of combat. Two or three battles left your precious store of veterans heavily depleted, and you had to make up the number with recruits, who were unskilled in the close-order drills required for the tactics of the time.

It was a matter of common observation that wars had a way of fizzling out after a few such campaigning cycles. Indeed, a state of gentle near-efficiency was probably the one best suited to sustain an eighteenth-century army over a long haul before the inevitable breakdown. If some institution or department of state happened to work too well, its effect was to shake the machine to pieces – like installing a racing car engine in a rickshaw. The *indelingsverk* system of recruiting sucked the Swedish state dry of manpower early in the eighteenth century, in a way that Frederick swore that he would never allow in Prussia. Few armies were ever supplied so well as the Austrian forces facing the Prussians in northern Bohemia in 1778, but the Austrian treasury was hit so badly in the process that (even if political considerations had not supervened) the Austrians would have been quite unable to keep up the effort.

Political constraints

The influence of the state did not usually reach far into the lives of individuals. When frontier provinces changed hands at the end of a war, the affair was normally managed with a sedulous regard for established local institutions, so that from being an 'Austrian' you could find that you had become a 'Sardinian' without noticing any difference in your everyday routine. We are a world removed from the twentieth century, when wars have frequently been fought with the purpose of eliminating the core area of an enemy state and imposing an alien regime and ideology.

In the eighteenth century, if one state showed signs of surmounting its physical limitations and attaining an outright military dominion, then an international regulating process came into effect. This was a flow of allies and other forms of support to the weaker party, a flow which continued until the equilibrium was restored. The first specific mention of such a stabilising effect among European states is to be found in the Anglo-Spanish Treaty of Utrecht on 13 July 1713, which commended 'an equal balance of power' as 'the best and most solid foundation of a mutual friendship and of a concord which will be lasting on all sides' (Keens-Soper, 1981–2, 19). The details of the thing could be calculated with some precision. A state could encourage one side or the other with subsidies, and stay out of the war altogether. Even if a sovereign engaged his forces directly in the struggle, he might still choose to remain legally aloof by representing himself as merely an 'auxiliary' of one of the principal belligerents. When the time for a peace congress finally came around the account could be settled by trading one conquest for another, such as the way the English and French swapped Louisbourg for Madras in 1748, or the deal whereby the Prussians evacuated Saxony in return for recovering Glatz at the end of the Seven Years War.

Ethical constraints

Most of the European wars were fought in a manner that reflected the urbanity and reasonableness of the age. On the battlefield the

English and French officers in particular sought to outdo each other in demonstrations of chivalrous concern. There were many episodes to match the one after the battle of Fontenoy in 1745, when a French colonel came across an English counterpart who had been seriously wounded. He gave him a guard for his protection and offered him the contents of his purse. The enemy colonel exclaimed 'an Englishman could not have done more for me!' and with tears in his eyes he held out his hand in gratitude (Ray, 1895, 228).

It was to the credit of the eighteenth century, rather than otherwise, that men justified their moderation in terms of self-interest rather than ostentatious virtue: 'we must be most careful to leave the peasants with enough grain not only to live, but to sow their ground for another harvest, particularly if we have reason to think that the next campaign will be waged in the same area' (Turpin de Crissé, 1754, I, 145). Wise commanders also knew that if they treated the local people reasonably well, they would not have to chase them over the landscape in order to obtain food or information.

Enemy armed forces, defended fortresses and public property were considered legitimate targets, but you were expected to refrain from deeds which might 'occasion loss and harm among the enemy, but inflict no essential damage to hostile interests and yield not the slightest benefit for us' (Schertel von Burtenbach, 1779, 9–10).

The eighteenth century had its share of atrocities. A number were deliberate, but the majority were the result of some kind of miscalculation rather than the consequence of a settled policy of *Schrecklichkeit*. The fortified towns of Zittau (1757), Cüstrin (1758) and Dresden (1760) all probably burnt more fiercely than the besieging bombardiers had intended or expected (see p. 293). The Russians devastated Pomerania and the Neumark in the Seven Years War only because the wild Cossacks were the only light cavalry available to them in any quantity. The Cossacks ran out of control just as badly in 1762, when they came under Prussian command and invaded Austrian territory, but this time the Prussian propagandists remained silent.

THE ORIGINS AND NATURE OF WAR IN THE CONTEMPORARY VIEW

Nearly all the writers who had seen war traced its causes to the restlessness, fears and passions of the human heart. It was an intermittent fever which 'may be arrested, but never cured' (Frederick to

Voltaire, 1 November 1772, Frederick, 1846–57, XXIII, 222). Impersonal forces were largely discounted. Even Jakob Mauvillon, who emphasised the role of power politics, set no great store by economic interests in bringing about the Seven Years War, at least on the continent of Europe (Mauvillon, J., 1794, I, 155. See also Ligne, 1795–1811, II, 42).

With the same near-unanimity, the military men maintained that war as such was not inherently evil. Again and again they advanced the same arguments. The soldier was entitled to respect as the protector of his country, and as the practitioner of a difficult and dangerous trade. All of the veterans could cite examples of heroic and humane impulses among the other ranks, and they knew from their own experience that it was possible to conduct war 'without unworthy passions, and without being moved by a personal hatred of the enemies of your state' (Loen, 1751, 17).

THE LARGE STANDING ARMIES AND THEIR CONSEQUENCES

Powerful regular armies were one of the most characteristic features of the age of absolutism. Their rise was linked with that of the centralised state, and especially its ability to raise taxes independently of the arbitrary will of the aristocracy. The relevant date in Brandenburg-Prussia is to be found as early as 1653, when the 'Great Elector' Frederick William dismissed the Brandenburg *Landtag* and prevailed on the magnates to make over annual taxes. The Austrian monarchy took almost one hundred years to win the same kind of freedom, and it is significant that it was only then that the Habsburgs could embark on a thoroughgoing military reform. In France the rebuilding of the army was self-consciously bureaucratic and state-centred, and it was above all the work of the two Le Tellier war ministers, the father Michel Le Tellier (d. 1685) and his associate and son François Michel Le Tellier, Marquis de Louvois (d. 1691). The size of the French regular army grew from 30,000 in the War of Devolution (1667–8) to an astounding 440,000 in the War of the League of Augsburg (1688–97). An essential core remained intact, even after the numbers of the French troops were cut in peacetime, and the Le Telliers built up an infrastructure of arsenals, magazines and fortresses that became the envy of Europe.

The absolutist rulers were just as determined to loosen the grip of private interests on the component units and sub-units of the armies. From the feudal and entrepreneurial past the colonels (regimental commanders) and the captains (company commanders) had inherited the assumption that their commands were private fiefs, which were to be raised, administered, clothed and trained according to individual fancy. By the same token, senior generals insisted that the state must regard them as partners in a joint enterprise, not as functionaries to be fitted into a hierarchy. In 1675, however, the French bureaucrats established the important principle that seniority, not birth, must determine the precedence of command among the generals. In the middle decades of the eighteenth century the monarchies not just in France, but in Prussia, Austria and Britain proceeded to launch a determined assault on feudal power at the regimental and company level (see p. 68).

The armed forces of Europe were therefore transformed into bodies that were more stable and more responsive to manipulation than anything known since Classical times. Weapons and clothing became largely standardised within armies in the later seventeenth century, and in the eighteenth century the central bureaucracy worked out prescribed codes relating to the conduct of war. In Britain as elsewhere 'it was the mid-1750s that marked the great take-off point, so much so that the drill and tactics practised in the army by the mid-1760s differed markedly from that known in the best of the battalions in the great North Brabant campaigns of 1748' (Houlding, 1981, 283).

The rise of military academies and military journals accentuated the importance of theory and study in the business of forming an officer. Old trades like that of gunner and engineer now became fully fledged military professions, and properly trained staff officers helped to lead military Europe into the nineteenth century.

On balance military efficiency was greatly improved. A young Prussian officer wrote on the eve of the Seven Years War:

> Never have the European powers kept such large forces in being
> as since the last peace at Aix-la-Chapelle (1748). Little or
> nothing is heard of troop reductions. The states vie with one
> another in training up their troops, and putting officers and
> men through constant military exercises. We keep our weapons
> sharp, and follow the principle that a large and well-schooled
> army is the best rampart of the state. (Rohr, 1756, xix–xx)

Frederick tried to convince his correspondent d'Alembert that there were also benefits for society. He maintained that the very expense of these huge organisations prevented wars from dragging on in the old style; they helped to circulate money, and they absorbed labour that was surplus to the needs of industry and agriculture. In former times the call to arms used to strip fields and workshops of productive hands, but nowadays the civilians got on with their work, leaving the conduct of war to the trained defenders of the fatherland (18 October 1770, Frederick, 1846–57, XXIV, 506).

It was still possible to harbour reservations about the standing armies. To a wide range of civilian authors they undoubtedly represented a 'new pestilence'. The Duc de Saint-Simon (1675–1755) resented the scandalous affronts to noble privilege. Archbishop Fénelon (1651–1715) and the Abbé de Saint-Pierre (1658–1743) were more concerned with the welfare of mankind in general, for they saw the standing armies as a threat to peace. In the middle and later years of the eighteenth century Thomas Abbt and other German writers objected on political or humanitarian grounds, while in France the economists of the physiocratic school maintained that standing armies inevitably diverted labour from productive toil.

In military terms the reforms were not always complete, or did not necessarily bring about an unqualified improvement. The commander of the French field army still had to pay due regard to the sensibilities of bodies like the Maison du Roi (which took its orders direct from the king), the sixteen companies of the Gendarmerie (each of which demanded a separate march route), and the regiments of Swiss (who refused to be brigaded together with the native French). In Poland the work of reform was hindered by periodic civil disorders (see p. 26) and the prominence of the Noble National Cavalry. The Russian army experienced an actual regression in the reign of Catherine the Great, who by 1766 had extended almost total liberty to the regimental commanders. There followed thirty years of maladministration, and it was left to the much-maligned Paul I to try to restore discipline and order.

Where 'defeudalisation' did indeed become effective, one of the results was to weaken traditional military relationships, and especially the bonds of loyalty and responsibility which had bound the captain to the soldiers of his company (see p. 69).

Some of the officers opposed the standing armies as resolutely as did the civilian writers, although not always for the same reasons. Most of the objections of the military men came directly or indirectly from the disparity they noted between the total size of the regular armed forces and the smaller numbers which could be usefully employed in the field.

In 1788–9, the last years of old Europe, the Russians had about 426,000 regular troops under arms, or some 1.33 per cent of the total population. Austria came next with 300,000 (1.11 per cent). Prussia stood third at 200,000 (3.77 per cent), or one-third less than Austria but proportionately much more in terms of population. The French army, which had undergone some reductions, could put forward only 170,000 troops (0.65 per cent), although in the Seven Years War there had been a maximum of 330,000 in the line units at one time, and the enormous total of 2,030,000 men had been called up in the course of the war.

Effective field armies were considerably smaller. They corresponded most closely to the total forces of the state in the Low Country campaigns from 1744 to 1748. The Netherlands were a classic collision zone of strategic interests. Moreover great cities and political capitals stood close together, trade was highly developed, the land was fertile and intensively cultivated, and armies could avail themselves of fortified depots and excellent communications by way of rivers and canals. Marshal Saxe had about 120,000 troops under his command at Rocoux (1746) and again at Laffeldt (1747), and the Allies opposed him with 80,000 and 90,000 respectively.

The scene of war in Central Europe was more extensive and less civilised. Frederick never led a larger army into battle than the 65,000 men he commanded at Prague in 1757, and it is perhaps significant that the combat almost completely escaped from his control. His forces in his other battles fall into three diminishing scales of size:

1   About 50,000 (Hohenfriedeberg, Kunersdorf, Torgau).
2   Between 36,000 and 29,000 (Lobositz, Kolin, Leuthen,
    Zorndorf, Hochkirch, Liegnitz).
3   About 23,000 (Mollwitz, Chotusitz, Soor, Rossbach).

In the wilds of North America the size of the field forces was minuscule. Altogether about 232,000 men served on the rebel side in the War of American Independence, including both the Militia and the Continental Line, but the largest body which Washington commanded in the field probably reached only 13,000 troops. The combined American and French forces amounted to only around

19,000 at the culminating siege of Yorktown in 1781 (Mitchell, 1974, 114).

Marshal Saxe put the most effective controllable number of troops at 46,000, which corresponds very closely to the 50,000 recommended by Frederick and Guibert. In other words, even after making allowances for detachments that had to be made to minor theatres of war, the establishments had swollen to what many military men regarded as a bloated size. In the field the large armies brought with them physical problems relating to supply (see p. 174), and positioning, control and movement (see p. 182). Morale and discipline came under stress, for the state recruited many unsuitable officers (see p. 46), as well as tens of thousands of ill-paid, badly treated and badly fed private soldiers. The solution must be to turn to élite forces of a more sustainable size (Qureille, 1771, 28–84; Algarotti, 1772, IV, 98–9; Guibert [1772], 1804, *passim*; Brezé, 1779, 6; Darut de Grandpré, 1787, II, 42). It is clear that the desirable revision of force was considered to be downwards, and that none of the authorities had any inkling that the age of the mass conscript army was almost upon them.

THE MILITARY NATIONS

National characteristics in general

Eighteenth-century officers frequently wrote about the great differences in character and attainment which existed between the armies of the various sovereigns.

On the largest scale the observers drew important distinctions between the 'cold' and 'hot' nations. The Germans, Swedes and Russians lived in chilly lands with thick atmospheres, where the blood coursed slowly through the veins, the thought processes were ponderous, the inhabitants ate too much and were given to drinking strong spirits or heavy beer. 'And since all of this reduces nations to a level of near-stupidity, they pay little attention to danger, and enter perilous situations as heedlessly – as wild beasts' (Santa Cruz, 1735–40, IV, 265). The Spanish, Italians, French and Hungarians were clearly counted among the hot peoples. The English occupied an intermediate state, appearing phlegmatic to some, hot and impatient to others, though invariably ferocious.

Regional differences sprang from physical conditions and styles of life. Hardy mountain folk were highly prized in many countries. Conversely the Prussian Rhinelanders were flabby, soft and drunken, and not to be compared with the sturdy peasants of Minden, Brandenburg and Pomerania, whom Frederick considered to be the core of his infantry. Field-Marshal Rumyantsev found that the peasants of Great Russia made excellent infantrymen but very poor cavalry, and could never be persuaded to take a ride on a horse, even after they had unhitched their teams from the plough at the end of a day's work.

The form of government was also influential:

> If you need proof, you just have to cast your eye on the troops
> of small, pacific states, like some of the republics of Europe
> or the ecclesiastical principalities. You will be struck straight
> away by their careless and boorish manner, so different from
> the martial mien which tells you that you are looking at good
> troops who have been in the wars, and whose spirit and
> motivation is sustained by constant drilling. (Bigot, 1761, II,
> 150).

We shall now examine the standing of individual nations in a little more detail, again emphasising the contemporary verdicts.

France

Liveliness, a questioning turn of mind, and a persistent tendency towards indiscipline were all recognised as characteristics of the French. The *enfants de la gloire* deeply resented corporal punishment, and in the middle of the century the vices of plundering, swearing and drunkenness were allowed to flourish almost unchecked. At Dettingen in 1743 the Comte de Stainville (later the Duc de Choiseul) three times heard Marshal Noailles order the army to reoccupy the position it had held on the day before, but

> all his efforts were nullified by ignorance, panic, the noise of
> battle and the lack of silence among our troops. A single
> cannon shot, which the enemy fired at random, was enough to
> scatter the royal army beyond hope of recall . . . what I saw
> at this battle became one of the main motives for the military
> reforms which I proposed to the king in 1763, and which I
> was able to put into due effect. (Choiseul, 1904, 9–10)

Marshal Saxe tolerated or even encouraged a degree of luxury and licence in his army in the Low Countries between 1744 and 1748, but he had the best possible vindication in his devastating offensives and his hard-fought victories. The rot set in when the easy-going ways were prolonged into the Seven Years War, without being compensated by any brilliance in the high command. The early and middle period of the Seven Years War indeed represented a nadir in French military reputation. At home the finances sank into disorder, and the leaders of society laughed at the reverses suffered by their own armies.

The French military renaissance probably dates from 1758, when the new war minister, Marshal Belle-Isle, raised and regulated military pay, and insisted that generals must wear proper uniforms and abandon their luxurious quarters in order to encamp with the troops. Already at Bergen in 1759 the French were fighting with imagination and tenacity, and as the war progressed the French armies displayed an almost perceptible daily improvement (Mauvillon, J., 1794, II, 280).

After the Seven Years War the work of reform was taken up in earnest. There were two main lines of development in military practice: advances in organisation, staff work and military topography laid the foundations for the divisional and corps systems which were exploited by Napoleon, endowing him with significant strategic advantages over the unitary armies of his enemies; in tactics, the culminating Ordinance of 1 August 1791 combined the advantages of the columnar formation for movement with those of the line for firepower.

All the time the improvement in discipline was maintained, and the French expeditionary corps won golden opinions for the fine order it observed in North America in 1780 and 1781. The troops made 'a very fine, soldierly appearance' (Feltman, 1853, 12), and it was considered noteworthy that 'Count Rochambeau's French spent more than three months encamped on Rhode Island, without disturbing so much as the fruit trees' (Hoyer, 1797–1800, II, 609).

Among the individual arms of service, the French infantry was believed to be unreliable on the defensive, but at its best when rushing at the enemy with cold steel. This view, which was a gross oversimplification, exercised a powerful influence on French writing about the form of tactics best suited to the nation. The French cavalry, which should indeed have been formed for shock action, was held back by the unprofessionalism of many of its officers, the indifferent quality of its horses, and the scanty attention which these animals received from their masters. The regeneration of the French artillery took place only after the Seven Years War, and military Europe had no proper opportunity to observe the significant progress which the French gunners had been making before the Revolution.

Nobody doubted that the French excelled all other nations in the sciences of building, defending and attacking fortresses. The French engineers formed members of a truly professional corps, which enjoyed a lavish range of supporting facilities, and a continuity of direction which stretched back for generations (see p. 289). The ordinary French soldiers also did well in the business of siegework, which seemed to run counter to many of the generalisations that were uttered about the national character. Perhaps, as Bonneville suggested, the French were more patient than was usually supposed (1762, I, 35). Perhaps also, good will and personal bravery were of more account in siege conditions than in battle in the open field, where tactical skill and tight discipline appeared to be the qualities which mattered (Warnery, 1785–91, III, 226–7).

Germany and the minor German states

Germany as a geographical region probably counted as the most highly militarised area of Europe. Its weakness, and its vulnerability to invasion, came from the fact that it was highly fragmented in the political sense. The nominal German Empire (*Reich*) had no permanent existence as such, and there was little real authority invested in the elective office of Emperor, which (except for a period between 1741 and 1745) was invariably held by the head of the Austrian house of Habsburg. Its *Reichstag* was a kind of irregular parliament. Its military organisation was in Circles (*Reichskreise*) or groupings of states, which were supposed to supply armed contingents when an 'execution' was declared against an offending power, as was done against Prussia in the Seven Years War. The resulting *Reichs-Armee* was of little account as a military force. One of the fundamental problems was that some of the most effective military states of the Empire – Prussia, Hanover, Brunswick and so on, were actually fighting in the opposing camp. The *Reichs-Armee* was therefore filled up by more or less loyal contingents which arrived from the rest of the Empire in penny packets, and were made up into Circle units.

In 1757, for example, the six cavalry squadrons of the Swabian Circle were compounded of no less than eighty-three state contingents, which can hardly have made for unity of purpose.

Leaving Prussia itself out of account for the moment, we may discern three main types of military culture:

1   A long band of northern central states, most of which were Protestant, and most of which were equipped and trained in the Prussian style. The most important of the states in question were Brunswick-Lüneburg, Hesse, Hanover, Münster, the Palatinate and Württemberg. The political allegiances of their masters were divided, but the British drew heavily on members of this group in order to make up the allied forces in Germany in the Seven Years War. In 1760, on top of the 22,000 English and 37,800 Hanoverians, the British paid for auxiliary contingents in the shape of 24,000 Hessians and 9,500 Brunswickers. The Hanoverians were in every way the heart of this force (Mauvillon, J., 1794, II, 274). The Hessians were state mercenaries *par excellence*, and they contributed a military cast of mind and a great depth of experience (see p. 33).

2   A perimeter of mostly ecclesiastical states like Mainz, Cologne, Trier, Würzburg and Salzburg. The 'Red' and 'Blue' Würzburg regiments fought well in the Austrian interest in the Seven Years War, but in most of the other states morale and military attainment were low.

3   Two largish central-southern states (Bavaria and Saxony) which had the misfortune to stand directly in the path of powerful neighbours.

Bavaria had last tasted glory in the far-off early years of the 'Blue Elector' Max Emanuel, who had conducted a series of celebrated campaigns against the Turks from 1683. In the eighteenth century, however, the electorate was exhausted by the efforts it put forth on behalf of the French against the Austrians. Max Emanuel died in 1725, leaving heavy debts and an army of only 5,000 troops, and in the War of the Austrian Succession Bavaria was trampled by the Austrians in 1743 and again in 1745.

Saxony was in a similar case. Bad administration and bad generalship squandered the loyalty of the Saxon troops (see p. 8), and the electorate underwent a harsh occupation by the Prussians from 1756 to 1763. After the war the Chevalier de Saxe tried to build up a balanced force of 30,000 men, but he could make no headway in the face of the regent Prince Xaver and the opposition of the noble assemblies.

Germany as a whole had been a great nursery of troops since medieval times, and in the eighteenth century Germans were reckoned to make the best all-round soldiers in Europe. The English admired the neat turnout of 'our great and warlike neighbours the Germans' (Bland, 1727, 115), though they were aware that English soldiers would never accustom themselves to German standards of exactitude and obedience. German cavalrymen looked after their horses well, and German infantry manoeuvred steadily under fire, which was a priceless asset. As an example of German discipline, the Duc de Crillon cited a soldier of the regiment of Alsace, who belonged to a detachment which had seized an isolated fort at Namur in 1746. The unsuspecting Dutch relief force arrived by boat and mistook the blue-coated soldiers of Alsace for their own men:

> One of our grenadiers was a little out of line, and he received a heavy blow from the commander of the new guard. The grenadier received the buffet impassively, but he marked down the officer for vengeance, and as soon as the enemy force had laid down its weapons he seized him by the collar and dealt him a number of punches and kicks. (Crillon, 1791, 109–10).

Charles-Emanuel Warnery was a Walloon who had first-hand knowledge of a number of European armies. He testifies that

> the German officer excels those of every other nation in his dedication to the service. He is a stickler for order, and he is outstandingly skilful in the way he preserves the alignment of his troops, whether of infantry or cavalry. He takes a great deal of trouble over this point, and in addition he possesses sound judgement, he is patient, he is obedient to his superiors, and he stays calm in action. While he is still young, however, you must keep him on a tight rein, and never suffer him to get away with the slightest mistake. (Warnery, 1785–91, II, 48–9)

Many of the senior officers were princes of the highest birth, who had been allowed to progress to field command only when they had mastered the details of every grade of subordinate rank. The Protestant noble was denied the ecclesiastical careers and the knightly orders that were open to the Catholic aristocracy. 'As a consequence, if he wishes to rise in a suitable manner, and make something of himself, the military profession is the only alternative to managing his estates or taking up one of the comparatively few posts in the central or local administration' (Pauli, 1758–64, I, 228). No less than three ducal brothers of Brunswick were fighting on one side or the other at the battle of Soor in 1745. Ferdinand was a brigade commander on the Prussian left; Ludwig was facing him on the Austrian right; the third brother, the young Albrecht, was killed on the Prussian right.

Prussia

Prussia was the most isolated and the least 'German' of the Germanic states. However this land is important in our story because it produced the foremost soldier of the age, in King Frederick II 'The Great', and because the Prussian army came to stand for the rest of Europe as a model of military perfection.

Apart from Frederick's genius for war, the causes of Prussia's military ascendancy lay deep in society and government. The Prussian officer was characteristically the product of the poor country nobility (the *Junkers*), and if he enjoyed a high status in company, he had to earn it by a lifelong dedication to his profession. Among themselves, the officers observed a most exact discipline when on service, but they cultivated an open and comradely manner in their off-duty hours.

The rank and file were composed of two elements. By recruiting a high proportion of foreigners, the kings of Prussia were able to keep up a large army on a small population base (see p. 17). The rest of the troops were native part-timers, raised by conscription, who did duty during the summer training season and during the wars. These natives provided the army with a reliable core, and they gave Frederick a long-term reserve after most of the foreigners had been killed or run away. As Frederick explained in 1748, 'our regiments are composed half of natives, and half of mercenaries. The latter have nothing to bind them to the state. They will make off at the first opportunity, and it therefore becomes important for us to prevent desertion' (*Principes Généraux de la Guerre*, Frederick, 1846–1857, XXVIII, I, 4).

The resulting discipline and constraints made the Prussian service notorious throughout Europe. Less well known was the fact that the Prussian army was sustained by excellent administration, which ensured that the soldiers were provided with regular pay, nourishing food and annual issues of new clothing. The Prussians also had the benefit of continuity and stability in their military institutions, because Old Fritz changed very little in the equipment and routine which he had inherited from his father.

After the Seven Years War military Europe tried to imitate whatever it was that made Prussia so successful in war, but the Prussomaniacs seldom saw any further than details of uniforms and tactics which were really of no importance. When foreign officers made their pilgrimage to Prussia, they were surprised to find that the authentic Prussians were more casual and far less artificially 'Prussian' than their imitators elsewhere in Europe.

Austria

The Austrian dominions were the possessions of the House of Habsburg, which sprawled across Europe from the North Sea to the Transylvanian Alps and the plain of Lombardy. The army took in decidedly 'hot' elements like the Hungarians and the hardy folk of the Croatian borderlands, but the regulars were recruited most heavily from Bohemia, Moravia, Austrian Lombardy, the Austrian Netherlands and the states of southern Germany, which made for a force that was long on staying-power but slow-moving on the offensive. The Austrian artillery was forged into a devastating instrument before the Seven Years War, and Austrian standards of staff work and administration became very high. The officer corps was the most heterogenous in Europe.

Poland

The Polish forces entered the Age of Reason much as they were described by Hanns Friedrich Fleming:

> The Polacks are not very good as soldiers . . . the best use you
> can make of them is in raiding parties, but they are not so easy
> to control as regular troops. They are proud, obstinate and
> pleasure-loving; they like alcoholic spirits, and they are given
> to forming factions. (Fleming, 1726, I, 41)

Poland was cursed by open borders, greedy neighbours, a system of elective monarchy, and a large and argumentative nobility. All the more credit is due to the perseverance of King Stanislas Augustus, who came to the throne in 1764 and undertook the herculean task of military reform. He had hardly begun work before a new period of civil strife opened in 1768, and four years later Russia, Austria and Prussia proceeded to help themselves to 221,200 square kilometres of the national territory (30 per cent), and 4,530,000 new subjects (35 per cent of the population).

Inside truncated Poland a measure of stability returned in the middle 1770s. Two reforming Diets came together, and the years between 1774 and 1777 saw the foundation of an artillery school, and the publication of codes of military law and regulations for the infantry and artillery. The king regained control of the four regiments of the royal guard, and he won the right to commission officers throughout the army except in the large and obstructive Noble National Cavalry. Tax revenues rose steadily from 1776, which enabled the state to stabilise its budget, and from 1788 the surplus was spent on items of military infrastructure like barracks and stores. It had been impossible to reach a projected military establishment of 20,000 troops in the middle 1770s, but 57,000 men were under arms in 1791, and 65,000 in 1792.

By now we are on the verge of another Partition, and the epic of national resistance which lasted until the fall of Praga to the Russians in 1794. We have made this excursion, not because Poland was of any real account as a military power, but to illustrate how even a country as remote and benighted as this could become the object of 'Enlightened' military reform.

Russia

In the view of many observers, Russia had one of the worst officer corps in Europe. It seemed to be full of scoundrels who were unprofessional, drunken, corrupt, comfort-loving, cowardly and insensible to 'honour' as that term was understood in the West.

The Russian army had three great strengths. The material and effectiveness of its artillery were outstanding. It produced, every generation or so, gifted and imaginative high commanders of the calibre of Rumyantsev, Potemkin and Suvorov. The third prop was the infantry, which was universally allowed to be the most solid in the modern world:

> The physical and mental attributes of the Russians are such as to make them the best people of all for war. They are long-enduring, tough and insensitive, and find it easy to withstand the hardships of campaigning. They devour great quantities of raw and uncooked food, they drink spirits like water, and their physical constitution is so hard that they bathe in rivers in the coldest weather. (Anon., 1758, 15).

Italy

In Italy, and in southern Europe generally, the military profession was held in low regard, and states like Piedmont-Sardinia, Genoa and Venice were forced to recruit very heavily among foreigners in order to make up the deficiency:

> I recall that when I was in Turin forty years ago, I was invited to see the interesting sight of fifty bandits who had been bound together and were destined for the galleys. An officer of a native Italian regiment had been given permission to enlist the strongest and tallest among them as recruits. Those whom he selected were plunged into the depths of despair. They threatened to take their own lives, and they begged in the name of God and all his saints to be spared, for their crimes were no worse than those of their comrades. Now tell me, are men like these fit to be soldiers?! (Warnery, 1785–91, II, 67)

This was in Piedmont-Sardinia, which was the most military of the Italian states. The Piedmontese officers were well paid, by Italian standards, but there was insufficient military employment for the native nobles, and many of these gentlemen had to find opportunities abroad, like the gallant Peter Guasco who defended Schweidnitz so well for the Austrians in 1762.

It is striking that so little use was made of the potentially excellent material that was at hand. The Piedmontese militiamen, like the citizen companies of Genoa, were loyal and brave, and Savoy, with its poor but courageous nobility, might have been the making of a Piedmontese Prussia.

Spain

It seemed to commentators that Spain had retreated from Europe, and virtually from the world of the eighteenth century. From the pages of Santa Cruz the Spanish soldiers emerge as savage and ignorant creatures, who were more reliably dangerous to their officers than to their enemy. Spain made something of a stir at the very beginning of the Age of Reason, thanks to the aggressive and reforming policies of Cardinal Alberoni and Queen Elizabeth Farnese, and yet a description of a Spanish expeditionary force at this period can represent the troops as a 'discouraged, suppressed, beggar'd, unpaid, naked-legged, barrel-headed, unofficered, undisciplined parcel of wretches' (*The Weekly Journal or Saturday's Post*, 15 February 1718).

No real improvement could be detected for the rest of the century:

> The Spaniards have never changed. Except for their hair, which is now powdered and curled, the soldiers remain in the same condition as seventy years ago. Their generals are totally ignorant of tactics, for they owe their promotion to favouritism, or to long service in garrisons where their only occupation was to arrange the processions to the burnings at the stake, and so on. (Scharnhorst, 1782–3, II, 138)

The basic failing was to be traced to the government, which 'set no store by having good troops, and allowed the generals and colonels to make officers out of their servants, or even the children of their servants. This does the military condition no good at all' (Gorani, 1944, 281).

Portugal

The Portuguese were historically at daggers drawn with their Spanish neighbours, but in the eighteenth century they resembled them very closely in the matter of general military incompetence. Such successes as the Portuguese enjoyed were almost invariably the work of able foreign commanders, such as Count Wilhelm Friedrich Ernst von Schaumburg-Lippe (1724–77), who led Portugal to victory over the Spanish in 1762, and built up an army of some 30,000 well-disciplined troops.

By the 1780s German officers reported that the Portuguese had reverted to the same pitiable state as before. The fundamental reason, as so often in southern Europe, was the lack of recognition and honour attached to the trade of arms:

> Most of the subalterns belonging to the garrison of Lisbon also have the honour of serving as valet to some *hombre ricco* or *hidalgo*. You may see a Portuguese lieutenant, fully-uniformed with his gorget under his chin, leave his post on guard and betake himself to his second master in order to pull off his stockings, hand him his night cap, or comb his wig. (Warnery, 1785–91, IV, 298)

Denmark

In matters military Denmark was a kind of Nordic Portugal, where civilian values were predominant. Denmark had known uninterrupted peace from 1720, and it had dropped from the ranks of second-rate powers, but even this most pacific of countries experienced its period of 'Enlightened' military reform. The agent was that abrasive individual Claude-Louis Comte de Saint-Germain (1707–78), who became a Danish field-marshal in 1761. He set up a centralised War Directorate in 1763, but he found that further progress was opposed by the nobility, who dominated the military administration and served as commanders of the territorial militia – an arrangement which helped to keep the peasants tied down to the lordly estates. The Danish professional army was a smallish force, and it had to compete on the international market for mercenaries (again the parallels with Mediterranean countries are close). Saint-Germain unhesitatingly purged the officer corps, and he set up a unitary army in which each regiment was constituted partly of professionals and partly of natives conscripted on the Prussian cantonal model.

Saint-Germain's patron, King Frederick V, died in 1766, and in the next year the Frenchman fell from grace. The Saint-Germain episode in Danish military history, like many of its counterparts elsewhere in Europe, lacked a broad institutional base and a continuity in political direction.

Sweden

After the Great Northern War (1700–21) Sweden was incapable of intervening with force on the mainland of Europe. When the Swedes joined the great coalition against Frederick in the Seven Years War they offered little threat to Prussian Pomerania, and only in their semi-amphibious operations against Russia (1788–90) did they show something of their old military prowess: 'The Swedes are no longer to be feared. Their state is poor and meagerly populated, and they have abdicated the heroic reputation they enjoyed at the time of Charles XII' (Algarotti, 1772, IV, 348).

The Low Countries

The Dutch Republic was another of those states which had last cut a figure at the turn of the seventeenth and eighteenth centuries. Dutch troops had been the backbone of the Allied armies in the Low Countries in the War of the Spanish Succession, and no less than 10,000 Dutchmen were killed or wounded on the field of Malplaquet (1709). They preserved their reputation for steadiness and discipline for some years yet (Bland, 1727, 145), but during the War of the Austrian Succession they stood out only through their obstinate defence of Bergen-op-Zoom in 1747. Dutch foreign policy tended more and more towards neutrality, and the republic held aloof from the dramas of the Seven Years War. By the middle of the eighteenth century, therefore, the Dutch had virtually ceased to be counted among the military peoples.

In 1715 the House of Habsburg assumed the sovereignty of the southern Netherlands. The Austrian Netherlands, as they were now called, corresponded roughly with the area of present-day Belgium excluding the area around Liège. The 'Belgians' (despite a general prejudice to the contrary) have for centuries shown themselves to be one of the more warlike populations of Europe. The Belgian army was to give an heroic account of itself in 1914 and 1940, and in the eighteenth century the Netherlanders, and more specifically the French-speaking Walloons, made an important contribution to the Austrian military effort. The Walloons also served in great numbers as mercenaries in foreign armies, and such glory as the Spanish gained on fields like Piacenza (1746) was due largely to the Netherlanders who fought in their ranks.

The English

There was a clear consensus as to the military character of the English (the word 'British' was little used in Europe at the time). Their materiel was of the finest: their artillery pieces were accurately bored-out and cleanly finished; their sturdy, beef-fed soldiers were clad in uniforms of good-quality cloth, and their horses were reckoned to be the fastest in Europe – equally suited for moving cavalry and senior officers.

The most pronounced moral traits of the English were violence and patriotism. The street battles of the London mobs were notorious, and continental Europeans noted how the populace flocked to bloody prize fights and the grisly tragedies of Shakespeare. Among the superior orders of society, political debate appeared to run with unbridled freedom. All classes were united in their contempt for foreigners. The French renegade Bonneville had the misfortune to serve with the English on the Rochefort expedition in 1757, and 'when I summon up in my mind all the remote quarters of the globe in which I have travelled, I say to myself that of all the peoples I have seen there are none who are more savage or unsociable than the English' (Bonneville, 1762, I, 85).

There was nothing exceptional or extraordinary about the hatred which the English bore against the French, even though they were hereditary enemies and their nearest neighbours. The English hated everyone else as well. The American provincial troops in the French and Indian War, the German auxiliaries on the continent of Europe in the Seven Years War and again in North America in the 1770s – they all found that the English were 'amazingly proud and haughty, and imbued with a scorn for all other nations' (Döhla, 1912, 145).

The fury and the xenophobia made for an 'epedmick bravery' which was recognised as unique. It was seen in the monstrous column at Fontenoy in 1745, and again at Minden in 1759, when six battalions of English infantry attacked and overthrew seventy-two squadrons of French cavalry (Scharnhorst, 1782–3, II, 129; Warnery, 1785–1, III, 38, 110; Mauvillon, J., 1794, II, 55, 270; Besenval, 1827–8, I, 92; Lehndorff, 1910–13, I, 217).

Dr Samuel Johnson examined the matter more closely. He found that the English bravery was dispersed among the ranks, yet had nothing in common with the machine-like order that was seen among the Prussians. It did not proceed from the leadership of superiors (for the English acknowledged no masters), nor was it inspired by any attachment to concepts of property or constitutional liberty. Johnson concluded that the bravery of the English proceeded from the Englishman's 'want of subordination' and his high opinion of his individual worth: 'they who complain, in peace, of the insolence of the populace, must remember, that their insolence in peace is bravery in war' ('On the Bravery of the English Common Soldier', Johnson, 1801–10, II, 430).

When considered in isolation, the English officer class nevertheless failed to impress the Europeans. Jakob Mauvillon had seen it at close quarters in the campaigns in the Seven Years War, and he testifies

> All their commissions may be obtained through purchase, and the consequence is that their officers do not bother about the service, and (with very very few exceptions) have no understanding of it whatsoever – and that goes for every rank from ensign to general. Their concept of life makes them into lovers of comfort, and they are nearly all given to long periods of luxurious sleep. (Mauvillon, J., 1794, II, 272).

The continental verdict is summed up by the Prince de Ligne: 'they are brave without being soldierly, and gentlemen without being officers' (Ligne, 1795–1811, I, 160).

The mercenaries

In the eighteenth century individuals of all ranks of society passed with almost untrammelled freedom from the service of one master to that of another. Many of Frederick's 'Prussians' were in fact Italians, Frenchmen, or Swiss like the compatriots whom Private Ulrich Bräker found in the regiment of Itzenplitz:

> As soon as drill was over we used to fly to Schottmann's beer cellar. There we would down a mug of Ruhin or Gottwitz beer, smoke a pipe, and warble one of our songs from Switzerland. The Brandenburgers and Pomeranians were fond of hearing us, and on occasion some of these gentry used to ask us to an eating house expressly to have us sing our herdsmen's songs. Mostly our reward was just some cloudy soup. (Bräker, 1852, 125–6)

The hire or formation of foreign units as integral bodies was another characteristic feature of military interchange. The British used to go shopping on a big scale in Germany, and hire whole contingents of auxiliaries for the duration of their wars. The French practice was to maintain regiments of foreign troops as permanent parts of the royal army. Thus, in the Seven Years War, the establishment of foreign troops in the French service stood at nearly 50,000 men, and comprised thirteen or fourteen regiments of Germans, between ten and thirteen of Swiss, five or six of Irish, two of Scots, two of Italians, and five of 'Hungarian' hussars.

The foreigners came in a variety of types. Bräker and his friends were recruited (or kidnapped) as individuals. The Irish, Scots and Hungarians had more the character of religious or political refugees. The Swiss, German and Walloon regiments had a greater resemblance to private commercial enterprises, while the contingents which were hired out by the German states were used to raise money for the sovereign and sometimes also as an indirect instrument of policy.

This 'trade in human beings' (*Menschenhandel*) came under attack from humanitarian writers like Friedrich Carl von Moser, but the ethics and justification of the thing had been worked out in some detail. States like Britain, France, the Dutch Republic, Spain and the other Mediterranean countries undoubtedly paid very heavily for their foreign troops. As the saying went, *point d'argent, point de Suisse*. On the other hand a hired foreign soldier not only added to the strength of the state, but he freed a native subject for productive labour and he deprived the enemy of a potential recruit. Thus one man became the equivalent of three. Schertel von Burtenbach added that it was misleading to talk about hired soldiers lacking genuine love, loyalty or zeal for their paymaster, for they were bound to him by something more reliable, namely 'their own advantage and welfare' (Schertel von Burtenbach, 1779, 183. See also General von Estorf, quoted in Jähns, 1889–91, III, 2, 165; Saxe [1748] quoted in Corvisier, 1963, 260).

This contention is borne out by the record of the Walloons in the Spanish employ at Piacenza (1746), and the Swiss regiment of Diesbach which fought so well in the ranks of the French at Rossbach (1757). The Hessian knew that he was

Born to be a soldier; from his youth he hears of nothing else. The farmer who bears arms tells to his son his adventures, and the lad, eager to tread in the footsteps of his elder, trains his feeble arms early to the use of formidable weapons; so when he has reached a size necessary to take a place in the valiant ranks, he is quickly formed into a soldier. (Quoted in Atwood, 1980, 20)

Altogether the employer of foreign soldiers seems to have received a good return for his money.

The sovereign who hired out his troops was not necessarily a heartless monster. Indeed Friedrich II, who became Landgraf of Hesse in 1762, was a model ruler after the pattern of his time. He reformed justice and the administration, and as an enlightened and cultivated prince he promoted learning and opened the first public museum in Central Europe. By placing his troops at the disposal of foreign powers, a sovereign like this could win friends, raise money for useful objectives, and keep up military experience and military values among his people.

Eventually, through the rise of nationalism in the nineteenth century, mercenary activity was confined to formations of the Foreign Legion type. More immediately the character of some of the most celebrated foreign units was threatened by processes of internal disintegration. The Swiss regiments, wherever they were found, were accustomed to running affairs according to their own rules, which gave rise to abuses like plural or hereditary companies, some of which were actually passed on by way of a female line. Moreover it became common for regiments that were nominally Swiss, German or Irish to be filled in the course of time with criminals and international riff-raff. The Baron de Besenval claims to have restored professional standards when he became Inspector of Swiss troops in France after the Seven Years War (Besenval, 1827-8, I, 21), but elsewhere many of the units of Swiss were in unmistakable decline.

2
The officer class

The aristocratic pre-eminence

The nobility derives its origins, and most of its
privileges, from the military establishment of our
ancestors.

(Wolff, 1776, 18)

To talk about the nobility was to use terms which carried a constant
reminder of ancient connections between high birth and leadership
in war. *Chevalier*, *Caballero* and *Ritter* all signified literally 'the man
on horseback', conveying images of physical and social elevation and
tactical superiority. The German *Herzog* was originally the leader of
an army, like the French *duc*, just as *Markgraf* had been a border
commander and *Freiherr* (baron) a freed soldier.

The link endured into the eighteenth century (and in some countries well beyond), and it was endorsed by authorities who were by
no means supporters of an exclusively noble claim to officer rank.
From what we have already seen it is evident that the military
prowess of a country often stood in a direct relation to the social
standing of its officer corps, which gave privilege a utilitarian aspect
which could not be overlooked.

The principal of natural justice was also invoked, for the nobility
'knows no other condition of life, no profession other than that of
arms. This prejudice is so deeply rooted that a gentleman who cannot
find a post in the army will choose to remain buried in his native
province, without employment or occupation' (memorandum of
1781, quoted in Tuetey, 1908, 1). It was assumed that when a bourgeois officer happened to fall from grace he could merge back into
civilian society without great embarrassment, but 'what resort does

a nobleman have, if he does not wish to dishonour his most precious jewel, his noble condition? A dishonoured noble is rejected by his kind, and not only injures himself, but shames his whole otherwise deserving family' (Pauli, 1758–64, I, 230).

The military nobility was brought up on fireside tales of heroic deeds, it risked its life on the hunting field, it measured swords with anybody who impugned its honour, and it exercised a daily habit of command on its lands. These connections were transferred to the military life, where 'the relations between the nobleman and the commoner remain unaltered; it would be demeaning . . . to require him to take his place among the crowd of common soldiers, who will often be his own tenants' (Cogniazzo, 1779, 109).

We must now ask how the nobles contrived to stay at the top of the pile. In the first place they enjoyed the great advantages which came from the example, teaching and help of relations and friends. François-Joseph Darut de Grandpré relates that when he was still only three, his father

> asked the Duc de L ★★★, who was then colonel of the regiment of T ★★★, for a second-lieutenant's commission. . . . It was granted at once. In 1736 all the places of second lieutenant were abolished as part of the general reduction of the army [i.e. after the end of the War of the Polish Succession]. However, there was no limit to the loving care which my father bore towards me. He bought me a lieutenancy, and I was therefore spared from the cuts. (Darut de Grandpré, 1787, I, 11)

Truly, 'our good fortune proceeds only from the support of the friends we make in this world' (Guignard, 1725, II, 484).

It does not take long to discover one of the reasons why there was a revolution in France before any other country of Europe. While Frederick insisted on noble birth as a qualification for commissioned rank in his infantry and regular cavalry, there was no exact understanding in Prussia or Germany as a whole as to what families were noble or not, which introduced a measure of flexibility.

> Whoever affords it, may become a count or baron irrespective of birth or service. I recall that when I first came to know the late General Winterfeldt I assumed that he was a count. He let me know that he considered this to be an insult, for he was a nobleman of an ancient house. (Warnery, 1785–91, II, 69)

Austria maintained a genealogical archive, but the officials often accepted documentation at its face value, and made no objection to far-fetched family trees such as those submitted by the Brownes, who claimed to be descended from Hengist and Horsa.

In contrast, the French practice was indefensible on two accounts. All too often the French nobility came forward to claim its privileges without any correspondence to real services; thus the young men from powerful court families could reasonably expect to become subalterns at around fifteen, captains at eighteen and colonels at twenty-three. Second, the predominance of the nobility was institutionalised to a higher degree than in probably any other state in Europe. In the expeditionary corps that went to bring freedom to America in 1780, about 85 per cent of the officers were of the nobility, and among these the leadership was clearly exercised by the 30 per cent whose titles dated from the middle ages. The newcomers who went back only as far as the sixteenth century were at a severe disadvantage, and they were virtually barred from becoming colonels (Bodinier, 1983, 78, 113).

The French nobility had experienced a collective *frisson* when, in 1750, a royal edict established a *noblesse militaire*, granted to a number of categories of deserving bourgeois officers (see p. 44). Already in 1758 this concession became a dead letter, and over the following years a number of fairly brutal actions were taken against individual officers from the middle classes. In 1764 Lieutenant Lantier, the son of a Marseilles merchant, was on leave at home when he received a letter from his colonel, the Marquis de Crenolle, informing him that his place in his regiment had been taken by a noble:

> You are well-off and young, and you will not be without an occupation as long as you devote yourself to the kind of life which was followed by your ancestors – it is a perfectly acceptable one when it is pursued honourably. However, by desiring to serve in the army you are out of your sphere; go back to your former condition, and you will be happy. I know, *Monsieur*, that high birth is the result of chance and that it should not be the object of vainglorious pride. But birth brings privileges and rights which cannot be violated without disturbing the public order. (Tuetey, 1908, 242)

The Marseilles bourgeoisie was outraged, but the minister of war supported the colonel's decision.

From the 1770s nobility was required of candidates for the traditionally broad-based corps of artillery and engineers, and finally a notorious decision of 22 May 1781 demanded at least four generations of full and unimpeachable nobility for every future officer. The domination of the nobles in the French army had never seemed more firmly buttressed than on the eve of the Revolution.

THE GRANDEES

In the leading military nations the nobility was divided by a surprisingly clear distinction between ancient and wealthy families of princely or nearly-princely status, and the mass of the poor country nobility:

> The first class simply walks into the leading offices as a matter of right, while the second class is condemned by birth or poverty to lifelong service in subordinate positions . . . The first class does not work in order to succeed; the second class does not work at all, for it knows that labour is useless. (Saint-Germain, 1779, 136–7)

In Russia, in the early eighteenth century, social power could be reckoned by the number of peasant households owned by the individual noble families. A family like the Naryshkins had a decided lead with 11,113 such households; then came lines like the Golitsyns (7,860) and the Saltykovs (7,758). The Volkonskys, Buturlins and Leon'tevs represented a second league of magnates (2,332–1, 313), but they were still comfortably ahead of all but a very few of the lesser nobility. The counterparts of these great men in France were the princes of the royal blood, the leaders of the greatest noble houses, and generally the 'presented' *noblesse de cour* who had titular proof of nobility deriving from the fourteenth century. Their young men were virtually assured of rapid promotion to colonel, after nominal service in a junior grade, and then of advance to field rank.

The great nobility at its worst lived out its days uselessly in the capital; when it went to war, it did so in circumstances of considerable luxury, and it returned home with the greatest speed at the close of every campaign. These men drew the hate of the poor nobility and all professionally minded officers. Langeron found a 'total lack of zeal and courage in the Russian magnates, and especially that mob of volunteers – courtiers, Muscovites and Guardsmen – who came out to the active army to deprive deserving officers of their rewards' (Langeron, 1895, 169).

In justice to the grandees it must be said that few of them expected any financial return from their military careers. Indeed, the lowest price at which it was possible to purchase a regimental colonelcy in France stood at 22,500 livres, and you would have to pay up to 120,000 livres for a really fashionable regiment. Once installed in place, the colonel in nearly every army was expected to pay handsomely from his own pocket to maintain open table for his officers, support a fitting regimental 'music', and provide ornaments and gratifications for his officers and soldiers. A number of prominent individuals ran through much of their own fortunes (and sometimes also those of others). Thus the regeneration of the Austrian and Russian artillery before the Seven Years War was the personal work of Prince Joseph Wenzel Liechtenstein and Prince Petr Ivanovich Shuvalov. Even Britain produced an authentic grandee in the person of John Manners, Marquis of Granby, who died in 1770 regretted by the soldiers and the public – and leaving debts estimated at £37,000.

Many a German reigning prince or his heir apparent entered the service of Austria or Prussia, bringing with him a well-found regiment and a genuine dedication to the military life (see p. 23). The arrival of a princely commander had the effect of calming rivalries among the generals (Lehndorff, 1910–13, I, 175), while at the regimental level 'the prestige which birth usually commands will spare a colonel from having to say, in effect, "respect me just because I am a colonel" ' (Ligne, 1795–1811, I, 141). The bourgeois officer was likely to find that an affable grandee made a more agreeable commander than the lesser noble, who was inclined to be on his dignity. A French staff officer warned deserving young men that self-made *chevaliers d'industrie* also made bad superiors, for they exploited subordinates to advance their own careers,

> but it is a different story when you associate yourself with
> houses of the first order, like those of the princes of the royal
> blood, the Princes of Soubise and Bouillon, the Dukes of
> Noailles and Richelieu . . . or the other houses of the same
> kind, renowned for their easy prosperity and their noble
> generosity. (Le Rouge, 1760, 4).

Regiments of the Guard

For the high nobility bodies of household troops incorporated the principle of highest privilege, as expressed in closeness to the person of the sovereign. As might have been expected, the three regiments of the Russian Guard carried matters to an extreme. Each regiment maintained on its books between 3,000 and 4,000 supernumerary NCOs, who were in fact young members of the higher nobility, who were waiting until in their mid-teens they were designated Captains of the Guard, and were therefore qualified to be admitted to the active army, if they so wished, as colonels or brigadiers – and all without ever having seen a private soldier. In our period the Russian Guard never went to war.

In the 1750s the French Maison du Roi was a glittering assemblage of rather over 9,000 men, comprising two infantry regiments (the Gardes Françaises and the Gardes Suisses), and the all-noble Maison cavalry – the eight squadrons of the Gardes du Corps, the company of Gendarmes, the company of Chevaux–Légers, the two companies of Mousquetaires and the single company of the Grenadiers à Cheval. The French Maison did most of its duties at court, but unlike its Russian counterpart it was not a complete stranger to the battlefield. One of the French regiments of the line, the Régiment du Roi, had virtual Maison status, for the king was its colonel proprietor, and all the officers and many of the NCOs and corporals were of good noble blood.

In Prussia the Régiment-Garde was 'formed of such handsome men that you might have thought you were among Amazons' (Prittwitz, 1935, 84–5). These beings figured prominently in peacetime parades at Potsdam, but they were also expected to earn their keep on the battlefield, and in the event they were very badly knocked about at Kolin in 1757. It is striking that the Austrians maintained no guard regiments at all.

The Comte de Saint-Germain reckoned that the Maison cost more than three times as much as the equivalent number of troops of the line. 'Just because a man is decked out in braid and lace, and has a higher pay, it does not mean that he is any better than a soldier of the line when it comes to war. In fact he is often worse' (Saint-Germain, 1779, 152).

Some powerful forces must have been at work to persuade the monarchs to support such expensive bodies of troops. The Prince de

Montbarey, who opposed Saint-Germain's projects for reform, argued that the Maison was 'indispensable for the brilliance and maintenance of the throne' (Montbarey, 1826-7, II, 163). The household troops indeed offered a last line of physical defence, as the Swiss Guard was going to prove in 1792. The Russian empresses Anna, Elizabeth and Catherine the Great owed their thrones to palace revolutions that were hatched with the help of the Guard, and with every change of rule this force accumulated more honours and privileges.

What Montbarey meant by 'brilliance' was a manifestation of the spirit of the age, which showed forth monarchical power through architecture, festivities, costume and etiquette. Thus in France, the office of captain-lieutenant in the Chevaux-Légers was hereditary in the house of Chaulnes, the leader of which had the right to commission suitably qualified officers in his own name. 'Another privilege which the Chevaux-Légers share with the Gendarmerie, is that when this company returns from campaign, an officer carries the standards into the king's bedchamber after the royal supper. He places them beside His Majesty's bed, and allows no one else to touch them' (Belleval, 1866, 5).

THE LESSER NOBILITY

The strength of the officer corps lay in the English 'private gentry', the French *noblesse d'épée*, the Prussian *Junkers* and their equivalents in other lands. The qualities of these people were idealised by their most eloquent champion, the Prince de Ligne, who desired a body of regimental officers drawn from

> that class of poor and honourable gentlemen. Their ancestors had attained nobility through some warlike deed. They grew up as the sons of valiant squires, who themselves were accustomed to country life and the hunt. From the age of twelve they conditioned themselves to hardship, sleeping in the woods with their dogs, arresting poachers, and fighting every now and then with a neighbour's son over the possession of a hare. (Ligne, 1795–1811, II, 149)

On the continent of Europe the small country nobility lived out the last decades of the old regime in a state of crisis, squeezed between the grandees on one side and the rising middle classes on the other.

At home the worst-off of the nobles were distinguishable from the peasantry only by their titles and the wearing of swords, and on campaign they existed in a state of near-starvation. In France the price of food and accommodation doubled within living memory, and there were very few sons of the squirearchy who could afford the three or four hundred livres of private income that a second-lieutenant needed in order to live in basic comfort (Tuetey, 1908, 15).

Such solace as the *hobereaux* enjoyed was to their pride rather than to their bellies. Frederick told his aristocrats to serve for the sake of honour, and that ideal was the only thing that 'could have made service as an officer tolerable for the poor nobility' (Seidl, 1821, 390). In France the nobles came under the protection of the measures that were taken to safeguard the officer corps against the influx of the bourgeoisie, and especially the edict of 1758, whereby the war minister Marshal Belle-Isle prohibited the sale of commissions in the infantry. One of his supporters claimed that 'promotions had been sold like goods on a stall. It was a trade which brought no advantage to the service of the king, and was not calculated to raise the prestige of the officer in the eyes of the soldiers' (Belleval, 1866, 12–13). Concessions like these illustrate the compromises which the so-called 'absolutist' governments were forced to make with established interests (Kunisch, 1983, 64).

GENTLEMAN RANKERS

In Prussia and some other German states, when a man of gentle birth was to be found among the private soldiers or NCOs, it was usually because he was serving a supervised apprenticeship before he was commissioned as an ensign or cornet:

> If an officer has young noblemen under his command, he must
> be no more indulgent towards them than to an ordinary
> soldier. He must make sure that they begin by carrying the
> musket and doing sentry duty like the others, until their good
> conduct makes them worthy of promotion. He must tolerate
> not the slightest symptom of ill-will, and he must visit severe
> punishment on any misdemeanour or display of frivolity. Even
> when such gentlemen have wealthy parents, he must keep

them short of cash, lest they should be tempted into all sorts of useless expenditure. (Fleming, 1726, I, 123–4)

France preserved more of the romantic traditions of early times, whereby noblemen were willing to sign themselves up from a sense of adventure or perverse pride. 'War is an honourable trade. Just call to mind all those princes who have borne a musket! – Turenne is one example. I have seen many an officer revert to the ranks rather than accept a demeaning condition of life' (Saxe [1732], 1877, 10).

THE MIDDLE CLASSES

In no country was there a totally effective prohibition against a commoner obtaining commissioned rank. Historians of British wars are familiar with the names of individuals like Sir William Draper (son of a customs official) who captured Manila in 1762, or the unfortunate Major John André, whose father was a merchant from Geneva.

Among the major continental powers, Austria pursued the most egalitarian policies of officer recruitment and promotion. The virtues of the established nobility were recognised, but the way was left clear for men of all conditions to become officers, and if they showed exceptional ability they could rise to high positions in the army and state. The *Nobilitätsdiplom* was awarded liberally, and in 1757 it was extended to all officers who had put in thirty years of unblemished service. The most brilliant example of the self-made man was Gideon Loudon, who came to Austria without friends or influence, and died in 1790 as field-marshal and the most celebrated soldier of the army. His funeral address gives some indication of the price he had to pay: 'Loudon had to make himself into what he was, and blaze his own trail. Consequently, when he had to appear among people of the first rank at court, he remained modest, reserved and bashful' (Kunisch, 1983, 71).

Men from the middle classes made their way with no great difficulty into the Russian officer corps, but they still faced interior bastions of privilege from where the aristocrats could bid defiance to the newcomers. The Guard was a notorious citadel of power and corruption, and even in the regiments of the line it was open to the officers to deny admission to any other officer whom they deemed unsuitable.

In France, the bourgeoisie had come nearest to effecting a break-through when, in 1750 (see p. 37), the war minister the Comte d'Argenson instituted a military nobility for the benefit of meritorious commoner officers, and especially those who had records of good service in the last war: 'They have ennobled themselves through their own actions, and deserved to become noble, even if they do not yet have the title' (Tuetey, 1908, 262). In this favourable atmosphere the middle-class element reached an estimated one-third of the total officer corps. The influx was restricted in 1758, as we have seen, and the aristocratic reaction set in with full force after the Seven Years War, with the result that the bourgeoisie accounted for only 15 per cent of the officers whom Rochambeau took with him to America in 1780 (see p. 37). About half of these survivors were veterans of the wars of the middle decades of the century, and the rest had successfully adopted a noble style of life, or had furnished themselves with false certificates of nobility or baptism.

The Prussian reaction was the handiwork of Frederick in person, who took it into his head to purge his officer corps after the Seven Years War. A veteran wrote:

> It greatly promoted an esprit de corps to have nearly all the officers of the regiments of the line drawn from the nobility. . . . The bourgeois officers were in a minority, and they commanded less respect unless they were really outstanding . . . This was reprehensible, no doubt, but it is in the nature of things. (Seidl, 1821, 381)

The dispossessed Prussian infantry officer had nowhere to go, except possibly to the gunners. The cavalry officers were more fortunate, since they could betake themselves to the regiments of hussars, where men of their background had always been admitted:

> Taken as a whole, the bourgeois officers were far better educated than the nobles, even in the higher reaches of knowledge, and they showed far greater decorum in their conduct. In fact there were many nobles who were total ignoramuses. These men from the middle class had an excellent effect on the spirit of the regiment. They nearly all hailed from respectable and decent families. Most of them were volunteers, who wished to advance themselves through military service, and they accordingly cultivated a certain dignity of manner in their off-duty hours.

Their example had an astonishing effect. The ordinary hussars strove to catch up with them, so as to be judged equally worthy of promotion. Our corps of NCOs was therefore of an exemplary standard. (Lojewsky, 1843, I, 294–5)

THE LOWER ORDERS

In Britain, France and some of the German services a special niche was reserved for 'officers of fortune'. These were reliable ex-soldiers, who lived out the rest of their military lives as lieutenants, doing tedious but invaluable work within the regiment. The colonel of the regiment of Provence explained: 'I make it an invariable rule to keep a number of lieutenants of fortune. They help the service along. They know the soldiers and their way of thinking better than we do. They put in solid work' (Tuetey, 1908, 281). In France in 1763 the officers of fortune accounted for 6.4 per cent of the officer corps of the infantry, 16.8 per cent of the heavy cavalry, 15.5 per cent of the dragoons and 33.8 per cent of the artillery.

Very occasionally one of these excellent people succeeded in breaking the bounds. There was almost universal admiration for François Chevert (1695–1769), a man of low birth who began his military career as a private soldier in the regiment of Beauce. He was commissioned lieutenant in 1711, and after a very slow ascent he was made lieutenant-colonel in 1739. He distinguished himself at the storm of Prague in 1741, and earned golden opinions from Marshal Belle-Isle, who took him under his wing. Chevert became brigadier-general in 1742, major-general in 1745 and lieutenant-general in 1748, and he went on to serve with great distinction in the Seven Years War.

Little evidence survives about the life and mentality of the officer of fortune. Warnery claims that such a man was usually an unhappy creature who had

become accustomed to a certain way of living, and the society of the cookshop, the beer house and the spirit cellar. He is in a still worse state if he is married, for the lady of the new ensign or lieutenant wishes to live like a woman of condition; her hands were made for doing the laundry and so on, but she no longer desires to apply them to toil. The man's pay hardly suffices for a cup of coffee, and his family, which was once comfortably off, is now reduced to dire poverty. (Warnery, 1785–91, II, 68)

In France, several generations of officers of fortune had been content to serve in the hope, however faint, of further advance up the officer ranks. All the greater was the shock and resentment when, on 10 July 1780 and 1 June 1781, orders were issued which barred them from promotion to captain. The officers of fortune as a class were therefore alienated from the established order, and many of these men ultimately became enthusiastic supporters of the Revolution.

Motivation

Men have always been fearful of how far their courage and abilities might fall short of the fearsome demands of war. There is no reason to think that the gap was any wider in the Age of Reason than in other periods, but the men of that time were more than usually inclined to put it down to a lack of aptitude and inclination. The root of the problem was that armies had been expanded beyond all measure without a commensurate attention having been given to choosing and training the necessary officers. The result might be called a 'crisis of motivation'.

A French officer declared:

> You must have an active turn of mind. You must rejoice at rising from your night's rest to be in the saddle at daybreak, when you can see with your own eyes the state of your weapons and your soldiers. You must delight in ranging them in rank and file, when you can read on their faces the revival of their hopes and their confidence in success. If you do not respond to such things, the trade of arms is not for you. (Comte de Chabot, quoted in Ray, 1895, 114. See also Ligne, 1795–1811, II, 3–4)

An officer who was inspired with this degree of motivation was a rare individual. Many perfectly adequate officers took up the military profession simply as a means of earning a livelihood; for people like that 'long service and good service are the same thing' (Frederick, quoted in Jähns, 1889–91, III, 2, 439). Others hoped to fill an inner emptiness, 'loving war as a means of satisfying their need for occupation or as a remedy for boredom, exposing themselves to danger for the same kind of motives as a man who goes hunting foxes' (Schaumburg-Lippe, 1977–81, II, 158).

As contemporaries insisted, a large group of men ended up as officers simply from inertia, for it was 'an accepted habit among men of quality to assign the eldest of their children to the profession of arms, and the others to the church' (Quincy, 1726, VIII, 5. See also Turpin de Crissé, 1754, I, 9–11; Bonneville, 1762, I, 25). All too little heed was given to the wishes and talents of the young people concerned, and the mis-matchings were very frequent, 'and so a man who would have made a fine captain of dragoons is made a priest, and another, who is suited for a quiet life, is made a captain of dragoons' (d'Espagnac, 1751, I, 76–7).

However, a number of more resolute individuals were able to break out of their cages, which gave rise to a significant cross-traffic between church and army. The counts Saint-Germain and Rochambeau and the Austrian field-marshal Andreas Haddik were all ex-Jesuit student priests who turned to a military career. The Comte de Clermont was abbé of Saint Germain des Prés, and received a Papal dispensation in order to follow his military calling. Turpin de Crissé, the highly regarded authority on cavalry affairs, retreated from the world as a Trappist monk in the interval between the War of the Austrian Succession and the Seven Years War.

Preparation

MILITARY ACADEMIES

The continuous history of formal military education dates from the Age of Reason. Most of the early training establishments were specialised schools of artillery and engineering, and here an important lead was given by Peter the Great, who set up two academies of gunnery and two of military engineering. The surviving schools were combined by Petr Ivanovich Shuvalov after he became Master of the Ordnance in 1756, and under Catherine the Great this joint establishment became the excellent Artillery and Engineering Noble Land Cadet Corps.

The Dutch artillery school dated from 1735, and the Woolwich engineering and artillery academy was founded in 1741. In France the Mézières engineering school opened in 1749, and it was a hard-driving establishment which soon gained the reputation for being the most professional of its kind in Europe. So much for the shape of technical education.

The Prussian Cadet Corps was opened in Berlin in 1717 to provide a general grounding for officers of the field arms. The Russian Noble Land Cadet Corps was established in 1732 in direct imitation of the Prussian model. The French followed suit in 1751 with the foundation of the École Militaire in Paris, while the Austrian military academy opened at Wiener Neustadt in 1752. By the late 1770s most European states had comparable institutions.

If the Prussian Cadet Corps set the tone in the early decades, then the style of the Württemberg military academy at Stuttgart became widely admired in the last years of old Europe. Private military academies flourished in Russia, and also in France, where the schools at Angers, Brienne and Caen acquired an international esteem.

Cadets in most countries were familiar with the routine of the kind established in the Prussian cadet corps, where the first waking hour of every day was spent in fastening back and plastering down the hair with wax and talc; the next half hour was devoted to buttoning up the gaiters with a special hook, after which attention turned back to the hair, which was dusted heavily with powder. Outright bullying was less likely to come from the directing staff or the NCOs than from powerfully built cadets who took advantage of interludes of weak supervision, as happened at Berlin in the Seven Years War. One of the victims remembered:

> Certain cadets assumed the role of mob leaders, and it amused and entertained them to break into the rooms of other cadets at night. When they wished to wreak some kind of vengeance, or extort money from them, they would maltreat them in various ways, such as dragging them under the pumps in the depths of winter and drenching them with water. A number of cadets . . . actually died as a result of these proceedings. (Anon, 1881, 88)

On the whole the technical schools furnished the potential officers with a good theoretical and practical grounding. However, the general establishments rarely lived up to the requirements of the field arms, and the principal reason was that there existed no settled idea of what military academies were supposed to do. The Paris École Militaire, for example, had the character of a philanthropic institution, which sought to provide an upbringing for the sons of poor officers. It was inefficient and expensive, it never attempted to furnish officers for the cavalry, and in 1776 it was disbanded into a number of provincial *écoles militaires*, leaving only a company of gentlemen cadets in Paris. In most of the academies the education was better suited for a citizen of the world than for a professional soldier, being of impressive scope but very thinly spread.

In every country the great majority of fledgling officers for the infantry and cavalry passed directly from home into their chosen regiments, without ever darkening the doors of a military academy. The formative influences on the young officer were therefore his domestic education and style of life, his professional reading, and his early experiences in his regiment. All of these matters now claim our attention.

THE COUNTRY LIFE

In one of the ante-rooms of the Royal Military Academy Sandhurst hang a series of watercolours entitled *Pink and Scarlet, or Hunting as a School for Soldiers*. The pictures are arranged in pairs, and illustrate how the pursuits of a country gentleman fit him for command in war. A huntsman who takes a good line across country will have a good eye for a covered approach which will bring his squadron within charging range of a battery. A rider who cares for his horse ('Well, Jim, has he fed all right?') will also be attentive to the welfare of his soldiers ('Dinners all right, men?'). The Sandhurst pictures bear the ominous date 1913, but they hark back to a much older understanding of the kind of upbringing that was best for an officer.

The mental conditioning began at an early age. According to the Chevalier de Ray,

> I spent my childhood in the castle whither my father had retired after the wars at the beginning of the present century, and I was entranced by the tales he told me. My imagination was fired by the accounts of his battles, and my soul took wing when he showed me his weapons and his scars. (Ray, 1895, 14. See also Pauli, 1758–64, I, 228–9; Garve, 1798, 161)

As an infant Charles-Joseph de Ligne had been carried in the arms of veteran dragoons of his uncle's regiment, who told him about the fields on which they had fought; he heard the battle of Fontenoy from his ancestral castle, he was in Brussels when it fell to the French, and he was taken by his father to see the sieges of Mons, Saint-

Ghislain and Ath. Hunting was an integral part of this schooling for war, for it

> inspires brave and cheerful spirits to despise fear and risk, it steels your temperament, and it schools the body to withstand all kinds of hardship through exposure to heat, frost and other kinds of adverse weather, through hunger, thirst and lack of sleep, and through the exertion of walking and running. It accustoms you to patience. (Fleming, 1726, I, 27)

It was *bon ton* to talk dismissively of the most appalling injuries which had been suffered in action or in the chase.

EDUCATION, ACCOMPLISHMENTS AND READING

Following ancient traditions, a number of young aristocrats were brought up as pages in the households of sovereigns or grandees. There were 158 places of this kind available with the king and the princes at Versailles, and in Germany the most celebrated product of the system was the Prussian cavalryman Friedrich Wilhelm von Seydlitz, who picked up his dissolute habits as a page at the court of the 'Mad Margrave' Friedrich of Brandenburg-Schwedt. A number of the more intelligent German Protestants made their way through university, and especially the one at Halle, and in the Germanic lands a good general education was available for the upper classes at the *Ritterakademien*, like the one at Liegnitz in Silesia which was attended by Franz Moritz von Lacy, who was to become head of the Austrian war machine in 1766.

Such experiences were exceptional, for most of the continental artistocrats were educated at home. This sheltered upbringing produced fiery Prussian hussars like Georg Christoph von Natzmer and Hans Joachim von Zieten, as well as deep-thinking individuals such as Prince Ferdinand of Brunswick:

> Ferdinand's education was entirely confined to his parental house. . . . This is not normally the environment best suited for forming a prince, but such an education can be most successful providing it is supervised by intelligent and vigilant parents who set a good example in all things. So it proved in this case. (Mauvillon, J., 1794, I, 18)

Suitable domestic tutors were to be found among clergymen, old

NCOs, retired officers of the artillery or engineers, or the unemployed university graduates who thronged Europe. Puységur and Guibert both had fathers who introduced them to the rudiments of the military trade with the help of sketches and counters.

One of the most valuable things a young officer could acquire was a fluent command of French, a language through which he could make himself understood in the ruling circles of army and state in all the major countries of Europe, with the possible exception of Spain. The linguistic demands on the Austrian officer were exceptionally heavy, because so many different nations were represented in the Habsburg service, but it was considered desirable for the officer of every army to have some comprehension of the tongue the local people spoke in the theatre of war.

A knowledge of geography, law and history was useful for every man of affairs. Mathematics and geometry were believed to sharpen the understanding, and in addition they provided the foundation for the science of fortification and helped the officer to calculate distance and movement. It is remarkable, however, that Frederick the Great was bad at sums and held mathematics in the utmost abhorrence.

A sense of proportion came with drawing and an acquaintance with civil architecture. Fencing endowed a young man with speed and strength, and dancing brought elegance and dignity to carriage and movement.

> Dancing is most necessary for the man of good education and for the officer. It makes him acceptable or even indispensable at parties when he relaxes in his off-duty hours. It is good for the officer to betake himself to such assemblies, and especially the mixed companies attended by ladies and pretty girls, which are an education for all persons of the male sex. (O'Cahill, 1787, 41–2)

Wealthy young men completed their civilian education by going on their travels, armed with sheaves of introductions to useful foreigners. They toured the famous sights and collections, they sampled the delights of society, and, if they were of a genuinely military turn of mind, they inspected fortresses, arsenals and battlefields.

By the 1750s the belief was current that experience alone did not enable the military man to progress in his knowledge: 'What distinguishes a man from a beast of burden is thought, and the faculty of bringing ideas together . . . a pack mule can go on ten campaigns with Prince Eugene of Savoy, and still learn nothing of tactics' (Frederick, 'Réflexions sur la Tactique et sur Quelques Parties de la Guerre', 1758, Frederick, 1846–57, XXVIII, 153–4). There was every confidence that men of insight would be able to reduce field warfare to firm principles such as those which had already been established for fortification and the natural sciences, and meanwhile an untutored courage was likely to do more harm than good. The bookish studies could not begin too early, for 'by means of theory a captain may learn what he has to do as a general, and it will be much too late if he postpones this task until he actually takes on the responsibility of field rank (Warnery, 1785–91, III, 115. See also Rohr, 1756, I, xv).

Where could the ambitious young officer look for guidance? He found little to inspire him in the day-to-day regimental routine, which had its own mindless life (Puységur, 1749, I, 76). Moreover the military regulations (like the musical scores of the time) were singularly uninformative on matters of execution and detail. Carl von Griesheim complained that 'I had hoped to learn the cavalry service from the Prussian cavalry regulations, but I found they were scarcely adequate to teach me about dismounted duty in a garrison' (Griesheim, 1777, Introduction). The regimental commanders supplied the rest from their instincts and what they knew of established custom, but they did not usually commit this corpus of knowledge to paper. Lieutenant-Colonel Humphrey Bland was one of the rare exceptions, and his manual of 1727 was still being cited in Britain many years later as 'that treatise, the best ever written upon the subject, at least in our language' (An Old Officer, 1760, 13).

Another notable gap in military literature was the dearth of reviews of the most recent wars. The military public seized avidly on E. Mauvillon's *Histoire de la Dernière Guerre de Bohème* (3 vols, Amsterdam, 1756) which supplied valuable details like the ratio of casualties to the expenditure of ammunition at Chotusitz (1742), but the first detailed treatment of the Seven Years War did not begin to appear until 1783, in the shape of Tempelhoff's expanded translation of Henry Lloyd's *History of the Late War in Germany*. Indeed, intelligent officers knew far more about Classical military history than they did about the events of their own time. An acquaintance with Caesar's *Commentaries* was part of the mental equipment of every well-read gentleman, and the writers defer constantly to the authority of figures like Polybius, Homer, Herodotus, Xenophon, and 'our historian' Thucydides.

The thought of Flavius VEGETIUS Renatus was absorbed so completely by the Age of Reason that he became effectively an eighteenth-century author. Oddly enough, when 'Vegetius' wrote his *De Re Militari*, some time between AD 385 and 450, it was already something of an historical exercise which sought to sum up the best military practice of earlier times. In Book I he wrote about the importance of selecting recruits from civilian trades that made for strength and toughness, and of subjecting the men to thorough training: 'Victory in war does not depend entirely upon numbers or mere courage; only skill and discipline will insure it' (Lieut. John Clarke's translation of 1767, reprinted in Phillips, 1940, 75). Book III, 'Dispositions for Action', tells how the Romans followed the Spartans in establishing military schools for their young men: 'Few men are brave; many become so through care and force of discipline' (p. 172). It was rash to give battle without very good cause: 'Good officers never engage in general actions unless induced by opportunity or obliged by necessity. To distress the enemy more by famine than the sword is a mark of consummate skill' (p. 174). If, having weighed everything up, the commander committed his army to action, he had six possible battle formations at his disposal, of which the best was the second, which was called the 'oblique order'.

The power of Ancient precedent in the eighteenth century was reinforced by the absence of any compartmentalised feeling for period and the belief that the principles of war and politics were unchanging. Thus, in support of one of his contentions (that it was bad to have women with the army), Santa Cruz cheerfully invokes the support of Aristotle, Moses, Judas Maccabeus and Thomas Aquinas.

It is significant that one of the foremost of the contemporary military writers was a man who sought to relate Classical military history to the modern time. This was Jean-Charles de FOLARD (1669–1752), author of the massive *Histoire de Polybe*, which was published in six quarto volumes between 1727 and 1730. Folard's exposition of Polybius was a platform for expounding his own ideas on the art of war, and particularly the advantages of the column, as outlined in his first volume.

For good or ill Folard remained one of the most influential military writers of the century. In his advocacy of the column, which he derived from what Polybius had to write about the Macedonian phalanx, Folard inaugurated a dogmatic and geometrical tendency in French military literature. As his friend Marshal Saxe noted, Folard regarded his soldiers as automata and assumed that they must be brave all the time (see p. 239). On the positive side Folard wrote usefully on matters of detail, he contributed to the growing belief that good generalship was a question of hard work and not just the happy result of inborn gifts, and he persuaded Europe that 'tactics' were worthy of serious study.

Young officers could derive much of value from the works of a number of Folard's near-contemporaries, who drew principally from the experience of the wars of Louis XIV. Frederick the Great was one of the admirers of Antoine Manasses de Pas, Marquis de FEUQUIÈRES (1648–1711), whose posthumous *Mémoires sur la Guerre* (3 vols, Paris, 1725; 4 vols, Paris, 1731) contain shrewd analyses of the campaigns. There were relatively compact surveys of the state of the military art in the Chevalier de GUIGNARD's *L'École de Mars* (2 vols, Paris, 1725), and the eighth and last volume of the *Histoire Militaire du Règne de Louis XIV* by Charles Sevin, Marquis de QUINCY (Paris, 1726). However, by far the most comprehensive and balanced work of the kind was the *Art de Guerre par Principes et par Règles* by Jacques-François de Chastenet, Marquis de PUYSÉGUR (1655–1743). Puységur's active military career lasted from 1677 to 1735, and he spent the final years of his very long life putting together his manuscripts. After a final editing by his son the work was published in two volumes in Paris in 1749.

Outside France the most influential writer of the earlier generation was Don Alvaro Navia Osorio y Vigil, Marqués de SANTA CRUZ de Marcenado (1684–1732). Santa Cruz was a man of political as well as warlike experience. He had been a student at Oviedo when he was overtaken by the outbreak of the War of the Spanish Succession, and he was precipitated straight into the military life as commander of the Asturian Tercio, which was raised in the Bourbon interest. Santa Cruz led the Spanish expedition to Sicily in 1718, but he then took up a diplomatic career, and as envoy to Turin and Paris he was able to complete his *magnum opus* and see it through the press. He was killed at Oran in 1732 when in action against the Moors.

The *Reflexiones militares* of Santa Cruz were first published in Spanish (11 vols, Turin and Paris, 1724–30) but read more widely in a French translation issued between 1735 and 1740. The little volumes of Santa Cruz still have the power to inform and entertain, and they were consulted with profit by Frederick the Great and Napoleon. They are an extraordinary compound of Classical quotation, hearsay, anecdote and old-soldier ruses. The advice is in many places frank or even brutal, but no other officer of the time writes so convincingly about the interplay of morale and tactics, or the influence of politics on the conduct of war.

A strong impression of backwardness is conveyed by the first substantial work by a contemporary German writer, namely Hanns Friedrich FLEMING (*Der Vollkommene Teutsche Soldat*, Leipzig, 1726). Fleming yielded much information about military law and custom to anyone who was prepared to follow his large and closely printed pages, but the arrangement and the framework of reference are antique, and the author is clearly more interested in semi-magical potions than in the theory of war as it was beginning to be understood in France.

The two most celebrated contributions by German authors were in fact strongly influenced by Gallic culture. Maurice de SAXE (1696–1750), an illegitimate son of Augustus the Strong of Saxony, had already been in the French service for a dozen years before he dashed off *Mes Rêveries* in 1732. The free and idiosyncratic style gives this work an enduring appeal, and what he has to say about morale and the conduct of operations in general has outlasted his tactical detail, which was soon outdated by the rise in the importance of firepower on the battlefield. For many years the *Rêveries* were known only from circulated manuscript copies, and the first printed edition did not appear until 1757 (2 vols, Amsterdam and Leipzig).

The second of the German writers was FREDERICK THE GREAT of Prussia. His *Principes Généraux de la Guerre* (1748) were compiled in the first place to clarify his own notions on the subject. The starting point was the character of the Prussian army, and how the presence of the large number of foreign mercenaries made it peculiarly liable to desertion. Frederick then proceeded through the conduct of warfare, from the planning of the campaign to the direction of a battle. A German translation, omitting some of the more confidential sections, was printed and issued to the Prussian generals in 1753 and 1754. One of the copies was captured by the Austrians in 1760, and by the end of the Seven Years War the work was known throughout Europe in a multitude of editions and translations. The *Principes Généraux* were at once recognised as a masterpiece, combining as they did the order and fluency of the best French writers with the experience of the foremost soldier of the age.

By this time the importance of military theory was almost universally accepted. The wars of Louis XIV had almost passed from living memory, and the age had new pantheons of heroes and newly-important modes of military action, like those of artillery and light troops, which demanded investigation. The bookish frame of mind was encouraged by the rise of the military academies, and by military discussion groups like the 'learned societies' which sprang up in all the Prussian garrisons from 1765. The first military periodicals entered circulation in the 1780s, though most of them disappeared from view after a short time.

Some of the monographs were held in high regard. 'Partisan' leaders like GRANDMAISON (1756) and the Hungarian hussar JENEY (1759) began to commit the secrets of their exotic trade to paper, and the experience of *la petite guerre* informed the pages of Lancelot TURPIN DE Crissé's wider-ranging *Essai sur l'Art de la Guerre* (2 vols, Paris, 1754). Turpin de Crissé won a reputation in Britain as a reliable guide to the detailed business of war, and he was commended to young officers for 'a serious and attentive perusal' (An Old Officer, 1760, 109). Specialist texts on artillery and fortification were more properly the concern of gunners and engineers, but there was an international welcome for the clear and practical exposition of fieldworks by the Saxon staff officer Johann Gottlieb TIELKE (*Unterricht für Feldingenieure*, 1769 and foreign translations).

It was unfortunate that much of the natural energy of the French military writers was dissipated in a most arid and boring debate on tactical minutiae. The contest was between the partisans of the *ordre mince*, which emphasised firepower and combat in line, and those of the *ordre profond*, who took their cue from Folard and advocated cold steel and deep formations. The 'deep' party made most of the running, and its most celebrated champions were the Baron François-Jean de MESNIL-DURAND (1729–99), and the less dogmatic Paul Gédéon JOLY DE MAIZEROY (1719–80).

The discussion was moved onto an altogether higher plane by the young Jacques Antoine Hypolite de GUIBERT (1743–90), the author of *Essai Général de Tactique* (Paris, 1772). Guibert's career was blighted by controversy and disappointment, but his work was of twofold importance. He combined the best elements of the deep and thin orders in a way that was enshrined in the Ordinance of 1791, which was the basis of French tactics in the Revolutionary and Napoleonic era. Guibert also succeeded in extending the range of debate to what he called 'grand tactics', concerning the multi-battalion divisions (see p. 182) that became the building-blocks of Napoleon's style of war.

Recent historians have been attracted by what Guibert wrote about the regeneration of France and the potential of a citizen army, as if these passages made him a prophet of the nationalistic mass warfare of the nineteenth century. In fact Guibert wrote as a man of the Age of Reason, concerned to reduce the scale of warfare. The small and highly motivated citizen army was proposed as an alternative to the large standing army of professionals (see p. 184), just as he believed that modern advances in tactics had made battles more scientific and less bloody, as befitted a progressive and enlightened age (Guibert [1772], 1804, II, 30–1).

The military career

THE ARRIVAL AT THE REGIMENT

By their early teens, and long before they had attained their full physical powers, the young men of military spirit burned to embrace the military life, or so they say in their memoirs. They claim that they found the instruction and well-meaning advice from parents and tutors less and less easy to endure, especially when their contemporaries might already be serving with the army and winning laurels and promotion. The young Chevalier de Ray set off for the army on the Danube without so much as a farewell, and his mother had to send his sword and a horse after him. More usually the parting was an affair of sadness and quiet dignity, attended with gruff words from the father and the proud tears of the mother (Andreu de Bilistein, 1763, 39–9). Tolstoy was only repeating long-established custom when in *War and Peace* he describes the last conversation between Prince Andrei and the harsh old Bolkonsky senior.

Probably the last service which the parents had been able to perform for the son had been to write to relations or old acquaintances, asking for a place in a suitable regiment. Louis-René de Belleval explains how matters were arranged for him in 1758:

The Chevalier de Floriville was an under-corporal and ensign in the Chevaux-Légers of the royal guard, and his brother was a member of the same company. He wanted to have me with him, and promised to take care of me, saying that I would be the comrade of a large number of gentlemen from Picardy. He added that my mother was acquainted with most of these people, and that their comradeship would be all the more agreeable since a number of them had also known my father and they would treat me well out of regard for his memory... My Cacqueray cousins were also there—it was like a family. (Belleval, 1866, 2-3)

The first duty of the young man was to pay his respects to his regimental commander, who usually received him affably enough. He then had to make his mark with the young officers, for whom he might be a stranger and a potential rival. Chevalier Tillette de Mautort arrived at his garrison at Perpignan in 1758. He wrote long afterwards:

The regiment of Champagne had the reputation of being stand-offish, as I can testify from my long and sad experience. I am timid by nature, but even if I had been more forthcoming I doubt whether I would have fared any better . . . . I made a point of spending several minutes of every day at a café, among my comrades. I believed that this was the only way to strike up friendships, and little by little this approach began to work. I was delighted when I once chatted for a quarter of an hour with one of our officers. Finally they introduced me into their circle, and my condition became much more tolerable. Such was the combined effect of time, patience, my outlay in money and social gambits, the fact that the officers became accustomed to seeing me around, and possibly also that they found something good to say about me. (Tillette de Mautort, 1891, 18-19. See also Lemcke, 1909, 21)

Relations with the first lieutenant remained on a strictly formal basis, but some of the Prussian and English authorities recommended the new arrival to cultivate the commanding officer of the regiment, who would ask one of the majors or captains to take him under his wing. However, the society of senior officers was not without its dangers. Some of these gentry might see the young man as a recruit for one of the factions that almost invariably divided the regiment. Others were less responsible still:

We cannot tolerate the common practice among officers of amusing themselves by leading astray some young man who

comes into the service directly from the care of his mother or a
Jesuit college. This does them no credit at all. They must
remember that he is still their comrade, and that he must serve
alongside them. (Esterhazy de Gallantha, 1747, 398)

For a number of weeks, or possibly much longer still, the youth
might not be accepted as an officer at all, but would have to take his
place among a crowd of supernumerary volunteers or begin service
as an officer candidate – the Austrian cadet, the Prussian free corporal
or *Fahnenjunker*, and the equivalent ranks in other armies. Whatever
his title might happen to be, the first responsibilities of every
newcomer were to acquaint himself with the names and faces of the
soldiers of his captain's company, and to master the intricacies of the
drill – for which purpose he usually hired one of the NCOs as his
instructor.

The most junior commissioned rank was that of ensign in the
infantry, or cornet in the cavalry. Acting under the direct authority of
the lieutenants, these hard-put-upon creatures attended the parades,
drills, roll calls and mountings of the guard. They kept exact lists of
accoutrements and stores, they supervised the care of the sick in the
hospitals, and they toured the soldiers' accommodation:

they should particularly . . . inspect the quarters of those men
who are billeted upon the houses of the lowest class, as they
are most likely to be prevailed upon, by the disobedient soldier,
to give him liquor for his meat . . . they are to attend [to] the
looks of the men, and if they are thinner or paler than usual,
the reasons of their falling off may be enquired into, and proper
means used to restore them to their former vigour. (Wolfe,
1768, 2)

The historical function of the ensign and cornet was to carry the
colour or standard of his unit. These were the rallying points of the
company, battalion or squadron. The number and allocation of these
flags varied considerably between armies and over periods of time,
but the two types were clearly established – the large square colour
of the infantry, and the smaller and heavily embroidered standard of
the cavalry. In the most important Germanic armies the old connection was lost. The Austrians abolished the ranks of ensign and cornet
in 1759, and the colours or standards were now entrusted to brave

and strong NCOs. In Prussia, less fortunately, the responsibility passed to the pathetic *Fahnenjunkers* who had

> only just left their parental house, where they were gently brought up and well cared for. Many of them are consequently incapable of withstanding the marches and other fatigues of a campaign, of carrying out the onerous duties of an NCO and of bearing the heavy colours. All too many of them succumb to deprivation and hardship. (Warnery, 1785–91, III, 478–9)

Occasionally we encounter further reminders of the extreme youth of such primitive forms of life. In the English and Prussian infantry, if these young gentlemen were not required to bear the colours, they were tucked out of sight in the rear of the battalion when it was on parade:

> I have seen some officers who, as soon as they have got to the rear, fixed their spontoons in the ground, and went to leap-frog, jumping or some other boyish tricks, to the great diversion of the rear ranks, who minded *them* more than their exercise. (An Old Officer, 1760, 140. See also Küster, 1793, 159)

The second lieutenants and their seniors, the first lieutenants, worked in a higher sphere of responsibility. They overlooked the training of the recruits and the work of the NCOs, and they received returns and forwarded them to the captain. One of the second lieutenants might be called upon to do orderly duty with a general, and

> when the general addresses him, or when he himself has occasion to speak to the general, he must make a suitable inclination of the head, then stand upright, look at him directly and say what he has to say with brevity, intelligence and modesty. When he has finished he makes further nod. (*Reglement für die sämmentliche-Kaiserlich-Königlich Infanterie*, Vienna 1769, 43)

The first lieutenant was the right-hand man of the captain, and in his absence he had to be able to take over the direction of the company, which was a unit of about 100 officers and men. With the advance from ensign to lieutenant, the young officer had already experienced a slight but agreeable improvement in his conditions of service. As he left his captain's table with a full stomach, or when he delighted in his new luxuries – say a little tent of his own when he was on campaign – his ambitions began to extend beyond physical survival to dreams of reward.

PROMOTION

> It will always be difficult to determine which means
> of military promotion best corresponds with
> justice and the good of the service.
>
> (Warnery, 1785–91, II, 289–90)

By an almost universal practice, appointments and promotions from colonel upwards were managed directly by the sovereign or his ministry of war, while those within the regiment lay wholly or in part at the disposal of the colonel or individual holders of commissions. The choice of the man for advancement was usually determined by one or other of three principles: purchase, seniority or merit.

Purchase

In the eighteenth century a high proportion of colonels and regimental officers attained their rank by private purchase. The practice endured in Austria, in spite of official disapproval; it was a wholesale and blatant traffic in Russia, and also in France, where it continued in the cavalry after Marshal Belle-Isle suppressed it in the infantry in 1758; in Britain it accounted for the placement of two-thirds of the officer corps. Prussia was remarkable in being free of this trade. The principle of purchase must appear outrageous to modern eyes, and it was just as offensive to many military men at the time: 'Nothing could be more dangerous or harmful to the service than the sale of commissions. Money brings neither talent nor merit, and we certainly need a good deal of both in the military profession' (Saint-Germain, 1779, 135–6).

There was no set scale of payments, for these were determined by the standing of the regiment in question, but in the 1760s the price for places in an average French regiment of the line could be reckoned at about 6,000 livres for a captaincy and 20,000–24,000 for a lieutenant-colonelcy. It is equally difficult to generalise about the precise circumstances of the arrangements. The majority of the deals were straightforward transactions, occasioned by the desire of an officer to buy himself upwards, or to sell off his military estate and retire to civilian life just like a doctor or lawyer at the end of his professional career. In some regiments, however, commissions were literally on sale to the highest bidder. In the middle of the eighteenth century the colonel of the French regiment of Piémont brought the business to a fine art, and fitted himself up with two fine houses on the proceeds. He was once able to oblige the son of a rich postmaster who came to Paris in search of a place. The first person that the young man addressed was a stiff and upright colonel who

> did not believe that a fellow of this sort would suit his regiment.
> He lightheartedly told him to betake himself to the far side of
> the stream to the lodging of the colonel of Piémont, who no
> doubt would be able to arrange things for him. A few days
> later the postmaster's son turned up in uniform to thank the
> first colonel for his good advice. (Comte de Gisors, quoted in
> Tuetey, 1908, 135–6)

The traffic in commissions did an obvious injustice to the low-born officer of fortune. It was also, as we have seen, bitterly resented by the class of the poor nobility, who were unable to compete with the grandees or the rich bourgeoisie. It contributed to the gross over-officering of armies like the French, which on 1 January 1758 owned 16 marshals of France and 348 other general officers for a force of about 300,000 men; there were 35 officers for the infantry battalion of 680 men, and 12 for the cuirassier or dragoon squadron of 160 troopers. By October 1787 the overall size of the army had been reduced to 170,000, but Guibert reported to the Conseil de Guerre that the military establishment still supported a total of 35,000 active or retired officers.

The justifications for the trade in commissions cannot be totally overlooked. Old, sick or bored officers thereby realised their invest-ments by selling their places, and made way for men who were likely to be younger and more active. The service generally was promoted by the influence of wealthy individuals who had set their hearts on a company or regiment. A well-endowed captain or colonel could pay for a better class of recruit, keep the soldiers' uniforms and shoes in good order, and help the subalterns and other officers who might otherwise be in danger of literal starvation. Private resources served as a cushion against disasters which ruined poor nobles like Thevet de Lesser, who in the course of his military career expended the equivalent of 45,000 livres, including the cost of his baggage which had been lost to the English twice over – at Klosterkamp in 1760, and again to a warship in the American War of Independence. His little estate in Saintonge brought him only 800–900 livres a year, and he was left without the means to pay so much as the interest on his heavy debts.

Seniority

Length of service was the most clearly equitable of the principles of promotion. In the Prussian army its rule was nearly absolute at the regimental level:

> The son of a great man, the favour of a mistress, a fortune in money – nothing is capable of intervening to deny a long-serving officer of due reward, as long as his conduct is beyond reproach. His seniority gives him a sound claim to advancement, and no colonel proprietor may stop his rise. As a further consequence this army has a multitude of experienced officers, and there are few captains who do not have twenty years of service behind them. (Griesheim, 1777, 77–8)

Seniority was also taken in Europe generally as the guide to the precedence of command among individuals who held the same rank. In normal circumstances a first lieutenant with a commission dated 25 January 1758, for example, would be the undoubted superior of one whose commission was granted on 8 May 1759. In the French service, however, the precedence was determined by the date when the individual officer's regiment happened to be raised. Thus a recently appointed captain from the regiment of Picardie, which was the most senior in the army, had automatic right of command over any captain of any regiment.

In most armies, seniority combined with purchase to produce an equilibrium in regimental affairs. Men of substance bought themselves as far up the hierarchy of rank as they could afford, while the other officers lived in hope that the death or retirement of a superior would eventually advance them a further step in their careers. The regiment gained from the presence of so many experienced officers. In the British army the length of service of lieutenant-colonels stood at an average of thirty years during the periods of prolonged peace, and in the middle of the Seven Years War, in 1759, it still amounted to a very respectable fifteen (Houlding, 1981, 109, 115). Outside France, the regimental officers as a whole can be taken to be settled men in their thirties and forties.

Seniority was less easy to defend as a guide to the appointment and precedence of general officers, and on occasion Frederick intervened with dramatic effect to interrupt the rule of seniority among his generals in the field. At Rossbach in 1757 he made the spur-of-the-moment decision to entrust the command of the entire cavalry to Seydlitz, who was the most junior lieutenant-general in the Prussian army. With less happy results in the next year he made Kurt Heinrich von Wedel the 'dictator' on the eastern theatre, with authority over four lieutenant-generals who were senior to him.

The most notorious shortcoming of seniority was its way of creating blockages of promotion, which condemned individuals to a lifetime of ill-rewarded service. Warnery encountered such a case in 1736, when he put in at the little port of San Stefano on the coast of Tuscany:

> When I went for a stroll in the town I came across a man whose face was almost concealed in a huge wig, and who was wearing a shabby suit of brown clothes. He showed no sign of military office, and did not even bear a sword, but he solemnly informed me that he was governor of the fortress, that he had served for fifty years, and that he had risen to the dignity of lieutenant-colonel. He was a Netherlander and a naturalised Spaniard. I heard elsewhere that all of this was true, and that his income, which amounted to the equivalent of two hundred thaler per annum, was paid to him most irregularly. I was also told that he frequently did not have so much as a crust of bread to eat, and that the lady governess had to spare her wardrobe, and ventured forth only on Sundays and feast days in order to hear Mass. (Warnery, 1785–91, IV, 133)

Merit

At first sight, the idea of advancing an officer on account of his talents and good service might seem to be the most positive and defensible of all, avoiding the outrageous injustice which so often came with purchase, and the stagnation which attended seniority. The most truly meritorious promotions were probably those made on the recommendation of a colonel or general immediately after an action. On a closer view, however, merit turns out to be a shifting concept, capable of bearing the most arbitrary interpretations.

It was in the first place not always easy to define what ought to be recognised as meritorious in an officer. The Age of Reason had already begun to confront the dilemma which has been explored by twentieth-century military sociologists, of how to reward two different kinds of good officer, as represented by the 'charismatic leader' with his traditional warrior virtues, and the better-organised 'military manager':

> We do not make sufficient distinction between the two kinds of merit in our profession – the officers who shine brilliantly in warfare and are good for nothing else, and those who are useful for training, instructing and manoeuvring the soldiers. Both sorts of talent are necessary in their way, and those who possess them are deserving of great reward. (Ligne, 1795–1811, I, 127. See also Santa Cruz, 1735–40, III, 96)

When a man was advanced on the personal intervention of a superior, it might be the return of a favour or the consequence of some other kind of entangling obligation, as Scharnhorst noted from his knowledge of the Hanoverian service (Jähns, 1889–91, II, 2, 368). Justice was better served when the prime mover could work on the basis of good confidential reports, such as the *Conduite-Listen* which Frederick received annually from his senior officers, or the most informative files that were kept up by the Comte d'Argenson, who was the French war minister early in the Seven Years War. Here are some of his entries:

> *Regiment of Poitou (infantry). Chevalier de Sons, captain*
> He is a good officer. He is highly regarded in his regiment, and the officers have such confidence in his judgment that they nearly always choose him to act as arbitrator in their debates. . . . He is said to be the finest player of chess in France.
> *Regiment of Beauvoisis (infantry). Chevalier de Douazac, captain of grenadiers*
> He is a strange individual, full of quirky humour. He is an enemy of discipline, and especially that imposed by de Lugeac his superior. This very spring he brought out a book which

bears the title *On Military Subordination*, the real purpose of which is to show that you need nothing of that commodity, or at least very little.

Regiment of Saint-Jal (cavalry). Louis de Fénelon, captain. An eccentric person who lives a reclusive life. He has a crazy obsession with writing poetry – he has a high opinion of the product, and will challenge you to a duel if you fail to agree. He has already fought two or three times in this cause. (Tuety, 1908, 342–8)

More often the instigator of the promotion had to work on third- or fourth-hand information, and he passed over many deserving cases out of sheer ignorance. Saint-Germain explains that when he became war minister in 1775 he had been out of France for many years, and that he discovered that the files were long out of date. When it came to choosing colonels he was therefore forced to rely completely on the well-informed Prince de Montbarey, who was a defender of the old order (Saint-Germain, 1779, 45).

OFFICER RANKS

We return to the career of the officer, and follow him further on his path to high authority. The nominal structure of ranks resembles a simple chain of command, as follows:

Rank	Level of command	Number of men (approximate)
Cadet, free corporal or equivalent	Within the company (squadron)	Not determined
Ensign (cornet)	,,	,,
Second lieutenant	,,	,,
First lieutenant	,,	,,
Captain	Company (squadron)	100 or more (160)
Major	Battalion, or regiment under authority of the lieutenant-colonel	500 or more
Lieutenant-Colonel	Regiment	1,600 (6–900)
Colonel commandant (if any)	,,	,,
Colonel proprietor	,,	,,

In practice there existed two parallel hierarchies. One was functional.

The other was primarily administrative and proprietorial, and represented a survival of the days when all military units were raised by feudal landowners or private contractors. It is therefore more realistic to set out the scheme as follows:

Functional	Proprietorial
Cadet, free corporal or equivalent	Captain
Ensign (cornet)	Colonel proprietor
Lieutentants	
Major	
Lieutenant-Colonel	
Colonel commandant	

The captain

The captain was the first of the proprietorial officers, and to a greater or lesser extent he 'owned' his company, at least into the second half of the eighteenth century. His prime responsibility was keeping the company in good condition. 'A full company is the pride of a good captain, as a weak one is the shame and reproach of him that commands it' (Simes, 1780a, 125).

The power of the captain was most fully shown in the Prussian service, where he received money from the state to provide the soldiers' pay and equipment, he promoted NCOs and he awarded punishments (up to about fifty blows with the stick). The Prussian captain was also directly responsible for recruiting his company, and for this purpose he sent out parties to enlist foreigners and exercised considerable control over the male civilian population of the native recruiting area (canton). Finally an agreeable custom allowed him to keep for himself the pay of the men who were absent from his company on leave, which in most peacetime months amounted to about half the regiment.

Hungry Prussian subalterns put in years of dedication to an ill-rewarded service in the hope of ultimately being granted a company, and an Austrian officer wrote that the Prussian system also had the advantage of giving the Prussian captain a direct stake in the welfare of his troops:

He and his subordinates lose no opportunity to encourage their men, and the kind of expressions you hear from them are

'Cheer up lads, things will soon get better!' Flattering
expressions like these cost no money, but they are most
effective in reviving the spirits of the ordinary soldiers, and
awakening an affection for their officers. (Anon,
'Verzeichniss', 1758, Haus-Hof-und Staatsarchiv, Vienna,
Kriegsakten 387)

One of the most characteristic features of Enlightened military
reform was an attack on the proprietorial status of the captain. In
France there was an important symbolic and practical breach in
1745, when a change in the system of regimental records altered the
formula '*soldat du sieur . . . capitaine au régiment de . . .*' to the bleak
and bureaucratic '*soldat au régiment de . . .*'. The French captains lost
most of their power over the economy of their companies in 1763,
and from the same year the foreign recruits for the Prussian service
were thrown into a common army pool and were no longer signed
up directly by the captains for their individual companies. In Austria
the tidy-minded Field-Marshal Lacy became President of the Hofkriegsrath in 1766, and he proceeded to supply the needs of the soldiers
directly from huge central magazines, which terminated the logistic
autonomy of the companies.

In Britain the comparable reforms were a cumulative and long-
drawn-out process, but by 1766 they had made considerable inroads
on the 'custom of the army' which had been so profitable for the
captains. A succession of royal ordinances gradually eliminated the
practice of a signing false names on the muster rolls (1716, 1740,
1747), restricted stoppages from the soldiers' pay (1717, 1721, 1749)
and regulated the allowances which were made over to the captains
(1747 and 1755–6) (see Guy, 1985b, *passim*).

The real or apparent bureaucratic efficiency came at a high price.
Prussia experienced a decline in the quality of its foreign recruits
which contributed significantly towards the decay of the army in the
last decades of Frederick the Great. In Austria the centralised economic regulations extended down to gaiter buttons and old soles of
shoes, and 'the endless accounts demanded reams of paper, and made
it necessary to enlist a miniature army of clerks, who had to lay aside
their muskets in order to take up the pen' (Berenhorst, 1798–9, II,
107). In France, as André Corvisier has pointed out, the cavalry in
particular forfeited the benefits it had derived from the ancient local
and feudal ties which had existed between officer and trooper, and

the soldiers became depressed and bewildered in a new and impersonal world which foreshadowed the ambience of the industrial age (Corvisier, 1964, 879, 897).

Things had been different in the 1740s. The Chevalier de Ray recalled that

> when the young noblemen set out from home, the young servants went with them. By the same token the young peasants followed the company baggage. Everybody wished to go on campaign, as long as it was with people of their own locality. You can imagine the advantages which ensue when warriors and servants are friends who form part of a larger whole! They go through the same experiences and dangers, and lifelong links are forged as a result. (Ray, 1895, 15)

The same dismal story is confirmed by the experience in Britain, where the reforms brought little detectable improvement in professionalism:

> Indeed, it could be argued that the removal of the captain's mercenary initiative, without the necessary compensating augmentation of personal pay, had, in conjunction with external factors, precisely the reverse effect. Restraints on customary dividends bore most heavily on men with little or no personal fortunes, the backbone of the mid-Georgian officer corps. From the late 1750s these restrictions coincided with an accelerating cost of living and a more extravagant gentlemanly lifestyle. (Guy, 1985b, 165)

So far we have considered the company purely as an administrative unit, and in fact the ordinary company of musketeers was seldom anything else. The main tactical units were the platoon, the two-platoon division and the battalion, and the company was significant as a fighting force only when it was composed of élite grenadiers (see p. 132). On campaign the grenadier companies were frequently detached from the parent regiment on dangerous service, like leading an assault, or they were combined with grenadiers from other regiments in battalions or larger bodies of crack troops. For this reason the captain of grenadiers had much more opportunity to stand out as an individual than his counterpart among the fusiliers, and to establish himself as a man marked out for promotion.

The major

The major, more than any other officer, was responsible for how the battalion or regiment performed on the battlefield. He supervised the progress of the training, he punished every serious shortcoming in drill or discipline, and he saw to the exactitude of the service – receiving the orders which came to the regiment, maintaining an exact journal, and keeping an eye on the NCOs, the provost and the sutlers and the butchers. In action the regiment or one of the battalions came under his direct command.

The ideal major was an exact, vigilant and industrious person – a professional military man *par excellence*, whose gaze inspired fear and respect. His relations with the colonel were often fraught with tension, for

> some delicate questions of authority arose from the association of officers of different ages, between young and often inexperienced people [the colonels] placed at the head of the regiments, and subordinates who had grown grey in the service and were often as old as their fathers. (Bodinier, 1983, 73)

In well-regulated armies the majors usually existed to the number of one, two or three to the regiment. In Russia, where everything was done to excess, some regiments were laden with up to thirty supernumerary majors, none of whom had done any real service in that rank. Lev Nikolaievich Engelhardt was still in his teens when he found himself elevated to major, and he was taken to task by one of his relations, a senior officer in the Vologdskii Infantry Regiment:

> my brother in law represented to me how unfortunate it was to be a major and still be ignorant of the service. He added that, when I was appointed to a regiment, I would not be respected by my superiors, and, what was worse I would be despised by my subordinates. He therefore proposed that I should learn the service in his regiment, to which I willingly agreed. (Engelhardt, 1868, 59)

The lieutenant-colonel

As a functional rank, a lieutenant-colonelcy offered a natural progression from a majority, and gave men without influence their best path for promotion to field rank. The lieutenant-colonel was responsible for commanding the regiment and defending its interests during the frequent absences of its colonel proprietor, and, in contrast to the duties of a major, who was a hard-driving executive, he had to bear the general welfare of the officers and men constantly in mind. He was characteristically a poor noble or a bourgeois who knew the regiment from long service, and no other rank was spoken about in warmer terms of affection or respect.

The colonel proprietor

The colonel proprietor takes us back to the world of privilege and money, for he owned the regiment as a whole in much the same way as the captains owned the individual companies. His influence for good or evil was very considerable. A colonel who was both wealthy and generous would enhance the outward show and the inner commodity of the regiment in ways that have already been outlined (see p. 62). He helped to feed up the starving subalterns, he paid the debts of erring officers and soldiers, and he provided for the widows.

In armies like the British or the Austrian the colonel managed his business affairs with the help of a regimental agent, who was his private appointee. The agent dealt with contractors and the commissariat and pay departments of the central government, and he acted as personal broker for the regimental officers as well as for the colonel, his direct employer. The agent repaid himself by taking a percentage profit on his deals, and some agents became so successful and skilled in their specialised work that they set up businesses which ran the affairs of several regiments at a time. John Calcraft was the most celebrated of the English agents in the Seven Years War, and he died in 1772 worth a reputed £250,000.

It is easy to imagine how a corruptly run regiment could experience all the abuses which might exist at the company level, but on a larger scale. Such was the case with the Russian regiments of horse in the reign of Catherine the Great:

> The cavalry is totally useless. This is because every colonel
> regards his regiment as an estate from which he desires to
> extract the greatest possible return. The condition of the
> regiment is of no concern to him, any more than the
> establishment of the horses, and he is in the habit of putting all

the money for the forage into his pocket. (Richelieu, 1886,
162)

When so much hung upon the character and inclinations of the
colonel, every change in the ownership of the regiment was attended
with a revolution in affairs. The turmoils were most frequent and
violent in the Russian service, for there (unlike the case in Prussia
and Austria) the former colonel was forced to abandon his regiment
when he was promoted to major-general. He was now besieged by
soldiers who came forward to require satisfaction of their grievances:
'The Russian soldier will never forgive you if you fail to hand over
even a single kopek which is owing to him, and he will be sure to
demand it sooner or later' (Langeron, 1895, 168). The departing
proprietor was simultaneously haggling with his replacement. He
asked a high price for any luxuries like musical instruments which
were left with the regiment, while the incoming colonel carried out
a detailed inventory of the official property and required compensation in full for deficiencies such as elderly horses, broken plates on
the cartridge pouches, or any screws that were missing from the
muskets. When everything was finally settled the new colonel
brought a complete set of officers from his last regiment, and evicted
all the sitting tenants. Langeron knew of officers who had served in
fifteen regiments, and had been driven out of each in turn.

In the West

> when a colonel has been nominated to a regiment and arrives
> to take command, there ensues an initial period in which the
> two parties size one another up – the colonel on his side, and
> on the other the officers and soldiers who are in his charge.
> The colonel wishes to discover the kind of men he is dealing
> with, and the ones he can draw into his confidence. His
> subordinates study the character and habits of their chief, so as
> to calculate how much consideration they should show him,
> and how they might obtain his favour. (Montbarey, 1826–7, I,
> 146)

A colonel might have to strive hard to establish his authority if
he was young and inexperienced, or if the captains joined forces
against him. When he imposed his will, it was sure to be in a
distinctive way: 'We may take it for granted that when a new colonel
comes he will be gentle, if his predecessor was strict. . . . You can

be just as sure that he will be tough, if the old colonel was easy-going'
(Ligne, 1795–1811, I, 206). However, in the eighteenth century the
reign of a colonel proprietor might last for ten, twenty or even thirty
years, which gave ample time for officers and men to grow into the
new style. They were certainly better placed than their counterparts
two centuries later, who are at the mercy of hag-ridden careerists
and caught up in a mindless cycle of two-yearly changes.

We take up the life of the general officers at a later opportunity
(see p. 137), for the generals were of virtually no significance in the
peacetime life of the army. Before leaving the regiment, it is
necessary to note that much of the detailed routine was the responsibility of particular appointments, which existed independently of the
rank of the officers who filled them. In this way a captain might find
himself detached as aide-major to help out one of the ranking majors.
Another useful appointment for a sharp and ambitious young officer
was that of the regimental adjutant, who saw the troops onto the
parade, noted failings in turnout and discipline, and kept up the
regimental returns and lists of duties. He was a figure of absolute
terror for the newly arrived subaltern. The regimental quartermaster
was usually an elderly officer, whose horizons were bounded by the
regiment. He and his assistants saw to the manifold duties relating
to the transport, lodging, supply and feeding of the regiment.

Volunteers

Volunteers were individuals who attached themselves to the army
or a regiment, without making any claim to pay or rank from the
force concerned. One sort of volunteer was a badly placed native
officer, who chose to cling to the service after his parent unit had
been reduced or disbanded. More typically the volunteers were types
like high-spirited young gentlemen, clerks or schoolmasters in search
of adventure, card-sharps, fugitives, or foreign princes completing
their knowledge of the world.

A number of the volunteers made themselves genuinely useful.
However, most of the surviving evidence indicates that the tribe was
a nuisance. The volunteers got in the way of busy men. They occupied accommodation which might otherwise have been available for
the wounded, and their horses chomped through precious forage.
They were accused of seeing too little, and getting themselves killed
for no particular reason, like young Duke Albrecht of Brunswick at

Soor (see p. 24). At other times these *Schlachtenbummeler* were accused of seeing altogether too much.

On occasion the conflict of loyalties was acute. After a brief spell in the Prussian service a roving Frenchman passed to Britain and became an aide-de-camp to General Mordaunt on the unfortunate expedition against Rochefort in 1757. He could tell the English little that was useful about their objective, and

> even if I had known Rochefort better, would it have been right for me to inform the English? I was a volunteer, I was a detached spectator of events, and I had entered into no commitments with these people. I would certainly have put my life at stake if it had been a question of actual combat, but I must tell *Messieurs les Anglais* that I would have been deficient in integrity and loyalty, and consequently dishonoured, if I had given them the benefit of what I might have learned about a fortress when I was in the service of a king who was its master. (Bonneville, 1762, I, 90)

Values and manners

THE CULT OF HONOUR

Its relation to other codes of conduct

In few respects do the values of the eighteenth century appear more alien than when we uncover what the men of the time understood by the concept of honour.

Patriotism in the eighteenth-century sense required only a limited dedication on the part of the individual, and it had little directly to do with race, language or nation. Rather it was a principle according to which you linked yourself with a chain of loyalty, obligation and profit (see p. 10). Bonneville has just explained the confusions he experienced at Rochefort. You were certainly dishonoured beyond recall if you forsook your master in the course of a war, but it was not considered unpatriotic if you went on your travels at the end of the conflict and found yourself a new home.

Honour was a principle which for many gentlemen stood in no firm relation to morality. Religion remained a motivating force for pious individuals like the Prussian field-marshal Kurt Christoph

Schwerin, but in leading circles of society in the eighteenth century faith was at one of its lower ebbs, and religious observance in the armies was supported primarily as a means of promoting discipline and cohesion (see p. 124). On the day before the battle of Zorndorf (1758) Lieutentant-General Forcade received the evening orders from Frederick, and then repeated them in his characteristically loud voice:

> During this litany the king chatted with Seydlitz, who was looking on with an amused and detached air. In due course Forcade came to the sentence 'Tomorrow, by the grace of God, we shall have a battle!' Frederick was apparently concerned that Seydlitz might think he had turned to God in his time of trial, and he muttered to him 'That's only for the baggage drivers!' (Kalkreuth, 1840, IV, 144)

Frederick, as a Frenchman by culture, was aware of the scorn which gentlemen of fine manners reserved for open displays of religious enthusiasm. Lazare Carnot, who practised a petty bourgeois piety, braved the jests of his comrades, but another of the French officers, Jean-Frédéric de Chabannes, was nearly broken by such an experience:

> Monsieur de Chabannes was handsome, young and rich. He was dancing at the queen's ball when he happened to fall and gave vent to the cry 'Jesus Maria!' He at once attracted such a weight of ridicule that he took off to America. There was no escape. He kept his nickname on the outward voyage and in the North American countryside, and he returned from America as 'Jesus Maria' just as when he had set out. (Quoted in Bodinier, 1983, 263–4)

Honour guided the officer in delicate affairs like paying debts and dealing with insults, and if the principle of honour indicated a course of action that ran contrary to the law of the land, then the gentleman of high mettle would obey the former rather than conform to the latter. Duty itself might have to defer to sentiments of honour, such as the ones which prompted the Marquis de Saint-Pern to keep the Grenadiers de France standing within open view of the allied artillery at Minden in 1759 (see p. 218). A French officer wrote of his comrades:

> The public good touches them only as far as their own good is

completely included therein, and they count as nothing the harm they do to the affairs of our master, the loss of so many brave men and the ruin of our army, provided that they achieve their purposes. (Quoted in Kennett 1967, 71)

Men like these observed a strict limit on how much of themselves they were prepared to devote to their professional duties. The French army was notorious for the modest demands it made on the officer, and when he searched for the reasons for its failures in the Seven Years War Marshal Broglie discovered one of them in the 'total ignorance displayed by everybody, from second lieutenant to lieutenant-general, of the duties of their estate and all those details which should properly concern them' (Ray, 1895, 348. See also Valentin Esterhazy, 1905, 97).

Its ingredients

Codes of honour have been described as 'an endlessly-prolonged initiation rite' (Dixon, 1976, 199–200), and the emphasis on physical courage probably brings the eighteenth-century definition of honour closest to the term as it has been understood in later times. The man of honour refused to remove his marks of distinction when he was under sniper fire. He cast aside protective armour with disdain, like Chevert at Hastenbeck, or the Comte de Gisors at Krefeld.

Courage of this order was not so much a virtue as a prerequisite, and the man who felt that he was lacking in this high quality was advised to stay at home rather than risk the anger of his peers. In 1748 the captains and lieutenants of a company of the regiment of Médoc turned on one of their number who had persistently hung back from danger. They dragged him in front of the regiment, pulled off his coat and ripped it up, broke his sword, beat him with sticks and chased him away.

Courage was peculiarly the property of the officer class, just as unthinking bravery was an attribute of the good soldier: 'Bravery is in the blood, but courage is in the soul. Bravery is instinctive, almost a mechanical reaction. Courage is a virtue, and a lofty and noble sentiment' (Turpin de Crissé, 1754, I, 6. See also d'Espagnac, 1751, I, 4–5).

These ideals were contaminated by the violence and indiscipline of the age. Rancorous and touchy, many officers in the eighteenth century seemed to have lived in a state of perpetual war with mankind. They pursued interminable lawsuits. They kicked waiters, beat night-watchmen and apprentices, and they broke the windows of their landlords. Even the Prussian cavalryman Seydlitz, who was taken as a model of reasonable conduct, was given to firing his pistol at persons or objects which excited his displeasure.

When they were among their social equals, the officers were prey to curious feelings of insecurity. Honour demanded to be constantly tested and reasserted, and it was a commodity which could so easily be lost, whether by a pure accident, or by pursuing an honest trade or a line of conduct whch in some respect was considered demeaning. Frederick was unrelenting. In the War of the Bavarian Succession he mistakenly beat an officer who was trying to restore order among a crowd of soldiers who were plundering a house:

> The officer was thunderstruck, and told the king that he was an officer and was on the spot for the best of reasons. The king simply replied 'I am not aware of having beaten any officer.' It was not long before news of this happening spread among the man's comrades. They appreciated at once that he had become involved in the encounter through no fault of his own, but they informed him that, however much they regretted his misfortune, they could serve with him no longer. (Anon., 1787–9, X, 37)

Duelling was an inevitable outcome of the seething violence and insecurity of the upper classes. The ostensible cause might be an unconsidered word, a disputed seat at the theatre or an argument at a gaming table, or the parties might find themselves fighting in a wine-sodden rage without knowing the reason why.

The formal duel was an elegant ritual, and the masters of ceremonies were the 'seconds', who went through the motions of trying to reconcile the principals, then proceeded to arrange the place, the presence of a surgeon, the availability of swords or pistols, and any necessary signal. Distinctive duelling pistols began to evolve in the 1760s. They came in cased pairs, and had characteristic ten-inch octagonal barrels, flattened and chequered butts (saw-handled from 1805) and hair triggers. It was at first the custom to toss coins to determine who was to fire first, but later the parties fired simultaneously upon an agreed signal. Deliberate aiming was forbidden.

Very often, however, the duel was a murderous fight, carried on with whatever weapons lay at hand. By no means all of the quarrels were capable of being settled by a token wound, and there are cases where the parties pursued their argument from country to country and even from continent to continent:

Two captains of the Champagne regiment, La Fenestre and d'Agay, had been mortal enemies for twenty-eight years, and had met seven times on the field of honour. La Fenestre had his head blown off by a cannon ball at Vellinghausen, but his partisans noted with a point of pride that a fragment of his skull put out d'Agay's right eye. (Kennett, 1967, 69)

In vain the codes of military and civilian law threatened the perpetrators of duels with draconian punishment. Writers also argued to no avail that there was no correspondence between the offended pride that drove men into duels and the genuine courage which sustained them on the battlefield: 'What a horrible prejudice it is to believe that when a man is insulted, he is also dishonoured unless he ends up bathed in his own blood!' (Bonneville, 1762, I, 57). It simply was not open to a man of honour to tolerate an affront or refuse a challenge. His best chance of avoiding such encounters was to keep a guard on his tongue, and to shun the company of proud and ignorant petty nobles, and officers like the notorious 'triers' who were to be found in some of the English regiments.

Some further peculiarities of honour are worthy of mention. One striking characteristic is the notion of a rough balance between obligation and reward. By embracing the trade of arms the gentleman accepted certain duties towards his masters and inferiors, and he unreservedly offered his life, if not his time and attention, to the service of his fatherland of the moment. He expected a due return: 'Nobles become extremely disgusted with war when they do not receive promotion. They believe that an injury has been done to their reputation unless, by suitable advancement, they are reassured that one is pleased with their services' (Santa Cruz, 1735–40, III, 110). Recognition might also come in the form of pensions, grants of land and nobility, arrangements for rich marriages (as in Spain and Piedmont-Savoy) and orders and decorations (the young Duc de Crillon was recommended for the cross of Saint-Louis after having his finger accidentally smashed by a pick at the siege of Pizzighettone in 1733). There were scenes of tumult at Potemkin's headquarters in

1788 when promotions, demotions, crosses and golden swords were announced at the prince's private whim, which gave rise to feuds, protests and refusals of duty. Gilbert Bodinier has examined the cases of hundreds of French officers who went to America during the War of Independence, and discovered only one who was not actively concerned with financial reward, and he was the Marquis de Lafayette who was an idealist and a grandee in terms of wealth.

A number of senior officers, like Zieten and Prince Ferdinand of Brunswick, refused to recommend a single officer for decoration throughout the Seven Years War, believing that courage and service were just part of the duty of the officer. However the statutes of the Military Order of Maria Theresa actually put the onus on heroes to offer themselves as candidates, and support their case with written attestations. An eighteenth-century officer could have given only qualified approval to the cry of John F. Kennedy: 'Ask not what your country can do for you – ask what you can do for your country!'

Ultimately the gentleman had the responsibility as an individual of determining what honour must mean to him. This notion of independence, and a good deal else besides, is enshrined in the Saxon *Dienst-Reglement* of 1753:

> The point of honour commands us to prefer duty to life, and
> honour to duty. The point of honour forbids kinds of
> behaviour which are permitted or even encouraged by the law,
> just as it allows certain conduct which is legally forbidden.
> The point of honour calls us to the dangerous and glorious estate
> of soldier, but it also motivates us to abandon that condition,
> if we are passed over unfairly in promotion, or have suffered
> some other injury through no fault of our own.... From
> these characteristics of the point of honour, it is evident that it
> cannot spring from the common people. (Jähns, 1889–91, III,
> 2, 136)

A sensation of particular poignancy was evoked by men of honour who chose to walk alone, like Major von Tellheim in Lessing's play *Minna von Barnhelm*, or the real-life Lieutenant-Colonel Johann Friedrich von der Marwitz who went to disgraceful retirement rather than carry out a brutal order from Frederick. Having encountered so much that was bizarre or selfish about the cult of honour, it is impossible for us to withold our admiration for the importance that the eighteenth century attached to the primacy of the individual conscience. Some of the atrocities of twentieth-century warfare would have been unthinkable if men in authority had still been guided by this principle.

Every age has its notion of honourable conduct, but the cult of honour, as it was understood in the eighteenth century, gradually lost its powerful hold over the succeeding generations. It had been the product of a small, hierarchical and relatively static society, where the reputation of an individual or a family was a matter of common talk, and where conduct could be measured against a consensus as to what made up honourable behaviour. An old lieutenant-colonel in a Salzburg regiment regretted having survived one of the *Reichsar-mee*'s actions in the Seven Years War:

> Woe is me! Would that I had been struck down by some bullet, for my only wish is to die on the field of honour! My father, my grandfather and my great grandfather were all killed on campaign, but I am left to carry my silvery head back over my threshold. (Schertel von Burtenbach, 1779, 66)

The ancient cult of honour, in all its complexities, gradually crumbled in face of the assaults of the industrial age. The ground that was once the preserve of the principle of honour has since been invaded by nationalism, political ideology or religiously based morality. Honour, which had once been the concern of the individual, now refers to loyalty to the group and the state. It is now tolerable for an officer to ignore an insult, but scarcely thinkable that he should let down the men for whom he is responsible.

PROFESSIONAL RELATIONSHIPS

Among the officers

When an officer or a private gentleman travelled through Europe, he noticed that in the various countries the relationships between the officers had a distinctive style. The English were the most open and unconstrained both in and out of the service. The Prussian officers, on the other hand, kept up a very clear distinction between their social gatherings (where everything was comradely equality), and what happened on parade: 'So cheerful, friendly and boyishly relaxed when he was off duty, Seydlitz became something of a despotic martinet when he was in the saddle, all dressed up with his pelisse and sabre' (Lojewsky, 1843, I, 167).

A note of servility could be detected in Austria, where junior officers might be seen waiting at table, or hastening to hold the stirrup when a senior hoisted himself into the saddle. In Russia it was possible for a commanding officer like Field-Marshal Münnich to rule as a tyrant:

> One day, when he was entering camp, a Russian officer saluted him with his musket. By a mischance the bayonet fell off. Münnich had the poor devil arrested on the spot, and he proceeded to strip him of his rank and made him into a private soldier. There were even instances when he had staff officers bound to gun carriages for trivial offences. (Warnery, 1785–91, IV, 294)

In armies generally the officers of the foot were more on their dignity than those of the horse, who preserved the traditions of knightly comradeship. The Chevalier de Guignard noted with disapproval how 'all the cavalry officers exist on terms of equality and friendship. The subalterns are in the habit of addressing their captains in over-familiar terms, while the captains call their lieutenant-colonel by his name, withut adding the proper *Monsieur*' (Guignard, 1725, II, 15).

The dining table was the most accessible meeting place between officers of different ranks. Frederick and his senior generals set an example to the rest of Europe, even if Old Fritz was notoriously economical in the matter of wines. A Frenchman discovered as much when he came to sit at the magnificent table of the Hereditary Prince of Brunswick:

> When we arranged ourselves at the table (Lieutenant-General) Prittwitz spoke to me: 'Sit yourself down beside me. My lackey has a bottle of wine in his pocket and we shall drink it together. The king's wine is dreadful.' I rejoined 'Surely you wouldn't dare to do this if the king was present in person?' 'Believe me, hardly any of us would do otherwise. The king sees it as a joke, and says that they are the equivalent of so many bottles spared for his cellar.' (Toulongeon and Hullin [1786], 1881, 148)

The open table was originally maintained in order to refresh the officers who happened to be on duty at headquarters, or who had come some distance in order to make a report or pay their respects. By the eighteenth century, however, the table had become a means of displaying the hospitality of the senior officers, and of getting to know the character and opinion of subordinates in a relaxed atmosphere. The Prussian generals usually kept a large table of ten places for guests, and a further table of six places for officers who dined with them daily. In other armies sittings of sixty were available in the grandest headquarters, and in semi-oriental Russia two hundred or more places were not unknown.

The colonels competed on a smaller scale, and Frederick gave allowances to the captains in order to enable the subalterns to sit at their table. Major-General Yorke noted this practice during the campaign in Moravia in 1758:

> By this means the young officers are constantly under the eye of their superiors, have no pretence for absenting themselves, and have nothing to attend to but their duty; whilst quarrels, caballing and all other inconveniences of too many young men messing together are avoided, of which I have myself seen many bad effects in other armies. (Yorke, 1913, III, 222)

When example or reprimands failed, discipline was enforced among officers by extra spells on watch, detention in the guard house and so on. In some of the smaller German states the hands of offending subalterns were bound with chains, and the young gentlemen were forced to appear in public with the regiment while still wearing these decorations. Major infractions of duty or subordination were properly the affair of courts martial, but Frederick and the Russian field-marshal Suvorov were both aware that it would have been subversive of discipline to drag a senior officer before such a tribunal when his offence was truly disgraceful, like stealing forage or failing to repay debts to soldiers. They preferred to wait until the wretched man had committed some minor mistake on parade or on manoeuvres, and then break him on the spot. They thereby avoided a public scandal, while astonishing the army by a spectacular display of tyrannical power.

Between officer and soldier

The cane, the sword, the gallows and all the other instruments of terror or death were at the disposal of superiors to reinforce their mastery over the soldiers. However, even in that age of close-order tactics, far more was required of the leader than the ability to inculcate fear among the private soldiers:

> Consider, that without *them* you would be of no consequence; and their good or bad behaviour reflects either *glory* or *shame* upon you; therefore make it your study to obtain their obedience by *love*, rather than fear. (An Old Officer, 1760, 27)

This sentiment was repeated in regulations and instructions in every land of Europe.

Knowledge of the soldier was the foundation upon which the officer could establish his means of communication. He naturally kept an eye on the progress of the drill, but he was also well advised to seek out opportunities to view the soldiers in their own environment, so as to ensure that their material needs were being kept properly supplied, and to gain a fresh perspective on their characters. O'Cahill recommended a visit to the quarters in the morning, when the soldiers were getting ready to appear on parade, and another in the afternoon, 'but on such occasions the officer must display a certain mildness and lack of formality, and ensure that the soldier does not have to put himself to unnecessary trouble, become paralysed with fear, or have to interrupt his duties and work' (O'Cahill, 1787, 246).

The soldiers probed endlessly for weaknesses among their leaders (see p. 99), but they responded to an officer who was assured enough in his authority to be willing to explain why such and such a thing must be done (see p. 285). Professionalism also commanded respect. The soldiers admired an officer who knew his business, who established a clear understanding of what he expected in terms of discipline and performance, who marched at their head into danger, and yet never subjected them to unnecessary fatigue or threatened to throw away their lives for no useful purpose.

The men were likely to be demoralised by any conduct which smacked of uncertainty, as when Clermont withdrew his first line to the Landwehr dyke at Krefeld (1758). A hint of cowardice was still worse. After being held back at Minden (1759) the English cavalrymen were gloomy and shamefaced, and 'cursed Mylord Sackville to the devil' (Westphalen, 1859–72, III, 697).

An element of paternalism entered into the relationship, and it was given specific expression in the orders of Peter the Great (Stein,

1885, 77) and in the usages of continental Europe in general, where 'children' was probably the officers' most common form of address to their soldiers. The vocabulary of military parenthood was brisk and affable, never descending into mawkish sympathy (which would have been despised by the troops), or a familiarity which might have smacked of egalitarianism. In Prussia Prince Leopold 'the Old Dessauer' was liked by the soldiers for his cheerfulness, accessibility and genial brutality. His pupil, Frederick the Great, established an equally successful relationship with his men.

The Russian field-marshal Rumyantsev was another master of the style, and soldiers compared him to his advantage with more overtly humane leaders like Prince Potemkin and General Petr Ivanovich Panin:

> Count Panin was much more indulgent towards the soldiers than Count Rumyantsev, yet it was striking that the troops actually liked Panin a good deal less – and possibly they did not like him at all. The reason is simply this, that he never talked to the private soldiers. His austere and reserved character held him back from such condescension. He strove instead to gain the regard of the soldiers and of mankind in general through his upright and honest conduct, and reckoned that any other way of winning people over was useless and downright ignoble. (Strandmann, 1882–4, 317)

STYLE OF LIFE

At a remove of two hundred years the eighteenth-century officer seems to have encumbered himself with a remarkable amount of clutter and appurtenances. If he chose to wear the regulation uniform he could still be distinguished from the private soldier by the ample skirts of his coat, his sash, his sword knot (a tasselled strip of cloth wound around the hilt), and his moon-shaped gorget, which was a piece of vestigial armour suspended from the neck. The wig or hair was curled into locks at the side, but drawn out at the back into a long military pigtail. The dress of this period demanded to be worn with confidence if it was not to look like a set of old garments draped over a clothes-horse. In fact 'the posture, gait, voice, and the movement of the body and hands must . . . all convey an impression of grace, avoiding that which is coarse and boorish, and equally that which is over-sweet and effeminate' (Wolff, 1776, 404).

The higher his rank, the more the officer was concerned to take his domestic comforts into the field. A young Quaker saw the English advancing into action at Brandywine Creek in 1777, and he noted that

> the officers who conversed with us, were of the first rank, and were rather short, portly men, were well dressed and of genteel appearance, and did not look as if they had ever been exposed to any hardship; their skins being white and delicate as it is customary for females who were brought up in large cities and towns. (Townsend, 1846, 23)

The baggage of a field officer could be expected to contain tents, beds, wardrobes, tables, chairs, kitchen utensils, table services and multiple changes of clothes. The whole could easily amount to 145 tons, like the baggage of the Duke of Cumberland. The transport train of the grandee comprised coaches, carts, and literally hundreds of draught horses and pack animals, in addition to a string of as much as twenty or thirty riding horses. Some of the necessary servants, attendants and drivers came from home, but most were detached from the ranks of the fighting soldiers, and further people were often picked up on the theatre of war, like the liberated blacks the English collected in America in 1780 and 1781 (Ewald, 1979, 305).

More telling in its way is the account of a Prussian first lieutenant, who tells how he managed his domestic economy in the War of the Bavarian Succession (1778–9). He hired one of the soldiers of his company as a servant:

> This lad had married just before we set out from Marienburg, and his wife was a splendid cook and a very good person generally. During our march through Poland I took on a fifteen-year-old youth, and at Ottmachau I had him dressed as a running footman. He was responsible for curling my hair, and carrying my spontoon and greatcoat on the march, and he also took with him a canteen which held everything that was needed to brew up coffee. . . . I had yet another servant to look after my horses, and he too was married. During the twenty-four months he was in my service my horses never went short of forage. He was willing to risk his neck in order to obtain it,

and his care for me and my horses cost him countless blows with the stick. (Anon., 1884, 27–8)

The officers would not have been men of their time if they had not gone to such a lot of trouble to fit themselves out. Their commitment to the military life was a conditional one, as we have seen, and they would have thought it wholly unreasonable to scale down their requirements to tactical ends. The headquarters of Marshal Saxe, whose campaigns were crowned with success, were no less brilliant than those of an obvious incompetent like Soubise. Economy was regarded as a bourgeois and demeaning trait, and the age set a great deal of store by displays of hospitality and outward show:

> These pleasant externals are not combat weapons, to be sure,
> but they are a perpetual reminder to the officer of his status
> and distinction, and by impressing his superiority on his soldiers
> they incline the men to consideration, respect and
> obedience. . . . At drill, on field days, marches and triumphal
> entries, and when the army is drawn up in line or on the battlefield
> – on all these occasions they make a magnificent impression, at
> once noble, martial and pleasing to the eye. (Andreu de Bilistein,
> 1763, 71)

It is perhaps easy to forget that in the early twentieth century people of quite modest condition gave employment to trains of domestic servants, and travelled in the company of a daunting collection of trunks, hat boxes and sports bags.

Some patterns may be discerned in the kind of life that the officers led in peacetime, in winter quarters, or during the lulls on campaign. An Austrian general drew a picture of

> what goes on for most of the time in the guardroom, which is
> the usual meeting place of the officers. They are not content
> with swapping tales about the governor or the affairs of the
> regiment, and similar tittle-tattle, but indulge in gambling with
> dice or cards, eating and drinking, and full-scale parties which
> often go on all day and night. (Esterhazy de Gallantha, 1747,
> 228)

Other common places of resort were sutlers' tents, coffee and gaming houses and billiard halls. In the more sociable regiments the officers organised balls and other entertainments, and even the ponderous gunners held a feast on 4 December, the day of their patron St Barbara. The theatre was considered as a school of morals and manners, and a number of senior officers followed the old custom of sitting up on the stage alongside the actors.

If the prevailing tone of military society was heavily philistine, many officers found solace in playing the flute, violin or harpsichord, and every army knew sensitive souls who escaped by burying themselves in their books or roaming the countryside. In Austria and the Germanic lands as a whole a more settled and serious mood overtook the officer corps in the 1770s, replacing the simple and boisterous pleasures of the rococo period (Ligne, 1928, I, 61; Adam Ludwig von Ochs, quoted in Atwood, 1980, 47).

Wives were the enemy of a 'free heart' (Frederick), and marriage was considered an undesirable state for a young military man. Many a Prussian officer spent his entire life in a state of enforced bachelorhood, and in France the officers of the lesser aristocracy and the bourgeoisie married significantly later and less frequently than was usual in civilian society (Bodinier, 1983, 221–3). It was perfectly acceptable, on the other hand, for a young officer to climb a ladder to keep a tryst with a pretty nun, to pay off a succession of trollops, or learn manners from the company of a lady of culture and standing. Men of the world, like the Prince de Ligne, drew a distinction between this kind of activity and the life of the unregenerate debauchee, who wasted time and fortune on supporting mistresses, or went in search of prostitutes on the street.

The Age of Reason also recognised what was, and what was not, truly dangerous in the other vices of the army. Thus the insidious and habit-forming regular tippling, what the British called 'dram drinking', was seen as more perilous than drunken carousels or heroic drinking bouts. The Marquis de Conflans emerged victorious after a succession of such contests when he was a prisoner of the English, but he was careful to spend the next eight days on water.

'Gaming is still the most tolerable and harmless recreation in large mixed assemblies, where people do not know each other, or in company where it offers an alternative to useless and empty conversation' (Wolff, 1776, 431). Equally innocent were those noisy sessions in the field, where cards were slammed down on some rough table amid groans or triumphal cries. The real harm was more likely to be done at small and intimate parties, where estates or companies might be gambled recklessly away. The addiction was as powerful as that for alcohol, and there was many an officer who, like the English colonel Daniel, 'scarce allowed himself time for rest; or if he slept, his dreams presented packs of cards to his eyes, and the rattling of dice to his ears' (An Old Officer, 1760, 79–80).

3
The private soldier

Origins

VOLUNTARY RECRUITING

Throughout our period more soldiers were recruited by voluntary enlistment than any other means. The most common agency of recruiting was a party from a company of a regiment which was led by the captain or a trusted officer, and consisted of well-set-up NCOs and soldiers and a little body of musicians: 'Your party must appear remarkably clean, very neat and smart in their dress, hats well-cocked, and worn in a soldierlike manner' (Simes, 1780a, 59).

Once a young man was prevailed upon to embrace the service he was given his bounty or first pay on the spot, presented with side arms and hat or some other tokens of the military trade, and told to append his signature or mark to the form of assent – which was a contract of service between the recruit and his captain. A full or preliminary oath was sworn, and the man began the first day of the three, six or more years of his engagement of service.

There is a discrepancy, which has yet to be resolved, between the appalling things which many experienced officers said about the background and motivation of the rank and file, and the somewhat different interpretations which may be drawn from our knowledge of individual cases and the scholarly study of the records.

We have it on the authority of the French war minister Saint-Germain that 'as things are at the moment, armies must inevitably be composed of the filth of the nation, and everything which is useless and harmful to society. We must turn to military discipline as the means of purifying this corrupt mass, of shaping it and making it useful' (Saint-Germain, 1779, 200–1). An Austrian colonel likewise testifies 'my experience has taught me that out of every hundred voluntary recruits, scarcely one will have a genuine calling to the trade of soldier' (Cogniazzo, 1779, 91–2. See also Dodart, quoted in Corvisier, 1964, 91).

In the eighteenth century the infantry regiments of the line certainly could not have remained in being without a substantial intake of men who enlisted out of inability to manage their affairs, or the need to escape punishment by civilian justice. A number of armies had a direct criminal intake, like the wretches who were voided from the galleys and prisons in Spain and Italy, the murderers and thieves who went from Hesse to the regiment of Hessen-Kassel (No. 45) in the Prussian service, or the convicted men who were consigned to the army by the English justices of the peace. By such means:

> the country gets clear of their banditti, and the ranks are filled
> with the scum of every country, the refuse of mankind. They
> are marched loaded with vice, villainy and chains, to their
> destined corps, where, when they arrive, they corrupt all they
> approach, and are whipped out, or desert in a month.
> (Dalrymple, 1761, I, 8)

Another poorly motivated element comprised innocent men who were forced or tricked into the service during some wartime emergency. In Bavaria and some of the minor German states there were instances where wedding parties or even entire Sunday congregations were put under armed arrest and combed for suitable men of military age. The arts of deception were brought to near-perfection by the French professional recruiters, or *racoleurs*, who operated from their headquarters on the Quai de la Feraille in Paris. One of this ilk was the notorious Colonel Collignon, who was hired by Frederick to do the rounds of Germany in the later stages of the Seven Years War:

> He travelled about in all sorts of garb and guises, and inveigled
> men to enter the Prussian service by the hundred. By dint of
> promises and actual written commissions he persuaded young
> fops, students, counter clerks and the like that he had made
> them lieutenants or captains in the Prussian army; it did not
> matter whether it was in the infantry, the cuirassiers or the
> hussars – they just had to choose. . . . They hastened with their

commissions to Magdeburg, where they were enlisted as ordinary recruits. Argument was to no avail, and the stick was applied until they were reduced to total submission.
(Archenholtz, 1840, II, 34)

Were such men typical of the rank and file? The question is debatable. Many of the recruits for the infantry of the various armies were men of the learned professions, or tradesmen or artisans who had been thrown out of work by economic changes. According to one estimate, as much as 20 per cent of the rank and file of the British army in the War of Independence was composed of former textile workers, chiefly from depressed areas like Lancashire or the counties of the south-west (Frey, 1981, 12, 21).

Poland, southern Germany, France and Italy were fruitful sources of such recruits for the Prussian army, where 'noblemen, runaway monks, doctors, lecturers and many other learned men, as well as merchants, apothecaries, former officials, craftsmen, artists, actors and jugglers all end up as private soldiers' (*Magazin für deutsche Geschichte und Statistik*, 1784, quoted in Jähns, 1889–91, III, 2, 238). By all accounts such folk made much more civilised and entertaining company than the native cantonal conscripts.

The raffish or rootless elements were leavened by the presence of genuine volunteers, such as those attracted by the cavalry, where throughout Europe the private trooper was treated well, and where service in wartime was attended with more excitement but less danger than among the foot. Even the Prussian infantry knew men like J. F. Dreyer, who looked back on a lifetime of happy soldiering and recalled how at the age of seventeen he was drawn from his native Alsace by the high standing of the military estate in Prussia:

I speeded to Aachen, where I asked for the Prussian recruiting house. I was duly shown the way. The horseplay, joyful shouts and din of the recruits could be heard for some distance. A splendid-looking man greeted me at the entrance, and from my demeanour he very soon detected what I was after. I was led in triumph to meet my comrades, and I was greeted with a loud cry of 'Long live the King!' (Dreyer, 1810, 13)

From all of this it is fair to conclude that there was a great diversity or character and motivation among the voluntary recruits. Most of them hailed from a rural background, and in the Age of

Reason it could scarcely be otherwise, for in a nation like France four out of five people still lived in the country. Writers continued to echo the sentiment of Vegetius to the effect that 'the best soldiers of all are the ones raised in the countryside. They are hardened against fatigue and accustomed to digging in the soil, and they have been brought up to endure coarse food and the rigour of the seasons' (Silva, 1778, 11).

The result was not necessarily an army of ploughmen. The agricultural labourers *per se* were leavened by large numbers of rural tradesmen and craftsmen whose work did not differ in kind from that of their counterparts in towns. Moreover it has been established that in France in 1763 the countrymen formed only about 66 per cent of the army, which is significantly less than the rural representation in the nation as a whole. The eastern provinces made a disproportionately large contribution, thanks to their military traditions and their heavy military presence, which establishes a further difference between the intake of the army and the character of civilian society.

CONSCRIPTION

Voluntary recruiting did not inevitably produce bad recruits, but it furnished manpower in an unreliable and unpredictable way. Some of the greatest military powers of the Age of Reason therefore had resort to various forms of compulsory enlistment.

The conscription in Russia dated from 1705, when Peter the Great abolished voluntary recruiting and began the first of a series of irregular levies from the male population of Great Russia. Service was initially for life, and was reduced to a still very formidable twenty-five years in 1793. However, in no sense did the Russian conscription call into being a 'nation in arms'. Not only were very few of the liable 'souls' called to the service in each levy, but the clergy were altogether exempt, and merchants, manufacturers and other privileged classes were permitted to buy themselves out of the system.

Conscription came to Prussia in 1732 and 1733. Every regiment was now allocated a 'canton' or district, where it had a pool of about 5,000 suitable men at its disposal. Again there were many categories of folk who were exempted, and in Prussia the demands were reduced still further by the requirement for the conscripts to join the colours for only about two months of every year in peacetime, which left them free to spend the rest of the time at home and going about their normal occupations. The freely enlisted foreigners always made up at least half the number of troops, and even in Russia, which had an all-native army, the service claimed only about 3.3 per cent of the male population in the 1760s.

After a prolonged internal debate, the Austrians slowly built up the foundations for a Prussian-style conscription for their 'German' infantry between 1770 and 1781. The vehicle for the French conscription was the *Milice*, which had been founded by Louis XIV in 1688. The militia was recruited by lot, and its purposes were to provide for local defence, especially along the coasts, and to furnish reserves for the field army. In 1757 the size of the *Milice* reached 80,000 men, and it made up about one-third of the strength of the field armies. The quality of the militiamen was generally poor, but they included a number of retired veterans, and the best men were fed into the regiments of the Grenadiers Royaux, from which in turn were recruited the two units of the Grenadiers de France.

The various kinds of conscription were intended to strike a balance between the military and economic needs of the state. On the battlefield the local loyalties certainly contributed to the staying-power of the Russian and Prussian armies. One of the Austrian advocates of the system also claimed that it

> makes for a closer link between the countryman and the soldier.
> Every district has its own regiment, which therefore becomes
> a second home and family for the peasant. When he leaves his
> native village he passes to a regiment which consists for a large
> part of his friends, relations and acquaintances. (General Creutz,
> *Nostitz-Rieneck Hofcommission* F IV 3, Kriegsarchiv, Vienna)

All the same the business brought with it an element of open force which remained shocking to many men at the time. In Russia the initial choice of conscripts from the list of 'souls' was left to the arbitrary choice of the landowner. Many of the potential victims fled to the forests, or they had fingers cut off or teeth pulled out so that they would be unfit to be presented to the acceptance board. Those that failed to escape were dragged off howling in chains, while their villages held funeral services in their memory.

The Prussian conscript knew that he would shortly see his home and family again, but his treatment during his time in the ranks might be barbaric, and the captains and colonels exercised a control over the life of the civilian community that was hotly resented, even in a patriotic town like Colberg. In Silesia a concerned father once addressed himself to General Rothkirch to protest about the conscription of his son, who was a slight and retiring young man:

> Immediately on entering the ante-room he encountered the general's wife, and he asked for her assistance. This gentle lady took the good little lad by the hand, presented him to her husband, and asked for his release as a proof of his love for her. You will probably say that the lady's action was unwise. Perhaps it was, but nothing can excuse the unbalanced behaviour of her husband, who drove – nay almost beat – her out of the room, swearing 'If God the Father came with the same request, I would throw him out too!' (Fiedel, J. (?), 1784, 65)

PHYSICAL ATTRIBUTES

An Austrian infantry officer complained that 'according to the principles of our time we pay no particular attention to moral character, nationality, profession, mental aptitude and so on. Size and external appearance determine our choice. . . . How the lad looks is his chief, in fact his only recommendation' (Cogniazzo, 1779, 96).

While truly colossal men were slow-moving and feeble, like the Giant Grenadiers of Frederick William I of Prussia, a certain stature was considered desirable:

> A large man can better sustain the weight of his weapons, his knapsack, his bread rations and the rest of his equipment. He is better at loading and aiming his musket, and thrusting with the bayonet. He finds it easier to jump a ditch, climb a breastwork and engage in other exertions. (Warnery, 1785–91, II, 35–6)

The stipulated minimum heights ranged from 5 feet 5 inches among the Prussian infantry, down to the 5 feet 1 inch demanded by the French infantry regulations – which was still taller than all but one in thirty Frenchmen in civilian life. Small and supple men were fitted for light cavalry work, but the regular horse called for individuals of 5 feet 4 inches or considerably more: 'The men can't be too tall, 'tis a vast advantage provided they are well chose, active not heavy' (Hawley [1726], 1946, XXVI, 91). Frederick believed that no rider under 5 feet 6 inches was capable of mounting the large cuirassier and dragoon horses without assistance.

The civilian trade of the recruit was of no great importance for service with the infantry, but for the mounted service

> huntsmen, butchers, blacksmiths and other men who pursue a trade which demands a strong and well-exercised constitution are better than craftsmen who lead a sedentary life. . . . But good young peasant lads are best suited of all for the cavalry, for they have been brought up with horses and have learned to like them. They are accustomed to hard work and all kinds of weather, and once they have been trained they possess more endurance than any other kind of soldier. (Griesheim, 1777, 26)

In armies like the Prussian, the gunners were left with whatever small or ugly men remained after the recruits had been combed by the infantry and the cavalry. However, the Russian artillery went in search of strong and lively men who could be trained in rapid fire, and this was undoubtedly one of the reasons why Russian gunnery became so formidable in the Age of Reason.

The professional soldier *par excellence* was a man of early middle age, who was on a long term of service or a second or third re-engagement. It might seem that somebody of this description might be unequal to the physical demands of war (Fann, 1977, 169), but a well-set-up man in his thirties or forties had the advantage in endurance and health over a slightly built lad in his teens or early twenties, and in addition he possessed the steadiness and experience which gave the superiority in close-order tactics:

> It still gives me pleasure to recall Prince Eugene's splendid regiment of cuirassiers. The men nearly all had grey moustaches, and their faces were weatherbeaten and tanned. There was something virile and intimidating in the way they carried their weapons, and they invariably put them to good use in combat. (Loen, 1751, 187. See also Lossow, 1826, 10–11, 13–14)

Up to six years of training was considered necessary to make a proficient trooper, and two or three years for an infantryman. This was why Frederick thought it worth his while to take such elaborate precautions against desertion:

> It hardly matters if a clumsy man deserts and is replaced by an oaf of the same kind. But it does us damage in the long term when we lose a man who has been schooled for two years on end to the requisite degree of physical skill, and we are left with a bad soldier, or indeed nobody at all to take his place. (*Principes Généraux de la Guerre* [1748] Frederick, 1846–57, XXVIII, 5).

It is notable, however, that the French army was a juvenile one by the standards of the time. Forty-six per cent of the men were aged twenty-five or below by the close of the Seven Years War, but by 1789, after a period of prolonged peace, the proportion had actually risen to half, which seems to run counter to the trends among the professionals in the other armies.

Training, conditioning and discipline

> A handful of men, inured to war, proceed to certain
> victory, while on the contrary numerous armies
> of raw and undisciplined troops are but multitudes
> of men dragged to slaughter.
>
> (Vegetius)

The process of acclimatisation to the military life began while the recruit was still on the march to the regimental garrison (and never more drastically than for the transport of raw Prussian soldiers which was ambushed by the Austrians at Unter-Gundersdorf in Moravia on 28 June 1758). In normal circumstances the route and the stopping places were laid down in advance, and

> when . . . the officer arrives with his transport he must make sure that the recruits enter wearing their full uniform, that they are clean and tidy and have their hair curled, and that they march according to the usage of the regiment in proper rank and file and with shouldered muskets. (Esterhazy de Gallantha, 1747, 315)

After the formalities of documentation and swearing-in were completed, the bewildered young man was assigned to a tent or room *Kameradschaft* in his captain's company, and given into the charge of

> a reliable and well-behaved soldier, who will teach the new man not only how to behave himself in an orderly fashion, but how to put on his shoes, dress himself, and make himself look presentable. He will school him to be diligent, bold, adroit and agile, and to rid himself utterly of his base peasant habits and vices, like pulling faces, or scratching himself when he talks. (Major-General A. I. Bibikov, [1764], in Skalon, 1902-*c*.1911, IV, pt 1, bk 2, section 3, p. 76)

The shock and depression experienced by the new soldier was known in the eighteenth century as *nostalgie* or the *maladie du pays*. Certain nations were recognised to be peculiarly susceptible, namely the Swiss, the men of Cleves in the Prussian Rhineland, and the Russians and French in general. Men like the Bretons, whose faith was based on the cult of local saints, began to doubt whether religion held any sway in these alien surroundings. The truly desperate recruits killed themselves or tried to desert, but others made the readjustment by fashioning a completely new life for themselves. The Russian soldier built up a home away from home in his *artel*, or association of comrades (see p. 131), and there is something jaunty and defiant in the way the French soldiers identified themselves with their chosen *noms de guerre* – *Beausoleil*, *Jolicoeur* and so on.

For some of the time the thoughts of the soldiers did not extend beyond the need for self-preservation. Ulrich Bräker tells us that in the Prussian infantry regiment of Itzenplitz the drill sessions might last for five hours at a stretch:

> We were dead-tired when we came back to our quarters, but we still had to throw ourselves into a frenzy of activity to see that our linen was in good order, and to clean every spot from our clothing – for the whole uniform was white, with the single exception of the blue coat. Musket, cartridge pouch, buckles and every button on the uniform had to be polished to a shining brightness. If there was anything amiss with any of these items, or if a single hair was out of place, we knew were in for a severe thrashing the moment we appeared on the drill square. (Bräker, 1852, 129)

Every item of equipment, dress or adornment demanded a

particular attention in those times. When a musket or carbine had been fired at drill, the barrel had to be removed from the wooden stock and swabbed out with a piece of rag that was wound around the head of the ramrod. It was dried with a fresh piece of cloth, and the exterior and the rest of the metal furniture – the lock plate, butt plate, trigger guard and ramrod pipes – was brought to a high polish by buff leather or cloth, with the help of agents like wood ash, iron filings, or powdered brick or coal. Gold lace could be brought up with urine, dry pipeclay or lumps of bread. Heel ball (a mixture of wax and charred bone) was applied to black leatherwork like shoes or cartridge pouches. Sword belts, the broad strap of the cartridge pouch and any items of white clothing could be restored to a state of immaculate brilliance through pipeclay, which was laid on with a damp sponge or a soft brush.

It was a fiddling affair to do up the gaiters, which were fastened by rows of little buttons. The crowning achievement, and the most difficult of all to master, was to arrange the hair into a sculptural form, with a pigtail, a swept-back crown, and the regulation number of locks on either side. Pins, curlers, powder and ribbon were all brought into service to this end, and the men spent hours helping one another out. When troops were due to go on guard the next morning, they might spend the entire night with their hair done up in papers.

Frederick the Great was extremely unwilling to award or confirm death sentences, but in other respects the Prussian army stood as an example of severity to the rest of Europe, visiting malefactors with confinement, branding, minor torture and mutilations, or to the ordeal of walking the gauntlet under a hail of blows with sticks. As in the armies of the other nations, kicks and buffeting were part of the vocabulary of NCOs and junior officers.

It is perhaps worth pausing to ask why the armies of the eighteenth century demanded so much of the private soldier, and why they seemed to treat him with such barbarity when he failed to supply it.

In the first place discipline was necessary to make the huge military machine function in an orderly way, and to compel its component parts to do what was frequently contrary to their will. This thought impressed itself on Frederick in 1740, while he stood beside Prince Leopold the Old Dessauer watching his troops assemble before the invasion of Silesia. The king asked the Old Dessauer what struck him most about the scene:

'Your Majesty! Can it be anything else than the splendid appearance of our troops, and the regularity and perfection of their movements?' 'All of that comes with time, attention and money. . . . No, my dear kinsman, what astonishes me is that we are standing here in perfect safety, looking at sixty thousand [*sic*] men – they are all our enemies, and there is not one of them who is not better armed and stronger than we are, and yet they all tremble in our presence, while we have no reason whatsoever to be afraid of them. This is the miraculous effect of order, subordination and narrow supervision'. (Hildebrandt, 1829–35, V, 45–6)

The strength of well-disciplined armies lay not in the motivation or prowess of individuals, but in the capacity for collective action: 'A regiment of Prussian infantry is like a machine which is directed by the officers' (Mauvillon, E., 1756, II, 102). Engrained battle drills enabled officers to rally troops who seemed to have been broken beyond recall, just as the principle of 'subordination' made it possible for the Prussian major-general Tauentzien to defend Breslau in 1760 with a garrison consisting mainly of deserters, pressed men and invalids. The most reliable troops were the one thousand men of the Garde, 'and most of these were foreign soldiers who served with bad grace, on account of their low pay, but who were bound to their colours by principles of honour and discipline' (Archenholtz, 1840, II, 59).

The private soldiers were drawn mostly from the common people, or in other words they were capable of conduct more foul and vile than can be imagined by the majority of historians. The officers and NCOs were therefore engaged in a constant duel with those who tested their authority, and they could not afford to relax their guard for an instant, 'for when a licentious, independent humour has prevailed amongst troops, it must be [a matter of] time, infinite pains and severity, to reduce them to their proper obedience' (Bland, 1727, 195).

The inculcation of discipline was the true reason for the perfection that was required on the drill square, 'for when you come down to it, all that manual drill of arms, which we practise every day with such care, is really only so much fiddle-faddle, necessary in its way to form the soldier and accustom him to obedience, but otherwise almost useless in action' (Guignard, 1725, I, 63).

In one respect it did not matter at all whether or not a musket sparkled in the sunlight, but a soldier who failed to maintain his weapon in this state in peacetime was unlikely to keep it in working order when he was on campaign. Enlightened commentators sought to do good by advocating browned musket barrels, realistic evolutions at drill, or a natural way of wearing the hair. They missed the point that the turnout and evolutions were totemic objects, and that a well-meaning amelioration in one detail would just have led to some other activity or object becoming a symbol of subordination in its place, like shining boots in modern armies. Meanwhile all the work kept the troops out of trouble, for 'soldiers, and especially French soldiers, want to be kept busy; if they are not employed doing something useful, they will get up to something bad' (d'Authville, 1756, 238).

With the passage of time the well-disciplined soldier began to take pride in his work. In the Prussian army

> every item of his equipment shone like a mirror – his musket, his sword, and the brass shield on his cartridge pouch. Many of the infantrymen and cavalrymen were adorned with rich aiglets, and gold and silver lace and braid. . . . The spontoons of the infantry officers were of glistening steel and gold. The mounted Gardes du Corps sported highly-polished cuirasses and elaborately-embroidered tabards, and they carried silver eagles in the style of ancient Roman standards. . . . Only unthinking people will condemn this splendour as useless. It increased the courage and esteem of the soldier, and enhanced the dignity of the army as a whole. (Archenholtz, 1974, 16–18)

This accounts for the paradox that troops who deserted from an exacting service like the Prussian army felt themselves strangely bereft in their new life. They now appreciated that their former masters had been paying them a kind of compliment by attaching so much importance to their standards of attainment, and it was unsettling to find that whatever they did for good or evil now counted for so little.

The Prussian style of discipline was not a code of unrelenting severity. When they were off duty, which was for most of the time, the soldiers were left entirely to their own devices. They went about in whatever order of dress they pleased, and they could relax or work for profit (see p. 127) as took their fancy. Indeed, a lot of the minute preparation needed to go on parade was the result of the licence that was allowed elsewhere.

We must also say in defence of eighteenth-century armies that, unlike their modern counterparts, they did not use drill as a deliberate instrument of breaking down the personality of the recruit. Initial training was concentrated on the individual, not the group, and the evidence suggests that it was carried out with patience, care and gentleness (see p. 104). The weight of discipline was brought to bear only after the young soldier fully understood what he was doing: 'At that period the . . . various drills and evolutions were easy to carry out, and when a soldier was careless he was called to strict account. Everything went like clockwork, as was only right and proper' (Dreyer, 1810, 20). The much-quoted Bräker concedes that he and his Swiss friends managed to escape the punishments which were visited on their negligent comrades.

Many soldiers in all ages are drawn irresistibly towards whatever will do themselves the most harm, which gives a further moral justification to the controls exercised by discipline in the eighteenth century. The records of military life were replete with stories of stupidity and improvidence. Soldiers sealed themselves up in over-heated rooms in winter time and consequently fell sick by the thousand. If they were given rations in bulk they traded them for alcohol, or they threw them away to save themselves the trouble of carrying them. Now that they found they were hungry, they gorged themselves on unripe fruit or some other stomach-churning substance. When the beer or spirits gave out they proceeded to drink from foul puddles when clear water could have been obtained with a little effort. The governor of Ceuta, the Marqués de Villadarias, knew that undisciplined warriors were also in the habit of discarding spades and other burdensome items of equipment. He kept the troops in a proper frame of mind by distributing old nails and similar useless objects among the soldiers, and punishing them if they failed to produce the ironmongery for inspection several days later.

The basic virtues of cleanliness and tidiness were likewise enforced thrugh disciplinary measures:

The first of these qualities preserves their health, and the other endows them with a noble appearance. For these reasons they must be compelled every day to wash their face and hands, comb their hair, bathe their eyes and rinse out their mouths. They will cut their fingernails twice a week, wash their feet once a week, and cut their toenails twice a month. In quarters they will go to the baths twice weekly, and if there is a stream nearby they must bathe in it. Every night, whether in quarters or camp, they are to remove their shoes. A number of them fail to do so, out of sheer laziness, and the leather rubbing against the legs gives rise to sores, which are difficult to heal. (Colonel Count Vorontsov, 'Instruction for Company Commanders' (i.e. of the First Grenadier Regiment), 17 January 1774, in Vorontsov, 1871, 34)

On campaign the welfare of the individual, his comrades and the service often went together. It was notorious that in sieges about half the casualties were the direct result of carelessness. Soldiers were given to stepping in front of cannon when the pieces were about to fire. They might walk unconcernedly behind a working party and be pierced through the head by a pick. They paid little heed to warnings that an enemy shot or shell was on the way, or if they survived the first graze, they might try to stop the rolling missile with their feet (which invariably resulted in the loss of a limb), or they might pick it up with the intention of selling it to their own gunners. At the siege of Mons in 1744 a French soldier took up what he thought to be a solid shot,

> and he clung to it even though the others shouted to him that it was a bomb, and that he must escape. The charge took fire and the bomb exploded in his hands. In a split second he was as dusky as a blackamoor. His uniform and hair were burnt, and his skin was a little singed. He was otherwise intact, and by a singular good fortune the splinters left him unscathed. (Mr R *****, 1759, 98)

Indiscipline brought still greater risks in action in the open field, for it put the whole unit at risk: 'Do not hesitate to smash in the skull of any soldiers who grumble, or gives vent to cries like "We are cut off! They are on our flanks! the enemy are coming at us from behind!" or other expressions capable of demoralising the men' (Bonneville, 1762, I, 74–5). Many of the casualties in the leading ranks were caused by badly handled muskets in the rear (see p. 246).

All of this helps to justify a far greater degree of formal discipline than would be tolerated in modern armies. We are left, however, with a number of indictments which withstand every attempt at mitigation. Warnery was surely correct when he drew attention to the lack of proportion which visited the same punishment for losing a hat during drill as for rape or bestiality (Warnery, 1785–91, II, 41). The element of artificiality was equally offensive, and it was encapsulated by the practice in some French regiments of painting false moustaches on the soldiers, or fashioning them out of horsehair and attaching them with pitch. Moreover the soldier in the eighteenth century had to endure extremes of discipline at the same time as he underwent an objective deterioration in his conditions of life. His cleaning materials had to be furnished out of his own pay, which in any case was falling far behind the wages in civilian life, and he was reduced to dire straits unless he was given the opportunity to work for private profit (see p. 127). Moreover he began to lose his remaining liberties when barrack accommodation began to replace the comparative freedom of billets towards the end of the Age of Reason.

One spectacle continued to revolt men of sensibility wherever it was witnessed in Europe. Thiébault once saw it in Berlin, though it was by no means confined to the Prussian service:

One evening Prince Ferdinand of Brunswick told me he had noticed me in the morning in the park, when he was drilling his regiment.

'You could not have seen me there for very long', I replied. 'Directly in front of me I had a *Junker* of about fifteen, who had seen a soldier of more than fifty years of age commit a slight mistake in the manual drill of arms. He summoned him from the ranks and proceeded to belabour him with repeated blows of his cane on the man's arms and thighs, using all the strength at his disposal. The poor victim burst into tears, but dared not utter a word. I must tell you, Your Grace, that I removed myself from this scene as fast as I could.'

'I must assure you, my friend, that measures of that kind are necessary.'

'I cannot answer for that, Your Grace, but I do know that it is not necessary for me to watch them.' (Thiébault, 1813,

III, 207–8. For the sadistic beating of veterans see also An Old Officer, 1760, 39; Berenhorst, 1798–9, I, 128)

The infantryman

THE NEW SOLDIER

The infantry was the foundation of the army. The foot soldiers lacked the impetus of the cavalry and the mighty firepower of the artillery, but they could do a far greater range of things than either – they fought with fire and cold steel, they held ground as well as attacking it, they defended and besieged fortresses, and they could act effectively in almost any kind of terrain.

The training of the recruits was slow and progressive, and at the beginning it was concentrated on the individuals. Once the men had mastered the basic skills they were incorporated in successively larger bodies, starting with the rank and proceeding to the complete platoon and the two-platoon division. These formations were in turn put through the increasingly elaborate 'firings' and manoeuvres.

For the first stage, acquiring the fundamental knowledge of the military life, the recruit was taken in hand by an experienced corporal or sergeant:

> The newly-arrived soldier almost invariably comes with the idea that he will be maltreated when he is learning the drill, and some of the effects I have seen are quite extraordinary. We must therefore build up the confidence of the ordinary soldier by speaking to him gently, so that he is not turned against his new condition of life from the outset. (Griesheim, 1777, 206–7)

In fact, if the instructor knew his work, he was careful not to hurry the young man. He first taught him to stand in the eighteenth-century military way, with heels about two inches apart, feet splayed out, and shoulders held back. There is little mention of soldiers having to 'suck in that gut', and indeed in many of the contemporary pictures they have a distinctly pot-bellied look. The Prussians stood relatively easily, but the military carriage was taken to an extreme in the French army when it went through its neo-Prussian phase after the Seven Years War. Guibert complained that

if you enter one of our typical drill depots you will notice that the wretched soldiers have all been put into a variety of artificial and enforced postures. As a result their muscles are completely seized up and the circulation of their blood is interrupted. (Guibert [1772], 1804, I, 78).

When the recruit had learned how to distinguish his left foot from his right, he was fit to be put through the elements of marching. The pace was slow (seventy-five to the minute in Prussia), and imprinted on the soldier by the tap of a drum or a chant of *'Ein und zwanzig! Zwei und zwanzig!'* or its equivalent outside Germany. The legs were unbending, and the foot was slightly raised, or it swept low over the ground as in the modern British march in slow time. In most armies the arms were immobile and fully extended, and the left palm or fingers supported the musket as near to the perpendicular as possible. Well-disciplined units took a pride in performing every motion with 'life and spirit' (MacIntire, 1763, 19), and in Prussia the 'shoulder arms' was brought to a state of near-perfection: 'This movement appears miraculous and well-nigh impossible to those who have not seen it before, until I tell them how we do it and give a demonstration' (Müller [1759], 1978, 12).

Not the least of the responsibilities of the instructor was to introduce the recruit to his uniform and equipment, and to pass on all the unwritten old-soldier lore as to how it was to be worn and maintained.

The colours of the infantry coats had pronounced national or regional characteristics. Green was as typical of the Russians as was blue for the Swedes and Prussians. Red or brownish red was worn by the Saxons, Hanoverians, Danes, English, the German and Irish regiments in the French service and the Swiss regiments generally. The Austrians, French and Spanish all wore white coats, which distinguished them immediately from the infantrymen of the Protestant or northern states with their stronger colours. Clothing was renewed most frequently in Prussia, where the soldier received a new outfit every year with absolute regularity. Uniforms in France were supposed to be renewed every three years, though in some regiments the corrupt colonels made them last much longer. Spanish uniforms were worn for six or seven years until they were full of holes.

Utilitarian uniforms were introduced for the Austrian infantry in 1767, as a result of the concern of the Empress Maria Theresa for the welfare of her troops. Prince Grigorii Aleksandrovich Potemkin did the same for the Russian infantry in 1786. Otherwise the clothing was modelled on the elegant civilian dress of the period, and serviceability was not always the prime consideration. A Piedmontese officer attacked the contemporary order of priorities:

> If you wish to decide on the most practical way of dressing the soldiers, you ought to banish from your mind the vision of how they look drawn up on parade on some splendid square, and instead imagine how they must appear when they are marching across fields, climbing hills, crashing through woods, fording rivers and digging in the ground, in all probability at a time when they are crushed by exhaustion, and exposed to rain, wind or appalling cold. (Brezé, 1779, 124)

Like the civilians, the ordinary musketeers wore tricorn hats of felt, which were 'invariably shapeless after two nights in the open air, and totally ruined by the end of the first campaign' (Silva, 1778, 33). The élite grenadiers sported characteristic caps or bonnets, with fronts of metal, bearskin or embroidered cloth. The men were proud of this headgear, which made them look tall and fierce, and they preferred it to the tricorns which they were usually given for everyday wear. They were more than willing to put up with the weight, the lack of protection against the elements, and the inconvenience of having the caps knocked off by low branches.

The undergarment of the eighteenth-century soldier was a shirt of coarse linen. The tails were long enough to be tucked under the seat (underpants were not invented until much later), and the sleeves were loosely fitting in the Douglas Fairbanks style. The shirt was bound at the top with a stock (neck cloth), which in some regiments was a virtual instrument of torture, forcing the soldier to hold his head upright.

On top of the shirt lay a waistcoat, which was frequently a substantial garment with sleeves. The coat itself did not differ greatly from the original in civilian life, and the cut followed the changes in fashion as the century wore on, tending more and more towards a swallow-tailed effect. The Prussian coat was a distinctively tight-sleeved and skimpy affair, and the hem came down only as far as the tip of a middle finger of a hand held at full stretch down the body. The Hungarian and Croatian troops of the Habsburgs were proud of their long tight pants, but almost all of the other infantrymen of Europe wore breeches, which were cut generously around the seat, and fastened below the knee. Black or white cloth gaiters protected the legs as far down as the shoes, which were high-heeled and broad-toed.

The reformers and the critics did not do complete justice to the commodity of the clothing here described, or the useful ways it could be adapted. In most armies the hats were left aside in camp and on fatigues, and the soldiers went about in comfortable woollen forage caps, which were usually cut up from old uniforms. The Prussian coat was certainly narrow and short, but it was not usually constricting:

> This item of clothing is made for agility, and compared with coats of more generous cut it absorbs less moisture and dries more quickly. We should bear in mind that dampness is the only thing which is truly dangerous to the health of the soldier, whose constitution should otherwise be inured to campaigning. (Mirabeau and Mauvillon, 1788, 99–100)

In popular imagery the English infantrymen fought through the North American summers in bewigged and scarlet splendour. In practice, however, the hair was frequently cropped short, the stock was loosened or discarded, and the brims of the hats were cut off close to the crown. It was also an English habit to shorten the coats to jackets, and the colour, which in any case was a dull brownish red, was at least as serviceable as anything worn by the American Continentals and the French regiments of the line (see p. 286).

In the middle of the century the cut of the coat was still ample enough in most armies to permit the lapels and turnbacks to be undone and fastened across the front in cold weather, and the cuffs to be lowered over the fingers. The Russians enjoyed the additional protection of their cloaks, which when not required were rolled up and worn in traditional style like a bandolier. In summertime both the Russian and Polish soldiers did without the coat altogether, and on occasion some of the Austrians did the same.

The gaiters were said to give better protection against cold, wet and mosquitoes than did the half boots which came into fashion in the later part of the century (Mirabeau and Mauvillon, 1788, 99), and the Prussian gaiters were softer and more comfortable than is generally believed: 'We should not bother if they do not lie smoothly, for gaiters are not intended for display but for the convenience of the soldiers' (Frederick, quoted in Kling, 1902–12, I, 51).

As in all periods, some of the worst damage to health was caused by damp penetrating through outer coverings to the legs and feet. The woollen stockings of the German armies became soggy and dangerous, but when the Prussians were on campaign they cut off the bottoms and followed the Russian custom of wrapping the feet in strips of cloth impregnated in tallow. Marshal Saxe writes that a similar practice was to be found among the French veterans, who knew from experience that grease gave the best protection against damp and chafing (Saxe [1732], 1877, 12).

When the soldier was fully equipped for the field, he was festooned with the great variety of objects which enabled him to live and fight. Most of his needs of a domestic kind were carried in his knapsack, which was a bag of canvas or untanned calfskin or goat-skin, suspended by a leather strap running slantwise over the right shoulder. The contents of the knapsack were a kind of military trousseau, and comprised spare shoes and clothing, brushes, hair powder and cleaning materials. Bread, flour or biscuit were stuffed into a canvas bag called the haversack, which was usually slung below the knapsack. A further strap supported a water bottle of tin, wood or leather. All of this weight pressing behind the left hip might be augmented by an axe or tentpegs (as in the Prussian infantry), and if the soldier was unlucky he would also be called upon to take his turn in carrying tent poles, kettles or other heavy items of communal property.

Hanging behind the right hip was the cartridge pouch, which was borne on a broad white leather strap which passed over the left shoulder. The pouch was a box of thick leather, and the open top was protected by a long hanging flap which was adorned with a metal medallion bearing the regimental coat of arms. By lifting the flap you gained access to the cartridges – little paper cylinders each containing a charge of powder and a leaden musket ball. The cartridges stood on end in holes drilled in the block of wood which lined the bottom of the pouch, and depending on the army and the period there was provision for anything from eighteen to sixty rounds. The cartridge pouch gave adequate protection against rain, but it was liable to let in water when the soldier was fording a stream, and it had to be held high or tightly shut when there was a danger of ignition. The Prussians took this precaution when they hurried through the smouldering ruins of Cüstrin in 1758, and the Hessian regiment of Lossberg did the same when it marched across a field of burning grass at White Plains on 28 October 1776.

The infantryman's sword was a short and slightly curved 'hanger', which was carried in a scabbard attached to a belt running around the soldier's waist, or (later in the century) a substantial strap passing over the right shoulder:

> 'Tis soldier-like and graceful for the men to have swords,
> especially in garrison, but too many inconveniences attend
> them. They are the loss of many men by their drunken quarrels,
> they are a hindrance to them in their exercises, and a great one
> in marching, a man having full enough to carry besides them.
> As to night parties, they make almost as much noise as the old
> bandoliers by rattling with the bayonet, and when are they ever
> used in the field or in action? (Hawley [1726], 1946, 93)

The hangers were sometimes put in store before a regiment went on campaign, which saved the trouble of recalling the weapons before a particular action, and obviated the danger of the soldiers selling their swords or simply throwing them away (d'Héricourt, 1748, I, 173).

The blade of the grenadier sabre was about 3 feet long, which made it a more genuinely formidable weapon. It was known to have been used in combat (see p. 204) unlike the hanger of the musketeers, and it had a powerful symbolic importance.

A sword or sabre might flatter a man's pride, but he was convinced that his survival in combat depended on his musket more than anything else. Some details of the musket's construction and use will be reviewed in due course, and it is enough for the moment to note that it was a weapon about 5 feet long (excluding the bayonet). It was the custom in many regiments to keep the barrel polished to a mirror-like perfection, and to loosen the screws in order to produce an impressive clatter when the weapon was slammed about, all of which might unfit the musket for real action.

The bayonet was a detachable knife, which was fitted to the muzzle of the musket by a slotted iron sleeve. The form of the blade was various, but it was most typically a slim needle-like object of triangular section.

FORMATIONS AND FIRE

Now that they had mastered the principles of deportment, and the care of their clothing and equipment, the recruits were gradually integrated into the training of the unit as a whole: 'each soldier is impressed with a religious observance of never relinquishing the touch of his neighbour: by this the idea of the necessity of order, mutual support is strongly felt and observed' (Dundas, 1788, 52). The unit in question was not usually the soldier's parent company, which existed primarily for purpose of administration (see p. 69), but the battalion and its tactical subdivisions.

The typical eighteenth-century regiment comprised two field battalions of up to 800 men each. These battalions were the fundamental building blocks of the line of battle. For drill and combat purposes the company demarcations inside the battalion were ignored (except for the grenadiers), and the officers and men were reconstituted into four, five or more 'divisions', of two platoons each. There was no permanent allocation of individuals to divisions or platoons (see p. 131), for these sub-units were being constantly remade according to the strength of the battalion (which might be well below establishment), but we should not go too far wrong if we imagined that the division was made up of between 60 and 100 men, and the platoon of between 30 and 50.

The eighteenth-century infantry drilled and fought in lines which were two, three or four ranks (rows) deep. The two-rank line was atypical, and was largely confined to the campaigns in North America (see p. 287). At the other extreme the four-rank line was characteristic of European tactics in the first half of the eighteenth century. It gave a useful depth against cavalry, but it was too thick to enable the rearward rank to use its muskets with any effect. Frederick adopted a three-rank line in 1742. The French went over in 1754, obeying a 'mania for imitation', and the Austrians followed suit during the Seven Years War.

Tacticians found it useful to imagine that the individual infantryman occupied a square with sides 1 pace long (taking the pace at about 2 feet). With the three-rank line this made for a line 3 paces deep, platoons about 15 paces long, and battalions about 220 paces long. In practice bulky individuals might exceed their allocation of 1 pace, just as skinny men fell below it, 'and so, once the battalion begins to move at any speed, the second and third ranks fall into inevitable disorder, the formation wavers on the march, the files get in each others' way, and the direction of fire loses its proper alignment' (Guibert [1772], 1804, I, 82).

By custom the tallest troops were allocated to the leading ranks. According to a Brunswick drillbook of 1751:

All the tall men with moustaches are placed in the first rank, with due attention being paid in the dressing to a uniformity of appearance – thus we do not like to place an old soldier next to a much younger one, or someone with a thin, half-starved face next to an individual with a strong countenance. The flanks are most in evidence when the soldiers march past, and so they must be covered by our most handsome men with good faces. Men who have moustaches, but are less good looking, are placed in the second rank, but if there are not enough moustaches to fill the whole rank, they must be positioned on one of the flanks. The shortest men go to the third rank, and the tallest men without moustaches to the fourth. (Jähns, 1889–91, III, 2, 570)

All will now be clear.

One of the eighteenth-century's most important discoveries about the Ancient art of war concerned the practice of marching in step in closely packed formations. Movement in compact blocks had been characteristic of the tactics of the Swiss and the Landsknechts during the Renaissance, and the Dutch and Swedes in the 'pike and shot' era of the early seventeenth century, but the rise of firepower in the later part of the seventeenth century brought about a considerable opening-up of the tactical formations. Marching in step fell out of use, and the columns of march became very long and were consequently difficult to form into line of battle.

Hesse and Prussia rediscovered marching in step after the War of the Spanish Succession, and in the middle of the eighteenth century the 'cadenced step' in tight formations was promoted by two formidable advocates – Marshal Saxe and Frederick the Great. It was adopted by the English infantry in 1748, and introduced to France by the ordinance of 1754. Effectively, by the time of the Seven Years War, movement on the drill square had been transformed into something much more speedy and controllable than before:

When men march in cadence, it gives them a bold and imposing air; and by the habit they acquire in regulating their pace, we may almost guess what time a body of men will take to traverse a certain length of ground. (MacIntire, 1763, 174)

It is, however, much more difficult to establish whether or not the cadenced step survived very long in the conditions of the battlefield (see p. 203).

The notorious goose step was an unauthorised aberration on the part of some Prussian drillmasters which was eventually accepted as the parade step of the German army at the end of the nineteenth century. The cadenced step, as it was known in the eighteenth century, corresponded much more to a stately walk. The French moved at 60 or 65 paces to the minute, which was tiringly slow, but the Prussian march of 75 paces was more easy, and looked like the natural gait of a man 'who is walking deliberately and solemnly to some chosen destination' (Berenhorst, 1798–9, II, 188).

A much quicker rate of marching was employed for certain rapid movements over short distances, such as wheels into column or line, and a faster pace generally was employed by the English in the American War of Independence. A German auxiliary complained:

Every day, to my disgust, I have to practice the lately-introduced quick step, which we do not have, nor do they have it in Prussia – nay, not in the world, except in the chase, with fast horses and good dogs! This is a splendid exercise for the men in winter; but in the summer, when the weather is warm, it is detrimental to the health of the men. It has no good result except to make the spectators laugh – for by this manner no closed ranks could be kept in an attack upon the enemy. (Captain Georg Pausch of the Hanau artillery, Pausch, 1886, 108)

Marching at a set pace could be best sustained when it had become an engrained instinct, as among the Prussian infantry. In the period of the Seven Years War the English sought to regulate their pace by fife and drum, but in the 1770s this practice fell out of use, except for helping to train the recruits.

Eighteenth-century columns marched by whole platoons or divisions, in other words they occupied a wide frontage measuring between about ten and thirty men abreast. When the force marched in the normal formation of open column, the gap between each platoon or division and the next was supposed to equal its width, which permitted the battalion to form line by a simultaneous quarter-wheel of each of these sub-units. Thus, a battalion in column of march ought to have taken up a length exactly equal to its line of battle. In practice, after an hour or two of marching, the columns became considerably strung out. No other army was able to imitate *tours de force* like that staged by the Prussians during the Silesian infantry manoeuvres of 1785, when, upon the signal of a cannon shot, a column of 23,000 infantry wheeled in a matter of seconds into a line estimated at two and a quarter English miles long.

There were obvious advantages to bringing your column into the field parallel to the enemy line of battle, as Frederick did by preference. The business was more complicated if the column approached the enemy head-on, for you then had to form your line either by diagonal fan-like movements of the sub-units (the *Deployiren*), or more reliably but more slowly by having each sub-unit of each column execute a successive right-angled wheel on a chosen spot, and then wheeling all the sub-units simultaneously into line in the normal way (the processional deployment).

A great deal obviously hung upon the speed and precision with which the troops could execute their quarter wheels. The procedure was as follows. The platoon or two-platoon division came to a momentary halt, whereupon the unit began to swing like a gate, with the troops nearest the wheeling flank executing their quarter-circle at a run or a very quick step, and the movement becoming less the nearer the files were located to the fixed or pivot flank, where the troops marked time. During this manoeuvre the men turned their heads to look along the line towards the wheeling flank, while they kept up a gentle pressure shoulder-to-shoulder towards the pivoting flank. With well-schooled troops the movement came to an automatic halt once the quarter-circle was completed:

> Whether on horseback or on foot, a regular wheel is just about the most difficult of all movements to accomplish. When a wheel is done well, you have the impression that the alignment has been regulated with a ruler, that one flank is tied to a stake, and that the other is describing an arc of a circle. You can employ these images if you wish to convey to the soldiers a clear understanding of what goes on in a wheel. (Griesheim, 1777, 283–4)

Practice alone brought speed and unison to loading and firing the musket, a process which might have seemed impossible to reduce to any kind of rhythm. The first motion was to hold the musket horizontally, or nearly so, in the palm of the left hand, while the right hand reached into the cartridge pouch and groped about for the next round. The soldier raised the paper cylinder to his mouth, and bit off the end containing the round leaden bullet. The opened cartridge was brought to the elaborate ignition mechanism at the breech end, and a little powder was shaken into a trough called the priming pan, from where a touch hole led into the interior of the barrel (the weapon was a muzzle loader). Now the soldier cocked the 'hammer', which held a piece of flint in its jaws, ready to strike sparks from the 'frizzen', a pivoting flap which was flicked back over the priming pan. The musket was up-ended on its butt, which permitted the soldier to empty the rest of the powder down the barrel, spit the bullet inside, and poke the paper of the empty cartridge a short way down the barrel. With his right hand the soldier withdrew the long ramrod from its housing under the barrel, and after reversing the stick in the air he used it to push the cartridge paper firmly on top of the load now resting at the bottom of the barrel. (Wooden ramrods were the norm until the Prussians showed the superiority of iron ramrods in the Silesian Wars). The ramrod was withdrawn, reversed, and returned to its place.

The loaded musket was now ready to be seated on the shoulder and fired. When the trigger was squeezed the head of the hammer shot forward, and the flint scraped down the rearward side of the frizzen, knocking it forward and sending a shower of sparks into the priming pan. The priming powder erupted into a miniature explosion, and a jet of flame communicated through the touch hole with the main charge inside the barrel, causing a second explosion which expelled the bullet.

The whole sequence was controlled by just three words of command, namely 'load!' 'present!' and 'fire!' Outside Britain, firing with ball ammunition was rarely practised in peacetime, but it appears nevertheless almost incredible that moderately proficient troops could fire three rounds of blank ammunition every minute, and that the Prussians ultimately attained a speed of six.

The complications did not end there. For a start, the tightly-packed ranks and files called for carefully co-ordinated movements in unison. In theory the musket barrels were long enough to permit the muzzles of the weapons of the third rank to project several inches beyond the heads of the men of the first rank. However this margin of safety did not prove adequate in peacetime, and when the troops were in full marching order for active operations,

> those seven inches can be curtailed or lost altogether. There are many reasons, but the principal cause is the crowding occasioned by all the gear which the soldiers wear on their backs – knapsack, haversack, water bottle and entrenching tool. Thus, when the men are ordered to 'present!', the soldiers of the first rank fall down on the right knee, while those of the second rank place their right foot about eight inches to the side, so as to make room for the ankles of the first rank, now projecting to the rear. The soldiers of the third rank simultaneously step a half pace, or about fourteen inches, to the right. The two rearward ranks accordingly win the space they need in order to level their muskets alongside the heads of the men of the first rank. (Berenhorst, 1798–9, I, 224)

This staggered arrangement of files was called 'locking on'.

The rank, platoon or division fired by simultaneous volleys, which could be co-ordinated with those of the other sub-units in various ways. Most celebrated was the platoon firing as perfected by the Prussians, whereby the eight or so platoons of the battalion loaded and fired in an elaborately designed sequence, which was designed to keep up a barrage of salvoes while retaining a perpetually changing reserve of loaded muskets.

The realities of combat (see p. 213) were very different from what has just been described, but the regularity of fire and movement was seen as the measure of the proficiency of the peacetime soldier, and it put a premium on the skills of the long-serving professional.

The cavalryman

WHAT HE DID

In battle the functions of the mounted arm were to attack the enemy cavalry by shock action, to support one's own infantry – and especially on the flanks, and to ride down the enemy foot soldiers and complete the victory by a pursuit. On campaign the cavalry helped to mount guards and outposts, protected and executed foraging expeditions, escorted officers on reconnaissance, carried out raids and in general helped the army to keep up the offensive.

There were three main types of cavalry, namely the heavy (cuirassiers), medium (dragoons) and light (hussars, lancers, etc). Oddly enough, Frederick claimed that the distinctions derived in the first place not from the need for particular tactical roles, but simply from the availability of different types of horses ('Instruction für die Commandeurs der Cavellerie-Regimenter' [1763], Frederick, 1846–57, XXX, 280).

The cuirassiers were big men mounted on big horses. They were the functional descendants of the armoured knights of the Middle Ages, and their main calling was to do battle with the enemy cavalry in the open field.

Dragoons were originally mounted infantrymen. They rode horses of middling size, and they showed traces of their ancestry in their infantry-style coats and their long carbines. According to army and period, the dragoons inclined more towards the cavalry or the infantry role. Their mode of action probably came closest to that of the cuirassiers in the Prussian army. In France the cuirassiers and dragoons had become organisationally identical by the end of 1757, but the dragoons still maintained their privileges against the cuirassiers, who in turn despised the dragoons as hermaphrodites whose hearts were not really in the mounted service.

Together the cuirassiers and dragoons represented the commander's mobile striking force on the battlefield. After a bad start at Mollwitz (1741) the Prussian cavalry went on to deal a series of mighty hammer blows. At Hohenfriedeberg (1745) a single unit, the Bayreuth Dragoons, destroyed five regiments of Austrian infantry, while at Rossbach (1757) the Prussian cavalry and artillery decided the day with almost no assistance from the foot soldiers. The Austrian cavalry performed respectably, if not brilliantly, and at Kunersdorf (1759) it combined with the Russian horse to sweep the exhausted Prussian infantry from the field. The French cavalry had a day of glory at Lutterberg (10 October 1758):

At the beginning the cavalry was positioned in the woods. The infantry was shaken by the enemy and broke, whereupon our cavalry turned the tide of battle and executed up to sixteen charges against the enemy infantry, dragoons and heavy horse. The French cavalry carried everything before it, and killed

almost all the enemy among scenes of terrible carnage.
(Mopinot de la Chapotte, 1905, 237)

Conversely at Minden (1759) the French cavalry covered itself with
shame, for seventy-two squadrons stood almost motionless and let
themselves be attacked and overthrown by 8,000 enemy infantry.
By then the mounted arm had lost its dominating position in the
French army, for the establishment of the infantry had been very
greatly increased. Sixteen new battalions had been raised in February
1757, and a further seven had come into being by the end of 1758.

The hussars (see p. 270) were the epitome of the light cavalry
service. The Prussian hussars were capable of taking their place in
the line of battle, but the classic role of hussars was that of raiding,
reconnaissances and any kind of detached duty in which speed and
agility were in demand. As the eighteenth century wore on, the
ranks of the light cavalry were swelled by newcomers like light
dragoons, chevaux légers, chasseurs à cheval, lancers and so on, who
helped to satisfy a demand for fancy uniforms and titles (see p. 134),
and enabled armies to make use of horses which were too light for
service with the cuirassiers and dragoons.

TRAINING AND EQUIPMENT

The proper choice and training of cavalry recruits were matters of
great importance. If the young man had not already been brought
up with horses he had at least to be an active and intelligent kind of
person, for the cavalry trooper had a 'multiplicity of things to do
more than a foot soldier, and ten times more arms, accoutrements
etc.' (Cumberland's 'Dragoon orders' [1755], Cumberland, 1945,
99). Seydlitz was fond of the simple test of putting the would-be
cavalrymen on unbroken horses, and watching to see who managed
to stay in the saddle.

Five years or more were required to train a trooper to full proficiency, and it was notoriously difficult and dangerous for units of
cavalry to incorporate large bodies of raw men. The veterans were
driven to distraction, and the health of men and horses collapsed, as
happened in the French army from July 1743, when the establishment
of the cavalry regiments was raised from three squadrons to four: 'it
seems scarcely credible that we should have dared to put a force of
cavalry into the field when it was in such a state' (d'Authville, 1756,

407. See also Puységur, 1749, I, 239–40). Among the infantry the platoon firings and the tactical minutiae did not usually survive in real combat, and were not expected to do so (see p. 213), but in the cavalry the uneasy and inexperienced rider was a menace not just to himself and his neighbours but to the whole unit. He tortured his horse by gripping tightly with his knees and grabbing the mane, 'and as soon as it sees the slightest opening in the ranks the animal makes off at an astonishing speed, unseating its rider or bearing him away' (Mottin de la Balme, 1776, 37).

The real schooling of the cavalryman began when he was introduced to his horse. In Britain, Holland and Hanover this was likely to be a dauntingly large creature, bred up by skilled farmers and nourished in its early years on fat pastures. The breeding of French horses had been neglected. Spanish horses were lively in battle, but lacking in endurance on campaign. Observers were surprised to note that the horses of the Prussian cavalry were of only middling size, and imported for the most part from eastern Europe.

Over the first weeks of his service the recruit was inculcated in the proper use of the comb, sponge and brush. He learned how to feed and water the horse well but moderately, and how to tidy up afterwards. For three or four months in the spring and early summer the horses were put out to graze in the open fields. In the late summer the gorged and lazy horses had to be brought back into condition, and then in the autumn the animals had to be protected by covers against the cold and the deadly rains.

The recruit was practised again and again in saddling up and unsaddling, and attaching the bridle and the many items of equipment – a procedure which a very skilled cavalryman might accomplish in 12 minutes (see p. 275). English and Hungarian saddles were hard, light and durable, but the main continental style of saddle was a heavy affair. The saddles in France still weighed between 30 and 40 pounds, even after attempts had been made to improve them following the Seven Years War: 'In spite of everything they are still massive chairs, laden down with woodwork, and the weight of large nails which split the fibres of the wood and weaken it, instead of adding strength as is usually claimed' (Mottin de la Balme, 1776, 190). The layers of stuffing and wood prevented the French cavalryman from sensing the reactions of his horse, and he rolled about like some Oriental potentate in his palanquin.

Stirrups were usually worn shorter than was the style in civilian life, so as to enable the trooper to rise in the saddle and give him greater height and reach for the use of his sword. The reins were the most immediately vulnerable items of equipment in combat with enemy cavalry, as Frederick appreciated before the Seven Years War: 'The king foresaw the storm which threatened to break over his head, and he made the Prussian cavalry more formidable than ever by giving the horsemen reins which were reinforced and braided with brass wire' (Haller, 1787, 56).

Exotic headgear for the light regular cavalry began to appear in the final decades of the Age of Reason, but the tricorn remained the characteristic covering of the cuirassiers and most of the dragoons. A wide hat gave a measure of protection against sword cuts, and a skull cap of iron strips was sometimes worn inside the crown for the same purpose, even though a heavy blow might break it into deadly splinters.

The coat of the dragoon was scarcely to be told apart from that of the infantryman, except for the aiglets dangling from the right shoulder. The cuirassier had a much more distinctive appearance, thanks to his breastplate (cuirass), which was a shaped slab of iron weighing about twenty pounds. The breastplate was usually painted black. It was padded on the inside, and it was fastened by straps passing cross-wise around the trooper's back. Nearly every surviving breastplate shows a characteristic dimple, for the cuirass had to be proved by a musket shot before it could be accepted for service.

The breastplate was attended with notorious inconveniences. Its weight tired the rider and the horse. It was very uncomfortable to wear in hot weather, yet unless it was fastened very tight it rode up and down, and was liable to inflict serious injury when the trooper fell off his horse. On the other hand the cuirass gave effective protection against infantry fire, and the French calculated that no less than 1,600 of their horsemen had been saved thereby at Laffeldt (1747) (Dalrymple, 1761, I, 250. See also Chabot, 1756, 54).

The dragoons were lightly shod, and the Duke of Cumberland reminded the officers of this branch of the service that

> they are still dragoons, and not horse, that they are to march
> and attack on foot, if there is occasion when dismounted,
> therefore the men's boots are not to be encumbered with great
> spur leathers and chains, to hinder them from getting over a
> hedge, ditch or works when they are ordered to attack, and

whenever they are ordered on such service, they are to sling their swords over their shoulders. (Cumberland [1755], 1945, 98)

The question of the proper boots for the cuirassiers was a matter of lively debate among cavalrymen. Warnery was an advocate of the traditional boot of thick leather:

It is my . . . contention that the rider with stiff boots actually takes up less space in the squadron than one who has soft boots. Moreover the squadron keeps its alignment better, especially when it has to execute abrupt movements. The cavalryman with stiff boots knows that his knees and legs are safe when he is drawn up in rank. He does not feel the impact of his neighbours' legs, stirrups, weapons or pistol holsters, and needs to harbour no fear of being crushed. He accordingly keeps his place in the rank. (Warnery, 1785–91, II, 172–3)

The opposing party drew attention to the clumsiness of the heavy boot. Puységur had seen actions when hundreds of cuirassiers had been checked by small parties of well-posted infantry, on account of the near impossibility of moving on foot, and he added that thick boots made it extremely difficult for a cavalryman to mount his horse without assistance (Puységur, 1749, I, 5). For tactical purposes, therefore, a dismounted cuirassier was as much use as a dead man.

The cavalryman's personal weapons usually comprised a pair of pistols, a carbine and a sword (for their use see pp. 222–7). The pistols were housed in leather bucket holsters, which were fixed on either side of the horse just in front of the saddle, and covered with elaborately embroidered cloths bearing the royal monogram. The carbine was fastened to the right-hand side of the saddle, or hung from a bandolier passing over the left shoulder. Both carbines and pistols demanded constant attention, for they hung muzzle-downwards and the load was liable to drop out. The swords of the light cavalry were long and curved weapons, designed specifically for slashing. The sword of the cuirassier and dragoon had a semi-enclosed guard, and a stiff and straight blade up to 3 feet long.

Altogether the upkeep of the horse and equipment absorbed several hours every day. Moreover all of the cavalrymen, and not just the dragoons, had to go through tedious sessions for dismounted drill, for the troopers frequently stood guard on foot, and they had to be able to defend themselves if they came under attack when they were in camp or billets or engaged in foraging expeditions.

The training in horsemanship began with the individual, and in winter-time it could be carried out in a purpose-built *manège*, or in a barn which had sufficient clear space. The English regiments had the advantage of well-paid professional riding instructors, but equestrian skills were probably at their highest in Prussia, where the cavalry drilled on horseback almost every day, and the men were at liberty to ride over the country in their off-duty hours. Conscientious officers in every army used routine marches and every other opportunity to reinforce the lessons which were inculcated in the formal training, and in time of war the preparations took on air of urgency. A Prussian officer of hussars recalls the hard winter of 1744–5:

> We carried out our instruction in barns, which were dilapidated and cold. Our riding ground was a meadow, which was a foot deep in snow every morning. In such locations we put our men through their training for five or six hours every day, until we had laden our pupils with sufficient torments, and we ourselves had lost our voices. (Lojewsky, 1843, I, 162)

Ultimately, after years of practice, the riders became masters of the elaborate movements of the *haute école*:

> All of this makes the horse supple and loose-linked, in the same way as a man acquires a comely appearance and nimbleness through dancing and fencing. The animal must be able to rear up on its hind legs, and the horse must also be schooled in the traverse, for this is a movement which a whole line of cavalry must be able to execute simultaneously, especially when a squadron wishes to restore its proper intervals. This can be achieved by the traverse without the necessity of breaking off files or sub-division, a procedure which takes time, always looks bad, and is a sign of incompetence in the unit. (Warnery, 1785–91, II, 153)

Cavalry regiments were bodies of between about six and nine hundred men, and this compact size helped to reinforce the sense of family identity which was already present in these semi-feudal organisations. Inside the regiment the tactical sub-unit was the squadron of 130–60 troopers: 'If the squadrons were any larger, they would be difficult to manoeuvre; if they were weaker, their charges would lack force, and they would be able to offer little resistance on the defensive' (Quincy, 1726, VIII, 64).

The usual combat formation was in two or three ranks (see p. 222), and it was accepted that the issue in combat was decided by the performance of the first rank, which was accordingly filled with the best men and a large complement of officers and NCOs.

The society of the regiment and the values of the soldier

THE CONTRIBUTION OF THE NCOs

On their fidelity and diligence a great measure of the service depends.

(Dalrymple, 1761, I, 48)

If the officers determined what was to be done in the regiment, the non-commissioned officers had a much more direct part in ensuring that those things were actually carried out, and carried out to an acceptable standard.

Within the company the sergeants were expected to have a fundamental understanding of drill and administration, for they trained the recruits, maintained alignment and order on the march, kept the men up to the mark, saw to the distribution of rations, and inspected the billets or barrack rooms. They worked closely with functionaries like the company clerk and quartermaster, and they kept a close eye on the activity of the corporals. The summit of the sergeant's ambition was to become the regimental sergeant-major.

The corporals and their assistants, the lance-corporals, were in one respect the most important people in the army, for they stood in direct control of the fundamental units of the military social order, which were the corporal's command of fifteen or so men, and the tent or billet *Kameradschaft* of six or seven. The corporal got the men on their feet in the morning, saw that they were properly dressed and equipped, and led them to the drill square, fatigues or guard duty. The Austrian regulations fully recognised the key position of this basic level of command:

The responsibilities of the corporal are some of the most onerous and exhausting in the whole company. He has no rest night or day. He must be the first to know what is going on, and he must render account of every detail to the sergeant. For these reasons . . . the corporal must strive to the utmost of his ability to get to know the men, not just by their appearance and name, but from their virtues and vices, acquainting himself with the ones who are the most inclined to gambling, drunkenness, arguing, fighting, thievery or other forms of bad behaviour. (*Reglement für die sämmentliche-Kaiserlich-Königlich Infanterie*, Vienna, 1769, 28–9)

The distinguishable weapon of the sergeant was the halberd, which he employed for beating down the musket barrels of the men if they were aiming too high, for pushing the soldiers forward in action, and for killing them if they tried to run away. Occasionally the sergeant took a direct combat role. At Corbach in 1760 the Prussian regiment of Markgraf Carl was being harassed by Austrian cuirassiers under the leadership of one Major Fischer. An NCO marked Fischer down and was ready to receive him when the next attack arrived:

At that moment the valiant NCO rushed forward a few paces and struck at the major's head with his halberd. This weapon is supposed to be purely ornamental, but he caught the rider's shoulder with a projecting barb, and with a mighty heave he plucked him from his horse. (Hildebrandt, 1829–35, III, 134)

It was essential for an NCO to be able to read and write, but when it came to choosing suitable men Frederick usually rejected ex-students in favour of those veterans whom he held in such high regard. When he passed down the ranks at 'special reviews' he frequently rejected young NCOs who were presented for his approval, and substituted old soldiers from the same company:

It seems to me . . . that he held the opinion that experienced veterans had a greater power over young people than did men who had seen less of life. . . . Seasoned NCOs of this kind are the real support of a unit, whether on the march, in battle or on other occasions of danger. (Lossow, 1826, 15)

The NCO was not necessarily immune from corporal punishment (in the Prussian service he was liable to be beaten with the flat of the sword), and he was forced to make repeated and unsettling transitions from despotic master to slave, and back again. This was one of the reasons why the soldiers were far more likely to be badly treated by the NCO than by their officers:

> Most of the NCOs I have seen, whether Prussian or not, remind me of nothing so much as those eunuchs who are supposed to guard the ladies of the Oriental harems. The NCOs (like the eunuchs) have to display their submission and obedience to their masters much more directly and much more frequently than do the private soldiers, and they are often maltreated and chivvied for their pains. In their turn the NCOs try to vent their ill-temper and injured pride on the soldiers, just like the eunuchs with the women. . . . In the event the artful soldiers often succeed in leading them by the nose, in the same way as the black eunuchs are bamboozled by the intrigues of the ladies of the seraglio. (Laukhard, 1930, I, 245–6 (from the experience of the regiment of Anhalt-Bernburg in the 1780s). See also O'Cahill, 1787, 245–6)

A number of regimental functionaries stood outside the main hierarchy of command. Such were the auditor, the provost marshal (who incarcerated prisoners and carried out punishments), and the clerks who proliferated in armies like the Austrian or the Russian.

The miniature staff of the regiment also comprised the chaplain. The most general complaint against this man of God was that he preached sermons which were not adapted to the understanding of the soldiery or conducive to military values. Otherwise the status of the chaplains differed markedly from one army to the next. They were least well regarded in France, for the regimental officers were scornful of religion and the French chaplains had the reputation of being time-servers, drunkards and sodomites. In the 1770s the war minister Saint-Germain sought in vain to give the chaplains a suitable training and salary, and obtain good candidates from the bishops. In the Austrian army the chaplain was often a figure of fun, for he was supposed to take the officers to task if they maintained mistresses under the guise of cooks, maids or washerwomen.

The Russian 'popes' were an essential support of the morale of the green-coated hosts of Muscovy, and the status of the chaplain also happened to be high in the army of cynical Frederick of Prussia. Religious observance was incorporated into the life of the Prussian regiments, and 'what they call a church parade is more like a military review than an ecclesiastical ceremony' (Bonneville, 1762, I, 161).

Prussian chaplains were said to be vigorous and brave. The celebrated Balke of the Seydlitz Cuirassiers was as effective in his way as Samuel Benedikt Carstedt in the regiment of Kalckstein, or Carl Daniel Küster of Carl Markgraf. *Feldprediger* Joachim Seegebart achieved European fame for helping to rally the cavalry at Chotusitz (1742):

> I made so bold as to address myself to the generals, gripping them by the hand, and urging them in the name of God and the king to get their men together again. They responded, and I ranged up and down the ranks pushing the soldiers into their places, until they began to arrange themselves in order. I used all the eloquence at my disposal, and I commanded total obedience. I cannot tell how it was that my little foxy-coloured horse was not trampled under foot by the huge and heavy chargers, but everybody seemed to give way and make room for me. (Berenhorst, 1845–7, I, 100)

The news of this deed spread through Europe, and even Voltaire found that he was impressed.

THE LIFE OF THE SOLDIER

In so far as eighteenth-century military life had a uniform routine it began at daybreak or soon after, when the roll was called to establish whether any soldier had deserted or fallen sick during the night. The NCOs and subalterns would then usually betake themselves to the company headquarters to make reports and receive orders, while the troops returned to their rooms or tents and made themselves presentable. The soldiers emerged again to be inspected, and in all probability they would be marched off to parade or drill. The after-noons were usually a time of comparative relaxation.

The general conditions of the peacetime soldier began to undergo an important change towards the end of the Age of Reason. During the earlier period he was seldom accommodated in barracks, unless he was stationed in a fortress or a capital city. He was quartered instead with the local population under a variety of arrangements.

In Britain a regimental surgeon complained that the billets were in public houses, and the landlord consequently

> never fails to look on the soldiery not only as a nuisance but as a great drawback to the profits of his business. They are treated

coldly and frequently lodged poorly. The places allotted to them are generally some uninhabited garret or lumber room where the very air they are obliged to breathe is so vitiated, as, at first entrance, considerably to affect a person unaccustomed to it. (Hamilton [1787], 1966, 131)

Where Russian soldiers were the troops in question, it was the local people who became the victims. The Russian troops got on well enough with the peasantry of Great Russia, but in the Ukraine (Little Russia), Poland and the conquered territories the Russian warrior behaved abominably, debauching the womenfolk of his hosts and turning the civilians out of their beds or even their homes:

He lives like a lord, summoning up all his needs and holding an open table to which he invites his comrades. I know of a sergeant who regaled himself with feasting twice a week, and of another, who had five or six houses at his disposal, from where he took all the mattresses and pillows, which he piled up on a bed until they reached the ceiling. (Langeron, 1895, 152)

Affairs were better regulated in Prussia. In Potsdam, which was the most important garrison town, the houses were built with a special chamber for the soldiers, who were supplied with provisions, firewood and services under carefully controlled conditions. In the Prussian countryside the billeting of soldiers was valued on account of the security it offered against thieves and bandits, and the stimulus to local trade. A. D. Ortmann writes:

The little town where I live has rather over 250 inhabitants. Two companies of grenadiers are quartered among them in an orderly fashion. Every month they receive more than six hundred thaler in pay, which they spend in the locality and bring this little place an annual income exceeding seven thousand thaler. (Ortmann, 1759, 145)

In Europe generally the cohabitation with the civilians went far to ameliorate the essential bleakness of military life, and for good or evil it preserved a close bond between army and society:

The shouting of orders provided a rhythmic accompaniment to the daily routine of the local people. Many military activities were staged in the centre of the town – manoeuvres, the drill of arms, or the beating or execution of offending soldiers, and these spectacles no doubt attracted an audience of bystanders and children. (Corvisier, 1964, 94–5)

These relationships began to change when the fashion for separate and purpose-built barracks began to set in during the 1770s and 1780s. The new Prussian barracks were dark and airless, and the Austrian accommodation was worse: 'it is made up of a huge room where a company of 160 men sleeps, dresses and does its cooking. The windows are low and narrow, and the stench is appalling' (Guibert, 1778, 132).

One of the remaining liberties of the soldier was the freedom to work for profit in his off-duty hours, which was conceded in most of the armies of Europe. This kind of labour kept the soldier active and happy, and gave him a welcome or necessary supplement to his military pay, which in some countries had not been increased for decades or centuries (see p. 103). A stream of orders of the day testifies to the attempts of the authorities to keep this kind of activity under a modicum of control. The French were worried by the penchant of their troops towards the smuggling of brandy, tobacco and other commodities, while Colonel James Wolfe observed in 1749 that his soldiers had of late been

> employed in all sorts of dirty work; such as carrying coals, filth etc. in the streets, and have been busy in the holds of several ships; they likewise have condescended to clean the kennels [gutters]: the colonel is ashamed and surprised to perceive that they are not below the meanest piece of drudgery for the meanest consideration. (Wolfe, 1768, 22–3)

Governments and colonels were less willing to concede the professional soldier the kind of independence which came from a proper family life. Frederick made an exception for his 'cantonists', for they were natives who spent most of their time at home, but in most of Europe soldiers were permitted to marry only as a kind of necessary evil, so as to provide the company with womenfolk who would wash the laundry, mend the clothes and help to tend the sick. On campaign the women went to swell the ranks of the marauders:

> When a German army is on the march, you will witness the hideous sight of a whole pack of those stinking Amazons, proceeding on foot or on horseback. You would take them for raiding parties, for they are to be found with the advance guard

and the rearguard and on the flanks of the army, and they cannot pass a village or hut without rummaging through the cellars, chambers, hidden recesses and chests, and making off with whatever suits them. (Warnery, 1785–91, II, 26–7)

Only about 16 per cent of the French rank and file ever married. The proportion among the German professionals was somewhat higher, but the unions usually turned out just as badly, for there were few respectable women who were willing to marry a soldier, and many of the wives were as pox-ridden as the full-time prostitutes.

When a soldier's wife brought children into the world, they were likely to turn into those ragged and feeble infants who scarcely had the strength to drag themselves up the staircase of a barracks. However, the boys who survived this ordeal had the potential to become some of the finest soldiers of the regiment. Maria Theresa of Austria recognised as much when in 1772 she set up the *Militar-Knaben Stiftung* at Pettau for the education of the orphan sons of NCOs and men. One of the last acts of her reign was to give her support to Father Felbiger's scheme to make provision for all the sons of the army, being convinced that military schools were 'essential, useful and practicable'.

Letters from home assume an extraordinary importance in the imagination of military men, and for many soldiers in the Age of Reason they provided the sole reminder of a life outside the army and daily work. Before the postal reforms in the nineteenth century letters were normally transmitted on a cash-on-delivery system, which put the responsibility of payment on the addressee, who in this case was the poor soldier. Frederick sagely instituted a free post for military men and their families in the Silesian Wars, but in France the soldier was in a cruel dilemma when he learned that the postmaster had a letter waiting for him:

Being bereft of money . . . the soldier is prepared to run the . . . risk of terrible punishment for selling a shirt, a pair of shoes or other items of equipment for small sum, and just to retrieve a letter whose postage might reach more than twenty sous. (Quoted in Corvisier, 1964, 878)

The solace of alcohol was particularly appreciated by English and

German soldiers. In 1751 the Prussian regiment of Forcade received the following order of the day:

> The regiment drills tomorrow, and the companies assemble at six in the morning on the counterscarp. Each man has ten cartridges. The companies must not allow their men to linger any length of time in the inns today, lest any soldier appears drunk on duty tomorrow. If a man does turn up in this condition, he is to be made to run the gauntlet on the spot, and for this purpose the provost will bring the appropriate sticks. (Witzleben, 1851, 9)

However the Italian and Spanish soldiers were generally abstemious, and drunkenness fell away considerably in the French army in the later part of the eighteenth century.

Smoking, unlike snuff-taking, was not tolerated in polite society, but it was an unfailing companion of military life: 'Tobacco is smoked in specially-made earthenware pipes. Experience shows that it is a magnificent cure for various afflictions and illnesses' (Fleming, 1726, I, 356).

Honour and the Private Soldier

Military authors in the eighteenth century found themselves in fundamental disagreement about the status and motivation of the ordinary man. Simes maintained that 'of all states and conditions, that of a soldier is most honourable to himself, and most advantageous to his country' (Simes, 1780a, 1), while his countryman Wolfe could write about 'vagabonds that stroll about in dirty red clothes from one gin shop to another . . . dirty, drunken, insolent rascals' (Houlding, 1981, 268). At this distance of time we can only seek to identify possible centres of the soldier's loyalty, and the ways in which his altruism or individuality might have been expressed.

In the conditions of modern combat the soldier fights fundamentally for the survival of himself and his immediate comrades, and he gives of his best in conditions that make for good 'small unit cohesion'. How well did the eighteenth-century regiment qualify as such a focus of communal effort?

The visible signs of regimental honour was incorporated in the trumpets, kettle drums and standards of the cavalry and the colours of the infantry: 'Like the Roman standards, the Prussian colours were held in holy awe. When they were paraded past the troops they were saluted like kings – the whole field music struck up, the battalion inclined its weapons and the officers stood with bare heads' (Archenholtz, 1974, 21).

Genuine regimental loyalty was probably at its highest in the Russian army, where it was promoted by the circumstance that the men were all natives, recruited from the same rural background, and by the excellent practice of giving the regiment the name and coat of arms of its home province (Vorontsov [1774], 1871, 470).

In the rest of Europe the regimental spirit had to contend with a number of hostile influences. Except when they were accommodated in the greatest garrison towns and fortresses, the regiments were broken down in peacetime into penny packets, which came together only on isolated occasions. The English regiments spent only about 16 per cent of their time in formed bodies (Houlding, 1981, 152), and

> the manner in which they are disposed in quarters over the country . . . naturally produces laxity of discipline: they are very little in the sight of their officers; and, when they are not engaged in the slight duty of the guard, are suffered to live every man in his own way. (Johnson, 1801–10, II, 428)

Things were hardly better in France, where military training was able to make little real progress from one year to the next. The strain on the French regiments was increased by the fact that the location of the garrison was frequently switched from one end of the kingdom to the other, which involved the units in tedious uprootings and marches. Even in Prussia there was a clear distinction between the professionals who spent the whole year nominally available for duty, and the native cantonists who stayed at home for more than nine months out of the twelve.

When war arrived, the French and Spanish governments not only augmented the strength of existing regiments, but created entirely new units:

> Peace arrives before the officers of such regiments have begun to learn their trade. . . . Every newly-raised unit is perfectly useless at the beginning of a war, and serves only to add to the size and cost of the army without increasing its strength.

Taking everything into account, you can began to rely on new levies only after five years of service, and sometimes, as Marshal Saxe has noted, they might be still good for nothing with ten campaigns behind them. (Silva, 1778, 14. See also Santa Cruz, 1735–40, I, 232)

Almost as damaging in its way was the English habit of stripping established units of large numbers of trained troops and drafting them to other regiments which were about to go on campaign.

At first sight, the corporal's command of about fifteen men appears to correspond directly to the section or squad-sized sub-unit so highly prized by modern military psychologists. It was divided again into a couple of still smaller groups which must be considered the basic military communities. These were the tent *Kameradschaft* of Western Europe, and the still more tightly-knit *artels* of Russia. The *artel* was managed by a veteran *artelchik* under the authority of the company captain, and it received all the capital and plunder of the eight or so members:

The Russian soldier is enlisted for life, and since he has no hope of receiving any private legacy, he has the habit of putting all his trust in this community. He frequently has occasion to draw on its help when he is on the march, or when he is in need of particular assistance – for example to buy a horse to draw his baggage, or to obtain extra food when the bread runs out. (Masson, 1859, 327–8)

These bands of comrades helped the soldier to survive on campaign but they counted for little or nothing in combat, for the fighting sub-units were the platoons and divisions, whose strength and composition were adjusted according to the needs of the moment (see p. 110). The necessary captains and lieutenants were being constantly reassigned, and it became a matter of pure chance whether a soldier found himself fighting alongside his friends.

According to another bad usage, when a party was put together for detached service, the officers and men were drawn not from a single sub-unit, but from as many of the different companies as was possible. The same principle applied among regiments when it was a question of assembling a larger detached force. The motive for this curious arrangement was to prevent all the honour or risk falling upon a single unit, but the effect was to break up the relationships which the soldiers had built up among themselves and with their officers in their everyday life. The evil was widely recognised, but nobody attempted to apply a remedy (Puységur, 1749, I, 249; Silva, 1778, 15).

Communal spirit was more easily developed among the regiments of cavalry, which at first sight appears somewhat surprising, since their way of life was still more fragmented than that of the infantry. The horses demanded a very considerable acreage of land for their forage and grazing, and the men were dispersed in packets of as little as one, two or three individuals in each village. In compensation, the cavalry regiment was a smaller and more homogeneous unit than the regiment of foot. The officers of cavalry were more likely to possess the ease and affability of the true aristocrat than their counterparts in the infantry, and something of the spirit of knightly community could be identified among the private troopers. French cavalrymen were addressed as *monsieur* or *maître*, just as the cuirassiers and dragoons in the Austrian muster lists were given the predicate *von*:

> Out of all the soldiers in the world, you will find few who are less likely to be beaten than the troopers in some of the Prussian cavalry regiments. It is striking that the same units do the best of all. Cavalrymen will never arise above themselves when they are drilled by the stick: pride, not blows, must be their motivating force. (Warnery, 1785–91, II, 91. But see p. 259!)

We are left with the impression that to belong to a regiment, as a regiment, was less important than what kind of soldier you considered yourself to be.

Vanity and the desire for distinction have always been sources of inspiration for military élites and special forces, and in the eighteenth century we encounter their influence in the grenadiers of the infantry, in the élite companies of cavalry, and in the more exotic forms of light force which proliferated towards the end of our period (see p. 228).

A body of grenadiers was a most imposing force in the physical sense – roughly equivalent to a couple of batteries of heavy cannon – and the moral effect was also by no means to be underestimated. The rattle of a Prussian grenadier march, or the sight of brass-fronted caps gleaming through dust and smoke, brought reassurance to

Frederick's soldiers and terror to his foes (Pauli, 1758–64, III, 43–4; Lojewsky, 1843, II, 53). In the Austrian army

> we have learned from experience that a grenadier . . . simply because he is called a grenadier, and is treated with a little distinction, is less inclined to desert and fights better. I have often noticed that when soldiers are assigned from other companies to the grenadiers, they take on something of the grenadier spirit at the instant they don their bearskin caps. The appearance and conduct are transformed. (Cogniazzo 1779, 106)

Such advantages were bought at a heavy price. For the regiments of the line the grenadiers were 'a constant drain of the tallest and most useful men' (Dalrymple, 1782, 10), and for the treasury they and the other kind of élite troops were an occasion of disproportionate expense. In January 1758 the French Gardes du Corps received a new uniform. 'Show it to me' (said Louis XV to Marshal Biron). 'Now that is something really fine and magnificent – just look at all those spangles embroidered along the skirts! I can hardly imagine the cost, but that is what they want, and they will have to pay for it if they can! Our funds are very short this year' (quoted in Dussauge, 1914, 181).

In combat, the work of the grenadiers proved difficult to co-ordinate with that of the other troops. Thus at Prague (1757) the massed force of Austrian grenadiers very nearly turned the battle against Frederick, but they found themselves isolated from the main body of the army and left a gap which was exploited by a lethal Prussian counterstroke. On occasion they did far too little, as at Krefeld (1758) where the French grenadiers were concentrated behind the right when Ferdinand of Brunswick aimed his blow at the left. More often the grenadiers were called upon to do far too much. Marshal Saxe recalled sieges where he had seen the companies of grenadiers replaced several times over, and expended on each occasion to very little purpose.

The conventional verdict on special and élite forces was delivered by the Prince de Ligne, who wrote as eloquently in his way as Field-Marshal Slim on the same subject a century and a half later:

> I like caps which are trimmed with fur and feathers as much as anybody. I set great store by military adornment, and I know that it is a most essential support for gallant escapades and for

every kind of dashing fellow. But, just because troops wear little boots or a particular sort of helmet, there is no reason to imagine that they should be devoted to a particular military speciality, and transported on that account from one end of the army to the other. Every sovereign should have two hundred thousand soldiers who are capable of fulfilling the same task, or as many different tasks as are demanded of them. (Ligne, 1795–1811, II, 182)

The sentiments considered proper for the ordinary soldier were instinctive ones, like impulsive generosity, or 'bravery' as it was understood in the eighteenth century (see p. 76). In Frederick's view the troops who displayed these qualities fully deserved the esteem of the *philosophes*, for combat was essentially a process of evicting the enemy from a piece of ground, 'and that can be done only with brave and determined men' (To D'Alembert, 23 July 1772, Frederick, 1846–57, XXIV, 570).

In its highest form the soldier's loyalty and honour survived the breaking of the chain of command. Such was the case with Corporal Todd and his companions, who were captured by the French in 1761 and resisted all the pressure to make them join the Irish Brigade in the service of France. After their exchange they were welcomed back by the officers of their parent regiment:

We returned the officers' thanks and the sutler brought us plenty of good beef and bread that we refreshed ourselves heartily and after that we drank some good punch for about an hour and then we returned to our quarters. . . . Everyone was glad to see us and crowded about us to hear how we had been used, but as we had gotten a very good refreshment we soon lay down to rest as it was the chiefest thing that we wanted and we slept all night. (Quoted in Savory, 1966, 507–8. See also p. 8)

A record like this is all the more valuable because it is so rare: 'Is it not extraordinary that soldiers do not write books, when they come out with so many well-chosen remarks, images and comparisons!' (Andreu de Bilistein, 1763, 58). The small library of private-soldier accounts is slimmed still further when we exclude the memoirs of men like Ulrich Bräker, *Magister* Laukhard and Joseph von Sonnenfels. They were first and foremost intellectuals, who treated their military service as a passing phase in their careers.

It would be entirely wrong to deduce from this that the ordinary soldier was an inert component of the military machine, capable of responding only to the direction of his officers. Those who knew him best were careful to draw attention to his remarkable powers of discernment. Carl Daniel Küster persuaded the old musketeer Hoppe to write down his recollections of the Zorndorf campaign, together with his shrewd judgments on the various armies of that time:

> This account shows how mistaken anyone is who denies the ability of the common soldier to think and judge properly. The old warrior proves to us that he could observe things with a keen eye, and that his courage was not merely blind rage, but arose from sound principles. (Hoppe, 1983, 11)

The soldiers were indeed 'strict observers' (Bland, 1727, 144), and the Chevalier de Ray found they were skilled at taking the measure of the Inspectors who came to review the regiments before the Seven Years War:

> These soldiers had only just come from their villages, where their sole concerns were their work and how to obtain their daily bread. Now, all at once, they became hard and discerning judges. They carried their verdicts back with them to their tents and their chambers, and they never relented. (Ray, 1895, 54)

Few soldiers resented the fact that they were not officers, but they all had a strong sense of what was due to them in their station. It was dangerous to ignore their displeasure. Thus, in the Seven Years War, the French had a way of humiliating their superiors by carefully controlled displays of insubordination. On 6 July 1761 the whole line applauded Marshal Broglie in the presence of his rival Soubise. The latter was despised by the corps of officers, and 'we must also take into account the mood of the soldiers in their bivouacs, and their feelings after having been put to several days of ceaseless labour – and that is something which a French army never forgives in a general' (Besenval, 1827–8, I, 365). On another occasion the brutal Comte de Lugeac was ill-advised enough to address the Grenadiers à Cheval in the following terms:

> 'Gentlemen, I am aware that a number of you have conceived some grievances against me. If anyone has genuine cause for

complaint, let him step forward, and I will be ready to hear him.'
At the words the company moved forward almost as one man.
Lugeac cried 'Halt!' and he hastened to begin the drill. (Ray,
1895, 41)

In the field the disaffected soldiers performed their duties without
spirit and lowered the morale of the others. Direct action against the
commanders was the eighteenth-century equivalent of the 'fragging'
of officers in the Vietnam war. Wounded Spanish officers were in
immediate danger of being robbed and finished off by their soldiers,
as Santa Cruz pointed out, and even in armies as well disciplined as
the Prussian or English the leaders were by no means immune from
a murderous bullet from their own men. At Blenheim in 1704 an
English officer was delighted to discover that the French had surrendered the strongpoint of Blenheim village:

> The major seeing this, faced about to the regiment and took off
> his hat to give an hussa; and just got out these words,
> 'Gentlemen, the day is ours!' when a musket ball hit him in the
> forehead, and killed him instantly. (An Old Officer, 1760, 30)

Far more weighty for the service as a whole was the practice of
desertion – a silent judgement on the part of the private soldiers
whereby an army could be damaged more severely than by an
outright defeat in the open field (see p. 172).

4

Generals and armies

Authority and promotion

Generals were literally 'general officers', high-ranking personages whose authority extended beyond individual units to groups of regiments or whole armies at a time. In ascending order the general ranks ran as follows:

Brigadier (France)
Major-General
Lieutenant-General
Full General (usually called simply 'General')
Field-Marshal

The wartime command of a major-general embraced a brigade of two, three or more regiments. It was recognised as a very demanding responsibility, and required men of 'great liveliness of mind, and experience and ability' (*Generals-Reglement*, Vienna 1769, 68). A lieutenant-general commanded a multi-battalion brigade, division, wing or line. On campaign he left the day-to-day running of his command to his hard-worked major-generals. In battle, however, the lieutenant-general had very important responsibilities, as we shall see. He could also find himself commanding a detached corps, though the authority over a main army usually went to a full general or a field-marshal.

It is not possible within the scope of this study to do justice to all the complexities of this basically simple hierarchy. For a start, the nominal rank did not necessarily correspond to function. There was little or nothing for a general to do in peacetime, in his capacity as a general, and in most armies his duty hours were occupied with his responsibilities as colonel proprietor of one of the regiments. As Frederick remarked: 'In peacetime and in garrison the general is really only a colonel' ('Instruction für die Major-Generals von der Infanterie' [1748], Frederick, 1846–57, XXX, 153–4). Even in time of war the possession of general rank did not necessarily bring command of a formation, and the French headquarters in particular were crowded with unplaced lieutenant-generals who competed for appointments and made all kinds of trouble.

In the Prussian army general rank was given to an officer primarily to enable him to act at a particular level of command. This straightforward criterion did not necessarily obtain in other services, where patents or marshals' batons were distributed as a reward, or for no better reason than to cheer the generals up. The result was monster promotions like those in the Austrian army on 15 October 1745, or in France on 1 January 1748 and 10 May 1749. Such *colpi di grazia* produced heavily over-generalled armies, and a significant log-jam of promotion at the level of lieutenant-general. In January 1758 the French army possessed sixteen marshals of France, 172 lieutenant-generals and 176 major-generals, or altogether 364 general officers for an army of less than 300,000 men.

If the silver-haired ranks of the superannuated lieutenant-generals were a characteristic of eighteenth-century armies, effective command in the field usually went to younger men. In the Austrian army in the Seven Years War Loudon advanced in four years from major to full general; his competitor Lacy became a field-marshal before the age of forty, and he could have taken this rank five years earlier if he had not wished to avoid an injustice to his comrades. In 1776, in the American War of Independence, George Washington was aged forty-four, Howe fifty-two, and Clinton and Cornwallis only thirty-eight.

Tel brille au deuxième rang, qui s'éclipse au premier. One of the recognised features of the military profession is the sudden and unexpected collapse of an officer who is promoted beyond his level of competence – beyond his 'ceiling', in the useful expression of Field-Marshal Montgomery. This phenomenon received a great deal of attention in the eighteenth century. Marshal Saxe noted that one of the signs was when a general began to issue a mass of confusing and over-detailed orders (Saxe [1732], 1877, 139). It was also betrayed by a timorous indecision on the part of a commander who had already given ample proofs of his physical courage. The Prussian hussar officer Warnery encountered such a man in a general who used to send him out to investigate every distant burst of firing. He once wasted a whole day in his presence, without being able to find out what was required of him, and

> I had scarcely returned to my camp when an orderly officer arrived with a message telling me to report to the general without delay. The night was dark, it was pouring with rain, and I had a good five miles to go before I reached his quarters. But there was no alternative – I had to obey. When I arrived I found that he was already dressed and wearing his sword. My presence seemed to occasion him some embarrassment, since he did not know what to say to me. Finally, after seven or eight minutes, he broke the silence and asked me whether I had anything new to report. Whereupon he wished me good night and let me go. This is an accurate description of what I mean by an anxious general. (Warnery, 1785–91, III, 48–9)

How do we account for these failings of decision and competence? Most commentators at the time were content to say that it reflected the simple fact that the higher reaches of the military trade were more complicated and difficult than the lower ones. However, later authorities have emphasised that the commander has to survive with much less comradely support than the men he leads (Dinter, 1985, 85), and even in the eighteenth century many writers were impelled to look more closely into the matter. There was, according to Schertel von Burtenbach, a clear distinction in mentality between those who executed what was ordered, and those who had to conceive an entire operation (1779, 61). Moreover, military life in the eighteenth century had peculiarities which forced a disproportionate number of officers through their natural 'ceiling'. Motivation (see p. 46) was frequently lacking in an age which was inclined to identify military rank with nobility, 'for it is difficult to excel in the onerous profession of war, when you have embraced that trade just to please your parents, or, as happens in certain countries, to conform with the virtual obligation on the nobility to take up military service' (d'Espagnac, 1751, I, 84).

Frederick believed that it was a good thing that peacetime generals were so caught up in regimental duties, 'unfortunately this narrowly-focussed activity confined the mental horizon of the generals to their particular arm of service, whether infantry or cavalry, and gave them little or no opportunity to appreciate how the different categories of troops were supposed to work together' (Lossow, 1826, 98). Even on campaign, many armies were so heavily-officered that it was possible for a man to become a major-general or even a lieutenant-general without ever having exercised independent command or learned the basic procedures of how to mark out a camp, conduct a reconnaissance or organise a march.

Military genius and its attributes

If we are to believe the eighteenth-century tracts on military affairs, the officer best qualified for high command was an assemblage of civic, political and military virtues. He had a wide command of languages, polite literature and history. He was cool and firm, enterprising but prudent, and he combined a mastery of detail with the capacity to keep the wider picture constantly in view. One day the Marquis de Brezé went to his library and he read as much in a whole series of ancient and modern authors. When, however, he turned to the lives of famous commanders, he found that these great men fell short in one or more respects: the Duke of Marlborough was consumed by avarice, just as the Old Dessauer was brutal and bad-tempered. He concluded:

> When you read their biographies with attention, you will see from the deeds of those great warriors that they were endowed with an active temperament, an invincible courage and an extraordinary toughness of mind. All the other virtues – good breeding, humanity, moderation, graciousness, generosity, sobriety and so on – will make you liked and esteemed, but it is through the qualities that I mentioned first that you rise above other men and command their admiration. (Brezé, 1779, 100–1)

So much for the temperament of the general. Among his skills, the one by which the eighteenth century set the greatest store was that of *coup d'oeil*, a facility which enabled a commander to grasp the essentials of a situation and make a speedy and appropriate decision (Pirscher, 1775, 17). Such a mastery of *coup d'oeil* was evident in officers like the French general Closen in the Seven Years War, who

> possessed, in the highest possible degree, the art of judging, by a quick aptitude of eye, of the advantages and defects of an

enemy's positions. . . . He fixed his batteries so judiciously that they produced, when opened, a decided effect. As soon as he reconnoitred the enemy, he immediately foresaw the nature and extent of the designs he meditated. In this, particularly, he was never deceived. (Wimpffen de Bournebourg, 1804, 131)

The process of acquiring *coup d'oeil* began in peacetime, while the officer was out walking, riding or hunting. One of the fundamental exercises was to fix a particular measurement in your mind, and then apply it over successively greater distances. The ordinary human pace was assumed to be about 2 feet, and the Prince de Ligne discovered that 80 such paces approximated to the maximum range at which he would consider shooting a hare. Three 80-pace units in turn yielded the length of an Austrian battalion, which came to 240 paces, including the 6 paces allowed for the battalion artillery. The estimation of numbers also demanded practice:

When you see labourers or a herd of cattle in a field, you should guess their number from a distance, then approach more closely and count them, so as to find your margin of error. By repeating this exercise over and over again you acquire a certain assurance of judgement, which will enable you afterwards to make an accurate assessment of a force of infantry or cavalry. (Bessel, 1778, 332)

Eventually it became possible to envisage the most peaceful landscape in military terms, and problems and their solutions crowded in upon the mind.

The Prussian cavalryman Seydlitz, who could see, judge and decide in seconds, was renowned for his long and keen eyesight. Many other commanders were not so well endowed, and they were too vain to help themselves out with spectacles. In 1757 Seydlitz happened to catch a force of French hussars in a hollow, but he was let down by one of his officers who mistook young fir trees for enemy infantry and failed to close the trap. In the same year the retreat of the army of Prince August Wilhelm of Prussia was bedevilled by a series of absurd blunders, which were again attributable to poor eyesight. The main road to Zittau was thought to be blocked by Austrian 'artillery', which turned out to be a herd of cattle. Further batteries were espied between Neudorf and Kreibitz, and only after the Prussians had burnt their pontoons and transport did they discover that the guns in question were tree trunks.

'Luck' was another attribute of successful military command which was much debated in the eighteenth century (Loen, 1751, 80; Pauli, 1758–64, I, Introduction). Frederick was supposed to have taken the brave Duke of Bevern to task because he was so rarely touched by this gift, but in his *Principes Généraux* of 1748 he writes about 'luck' as something that was entirely capricious in its visitations. In his experience the best-thought-out schemes were at the mercy of fog, a poor harvest, sickness in the army, misunderstood orders, the illness or death of a general, the loss of military intelligence or the negligence of subordinates (Frederick, 1846–57, XXXVIII, 85).

Relationships

The Prince de Ligne had some excellent advice for the commander in chief:

> I would beg the field-marshal to make a habit of touring the length of his army with a brilliant retinue, stopping every now and then to talk to some brave officer, or question a number of soldiers. It is agreeable to see how all the other men will come crowding up to hear what is going on. They admire the kind of field-marshal who takes the trouble to make himself popular by uttering a few pleasantries or distributing a few coins....
> I would further advise the field-marshal to be the last man in the army to return to his shelter, when the weather is atrocious, but he must be the first in line if there is a prospect of action. He must deny himself every convenience, rather than deprive his subordinates of any. (Ligne, 1795–1811, II, 74–5. See also in similar vein Quincy, 1726, VIII, 20; Frederick *Principes Généraux* [1748] Frederick, 1846–57, I, 51; Chabot, 1756, 69; Donkin, 1777, 65)

On several occasions we have touched on the kind of bond which could thereby be established between the commander-in-chief and the private soldier. It was much more difficult to strike a satisfactory relationship with the generals under your command (or possibly it just seemed so, because discord leaves a stronger impression than harmony). In the Seven Years War Marshal Broglie discovered that the commander had to battle with the limitless professional ignorance of the French officer corps, and

> for that reason the general has to do everything by himself — array the whole army in line of battle, determine all the movements, provide for every eventuality and be everywhere. This proves to be impossible in a large army, however young the commander might be, however well mounted or however active. (Ray, 1895, 349)

In the enemy camp, Prince Ferdinand of Brunswick was simultaneously contending with touchy allies and unwilling subordinates. Officers of this kind could stop short of open defiance, yet still do a lot of damage by letting favourable opportunities slip by unexploited. 'The army consequently makes no progress, but nobody can say exactly why' (Mauvillon, J., 1794, II, 268).

Among generals of equal rank, relationships were frequently soured by the spirit of faction. Mopinot de la Chapotte wrote that in western Germany in the Seven Years War there were 'four opposing parties in the army, namely those of Estrées, Soubise, Broglie and Stainville. Each of the factions is set on the rise of its own party and the fall of the others' (1905, 392). Marshal d'Estrées was a brave and honest commander who did not shine at court; Marshal Soubise had been disgraced in the eyes of the army and the public by his defeat at Rossbach in 1757, but he was sustained by his charm, his lack of shame, his high birth and the support of the Pompadour; Marshal Broglie was a professional soldier through-and-through, and he was adored by the more humble officers; Stainville (later the Duc de Choiseul) had shown great intelligence and ambition in the course of his military and diplomatic career, and he was supported by some excellent officers, as well as by the courtiers and the careerists.

The feuds in the French armies were stoked by the large number of idle lieutenant-generals who hung around the headquarters (see p. 138), and by the way the factions were encouraged by interests at court. However something of the same could be observed in all the armies. In Austria the contest between Lacy and Loudon endured for more than thirty years. Frederick of Prussia kept his generals on a tight rein, but even so the Prussian service was split by a rivalry between a hard-nosed party represented by the family of Anhalt-Dessau, the generals Winterfeldt and Fouqué and other individuals close to the person of the king, and a more liberal tradition which was championed by Field-Marshal Schwerin, Prince Ferdinand of Brunswick and the royal brother Prince Henry.

The peacetime army

In times of peace during the eighteenth century it was difficult to discover anything which could properly be called an army, if by that term we understand something more than a collection of individual regiments.

Only a few functionaries were given a measure of authority over substantial parts of the army at a time. Such were the roving Austrian commissaries, or the French and Prussian inspectors. Their duties were to ensure that the regiments were up to strength in men and materiel, and that the drills (and especially the new ones) were performed to a high and uniform standard.

The Prussian inspectorate was established on 9 February 1763. Some of its representatives were truly formidable figures, like Friedrich Wilhelm von Seydlitz, who ruled the cavalry regiments in Silesia, and Friedrich Christoph von Salders, who became head of the Magdeburg Infantry Inspection. Inevitably the colonels (who in Prussia were also generals in their own right) resented the infringement of their authority over their regiments, which they had been accustomed to ruling like petty kingdoms. The offence was all the greater if the inspector or the other royal representative happened to be a young man who overset the normal hierarchy of command: 'The principle of subordination suffered severely in the process. Generals and staff officers found it demeaning to be under the orders of a mere adjutant, who was rarely intelligent enough to carry out his task with due modesty' (Berenhorst, 1798–9, I, 245). Orders from such people were received with grins and shrugging of shoulders. In Russia Emperor Paul I established inspectors as part of the very necessary reform of the army which he began in 1796, and Suvorov and the other old commanders responded just as angrily as did their counterparts in Prussia.

The colonels hastened to cover themselves against detection, once they knew that an inspector was on the way. In Russia they prepared bribes and entertainments to beguile the visitor, and they arranged among themselves to cover any deficiencies in their establishment. Langeron noted how in 1796 an inspector saw one and the same horse in four different regiments, and never appreciated how he was being deceived. Such elaborate precautions were seldom necessary in France:

> Nowadays most inspectors go through their reviews with about as much . . . interest as you might watch a procession which happens to be passing beneath your window. . . . When the season for the inspections comes near, the regimental staffs make ready for this great ceremony, and are especially attentive to dressing their troops in full parade uniform. . . . The inspector arrives, and the troops are drawn up. He puts them through a few pirouettes to the right and the left, and then he makes his stately progress down the ranks, rejecting the occasional idiot or dwarf who, as he had noticed, had committed some appallingly clumsy misdeed during that vital manoeuvre. Finally the troops march past. A regimental feast will have now been prepared, and the party goes off to eat. (Bonneville, 1762, I, 42)

During the period of the rococo the camps and field days of most of the armies were primarily occasions of a social nature. Their spirit was caught by a young cheval-léger of the Garde, who took part in the review of the Maison du Roi which was staged on 4 July 1759:

> I was mightily pleased with myself, for I was wearing my red coat with gold lace, and I was mounted on a splendid horse, which was black and full of spirit. At two in the afternoon the king arrived from Versailles. He was on horseback, and all the royal family was present in open carriages. There was also a great concourse of coaches, belonging both to the courtiers and to spectators from Paris, as well as an immense throng on foot, for this was an excellent show which was well worth travelling to see. The sun was blazing, and the heat was intense. The king passed along the ranks, examining each of the chevaux-légers, and especially those whom he had not seen before. When his gaze rested on me I was so agitated that all that I could take in was his blue sash, which passed over his velvet coat, all embroidered with gold along every seam. (Belleval, 1866, 23–4)

The manoeuvres and exercises of the Prussians had a much more serious purpose. As a young man Frederick had despised what he saw at the Saxon camp at Mühlberg in 1730, and at the gathering of the gilded youth of Europe at Heidelberg during the singularly bloodless campaign in western Germany in 1734. As reigning king, Frederick continued to hold the springtime reviews of groups of regiments, but as his reign wore on he gave more and more attention to the great manoeuvres of thousands of men which were arranged for the high summer and early autumn, when the ground was clear of the harvest. The higher officers now had a rare opportunity to move large bodies of troops, just as the smaller concentrations at Potsdam gave Frederick the means of experimenting with new tactics.

The Austrians responded in kind. The initiative was taken by Lieutenant-General Maximilian Ulysses von Browne, who became commanding general in Bohemia in 1752. He arranged contested manoeuvres which outdid the Prussian originals in realism, and genuine battles developed when Hungarian infantry faced the 'German' troops.

In France, the first one-month camps were staged in 1753, and here, as in Britain, the larger encampments also served the strategically useful purpose of concentrating forces near the coast. In the 1770s the French camps on the coasts and the inland frontiers were utilised to inculcate the new Prussian-style tactics, or to test new ideas, like the *plésions* of Mesnil-Durand which were tried at Metz in 1774 and again at Vaussieux near Bordeaux four years later.

However, the best of the manoeuvres still provided only a simulacrum of war, and the experience became less and less valuable the lower the level of command. Even in Prussia

> the captains and the other officers with the platoons have nothing more to do than they would if the battalion was drilling in isolation, and hardly any of them could explain the purpose of a particular movement. . . . A captain can serve for twenty years, and still know little more than the day he received his company. (Warnery, 1785–91, III, 116)

Officers noted with dismay how the proficiency of the army declined during peace: 'The armies gradually lose the higher officers who have distinguished themselves on campaign and who have acquired an experience of warfare. . . . They are carried away by illness, age, incapacity or other causes, and the passage of just ten years makes a perceptible difference' (Rohr, 1756, I, xv). Thus, by 1740, Field-Marshal Schwerin was almost the only serving senior officer in the Prussian army who had any experience of large-scale operations. The military spirit declined noticeably in Spain and Portugal over the course of the century, and in Denmark it was extinguished almost altogether. In continental Europe generally the atmosphere of pedantry reigned supreme by the 1780s, because there were so few generals who could distinguish what was, and what was not, genuinely important in war.

When the regiments were split up and dispersed over the country-side the soldiers fell into 'lazy and dirty ways, and assume the habits of the people among whom they live. You can say goodbye to competition – which should be the driving force of armies!' (Ligne, 1795–1811, II, 54–5). The contagion of the larger garrisons and fortress towns was just as dangerous in its way, for the officers contracted marriages and debts, and fought each other with swords, pistols and legal writs.

Little was done to remedy the deterioration of physical condition which set in among the warriors:

> If the peace continues very long, I may live to see the foot of England carried in waggons from quarter to quarter, for what with their vast size and the idleness they live in, I'm sure they can't march. . . . Take the case of a peasant. He is strong and vigorous when he leaves his village, and his arms are muscular and inured to toil. Soon he is incapable of wielding anything more than his musket. His hands become as delicate as those of a young girl, and are no longer equal to gripping a spade or a pick. (Hawley [1726], 1946, 93; Bonneville, 1762, I, 31)

Conscientious officers recognised the need to ride frequently and hard, but they did not appreciate the value of other kinds of exercise. Before he became king, Frederick and a companion once ran down the sandy forest path from Zegelin to the palace of Rheinsberg. The distance only came to a couple of miles, but they were so afflicted by heat, breathlessness and pains in the side that they truly believed they were near death. Frederick could never bring himself to repeat the experiment.

With the passage of time entire armies became *hors d'haleine*, in the eighteenth-century sense. National security was imperilled as a result, and some commanders came to believe that the state must go to war so as to restore the physical and mental fitness of its defenders. Almost any war would do, for the nominal occasion hardly mattered

(Field-Marshal Münnich, quoted in Mediger, 1952, 325; Santa Cruz, 1735–40, XII, 35).

Part II

War

5

The campaign

Central direction

In the Age of Reason warfare and the military machines were managed in two ways. One was the style of Frederick the Great, and the other was followed by everyone else.

From the beginning, Frederick concentrated the control of politics and strategy in his person. During the winter of 1760–1 his friend d'Argens got into the habit of dropping into the king's headquarters at Leipzig after the daily concert, and one evening he discovered the king sitting on the floor, feeding his greyhounds with stew from a dish. He had a little stick, with which he maintained order among the pack, and pushed the best morsels in the direction of his favourite bitch. D'Argens clapped his hands and exclaimed:

> Five great powers of Europe have sworn to destroy you, the Marquis of Brandenburg. They think that you must surely be hatching some deadly plot for the next campaign, collecting the funds to see it through, assembling your stores of food and forage, or launching negotiations to divide your enemies and gain yourself new allies. Nothing could be further from the truth! Here you are sitting peacefully in your room, feeding your dogs! (Nicolai, 1788–92, I, 46)

The operational advantages of such a centralisation of power were priceless, but they exacted a heavy penalty of Frederick in terms of isolation and strain. He was prostrated by psychosomatic collapse on several occasions in the Seven Years War, and during those terrible episodes he removed himself from human contact for days at a time.

The Frederician war ministry was reduced to little more than an office of clerks, and it was allowed no authority over the personnel of the army, which was managed by Frederick in person. For more than forty years he directed and shaped the army through leadership in war, instruction and training in peace, and the compelling magic of his presence. The charismatic ways of Frederick were inimitable, and Old Fritz himself proved incapable of sustaining them towards the end of his days. There was nobody fitted to take over from him, and the arbitrary ways of Frederick's management now stood out in sharp relief. The very well-informed Carl Alexander von der Goltz wrote in the early 1780s:

> If you examine our present military constitution with any care, it will not take you long to discover the lack of harmony which proceeds from the diversity of the various elements, the vagueness of the laws, the unsystematic and inappropriate regulations, and finally the arbitrary interventions of the inspectors. (Jähns, 1889–91, III, 2, 264)

Compared with the brilliance of Frederick in his prime, the leadership provided by the other sovereigns of Europe appears tentative and indirect. Maria Theresa of Austria was loved by her army, she had a sound grasp of strategy and military detail, and she was a more creative military administrator than Frederick himself, yet she never commanded an army in person, and a veil of bureaucracy, established interests and family and personal obligations came between herself and her officers and men. Louis XV earned the fawning title of 'Louis le Bien-Aimé' by nearly expiring from illness on the journey from Flanders to the threatened Rhine frontier in 1744. He was present at the battle of Fontenoy in 1745, but in the Seven Years War he sank into inertia at Versailles, and contented himself with offering occasional comments when the reports from the field were read out in his presence. Empress Elizabeth of Russia was comatose for days on end.

It followed that in the Seven Years War the leaders of the ponderous anti-Prussian alliance spent a substantial part of every year trying to fix their plans of joint operations. In Vienna, Versailles and St Petersburg the first projects were evolved in the winter, and then underwent weeks or months of internal debate during which it was usual to consult a variety of serving or retired generals, and foreign envoys or military representatives. Small wonder that the next campaign was often well advanced before any kind of common strategy had been evolved.

Outside Prussia, it was in fact difficult to establish the precise centre of military control. Every country had one form or another of bureaucracy, whether the Russian War College, the Austrian *Hofkriegsrath*, the French war ministry, or the British War Office, Board of Ordnance and Admiralty. However, the staffs were small and scattered, and they frequently had to contend with squalor and inconvenience in their immediate surroundings. The wretched clerks of the French war ministry were accommodated in rented houses at Versailles, and they slaved at tables which were made of planks laid across barrels. Even the proceedings of the British Board of General Officers, which was an august consultative body, were interrupted every now and then by debris which showered from the ceiling of the Great Room in Horse Guards. The chiefs consequently lacked the basic wherewithal to assess the resources of the nation, or even to find out what was going on in the armed services. After a bruising encounter in the 1770s the Comte de Saint-Germain admitted that 'this episode made me appreciate how easy it is to deceive a minister and abuse his confidence' (Saint-Germain, 1779, 50).

Effectively, the most important military questions were determined by *ad hoc* cabinets of shifting composition. Making allowance for differing titles, these inner cabinets usually comprised the head of state or his or her representative, together with the foreign minister, the chief of the treasury, the war minister, and one or more of the leading military men or other persons who had a specialised knowledge of the matter under discussion.

One historian has concluded that Britain attained her brilliant conquests and victories in the Seven Years War without the benefit of any long-sighted strategic guidance from London. It was enough that the local military leadership was sound, that the fleet was powerful, that British financial credit was strong, and that Pitt the Elder was effective in Parliament:

> The eighteenth century has been called the age of reason. If the machinery of government is considered, it might equally be called the age of irrationality. In practice, reason penetrated no further than the doors of fashionable society; and a study of eighteenth-century institutions shows how shallow was the belief in unimpeded progress. (Middleton, 1985, 215)

This argument is unimpeachable as it stands, but we should not suppose that the direction of war was necessarily more enlightened in the twentieth century. In fact the contrary is indicated by examining the political and military command structure of the Germans in the Second World War, or of the Americans in the Vietnam war. Pitt's style of management was no less effective for leaving so little trace at the present day. One of his rivals, the Austrian chancellor Kaunitz, wrote in the middle of the war that he could see no likelihood of the British wishing to make peace, 'and not least because Pitt has his hand on the tiller. His former conduct has furnished convincing proof that he does not live from day to day, but goes to work in a systematic fashion, and knows how to direct the decisions in his part of the world towards a single aim' (Kaunitz to Maria Theresa, 28 May 1758, Haus-Hof-und Staatsarchiv, Vienna, *Staatskanzlei Vorträge* 82).

The connection between war and politics was clearly understood in the Age of Reason, even if nobody summed it up quite as neatly as Clausewitz was going to do in the next century. Friedrich Wilhelm von Zanthier spoke long-windedly but well:

The art of war and political matters go hand in hand, and together they determine the general plan of war. You will go astray if you choose one as your guide to the exclusion of the other. Let us take the matter of how far you ought to carry a successful offensive. Is it permissible to push your advantage over all your enemies as far as you possibly can? A soldier who is a soldier, and nothing else, will answer 'yes'. A statesman, however, is acquainted with the limits which political considerations all too often impose on conquest. (Quoted in Jähns, 1889–91, III, 2,906–7. See also Christoph Conrad Frederici, quoted in Jähns, 1889–91, III, 1,909; P. A. Rumyantsev to N. I. Panin, 2 February 1771, Rumyantsev, 1953–9, II, 226)

Statesmen also appreciated that it was advantageous to allow the theatre commanders freedom of action within the overall framework of the campaign. As minister of war Marshal Belle-Isle wrote to Contades in 1759:

It is certain that the general must be master of his movements. I know more than anyone else that I cannot command an army from Versailles. All that the minister can and should do is to make known to the general the political and military objectives and the king's manner of thinking. (Kennett, 1967, 20. See also Empress Elizabeth to A. B. Buturlin, 28 September 1760, Vorontsov, 1870–95, VII, 442; Lord George Germain to Clinton, 3 December 1778 and 23 January 1779, Clinton, 1954, 397, 398)

As a matter of routine, the commanders of armies and detached corps were furnished by their governments with detailed explanations about the political context of their operations. Frederick, who was normally so secretive in matters of statecraft, opened his mind freely to Winterfeldt, Dohna, Ferdinand of Brunswick and his own brother Prince Henry, which shows how earnestly he took this principle to heart.

Altogether wars in the eighteenth century were managed at least as effectively as the generality of wars in any other period of history. This is not to deny that many of the field commanders in the Age of Reason ended up by living on bad terms with their political masters. A number of possible explanations suggest themselves. For a start we must not underestimate the physical difficulties of communication. In the Seven Years War it took a week or more to effect an exchange of correspondence between Versailles and the French army in Germany, and up to three or more months to send a communication in a single direction across the Atlantic.

Also, despite their protestations to the contrary, a number of politicians and bureaucrats could not resist the temptation to send operational directives from the capital. Marshal Clermont wrote from Germany:

> The court has an ancient and thoroughly bad custom of trying to direct military movements. My friend Marshal Belle-Isle agreed as much with me before I set out, but he ended up doing the same thing, being carried away by what he conceived to be the general good, and his fear that other men might not have such good ideas as himself. All of this causes embarrassment to a commander on the spot who happens to know his trade, and who is informed of our political intentions. (To the Pompadour, 27 March 1758, Dussauge, 1914, 143)

There were campaigns, like those of the English in the War of

Independence, in which the interference was obstructive and harmful, but on the whole the politicians and the chair-bound officers in the capital deserve a better treatment than they receive from the historians. The generals in the field were seldom wild-eyed men of action, impatient of all restraint. On the contrary, the politicians were usually the men who were in favour of offensive action, and they would have liked nothing better than for the commanders to trust their own judgement and act 'according to time and circumstances', in the favourite Austrian phrase.

Few commanders were willing to exercise the degree of freedom that was actually allowed to them. They were anxious to unload or share the awesome responsibility of giving battle, and they were under a compulsive urge to communicate with their governments. We may cite the rambling correspondence of the Austrian commanders Daun and Loudon with Vienna, or the lengthy epistles which Marshal Soubise addressed to the war minister in Paris: 'He sent letter after letter, and what letters they were! Some extended to twelve pages, and every letter was written in his own hand. How did he leave himself with any time for action?' (Dussauge, 1914, 318). It was as if this activity provided the generals with a solace for the loneliness of high command.

The departure

Once a war was fairly under way, most departures for the field involved experienced troops, who set out from winter quarters in the late spring or early summer. The quarters in question were usually billets which had been established in towns or villages near the theatre of war. Only the light cavalry – the dragoons and the hussars – were exposed to the rigours of maintaining a cordon against the enemy during the winter months, and the rest of the troops were kept under cover for as long as the winter lull permitted. It was an old maxim that 'the meanest hovel is better than the finest tent.'

The change to the campaign footing made a considerably greater impact when the troops were embarking on the first campaign of a new war. It so happens that the most vivid accounts derive from Prussia, but something of the experience was shared by all armies.

Acute distress was felt by the native troops and their families, and by long-serving professionals who had contracted marriages in the garrisons. These sentiments were not shared by the foreign troops, many of whom literally sang and danced at the prospect of the relative freedom which could be enjoyed on campaign, and the opportunities for plunder or desertion. Finally the shrilling of the cavalry trumpets or the drumming of the infantry *Generalmarsch* summoned the troops from their billets for the last time, festooned with their full equipment and rations. In August 1756 the appointed assembly place for the Prussian hussar regiment of Putkammer was its garrison town in Silesia:

> It was a splendid summer morning when the sun rose and we drew ourselves up on the market square of the little town. We stood in a grave and solemn silence, for we knew the work that lay before us, and we could see that a dense circle of townspeople of all conditions had gathered to see us for the last time. There were streams of tears on all sides, and many a veteran hussar rubbed his eyes with the back of his hand after he had noticed his wife and child in the circle of long-faced spectators. . . . This solemn and mournful mood dominates the first hour of the march, but then it gave way to the innate cheerfulness of the soldier. The men joked or broke into jolly popular song, and gradually their countenances began to lighten. (Lojewsky, 1843, II, 8–9. See also Thiébault, 1813, III, 207; Bräker, 1852, 138; Anon., 1884, 22)

To begin with the armies marched non-tactically and in a multi-tude of columns, which permitted every battalion or regiment to be directed to a suitable village or town for its overnight rest. Here the soldiers threw themselves down in barns or rooms which were packed with straw. The men were in a state of acute distress, for their life in peacetime had left them totally unfitted for the rigours of the march (see p. 147). Frederick noted: 'When the troops are setting out after a long period of rest, you will ruin them if the initial marches are too long. In the first days they should not be made to cover more than 3 German miles [about 15 English miles] at the very most' ('Des marches d'armée [177], Frederick, 1846–57, XXIX, 98).

For many of the French, Spanish or English troops, the first marches took them only as far as the nearest seaport, where they took ship for a destination overseas. The English accumulated a considerable experience of sea-borne expeditions, and by the time of the American War of Independence their arrangements were recognised as admirable. The troops were allocated to the transports at a ratio of one man for about every two tons of ship. Rations and bedding were generally good, the decks were swabbed clean regularly, and every day the blankets and the men were brought up to air, although

> when they were seasick, nothing but force could make them come on deck – We were obliged several times to tie a rope about some of the lazy fellows as they lay in bed, and give the other end to the men on deck, who hauled them out in an instant. (Lieutenant Frederick Mackenzie's account of the voyage of the 23rd Foot to New York, Mackenzie, 1960, 51–2).

Unfortunately, the best-provided and the most tightly-run ships were still at the mercy of contrary winds. A passage from England to Ireland or the Low Countries might take a couple of days or as many weeks. A normal voyage from England to North America lasted between seven and thirteen weeks, or it might be prolonged still further if the ships were blown down to the West Indies.

The accepted human relationships underwent a literal sea-change, even when everything went well. The sight and smell of one's companions became intolerable if, like Baron von Closen and his French comrades in 1780, they had to crawl around in a wardroom which was 4½ feet high (Closen, 1958, 6). Military authority lost the support it had enjoyed in former places and circumstances:

> Nothing can be more hilarious than the condition of a colonel on board ship. He now has to entrust his sacred person to a swaying hammock, and he must now beg for a little water with which to make his grand toilet. He is elbowed aside by dirty and tar-stained seamen, and he has to engage in a competition of hat-raising with a troop of young ensigns who amuse themselves by making jokes at his expense. He has no alternative but to be polite, lest he should compromise his high dignity in the presence of these young scallywags. (Perron de Revel, quoted in Bodinier, 1983, 183)

When they could bear to look up from their misery, soldiers cowered at the sight of those ranks of mountainous water which they could see marching upon their ships in daytime, or breaking over the bulwarks during the night in a rush of phosphorescent foam. A howl of terror went up from Johann Konrad Döhla and his German companions on their way to America, when during one of the storms their equipment broke loose and the water swirled around in the ship. The English sailors came down with lanterns to see what was afoot, and they laughed at their distress. They imposed on the German troops' credulity during the voyage, and Döhla was convinced that the sharks shadowing his ship were really murderous lobsters twelve feet long. Altogether the English seamen were discovered to be a 'thieving, arrogant, debauched and drunken species of mankind, much given to profanity and swearing. They scarcely utter a word without adding their favourite oaths 'God damn my soul! God damn me!' (Döhla, 1912, 95).

The English and Hessian soldiery had to concede that the sailors of the transports and warships were masters of their trade. Such was not always the case among the French, for the officers of Rochambeau's expeditionary force (1780) were appalled by the professional ignorance of their naval opposite numbers, who seemed to know very little about navigation, basic geography or how to manage their ships.

The experience of the march

As he lay in his tent or under the open sky, the soldier was awakened from his sleep by the 'general' drumbeat, which was the signal that he must get up and don his equipment. At the beat of 'assembly' the troops packed up the baggage and tents on the carts, and arranged themselves in their ranks and files ready to march.

In midsummer a departure at four o'clock was by no means too early, if the army was to complete the designated distance by about ten in the morning, before the sun reached its height.

> To see just a single battalion setting off is quite a performance. It is like some ramshackle machine which is on the verge of disintegrating at any moment, and which moves only with infinite difficulty. What happens when you wish to get the head off to a brisk start? The tail is left unaware that the leading troops have marched off at speed. Gaps inevitably result, and in order to make them up the troops at the rear have to run as fast as they can. The head of the following battalion must do the same, and soon the whole sinks into disorder. (Saxe [1732], 1877, 20)

When an army was in no particular hurry it progressed at a rate of 6 or 8 miles a day, and this leisurely pace permitted the baggage and heavy guns to keep up with no great difficulty. During urgent phases of a campaign the rate might be increased to a dozen miles, and sustained at this speed for up to a fortnight. Lightly equipped raiding forces moved at between 15 and 20 miles a day, and occasionally a formation or unit achieved a remarkable tour de force, like that of the 10th Regiment of Foot following Thurot's landing in Ireland in 1760, when the troops dashed the seventy-odd miles from Kilkenny to Dublin in twenty-four hours (Donkin, 1777, 171). In terms of distance the performance eclipsed the celebrated march of Craufurd's Light Division to Talavera in July 1809, and Lossow wrote perceptively

> in this respect it would appear mistaken to claim that recent wars are the only ones which have demanded great physical exertion, or that these exertions were greater than those of our ancestors. We would be just as wrong to suppose that the soldiers of those times, most of whom were probably aged between thirty and forty, could not have been a match for our present soldiers, the majority of whom are between twenty and thirty. (Lossow, 1826, 10–11. See also p. 95)

On campaign the soldiers were allowed to march at their ease:

> Just look at a column of infantry on the march, and you might see about four soldiers carrying the musket with the stock to the front. Most of them in fact carry it with the stock resting on the shoulder. They hold the barrel by the muzzle, and shift the musket every now and then from one shoulder to the other, for the sake of relief. A few soldiers carry the musket cradled in their arms, while others sling it over their backs. (Puységur, 1749, I, 228)

When the men were marching through wooded country, it was a good idea to order them to shoulder arms with the butt downwards in something like the regulation manner,

> the necessity of this is obvious enough, because if their arms are clubbed, the cock will be uppermost, and some pendant branch may catch hold of it, and pull it so far back, that when it quits the branch, it is with such a spring as to give fire to the charge;

and the musket going off, will, most likely, kill the man before it. (An Old Officer, 1760, 173)

Soldiers chattered at the beginning of each day's progress, but they gradually fell silent when exhausion began to sap their strength and spirits. Their view of the world was confined to the knapsack of the man in front (as Napoleon observed), and only the ex-farmers were likely to be alert to the weather, the landscape and the crops.

The regimental quartermaster and his assistants had meanwhile gone ahead, and while the troops were still on the march the lines for the next night's camp were being marked out with flags and lengths of rope. 'When the infantry arrives in the new camp, some of the soldiers set to work to pitch the tents, but most of them go out into the neighbouring villages to obtain straw' (Ray, 1895, 171). The soldiers were crowded at about six at a time into simple ridge tents of canvas, where they slept on whatever straw had been gathered in, with their breeches lowered to their ankles and their coats or cloaks serving as blankets. The Prussian coats were too short to give much comfort, but in compensation the Prussian tents had canvas floors which insulated the men from the ground. Subalterns had the relative luxury of one- or two-man tents, and senior officers enjoyed bell tents or commodious pavilions, in which it was possible to entertain in some style.

The muskets were piled in pyramids and covered with a waxed cloth (the bell of arms), or were left in the open in racks as was the Austrian practice:

this is no doubt the merest trifle to the gentlemen who elucidate higher tactics and logistics, but I can assure them that there is considerable disorder throughout the camp when the soldiers have to bring their muskets into the tents at any suspicion of damp weather, and take them out again when the sun sheds its welcome rays. (Cogniazzo, 1779, 148-9).

The standard basic ration was bread, which in Western armies was baked centrally and issued to the soldiers on a scale of 2 pounds a day. This unappetising substance could be eaten as it was, or boiled up with lard, salt or other substances into a soup. Beer, wines or spirits might also be on issue, and wherever possible Frederick of Prussia bought herds of cattle and distributed them among the regiments, where the animals were slaughtered one by one during the course of the march: 'This consideration is something which we owe to our poor soldiers, and especially in Bohemia, where they go to war in a virtual desert' (*Principes Généraux* [1748], Frederick, 1846–57, XXVIII, 20).

Latrines were simple trenches dug in the earth, and since at least the time of the ancient Romans they have afforded warriors an opportunity for social concourse as well as physical relief. Camp fires (which have been banished from modern warfare) went further to reinforce the basic military communities. They not only provided the soldiers of the tent *Kameradschaft* with the means of cooking their food, but offered a focus for smoking, or delousing the seams of their clothes. For the rest of his life no veteran could smell wood-smoke without recalling one of the more agreeable odours of military life.

In camp, the activity of every twenty-four hours was regulated by the *Parole* – a little ceremony in which the army and regimental commanders issued the password and other appropriate instructions. Individual regiments had their own 'quarter guard', intended 'rather for preserving the peace and tranquillity within the regiment, by quelling all disputes that may arise, either between officer and officer, or amongst the soldiers, than for a security against the enemy' (Bland, 1727, 209). Distant protection was provided by pickets of infantry and 'grand guards' of cavalry. Vigilance was supposed to be at its highest around dawn, when the cavalry stood ready mounted, but experience showed that the system of passwords did not really work:

> The headquarters of the army and every regiment duly issue the orders, with the names of the saints or towns which have been chosen for the sign and countersign. It is a different story when you go to the outposts. The men are distracted and half asleep, and when somebody turns up and they demand the appropriate word, they are quite content with an inaudible reply. (Ligne, 1795–1811, I, 230).

If the soldier was unlucky, he might find himself under attack:

> Ill-disciplined troops are the ones most likely to disintegrate in small-scale actions . . . you will see whole platoons scatter like fleas. Some of the men make off in search of cover. Some advance and open fire without order, while yet others fire

blindly into the air. All experienced officers will recall having seen more than one of these regrettable episodes. (Bigot, 1761, I, 168).

However, skirmishing of this kind was usually left to the light troops, and the regular soldiers of the line were unlikely to find themselves engaged in combat in anything short of a pitched battle. When the rival armies were in close proximity the troops were in the habit of concluding informal truces, with or without the knowledge of their officers. Streams offered a natural line of demarcation, but in December 1757 the Comte de Gisors noted that the enemy took no offence when the grenadiers of the Regiment of Champagne crossed to the 'Hanoverian' side of a river and proceeded to uproot some palisades for firewood.

A Hanoverian post was stationed at the actual barrier, but it let us continue our work with a benevolence that was agreeable to see. The enemy sentry asked me for some tobacco, which was passed to him hand to hand by our workmen, and his officer duly raised his hat to me. (Rousset, 1868, 335).

Soldiers usually experienced a great repugnance when they were ordered to kill a sentry. Not only did such a deed break the hallowed truce, but it involved the troops in a deed of violence against somebody who stood before them as an identifiable individual. In 1778 John McAsland of the Pennsylvania Militia was in a patrol which discovered a Hessian sentry, a large man, who was posted outside a mansion near Philadelphia:

We cast lots, and it fell to my lot to shoot the Hessian. I did not like to shoot a man down in cold blood. The company present knew I was a good marksman, and I concluded to break his thigh. I shot with a rifle and aimed at his hip. He had a large iron tobacco box in his breeches pocket, and I hit the box, the ball glanced, and it entered his thigh and scaled the bone of the thigh on the outside. He fell and then rose. We scaled the yard fence and surrounded the house. They saw their situation and were . . . disposed to surrender. (Dann, 1980, 156).

If time permitted, the officers and soldiers repaired to the tents and stalls of the licensed regimental sutlers. When the Prussians were blockading Pirna in 1756, life went ahead just as in a city, with a full complement of shopkeepers and butchers. For the entire day food was being boiled or roasted over long rows of fires, and you could partake of whatever you wanted, or rather whatever you could pay for – meat, butter, cheese, bread, and fruit and vegetables of every kind. Except for the soldiers on guard duty, the men were free to follow their own pursuits, playing at skittles, perhaps, or gambling or going for walks in the camp and the neighbouring country. When you looked into the tents you found that only a few of the men were idle; the rest were cleaning a musket, or out doing the laundry, cooking, repairing breeches, mending shoes, or carving something from wood to sell to the peasants. (Bräker, 1852, 142–3).

Together with the military transport trains of the regiments and the army, the sutlers and their carts made up the 'baggage', which amounted to thousands of personnel and vehicles, and extended for miles on the march.

French, Russian and Saxon higher officers succeeded particularly well in insulating themselves from the unnecessary hardships of warfare. Festivities and plays were the order of the day at the head-quarters of Marshal Saxe during his campaigns in the Netherlands, and in the Seven Years War Pastor Täge once had the unforgettable experience of seeing part of the train of Prince Charles of Saxony pass before his eyes. First came ten splendidly liveried servants, each leading a large mule, hung about with silver bells and bearing a load under yellow cloth covers worked with gold. This was part of the canteen. Next onto the scene were thirty-eight richly dressed attendants, walking in pairs, and these were followed by the *Ober-Stallmeister* and his grooms riding the princely string of thirty horses. Two large carriages were intended for the use of the prince and the most important members of his suite 'in case of illness or bad weather' (Täge, 1864, II, 290), and further coaches were at the disposal of the chaplain, the doctor and two lady acquaintances. The procession was closed up by a train of carts for the kitchen.

Female company provided further compensations. The Duke of Cumberland reviewed the Austrian army in the Netherlands on 15 April 1747, and

What was a little surprising to the British, was to see Madame Harrach, the ambassador's lady, and another lady of quality mounted on horseback, riding astride like the men, and differing little from them in dress. In this manner they were introduced to the Duke at the head of the troops. . . . they commanded their steeds with a martial air, and seemed to resign the delicacy of the sex to a masculine carriage more appropriate to the field. They by far outdid those English heroines, who so much affect the hermaphrodite habit. (Colville, 1948–9, 76).

The Prussian and Hessian officers were usually forbidden such indulgences, but even some of these hard-living gentry found that 'for the enlightened intelligence and a sensitive heart there is a source of endless delights in the contemplation and investigation of the beauties of nature, and the graphic arts which model themselves thereon' (Wolff, 1776, 416). In the Seven Years War we hear of the young Prussian officer Scheffner roaming the Saxon hills, his head turned by Shakespeare and Rousseau, or George Heinrich von Berenhorst contemplating fallen blossom and recalling his intense friendship with his young kinsman the Hereditary Prince of Anhalt-Dessau. Thus by the 1770s the more cultivated of the Hessian officers arrived in the New World with their sensitivities fully attuned, and they exclaimed in admiration at the wonders of the American South, with its waterfalls, wild laurel, tulip trees and magnolia.

Agents of destruction

The normal campaigning of an eighteenth-century army involved the troops in activities which told heavily against their discipline and effectiveness.

As soon as they arrived at their campsite the infantrymen went in search of straw, as we have seen. For the cavalry, the immediate priority was to obtain feed for the horses. A security cordon was first thrown around the chosen foraging area, and then the cavalrymen set to work with scythe or sword to mow the grass, which was gathered and tied in bundles, and carried off with geese, ducks, hens, piglets or whatever other small livestock took the troopers' fancy. The dry forage – hay and grain – was obtained from the barns of the peasants. For this purpose the monkish Turpin de Crissé recommended that the commander of the party should seize a couple of burgomasters or estate stewards as hostages, and 'command them to inform the inhabitants that, if they fall short by so much as a single sheaf, he

will plunder the village then set it on fire' (Turpin de Crissé, 1754,
I, 145).

The hunger of the soldiers recognised no laws, unless a good
disciplinarian was in charge of the army, and the passage of the troops
resembled that of a swarm of locusts. The demand for firewood
was still more destructive. On the march into Bohemia in 1757
detachments went out from the Prussian regiments to dismantle the
houses, and

> we carried shingles, laths, rafters, faggots and finally the
> equivalent of an entire village into the camp. The unfortunate
> people raised a chorus of cries, howls, pleas and curses, but we
> carried on regardless, for we could not live without wood.
> (Prittwitz, 1935, 105)

'Contributions' were a form of blackmail, whereby an invading
force compelled a town or district to make a heavy payment under
threat of physical force. This procedure was a recognised one, and
the local authorities usually hastened to supply the cash or promissory
notes. When the Austrian general Haddik descended on Berlin in
1757 he is said to have demanded not only a large sum of money
but two dozen gloves for Maria Theresa. When, however, the gift
arrived in Vienna, it was discovered that the Berliners had taken
their revenge by providing only left-hand gloves. This, according to
legend, was the origin of the custom among Austrian officers of
carrying their right-hand gloves in their left hand, so as not to put
themselves above their sovereign.

In Saxony in the Seven Years War Frederick exacted huge contributions in money, provisions and recruits from the electorate, and
(to the scandal of his own officers) he proceeded to carry out acts of
vandalism against the property of the ruling family of Saxony-
Poland. In July 1760 he turned his attention to the Grosser Garten
at Dresden, just before he broke off his siege of that city:

> All the surrounding walls have been levelled to the foundation.
> On the night before his departure all the trees of the avenues
> of this garden were cut down by the pioneers of his army, who
> had been detached for this shameful operation. The Prussians
> had already hauled away and smashed the marble statues which
> they found in the places where they had been hidden in the
> pavilions of the royal palace. Some of these works were of great

value. Every growing thing has been hacked to pieces, down
to the orange trees. (Comte de Marainville, 8 August 1760,
Broglie, 1903, II, 611).

In 1761 the electoral palace of Hubertusburg was plundered so
thoroughly that the Prussians carried away the copper roofing and
the clock and bell from the tower, and scraped the gold from the
gilded doors and walls.

'Marauding' was the plundering of the countryside by the scum
of the army – straggling troops, the soldiers' women, and drivers,
servants and wolfish hangers-on – a shadow army which comprised
thousands of damned souls. Some of the marauders were killed by
the vengeful peasants, while others were hanged by the military
authorities as an example. However, many of the English junior
officers were tolerant of marauding, which they recognised as an
activity which differed only in degree from the normal foraging and
raising of contributions. Marauding in the French army had an almost
institutional status, which enabled French soldiers (long before the
Revolutionary Wars) to develop a high degree of skill in living off
the country. French soldiers could be relied upon to return to the
colours as soon as the alarm sounded (Santa Cruz, 1735–40, III, 195),
and 'when a [French] soldier is lucky enough to escape detection he
commands all the greater esteem among his comrades, who admire
and envy a man who has thereby cheated the hangman's noose'
(Warnery, 1785–91, II, 42).

Even the well-motivated troops were not entirely exempt from
the general deterioration of standards:

> However good an army might be, it will inevitably lose some
> of its old, strict discipline. If a soldier is otherwise brave and
> orderly in the service, if he looks after his horse and is guilty of
> no base conduct, then we must permit him his odd word of
> protest, and the occasions when he has a little too much to
> drink. (Lojewsky, 1843, II, 149–50)

The authorities sought to make up the lost ground in winter quarters
and peacetime, by imposing harsh regimes of discipline and formal
drill.

Meanwhile the strength of the army was being eaten away by
the physical demands of the march. Until the truck and the armoured
personnel carrier were invented in the twentieth century, those

requirements had differed very little over the centuries. With remarkably consistency the load of the foot soldier has amounted to as much as any man can bear over a length of time, which comes to about 60 pounds. By English, Hanoverian and Prussian calculations the approximate weight of the components amounted to 10 or 11 pounds for the musket and its bayonet, 10 pounds for the cartridge pouch with sixty rounds, 3 pounds for the sword and its belt, the empty knapsacks at 3½ pounds, brushes, shirts and other small items of clothing or equipment at 8 pounds, and bread for one or two days at 2 pounds per day, to which must be added the clothing which the soldier wore on his person, the water bottle, and extra items like shovel, axe or light pick, tent pegs or tent poles, or the *Kameradschaft's* field kettle (see p. 108).

Over the course of history the soldier's burden has been carried in styles which have proved equally uncomfortable in different ways, according to which part of the anatomy bears the main load. For most of our period the belts of the knapsack and haversack crossed with that of the cartridge pouch over the chest (with the sling of the musket sometimes added on top), which caused deep and permanent bruising and an actual indentation in the chest. Towards the end of the century a fashion set in for transferring the weight of the knapsack to small straps which passed over the shoulders and under the armpits. The soldiers considered the new style unmilitary, and they found that it caused the arms to swell up and grow numb.

Frederick's friend Captain Charles Guichard, or Guischardt ('Quintus Icilius'), had once written a book in which he claimed that nobody had equalled the ancient Roman soldiers in their ability to bear hardship. One day in 1758 the king called Guichard to his chamber, and upon a royal command a grenadier of the First Battalion of the Garde entered the room, deposited all the equipment of a private soldier on the floor, and left without saying a word:

> The king proceeded to station him in the middle of the room, and made him stand like a soldier at drill. He pushed up his chin, and emplaced the hat in the proper style, jammed well onto the head. He attached the sword, put on the cartridge pouch with its sixty cartridges, then the haversack, and finally presented him with the musket. (Catt, 1884, 26).

Guichard was left standing for three quarters of an hour, and after this ordeal he had to concede that he had been mistaken in what he had written.

When the troops were on the march, the fresh air penetrated with difficulty between the packed ranks and files. The men were crushed and sweating, and they breathed a miasma exuding from their bodies and their stained clothing and leatherwork. They became insensitive to their own stench, but it was offensive to civilians and the higher officers, and in hot and still weather it hung in the air for hours after the regiments had passed through.

The soldier entered physical danger when his 'core temperature' rose above 38.5 degrees Centigrade. Beyond that point he was liable to be prostrated by heat exhaustion, or drop dead on the road like the hundreds of Prussians and Austrians who expired on the forced marches across the Saxon hills in the Seven Years War.

When the soldiers arrived at some blessed stream, pond or well, the longing for water became a compulsion. Well-disciplined troops might be content to wait in ranks while their bottles were collected and filled by corporals or other selected men, but frequently the officers and NCOs were swept aside in a gadarene rush for the water. The Russians experienced heavy losses from sickness on their march through East Prussia in the hot spring and summer of 1757

> for when the soldier is overheated, and covered with dust and sweat, he gulps deeply of the stinking, muddy and foul water, and pours it over his body. No force, no kind of punishment is capable of deterring or preventing him from doing so, as experience shows. (Weymarn, 1794, 26–7).

The medical opinion of the time held that not just dirty water but any kind of refreshment was dangerous in these circumstances.

The cavalrymen were spared some of the hardships of the footsore infantry, but the cuirassiers were tormented by their breastplates, which became very hot in the sun, and all the horse soldiers knew the tiresome business of falling out of rank and file on the march and having to spur their horses to catch up again (Saxe, [1732], 1877, 51). The cavalry, like the infantry, were liable to fall into a comatose state after several hours on the road, which at night-time led to the whole column losing cohesion 'for when the horse of a sleeping man stands still, all the men to the rear believe that the column has encountered some obstacle, and they too come to a halt' (Generals-Reglement, Vienna 1769, 139).

During such episodes the veteran was much better than a recruit at recognising what was going on. He had further advantages. Years of campaigning had schooled him in how to manage his life on the march – how to adjust his equipment to the most tolerable position, how to make himself comfortable in his tent and so on. Having survived his first months in the field, he was in better condition to survive the rest: 'while it is wrong to maintain that only a large man can be a useful soldier, it has been shown that a measure of bodily size, together with a certain age, are necessary to enable a man to endure severe fatigue' (Lossow, 1826, 13). Wispy, ectomorphic types of men excel in the conventional demonstrations of physical fitness, but the Falklands War of 1982 indicated that their generously covered colleagues are better at withstanding the hardships of campaigning.

In the eighteenth century the losses from disease were actually less when the troops were on the march than when they were mewed up in garrisons or winter quarters. However, even during the height of the campaigning season, illness was still much more deadly than hostile action. It is difficult to retrieve accurate figures from the eighteenth-century evidence, but the main killers or incapacitators appear to have been typhus, lung and intestinal infections, and malaria and rheumatic diseases. The swampy area of Italy around Mantua was a notorious sink of infection, and Hungary was worse, the 'graveyard of the Germans' (Karl Graf zu Wied, in Wengen, 1890, 32). It was a spotted 'Hungarian fever' from the Austrian prisoners which struck down the Prussians after their victory at Leuthen (1757), and pits for thousands of corpses at a time were dug in front of the gates of Breslau.

Three levels of attention were available for the soldier who was wounded or who fell sick. Many of the unfortunates were treated on the spot by the regimental surgeon or physician and their assistants. More serious cases were received in the churches, barns or other spacious buildings taken over by the field hospitals (*hôpitaux ambulants*) which accompanied the army on the march. Long-term invalids and men who fell ill in garrison usually ended up in the large and static *hôpitaux sédentaires*.

Within the limits of the medical science of the time, some of the best care was available in the Austrian army, after the reforming work of Gerhard van Swieten and the *Protomedicus* Dr Brady in the middle of the century. The Austrian hospitals were by no means immune to abuse and corruption, but as a general rule they were much better run than their Prussian and Russian counterparts, which existed in a state of near-total neglect. The most actively vicious administration was that of the French, which was in the hands of private contractors:

> Desirous to gain the favour of his contractor . . . the hospital orderly deprives the sick men of items which are essential to their cure, and when a shirt is soaked in the sweat of one soldier he will be content to dry it out, and then pass it on to another. (Darut de Grandpré, 1787, II, 99. See also Chenevière, 1742, 231)

Dr Shippen could at least invoke the force of circumstances to explain the collapse of the American medical system in 1777. The sufferings of the rebel soldiers were

> not owing to my neglect, to a deficiency of stores or to a want of surgeons, commissaries, nurses, medicines, or other things that I ought and could supply. They arose partially from a want of clothing and the covering necessary to keep the soldiers clean and warm; articles that at that time were not procurable in the country; they were also partially due to the fact that our army was raw, unused to camp life, exposure, fatigue, discipline and great hardship. (Gibson, 1937, 285).

Outside Austria the quality of medical staff was notoriously low. The doctors and surgeons were frequently workless medical students who had come to the end of their studies, and the experience of their assistants, if they had any experience at all, was confined to opening veins in barbers' shops. The feeding and cleanliness of the patients was the responsibility of unskilled male and female auxiliaries. Major Richard Davenport of the 10th Dragoons reported the end of one of his troopers in hospital at Münster in 1759:

> I am sorry I can give Mrs. Moss no other account of her husband than that he died at Münster. As to his things, whatever he had is lost. When a man goes into hospital, his wallet, with his necessaries are sent with him, but nothing ever returns. Those that recover, seldom bring anything back, but those that die are stripped of all. I have lost nine men and have not heard of anything that belonged to them. It is a common practice of a nurse, when a man is in danger, to put him on a clean shirt,

that he may die in it, and that it may become her perquisite. (Davenport, 1968, 131).

Forty French soldiers died, out of every hundred who were admitted to hospital in the Seven Years War (Kennett, 1967, 136), and no military experience in the Age of Reason was more justifiably dreaded. A Prussian lieutenant wrote that 'In my opinion the main cause of the prevailing and heavy desertion is to be traced to the fear of the soldiers that they will fall ill, and then be virtually buried alive in one of our overcrowded hospitals' (Anon, 1884, 148).

Desertion was itself a characteristic evil of eighteenth-century armies. It was certainly known in peacetime garrisons, but the opportunities naturally multiplied on campaign. Desertion could destroy an individual regiment outright, or undermine an entire army, like that of the Spanish in Italy in 1742, or the Prussian force in Bohemia in 1744 and 1778.

Small wonder that Frederick placed a list of fourteen precautions against desertion at the head of his *Principes Généraux de la Guerre* of 1748. Among the accepted remedies were to keep the soldiers busy, to attend to their needs, to keep them under heavy supervision, but also to get to know the character and circumstances of the individuals, if necessary by planting 'confidential and artful' informants among the ranks (*Reglement für die sämmentliche-Kaiserlich-Königlich Infanterie*, Vienna 1759, 58). Punishment by itself was no deterrent:

> Desertion is an illness which can be cured only by depriving soldiers of the opportunity. . . . I have seen several hangings of men who were due to go on leave in a fortnight. . . .
> Desertion is so enticing that when a deserter is strung up, someone else will almost invariably make off on the same day. (Ligne, 1795–1811, I, 186).

Desertion became something of an institution in its own right, and the case of the authorities was weakened because they so often proclaimed amnesties, and because so many unscrupulous captains bribed soldiers to come over to them from other companies or regiments. These 'interior' fugitives were called *Deserteurs* in Austria, and *billardeurs* or *rouleurs* in France, but they were a special characteristic of the Spanish army where 'most of the soldiers have served since a very early age and know no other trade than the army' (Santa Cruz, 1735–40, III, 91).

What the Austrians termed *Ueberläufer* were men who took the more drastic step of going over to the enemy. These too had an established place in the eighteenth-century scheme of things. You did what you could to encourage troops to leave the enemy ranks, and you sent brave troops from your own army in the guise of deserters in order to spy out the land or convey false messages.

The most circumstantial account of a genuine and successful desertion comes from the pen of Ulrich Bräker, who escaped from the Prussian regiment of Itzenplitz in 1756. On the march through Saxony the officer kept the men under narrow surveillance, to the extent of observing the expression on their faces, but Bräker at last found his opportunity during the scrappy fighting on the Lobosch Hill towards the end of the battle of Lobositz. At first he sidled away cautiously, then he broke into a fast walk, and finally he made his escape at a run. He and the rest of the Prussian deserters were received by the Austrians, who gave them passes and travel money. Bräker and five others afterwards made up a party which journeyed to Regensburg:

> It was already evening when we marched out of Prague. Before long we climbed a hill, from where we had an incomparable view over the whole royal city. We were entranced to see how the welcome sunlight gilded the countless points of the towers, all clad in copper. . . . I drank in the scene, but otherwise my only desire was to return to my house, to my own folk, to my Anneli (Bräker, 1852, 155–6).

Together the exhausion, disease and desertion commonly deprived an army of about one-fifth of its strength in the course of a campaign. Small wonder that Clausewitz counted marching as one of the active principles of destruction, or that Santa Cruz advocated striking a blow when an army was exhausted by miles spent on the road in adverse weather (Santa Cruz, 1735–40, X, 88–9).

The management of the campaign

COMMISSARIES AND DRIVERS

In all periods of history there has been a great difference between the wartime and peacetime conditions of an army. In the eighteenth century the contrast was more than usually extreme, for the outbreak of war summoned into being institutions and functions which had existed during the peace only in a rudimentary form, or which had not existed at all.

To some extent the armies lived off the country in time of war, as we have seen, but the supply of the basic rations, as well as remounts for the cavalry, and clothing and equipment was managed by commissary officials and private contractors. Some of these men became significant personages in their own right, like Parîs-Duverney who influenced French strategy in the Seven Years War, and who trained up a considerable number of relations and young men in this specialised trade. Two further French officials, the provisions contractor Bourgade and the bread supplier de Peyre, won golden opinions for the skill they displayed in the same war. The American Congress looked more to bureaucratic safeguards, and on 14 April 1778 it passed a number of resolutions which were designed to keep its commissaries under strict control. Epaphroditus Thompson tells us that he had to lodge a bond of 10,000 dollars with the Treasury Office, and that he received in return a commission of 1 per cent on the purchases of livestock which he made for the American forces:

> During the 542 days I was with the army . . . I received alive and delivered slaughtered or dressed for the use of the army 3,019,554 pounds of beef, 40,275 pounds of mutton, 18,639 pounds of pork [and] 19,913 pounds of fat. Also, I received and delivered alive 3,257 beef cattle, 657 sheep, and 35 fat hogs. (Dann, 1980, 371)

In general, however, the officials and contractors were associated with lack of principle and unbridled corruption. Many of them were the product of notoriously sharp and entrepreneurial families, or were shameless upstarts like the Austrian ex-valet Koschinna 'von' Freudenthal. Frederick of Prussia took it for granted that his commissaries were criminals, and on 28 January 1778 the Silesian minister of state von Hoym (who was himself a corrupt individual) received the following communication:

> His Majesty in person will draw up an Instruction whereby you will regulate the conduct of these people, who in the last war [the Seven Years War] devoted themselves exclusively to theft and the most unholy oppressions. When these men are taken

on they are to be told that they had better behave themselves honestly, otherwise His Majesty will have them all nailed up like vermin. (Preuss, 1832–4, IV, 197).

In Russia, the scandals reached further imto the substance of the army, for the commissaries of the Supply Department were uniformed military officers. Langeron wrote:

For two years a certain Major Petr Nartov was commissary of my regiment. . . . A more despicable and villainous individual it would be difficult to find. He already had two or three crimes on his conscience . . . he cheated openly at gambling, and yet he was entrusted with administering a considerable district (which he bought for himself at St Petersburg) as well as the management of huge sums of money. In the course of those two years I saw how he proceeded to rob the official funds with total impudence and lack of shame. Finally, when he had accomplished this task, he turned his attention to me and made off with several thousand roubles which I had left lying on a table. And still, as commissaries go, he must be reckoned one of the more honest members of that profession. (Langeron, 1895, 151)

Why were such phenomena so widespread? The opportunities for fraud were almost unlimited in this primitive period in the history of public administration, when individuals were left to manage great wealth in money and supplies without bureaucratic control. The fighting officers were children in such matters, and they were inclined to take the commissaries at their word (Guibert, [1772], 1804, II, 113). At the same time something more was involved than criminality. A wholly honest contractor or commissary (like a wholly honest waiter in a restaurant) would probably not have been very good at his work, for he would have lacked flair and motivation in his trade, and been deficient in some very necessary skills of manipulation. Von Hoym in Silesia certainly feathered his own nest, but he was also complimented by Frederick for the ability with which he assembled supplies for the new war against the Austrians in the summer of 1778. Similar ambiguities were linked with the name of the French commissary Foulon, who managed to evade prosecution over the course of forty years of public service:

Even now it is not possible to speak confidently about the

honesty of Foulon. All that we can and must agree is that his facility at his work, his agreeable appearance and his resourceful imagination all ensured him a useful place at the right hand of the ministers of the various departments. (Montbarey, 1826–7, I, 69).

If this had been a book about the art of war, and not the experience of war, we would have been compelled to follow a lengthy detour to explore the way in which the provisions were gathered and transported to the army. As it is, the lack of eyewitness accounts leaves us with very little to say. Humble folk like waggon drivers occasionally drew attention to themselves by running away from battles or causing traffic jams at bridges, but they scarcely emerge as individuals. Probably the single exception is the testimony of William Burnett, who was a driver for the American forces in the War of Independence. It is a pathetic story. As a young lad Burnett ran away from servitude to a master, but he found that he had merely changed one condition of near-slavery for another:

> He cannot recollect the names of many of the places that he was at during his term of service, as he was kept very close to his team and knew but little else, only what related to them. He hardly ever knew when he started where he was going till he arrived at the place of loading, and when he received his loading, he knew not where he had to take it, as the wagon master did not allow the wagoners to question him, and it seldom happened that the wagon guards knew more than the wagoners. (Dann, 1980, 373).

His single experience of combat was as an observer. A noise of clashing metal happened to draw him to a field, where he saw English and American cavalrymen hewing away at each other. He gripped a little pine tree, and he was trembling so violently that the whole bush shook. His one wholly agreeable memory was that of the old-time courtesy of George Washington, 'and will never forget while he retains his memory the polite bow that the general made to the poor wagoners as he passed them' (Dann, 1980, 373).

THE OFFICERS OF THE STAFF

We move to altogether higher circles to make the acquaintance of the officers who stood closest to the persons of the commanding general on campaign. These gentry were of two kinds – the commander's private circle of aides-de-camp, and men who represented the emerging profession of staff officer.

'An aide-de-camp is an officer who serves with a general, to carry his orders wherever is necessary' (d'Authville, 1756, 6). The classic aide-de-camp was young, pretty, high-born and mounted on a fast horse. He and his kind had formed part of the military families of generals for centuries, and they functioned as the equivalent of the vast signals apparatus of armies today.

Some of the aides-de-camp, like Frederick's favourite *Flügeladjutant* von Oppen, were experienced and dedicated officers. However this post also exercised a powerful appeal for well-connected young gentlemen who wished to escape the hard daily grind of regimental duties. Rochambeau affected to scorn the crowd of aides-de-camp he discovered in the suite of Clermont in the Netherlands in 1747, and yet his own expeditionary corps to America in 1780 was accompanied by thirty-eight officers of the same kind, and most of them owed their appointments to favouritism.

Le Rouge noted that noblemen naturally gravitated to the general's suite.

but these young people are the last folk I would use to convey orders on a day of battle. Here are the reasons. The desire for glory all too often induces them to stop on the way, so as to fight at the head of some unit or other. They seldom have any conception of the confusion which can be caused by altering just a single word in the orders entrusted to them. Finally they are incapable of judging the state of the troops they find at their destination, and therefore of making an appropriate report to their general on their return. (Le Rouge, 1760, 8).

The staff proper had much more lowly origins, for it had consisted of nothing more than the men who had toured towns and villages, chalking signs on the doors of the houses they selected as lodgings for the higher officers. This was the literal meaning of the terms Quartermaster-General, *Generalquartiermeister* and *Maréchal-Général des Logis de l'Armée*.

The quartermaster-general and his assistants naturally performed the same duties in camp, where they chose the sites for the generals' tents. In the course of time they took over responsibility for determining the place of the camp itself, then the routes between one camp and the next, and ultimately for everything to do with movement and the working-out of orders.

With minor variations, the staffs of field armies in the first half of the eighteenth century had a nearly identical structure. At the head was the quartermaster-general, who was now a general in his own right. A general-intendant was responsible for organising supply, a general-treasurer saw to the disbursement of monies, and an adjutant-general kept up the lists of the strength of the army and wrote out and issued orders. The Prussian *Capitaine des Guides* and the Austrian *Wegemeister* procured reliable guides. Brigade majors were effectively the chiefs of staff of the individual generals in the army.

Certain skills and activities were peculiarly the concern of the staff and the officers who reported to them. Written communications were much more satisfactory than verbal ones, and

> on this account every officer must carry with him a writing tablet, or one or more sheets of white paper and a pencil. He must train himself to compose reports and make effective use of these materials, whether on foot or horseback. Without bothering with titles or other formalities, he must enter the place, date and time, and proceed to add a concise but accurate review of what he thinks the enemy intentions might be, and what he himself proposes to do. (Wissel, 1784, 135).

The great point in organising marches was to divide the army into as many columns as was consonant with safety, so as to take advantage of all the available routes and provisions, and to prevent the troops from becoming strung out at great length along the axis of movement. The appropriate *Marsch-Zettel* was worked out by the staff, and specified the composition of the advance guard and the order of the regiments in each column.

Routes and camp sites could rarely be determined from the available maps, and the staff had to make its own intensive studies of the ground. Military itineraries were a useful exercise on such occasions, and a typical extract might read

> The village of . . . is at nineteen hours' marching distance from our camp. It is situated in a wide plain and contains 220 houses. On the southern side it is enclosed by very thick hedges, and on the other sides by fences and garden walls. The village is divided into two equal parts by a stream which is nine or ten

feet wide. The church is well and strongly built, and the cemetery is surrounded by a stout wall, behind which we could draw up three battalions on a depth of four ranks. (Bonneville, 1762, I, 51).

New maps were compiled with pencil, pen or brush, using conventional symbols. Contours were not yet in use to represent elevations, and

the best way of showing the smallest and most exact details of the hills, and at the same time of giving some idea of their height, is to draw them with a pen (this work demands long practice before one acquires the necessary facility, and here the French engineers and geographers lead the rest of Europe)... the blacker the hills are hatched in, the steeper and the higher they are supposed to be. Towards the valley or the foot of the hill the pen strokes must be diminished almost imperceptibly. (Pirscher, 1775, 26–7. See also Bourcet, 1875, 2–3).

It is easy to comprehend why the old warrior aristocracy of Europe was unwilling to apply itself to this kind of labour.

At the beginning of our period the training for the staff was entirely a matter of experience. The Marquis de Puységur (1655–1743), who set standards for chiefs of staff throughout Europe, began his apprenticeship when he was made a regimental *aide-major*, a post which involved him in processing all the orders of the regiment. In 1690 he was attached for the first time to field armies as *maréchal-général des logis*, but he was aware that he was short of the necessary expertise and that a long period of self-instruction still lay ahead of him.

The old-time staffs had some impressive feats to their credit, as witness the French offensive in the Netherlands in 1748, or that of the Prussians in Bohemia in 1757. On each of these occasions the attacking columns began the march on a wide frontage, then swiftly coalesced into a single striking force.

However a number of officers began to urge that staff work must be put on a regular footing, with rules to determine 'the clear and simple setting-out of every order, every disposition and every instruction and every plan and project'. A systematic training should also be made available, for otherise it was impossible to find expert chiefs of staffs and assistants to provide for the army at the beginning of a war (Darut de Grandpré, 1787, II, 52, 54).

The first of the modern staffs was founded in Austria by Lieutenant-General Franz Moritz Lacy on 20 February 1758. He assembled and trained the necessary personnel, worked out the paths for the transmission of orders, and formed units of staff dragoons, jägers, infantry and pioneers to protect the officers of the staff and facilitate their work in various ways. Lacy was able to send skilled officers to assist every detached general, and not just the commander-in-chief, and he perpetuated the Austrian staff in cadre form after the close of the Seven Years War.

The progress of the rest of Europe was highly uneven. In Frederick's Prussia the nominal titles of the staff officers signified little, for the king sought to control everything in person, and his real interest was in the troops of the line.

Prince Ferdinand of Brunswick was a Prussian general, but he escaped the supervision of Old Fritz as the independent commander of the allied army in West Germany in the Seven Years War, and he evolved a very effective routine of staff work. He first discussed his plans with his private secretary, the civilian Christian Heinrich Philipp von Westphalen:

> Having left his office the prince determined that the army would make such and such a march, or take up such and such a camp. He then summoned his quartermaster-general, so as to discuss the details of the march, the actual position of the camp, and the other main provisions which had to be made. When questions arose concerning supply, the artillery or other specialised matters, the prince was careful to hear the chiefs of all these departments, so as to learn what could or could not be done. The outcome of all these deliberations was afterwards put together in the office in a general scheme, which was transmitted to the general-adjutants, who used it as a basis for the necessary orders and instructions. These or other trustworthy adjutants were then chosen for special tasks, and so from one hand to the next the whole plan was worked out to the tiniest detail. (Mauvillon, J., 1794, II, 350–1).

One of the veterans of Ferdinand's staff, Friedrich Wilhelm Bauer, went in 1769 to reform the Russian staff, which had first been set up six years earlier. The new staff worked very effectively in the campaigns against the Turks in 1770–4, but the work of Bauer was not sustained after the peace, for Catherine the Great was more interested in the society of her young and decorative aides-de-camp than in encouraging senior German staff officers.

In France the cause of professionalism was championed by Marshal Maillebois and General Crémilles in the War of the Austrian Succession, and by G. L. Le Rouge (*Le Parfait Aide-de-Camp*, Paris, 1760) who assailed the amateurism of the traditional noble aides-de-camp during the Seven Years War. Another skilled military topographer, Pierre Bourcet, opened a staff school at Grenoble in 1764, and two years later he created the embryo of a permanent general staff. These pioneers drew down the anger of entrenched interests which maintained that the authority of the commander-in-chief was under attack:

> The commander of the army must be the one who composes his general staff. Since he shoulders the whole responsibility for the army and is answerable for its success, it is only right – indeed it is for the good of the service – that he must be free to choose his associates and assistants. It is in his own interest to prefer men on whose ability he can safely rely. (Saint-Germain, 1779, 230–1).

The war minister Saint-Germain proceeded to abolish the remnants of Bourcet's staff in 1776.

The defenders of professional staff work nevertheless kept up their battle, and they were rewarded when a new French staff was established in 1783. From the beginning it drew its personnel from a wide social range. Nine of its officers became generals under the Revolution or the Empire, and six among the émigré forces or in the army of the Restoration.

Where the French led clearly and consistently was in the way armies were put together. Old feudal relationships were predominant in the conventional organisation of armies, where there was no permanent intermediate authority between the commander in chief and the individual regiments, and where generals as a result had no settled commands. In some armies the orders of battle had to be remade almost daily, to conform with the fads and prejudices of the generals. Locations and assignments were also in a state of constant flux, and the exhausted troops had to drag themselves from one end of the army to the other, so as to undergo inspections or make up detachments. Meanwhile all the commotion gave the enemy ample notice of what was going on.

Marshal Belle-Isle proposed a system of permanent commands as early as 1752. He developed his ideas in a correspondence with the Comte de Mortaigne, who went to Germany in 1758 as *maréchal-général des logis*. Marshal Clermont became convinced of the merits of this principle, and so did the gifted Marshal Broglie, who reconstituted the army accordingly at the outset of the campaign of 1760, reorganising it into two divisions of cavalry and four divisions of infantry. Every division was ready to move off as a formed body:

> All the rest of the army was left in peace, and even remained unaware that the other divisions had departed. They were the equivalent of miniature armies, each with its own general, its own staff, and its own means of subsistence, and they were free to take up whatever positions best suited their tactical advantage. This experience was also a magnificent education for the lieutenant-generals! (Ray, 1895, 172–3).

Moreover the division for the first time established a stable relationship between the soldiers and officers on the one hand, and the generals on the other. The latter, as Mortaigne had anticipated in 1758, were 'forced to live alongside their officers, and in a military style, instead of living by themselves and in their own luxurious society' (Dussauge, 1914, 285). We can already taste the flavour of Napoleonic campaigning.

The Russian field army was formed into divisions in 1768 for a war against the Turks, and the divisions were retained as a permanent feature after the subsequent peace in 1774. Such was not the case in the French army after the Seven Years War. However the advantages of the new formations had been clearly established, and the use of divisions on the strategic scale was explored by Pierre Bourcet in his memorandum *Principes de la guerre de montagnes*, which was compiled for his staff school at Grenoble and sent to the war ministry in 1775. Ultimately, in the Revolutionary and Napoleonic period the system of divisions became the means of controlling forces far larger than the 50,000 men which had been considered the effective maximum in the middle of the eighteenth century (see p. 18).

THE ACTIVITY OF THE COMMANDER

There was a limit to what it was proper for a leader to delegate to his associates. For a start, all the old-soldier instincts of the commander in chief were needed to evaluate the worth of the available intelligence. 'For that reason, no commander should think himself too grand to enter into conversation with a peasant, a miller, a forester or other men of the same kind' (Bessel, 1778, 16).

Experienced generals were aware that a man who wished to please, or one who was bent on revenge or booty at the expense of his former master, was likely to represent a particular route as easier than it really was. Agricultural labourers were also inclined to give over-optimistic reports, because they assumed that a path that was accessible to a peasant could also be used by an army. In fact

> the best men for guides are people whose condition or trade encourages them to seek out new or hidden routes, such as partisan leaders from earlier wars, huntsmen, shepherds, drovers, or, in a number of countries, the local bandits or the officials who are responsible for tracking them down. (Zanthier, 1778, 47)

Force or blackmail might be used if the local people were of the opposing religious party, or otherwise disaffected from you. The Saxon Wends suddenly discovered a command of German when Frederick had them beaten in 1760, and the same monarch recommended an expedient which he himself conceded to be cruel,

> that is, you take a prosperous citizen who has a wife, children and house, and you assign him an intelligent fellow who is disguised as a servant. . . . You make the citizen take him on as his coachman, and repair to the enemy camp so as to seek redress of the violence which he suffers at your hands. You threaten to cut the throats of his wife and children and plunder and burn his house, if he fails to bring your man back after their stay in the enemy camp. (*Principes Généraux* [1748], Frederick, 1846–57, XXVIII, 47–8).

Some of the best spies were clerks at enemy headquarters. Double spies were also extremely useful, like the Italian who lured the Austrians and Saxons to their defeat at Hohenfriedeberg in 1745, though their loyalty had to be tested with some care.

A sharp faculty of *coup d'oeil* (see p. 140) was of great service to the general when he was on reconnaissance. These rides occupied many of his waking hours, and the histories of the wars were replete with sorry stories of mistakes or omissions in this vital activity. At Luzzara (1702) the Duc de Vendôme contrived to run into an Austrian army on a seemingly open plain, because he had not appreciated that the enemy had made an overnight crossing of the Po and ranged themselves behind a dyke. The Duke of Cumberland did not notice that his right flank at Hastenbeck (1757) was open to a march over the Obensburg ridge. In the following year the far more able Ferdinand of Brunswick examined the terrain at Krefeld from the church tower of St Tönis, but failed to see the obstructive ditch at Berschelsbaum.

As recommended by authorities like Puységur, Frederick and Scharnhorst, the basic procedure was to ride from one piece of high ground to the next, and keep yourself orientated with the help of map and telescope and whatever local guides were at hand. Frederick had an excellent eye for commanding ground, and it is remarkable how many of his standpoints in Central Europe in the Seven Years War are now occupied by radar stations or batteries of anti-aircraft missiles.

The reconnaissance parties were usually small, and the effectiveness of the operation frequently depended on the skill and intelligence of the escorting troops. The French reconnaissances in the Seven Years War were generally poor, since the cuirassiers and dragoons considered such work beneath their dignity and the French hussars were of miserable quality. The hussars of the Austrians and Prussians were much better at their trade, and the Austrians in addition created specialised units of staff infantry and cavalry (see p. 180).

The typical main road in the eighteenth century was a network of wandering tracks, complete with short-cuts and detours which had been carved out by vehicles and travellers over the years. The artillery and baggage needed the best possible surface, but the main requirement for the infantry was for enough space on the road and the ground on either side to permit the troops to march on platoon or divisional frontages. All the time the commander was alert for traces of the enemy: 'The tracks of men, horses, pack animals and carts . . . have characteristic features. If, on a normally busy road, nobody is to be seen, you may deduce that the enemy has detained all the travellers, and that he has in mind some important enterprise which demands great secrecy' (Saxe [1732], 1877, 211).

Old officers knew that woods and forests were often less impenetrable than they appeared to be. The Prince de Ligne writes:

> When you see them from a distance, and they are held by infantry, it is easy to imagine that the vegetation is very thick and that the troops are unassailable. The Zieten Hussars once taught me differently, when I saw them charging through one of these so-called forests, cutting down our brave Warasdiner Croats at every pass. (Ligne, 1795–1811, II, 65).

In western Germany in the Seven Years War the only forested areas which proved to be genuinely impassable were the Harz Mountains and the Thüringer Wald (Bourcet 1875, 23–4).

Rivers could be passed by means of permanent bridges, and at suitable places by pontoons or fords. The Cossacks used to find their passages by extending themselves in line 15 or 20 paces apart, and sounding the bottom with their lances. The presence of a ford might also be detected by the direction of old cart tracks. Sandy and muddy bottoms deteriorated under the passage of troops, and regard also had to be paid to both the velocity and the depth of the water, for a fast current made a depth of as little as 2½ feet almost impassable for infantry. However something of the force could be diminished by making the cavalry cross immediately upstream.

At Prague (1757) Old Fritz felt too ill to carry out a personal reconnaissance, and after a sketchy view of the ground Schwerin and Winterfeldt launched the left wing of the Prussian infantry into what turned out to be a zone of drained fish ponds, where the troops stuck fast:

> Marshy meadows deserve at least as much attention as swamps. In summertime they might appear eminently practicable, and then turn out to be incapable of bearing a column of cavalry. You must examine them with care, and be invariably suspicious of meadows where the grass is high and tussocky, and where there are patches of greenish-yellow moss. (Bourcet, 1875, 22).

Bourcet, who was the foremost topographer of hill country, pointed out that mountain ridges nearly always had a perfectly good track running along the top, and that by making for the high ground you could overcome most of the difficulties associated with broken terrain (Bourcet, 1875, 26–9).

> For the occupying troops, hills give commanding views, and offer good protection against artillery fire, and ricochet in particular. . . . These, however, are only what you might call defensive advantages. On the other side the enemy suffers less when attacking uphill than on level ground, since fire coming from above is much less effective and accurate than fire on a horizontal plane. (Zanthier, 1778, 107).

When an action seemed likely, it was advisable to check whether the neighbouring villages could be put into a state of defence. The villages in Central Europe were usually too open or too lightly built to be of any use, but in Flanders and Italy the massive walls and embankments made the farm enclosures the equivalent of citadels.

The skills and experience of the commander were tested to the utmost when he sought to bring together his knowledge of the ground with what he could see of the enemy. Saxe and Frederick were among the leaders who set great store by *indices* which might betray the intentions of the foe. Dust itself had certain qualities, when seen from a distance of several miles. A generalised cloud of dust usually signified that the enemy foragers were about. The same kind of dust, without any sighting of the foraging parties, suggested that the sutlers and the baggage were being sent to the rear and that the enemy were about to move. Dense and isolated towers of dust showed that the columns were already on the march.

The same landscape appeared quite differently, according to whether the sunlight came from your front or back. With the naked eye the muskets and bayonets of the enemy could be seen glistening in the sun at more than a mile: 'if the rays are perpendicular, it means the enemy is coming at you; if they are broken and infrequent, he is retreating'. (Saxe [1732], 1877, 135–6).

At night-time 'it is well known, that when an object is darkened by the interposition of a cloud between it and the moon, as the cloud withdraws, the object seems to move' (An Old Officer, 1760, 176). The enemy camp fires presented a picture of great beauty, and on a clear night they appeared to merge with the stars. It was, however, a standard ruse to leave parties to tend the fires while the main force moved elsewhere, and Field-Marshal Daun caught Frederick off his guard in this way at Hochkirch (1758). Two years later Old Fritz repaid the Austrians in the same coin at Liegnitz.

In fine weather large bodies of men could be made out with a telescope at a distance of several miles, and they became evident to the unassisted eye at about one mile. Infantry could be distinguished from cavalry at about 1,900 paces (1,300 yards), and at 750 paces you discovered the movements of individuals and the colour of uniforms. A variety of further information became available at these close distances:

> When you are encamped near the enemy, and you hear a great deal of firing in the enemy camp, you can expect to have a battle on your hands the next day, for the soldiers are firing and cleaning their muskets. When, again, the two armies are under arms and in close proximity, and you see the soldiers changing their shirts, you will certainly be attacked, because the troops have the habit of putting their shirts on top of one another, so as not to lose them during the action. (Saxe [1732], 1877, 135).

THE ISOLATION OF COMMAND

The commander in chief faced the burden of command alone. His major-generals were engaged in hard executive work throughout the campaign, for they had to make sure that their brigades moved and encamped in an orderly fashion. Day-by-day the lieutenant-generals and the full generals had less to do, and so the commander might occasionally summon them to headquarters to participate in a council of war. However, authorities like Prince Eugene and Frederick the Great set their face against such gatherings, for gloomy sentiments usually prevailed, and councils of war were the characteristic resort of commanders who were fearful of responsibility.

A fortunate commander might enjoy a measure of companionship and truly helpful advice. Marshal Broglie had the support of his brother the Comte de Broglie, who was his *maréchal-général des logis*. In the enemy army Prince Ferdinand of Brunswick looked to his secretary Westphalen:

> The prince came to take command of an army in which he did not know a single person, and where he had no relation of any kind. It was scarcely surprising that he invested his full confidence in a man of outstanding ability, and whose loyalty

and devotion to him he had already known and tested. (Mauvillon, J., 1794, II, 346)

Broglie and Ferdinand nevertheless reserved the difficult decisions for themselves, and the hardest of the hard choices was whether or not to give battle.

6

The battle

The most brilliant of all military actions, the
consequences of which frequently determine the
destruction or aggrandisement of states. Battles are
the making of a conqueror, and more than any
other deed they endow him with the reputation of
being a great captain.

(Quincy, 1726, VIII, 51)

The option for battle

By a battle the eighteenth century understood a general action
involving most of the frontage of rival armies. The issue was usually
decided in a matter of a few hours, and if it went very badly for
the loser he would forfeit his artillery and baggage, along with his
reputation and a great tract of territory.

Eighteenth-century military authors were fond of compiling elaborate lists of the reasons for giving or avoiding battle. It is rare to
find a writer who, in the nineteenth-century style, puts 'the hope of
victory' at the top of his table. When the idea of a knockout blow
appears at all, it is usually put some way down the column, and in
association with the notion of ending a war which, if it dragged on
much further, would actually prove more destructive than a bloody
but 'clean' battle (Frederick, *Principes Généraux* [1748], Frederick,
1846–57, XXVIII, 83. See also Turpin de Crissé, 1754, I, 381–2;
Grimoard, 1775, 10).

Everybody agreed that the worst kind of battle was one into
which you were forced against your will. However you could not
evade battle if the alternative was to lose one of your key fortresses,

like Turin for the Piedmontese and Prince Eugene in 1706, or Prague for the Austrians in 1757.

In less extreme circumstances the question was reduced to identifying 'whether the advantages you would derive by winning, exceed in degree the damage you would sustain if you lost' (Turpin de Crissé, 1754, I, 382). This mechanical formula was widely accepted at the time, and it was cited by Field-Marshal Daun and Prince Henry of Prussia. In the event, the decision was usually against fighting,

> for the greatest generals refrain from giving battle, except for urgent reasons. There can be no guarantee of victory, even after the finest possible preparations have been made. Some small blunder, some unavoidable accident are enough to lose you the encounter. (Saxon *Dienst-Reglement*, 1753, quoted in Jähns, 1889–91, III, 2, 031).

Tempting alternatives were at hand, for 'to capture the enemy's convoys, and deprive him of the means of subsistence, is tantamount to winning without fighting . . . this kind of war . . . is beyond doubt the most useful, refined and scientific of all' (Turpin de Crissé, 1754, I, 286).

When the authors considered the case of a general who, despite everything, had decided to commit his army to battle, they usually advised him to take the offensive. The attacking party had the technical advantage of being able to concentrate his forces on a chosen point, as Frederick taught military Europe in the Seven Years War (e.g. Belle-Isle to Contades, 10 July 1758, quoted in Dussauge, 1914, 304). The moral advantage was also with the attacker. The act of moving forward was considered to be cheering to the soldiers, and when men began to fall the corpses and the wounded were left behind, whereas the defenders found that the casualties were piling up around them in a most distressing fashion.

Preparations

PLANS AND BRIEFINGS

The commander in chief conducted his final reconnaissance in an atmosphere of considerable tension. Many of the troops were able to see him talking for the last time with his senior generals, and they knew that their survival hung on what was being debated (Lojewsky,

1843, II, 41). Small miscalculations were now likely to be attended with terrible consequences:

> It is one thing to sit down at a writing table, and cold-bloodedly investigate what did happen, and what should have happened at a battle. It is something altogether different to draw up a scheme for a battle on the actual field, to put it into effect, and to improve and amend it when all the passions are racing, and, if I may put it this way, human nature is on trial. (Tempelhoff, 1783–1801, I, 130)

Most probably the commander would follow convention and arrange to draw up his army in a first line, a second line and a reserve (see p. 200). He had to make certain that the battle frontage was in proportion to the strength of the army, so that the formations and units were neither jammed together nor separated by vulnerable gaps. The various arms of service were, if at all possible, to go into action on terrain which best suited their peculiar ways of fighting – the heavy artillery, for example, on low hills, or the cavalry on open ground. These requirements had to be reconciled with the principle of mutual support.

The next procedure was to work out the 'order of battle' and determine the make-up of the columns and their routes to the battlefield. In all of this the commander had to pay due regard to precedence and seniority in those semi-feudal armies (the details are explained in Bland, 1727, 252). At Campo Santo (1743) the Spanish right wing came under a surprise attack from the whole of the first line of the Austrian infantry. In this emergency Lieutenant-General Macdonnell brought up the Irish regiments of Irlanda and Hibernia from the rear, and

> when these regiments arrived he placed them to the right of the Spanish Guards. The Guards now raised a very ill-timed objection against the affront to their honour, and in order to satisfy them he had to leave an interval to signify that the new regiments stood outside the line proper. (Power, 1784, I, Part 2, 240).

This gap acted to the advantage of the Austrians, and was the occasion of some entirely unnecessary casualties.

The plan of battle also had to make provision for a number of important particulars. The teams of surgeons were allocated to their stations on the battlefield, where fires were made ready to advertise their presence. Every soldier received his full allowance of ammunition, and arrangements were made to send vehicles with reserve ammunition to where the fighting was expected to be heaviest. The soldiers might go into action wearing their knapsacks and haversacks, or be ordered to deposit them in rows on the ground, ready to be picked up after the battle.

Specific orders were sometimes issued to have the tents struck and packed away, but in the Russian and French armies the soldiers were in the habit of taking this matter into their own hands. At Krefeld (1758) the French camp was left standing until the afternoon, but then

> the love which every man naturally has for his own possessions induced the troops to strike their tents, load up their bundles and send the whole lot in the direction of Viecheln, which was the location of headquarters . . . the troops set to work without orders, and they did so only in the nick of time, for while they were still loading the baggage the enemy cannon shot began to roll through some parts of the camp site. (Mopinot de la Chapotte, 1905, 190)

Wise commanders made contingency plans for a possible retreat, and equally sagely made sure that the troops knew nothing about them.

In the Seven Years War the French and Austrian staffs were in the habit of working up the battle plan into elaborate written *Dispositions*, which were distributed among the generals on the day or night before the action. Mercoyrol de Beaulieu describes how the instructions were made known to the column of Lieutenant-General Nicolay, near Minden on the misty night of 31 July/1 August 1759:

> Our colonel, Monsieur Bréhant, told the officers of our regiment to ensure that the muskets were put under proper cover. This order was duly carried out. All the regimental tents were struck, with the single exception of the tent of our colonel. Here he received General Nicolay, together with as many of the officers as could squeeze in, for it was raining. A solitary candle provided the illumination when Nicolay made a few conversational remarks, then announced: 'Gentlemen, I must acquaint you with the battle orders, a copy of which has gone to the commander and guide of every column.' This order extended

over two and a half pages of large-format paper. (Mercoyrol de Beaulieu, 1915, 223–4)

It was, in fact, an example of excellent staffwork.

As we might have expected, Saxe and Frederick liked to manage their battles in their own style. Little bureaucratic preparation was needed for the French victories at Rocoux or Laffeldt, or for Frederick's combats in the early and middle period of the Seven Years War. The great men led their forces onto the field, made an appraisal of the ground and the enemy forces and issued a verbal briefing, after which everything proceeded according to well-established routines. The most circumstantial account of such a briefing comes from a royal page, who was present when Frederick addressed his commanders on the upper floor of the inn of Zlaté Slunce at Kolin (1757):

> The king announced to the assembled generals 'We must confine our attack to the enemy right flank, where they can oppose us on a frontage of only six or eight battalions. We march until our left wing reaches the Kolin stream, and then we proceed to roll up the enemy line and throw their right flank into their left, so that they will either end up in the marsh or lay down their arms. Our right flank must be held back so that if possible it does not hear a single enemy cannon shot, let alone sustain any casualties. Look, gentlemen, over there on the left you can see that large building or granary! Next to it is a little village and some ponds, and that's where our right wing must come to rest. If for any reason it has to move any further to the left, when our left wing attacks, it must still hold back, as I have just said. Gentlemen, if you do not understand I ask you to say so. I will not take it amiss, and I am happy to go over the plan again.' All the generals assured him that they had indeed understood, and Prince Moritz of Anhalt-Dessau added: 'Nobody can possibly fail to grasp it. It's so clear that nobody can go wrong'. (Duncker, 1876, 89–90)

These improvised and intuitive briefings failed to answer the conditions in the final campaigns of the Seven Years War, for the enemies of Frederick were becoming more expert, and the quality of the Prussian army was in decline. Frederick briefed his generals most carefully before the action at Burkersdorf (1762), and in the same year Prince Henry distributed a detailed *Disposition* before his attack at Freiberg.

Finally a touch of theatricality was not out of place. On the day before Rocoux (1746), Marshal Saxe arranged to have an actress announce the forthcoming battle from the stage at the close of a play. A personal harangue from the commander in chief was a physical impossibility in the eighteenth century, but he could still do a lot of good by riding along the columns, calling out to officers and soldiers he recognised (or pretended to recognise), and he could convey a message to the army as a whole through the medium of the senior officers when they dispersed after the briefing. Santa Cruz recommended that the commander should emphasise to the troops that they were fighting for their homes and families, and that good care would be taken of any widows or orphans, 'for soldiers are often demoralised by the thought that if they die, they will leave their wives and families under the hard necessity of having to beg for alms' (Santa Cruz, 1735–40, V, 252). This passage was almost certainly the inspiration for the famous 'Parchwitz Address' which Frederick delivered before the battle of Leuthen (1757).

MORALE

Ideally the troops went into battle after their weapons had undergone a careful inspection, and they themselves had passed a peaceful night and eaten well, 'for there can be no comparison between an army which is exhausted by a long march, and another which might be weaker in number but has enjoyed a rest' (Turpin de Crissé, 1754, I, 392). The Russians slept particularly well on the night before their victory at Gross-Jägersdorf (1757), and Andrei Timofeevich Bolotov recalled how

> a purple tint gradually suffused the horizon, foretelling a splendid day. The mist had set in heavily again before daybreak, but now it began to thin and the air became limpid and transparent. The sun, rising over the hills, had already illuminated the whole horizon when the sonorous signal of cannon fire broke our sweet slumbers and set the whole army in movement. (Bolotov, 1870–3, I, 517)

All too often, however, the last night was spent in conditions of extreme discomfort, with the troops bivouacking in the open, or executing the last stages of a forced march. If there was an opportunity to cook food there might be no chance to eat it, as was the experience of Wedel's corps at Paltzig (1759), when the Prussians had to pour away the steaming soup and stuff their half-cooked meat into haversacks. The Prussian defeat at Kolin (1757) was due in part to the heavy demands which Frederick had made on the troops before the action. It was the same story at Kunersdorf (1759), where on the evening before the battle the hot and still air carried the mournful sound of the bells of the village churches to the Prussian troops, who lay exhausted and despondent on the sandy ground:

> They were not lacking in courage. They were not stricken with fear, or anxious that they might lose the coming battle. Rather the cause of their mood was physical, for many of the regiments had been on the march for three weeks, during which they had contended with dust, heat, hunger and thirst, without enjoying a single day of rest on the endless road. When the body is spent and exhausted, this condition has a direct effect on the spirits. (Lojewsky, 1843, II, 254–5)

Few people who were present on the morning of a battle were exempt from feelings of agitation, however well they might be concealed. Soft or sensitive parts of the anatomy never felt more vulnerable. A man who wore a calm expression might give his inner sentiments away by the exaggerated attention he paid to adjusting his weapons and equipment. Personal rituals or long-forgotten religious beliefs now became a matter of urgent concern. Certain individuals were afflicted by a very clear presentiment that they would not survive the battle. Frederick and many other veterans had seen relations or friends overcome in this way, and they testified that the instinct was rarely wrong.

Among groups, the heightened powers of imagination and observation frequently became focused on omens. On the day of Prague (6 May 1757) a Prussian musketeer noted

> a large, tall crucifix standing by the wayside. A sizeable white dove was perched on the right arm, and it looked at us as we marched by, extending its neck but otherwise remaining motionless. It repeatedly turned its head to face the Austrians, as if to show us the way. The soldiers pointed to the dove and

cried out: 'This means we're going to be lucky today!' (Grosser Generalstab, 1901, I, Part 2, 54)

To a limited degree the sentiments of the soldiers were still capable of manipulation at this late stage. The troops might take their lead from the 'serene and cheerful' air of an officer (Bland, 1727, 144), and experienced leaders like the Prince de Ligne were alive to what a later age would call 'crowd psychology':

> Your demeanour, or a single word on your part, will make
> them shiver; another word will bring them back to life, or
> make them laugh. . . . You never hear greater merriment in a
> theatre than when the house is full, for crowds are easy to
> move, and then you can lead them as you wish, if you know
> their nature. This is a subject which is well worth our attention.
> You must give the impression that you have your task fully in
> hand, even when you do not. (Ligne, 1795–1811, II, 91)

Sieges were an accepted way of accustoming troops to musketry and artillery fire in controlled conditions (see p. 292). In the normal course of campaigns, however, the patrolling, skirmishing and other small-scale actions were left to the light troops (see p. 163), and so when the first battle of a war arrived the whole of the rest of the army might be 'new and inexperienced' (Saint-Germain, 1779, 176). After the success of his advance guard at Leuthen, Frederick went to the trouble of leading the prisoners past the columns of the main army so as to give confidence to the soldiers. On the other hand

> nothing can destroy the morale of an army before a battle more
> completely than to have its forward detachments surprised or
> beaten by an approaching enemy. Then the beaten troops stream
> back to the camp in some disorder, with bloody faces and
> mutilated arms, spreading fear and panic in their path. (Warnery,
> 1785–91, III, 336)

Cavalry certainly benefited from previous exposure to combat, but the infantry fought in a more mechanical way and providing the foot soldiers were adequately trained there was something to be said for preserving them from the risk of action until the day of the big battle. ' "What a pity!" some officers say. "The only troops we have are recruits!" As for me, I love the recruits. They do not know what danger is, and they stand up manfully in their first battle' (Ligne,

1795–1811, I, 167–8. See also Warnery, 1785–91, II, 33–4; Retzow, 1802, II, 55; Savory, 1966, 180). Unfortunately it was impossible to arrange in advance for a bloodless initiation like that of the Russians at Gross-Jägersdorf, where they came under two totally ineffective Prussian volleys at the outset of the battle, and were persuaded as a result that they were invulnerable.

The opening of the battle

THE BAPTISM OF FIRE

The first sight of the enemy was often enough to terminate the unfocused anxiety which had afflicted the armies before the battle.

> During the action, every apprehension and the idea of danger forsakes the mind, which becomes more animated and determined the nearer the time of attack approaches. Every soldier feels inspired with an impatient ardour, as if he conceived the fate of the battle would be decided by the heel of his musket, or the point of his bayonet. (Anburey, 1969, I, 337–8).

A crackling of thousands of musket shots carried back to the main forces from the first encounter of the light troops or the advance guard. The heavy artillery meanwhile moved forward, and after some ranging shots the gunners opened a general cannonade, during which the sound of one discharge merged with the next, and the cannon balls bounded over the field as if somebody had upset a tray of tennis balls. When Frederick's artillery opened fire at Zorndorf (1758) it appeared to the Russians

> as if heaven and earth had fallen in on themselves. The roar of the artillery and musketry swelled in a most intimidating and terrible fashion, and from the scene of the attack a thick cloud of smoke enveloped the whole of our army as it stood in square. . . . The cannon shot were screaming ceaselessly through the air, and then they suddenly began to plunge into the wood which surrounded us. Many of our soldiers climbed the trees to get a better view of the action, and some of them fell dead or wounded at my feet. A young lad . . . said something to me, walked away and within fourteen paces he

was killed while I was still looking at him. In the same minute a Cossack and his horse were struck down at my side. (Täge, 1864, II, 296)

Early in the battle the attacking army sometimes found that it had to evict the enemy from defended villages, where the troops were holding out in loopholed houses and behind walls or hedges. Churches were best defended not from the building itself, but from the surrounding cemetery walls, and 'those of brick are best, for they withstand cannon fire better than those of stone, and they are less inclined to throw out flying splinters' (O'Cahill, 1787, 153). The fights for such villages often became the most bitter actions of the whole battle, for the enclosures offered 'defensible space' which the troops were reluctant or unable to leave. The battles at Kesselsdorf (1745), Rocoux (1746), Laffeldt (1747) and Hochkirch (1758) all opened with a contest for villages.

FROM COLUMN INTO LINE

The armies approached the battlefield in lengthy columns, each of which corresponded to an element of the intended lines of battle. At this stage of the action it appeared at Prague (1757) and Brandywine Creek (1777) that the ground was literally covered with troops. However, the most comprehensive descriptions of the approach to the field derive from the day of Rocoux (11 October 1746), when the French were advancing in twelve columns of infantry and eight of cavalry. Mercoyrol de Beaulieu had a good view from the column of the Prince de Clermont on the far right:

We could espy the whole length of the enemy line, as far as the irregularity of the terrain permitted, and our position was directly on their left flank. We stayed there motionless for nearly an hour, at the end of which we could see the royal army and a large number of columns snaking onto the immense plains under our gaze. We noticed many individuals passing from one column to the next, and it seemed that the various formations of infantry and cavalry were much concerned with keeping their heads in an even alignment. We could not see every single column, but those within our view came to repeated halts, and we found that everything was proceeding with great slowness. (Mercoyrol de Beaulieu, 1915, 64)

The preliminaries lasted for a couple of hours, for Marshal Saxe was making his usual reconnaissance (see p. 193), and during the interval the French soldiers amused themselves with horseplay, or talking and dancing with the girls who came out from Liège to sell them provisions. Finally 'a drum beat was taken up along the length of the army, and recalled everyone to their positions' (Montbarey, 1826–7, I, 32–3).

According to the conventional practice, columns were nothing more than a tool – an order of march whereby the platoons, tactical divisions or other sub-units reached the ground where they were to move by simultaneous wheels into line of battle (see p. 113). However, a notion of employing the column as an attacking formation in its own right was originated by the Chevalier de Folard in the 1720s (see p. 53), and developed by his countryman Joly de Maizeroy: 'The true strength of a unit consists in the thickness or depth of its files and in their cohesion and pressure' (Folard, 1727–30, I, vii).

The column as a battle formation never won wide acceptance in the Age of Reason. Those two great authorities Frederick and Saxe talked about it at Sans Souci after the War of the Austrian Succession, and they concluded that its narrow frontage and great depth made it singularly vulnerable to cross fire. Other critics pointed out that the column was deficient in firepower, and that it was impossible to imagine how soldiers somehow managed to step on each other's heads and shoulders to produce the magical 'shock'.

In fact the great majority of columns were created not by deliberate design, but by a herd-like instinct on the part of the soldiers. At Hochkirch (1758) and Maxen (1759) the Austrians made successful use of columns of deployed battalions, so as to deliver masses of troops at selected points of the field, but the most celebrated column of the period was that of the English at Fontenoy (1745), and it was formed purely as an accident, when the British were trying to break the French line between two strongpoints.

The compulsion to crowd together might conceivably have been of some utility to primitive men when they were faced by wolves or bears, but in the age of firearms it produced the dreaded 'bunching', which continues to be of concern to tacticians at the present day.

> Columns are the product of fear, and courage is needed to
> deploy them again. . . . I cannot recall an action when I did

not have to try to break up a multitude of such columns with blows with the flat of my sword, while my corporals were wading in with their sticks. (Ligne, 1795–1811, I, 20).

We return to the arrival of the columns on the field in the conventional style. There now ensued a critical moment when the columns of march, having reached their assigned positions, were wheeled by their component sub-divisions into line of battle. This manoeuvre was accomplished several hundred paces from the enemy, and could normally be disrupted only by the fire of heavy artillery. However, at Campo Santo (1743) the Austrians came into the view of the sharp-eyed Lieutenant-General Comte de Sayve, who commanded the right wing of the waiting Spanish:

> He was standing on foot near the Duke of Atrisco, who was at the head of the Carabiniers. Sayve kept a close eye on the enemy cavalry, and, when he saw that it had nearly reached the dyke, where it was supposed to make its quarter wheel into line . . . he uttered a mighty shout:
> 'Now is the time to attack!'
> 'Do you really think so?' enquired the Duke of Atrisco.
> 'Yes, for God's sake!'
> The Queen's Dragoons joined in the charge, and thanks to the speed of their native horses the Spanish cavalrymen caught the Austrians just when they were attempting to form line to meet them. (Power, 1784, I, Part 2, 240–1)

Assuming that the approach in columns and the wheel into line took place without interruption, the army proceeded to arrange itself in battle formation. The first line was the longest and the most powerful. The second line was stationed about 300 paces to the rear. This interval placed it beyond the reach of enemy small-arms fire, and provided enough space to allow movements and transfers of forces between the two lines to be effected without confusion.

The reserve was a potentially vital force which was positioned well to the rear of the second line. It gave moral as well as physical support to the rest of the army, as Saxe used to explain to his officers.

THE ADVANCE IN LINE

The primary advantage of the line was the weight of infantry fire which it could bring to bear, for, in a battle formation which was only two or three ranks deep, every infantryman had the capacity to make some use of his musket. In addition the linear formations permitted the heavy artillery to be established in rows of batteries, while the long lines of cavalry, which were usually extended on the wings, deterred the enemy from turning the flank of the army.

The great difficulty came when you tried to move the lines forward in any kind of order. Drawn up in three ranks, a single Prussian battalion was 214 paces wide, assuming that every pace was the equivalent of about 2 feet or one file of soldiers. A line of ten battalions amounted to no less than 2,260 paces, allowing ten intervals of 12 paces each for the battalion artillery. The frontages in other armies were roughly comparable (see p. 141). Well-drilled troops like the Prussians gained great tactical advantage from the regularity of their march in columns, and the accuracy of their wheelings into line, but 'once the battalions are completely deployed or extended in line these advantages come to an end. The Prussians find themselves embarrassed by the length of their formations, and they have to contend with undulations and delay' (Silva, 1778, 82). In the allied army of Prince Ferdinand of Brunswick in western Germany the experience was that

> the advance in line had to be an extraordinarily slow affair, if it was to proceed in any kind of order. We need only recall the example of the battle of Wilhelmesthal (1762), when the allied army took a good five hours to cover the equivalent of one hour's march. (Mauvillon, 1794, II, 281)

The advance in straight lines was in fact one of those things which are simple in concept, but very difficult and complicated to carry out in practice. Armies learned to follow the basic procedures which were worked out by Frederick the Great. The first rule was to 'select points of view for the wings. We must say, for example, that the right will align itself on that bell tower, and the left on that windmill' (*Principes Généraux* [1748], Frederick, 1846–57, XXVIII, 77). By keeping these landmarks in view, and regulating the ends of the wings accordingly, the generals and their staffs controlled the direction of the march of the army as a whole. The geographical points of view could be supplemented by reliable mounted aides-de-camp, who rode ahead along the chosen alignment to act as mobile markers – the *points de vue ambulants*. An ex-Prussian officer, Baron Johann Ernst Pirch, introduced the principles of the points of view to France, and their influence was shown in the Infantry Instructions of 1774 and 1775 and the full tactical Ordinance of 1776.

Like some kind of sacred flame, the assigned direction was communicated to the formations and units of the army. Within each brigade an individual squadron or battalion was designated the 'regulating' unit, upon which all the others conformed. In the Prussian army the regulating squadron was usually on the right, and the regulating battalion in the centre.

The commander of the regulating battalion selected a point of view of his own, so as to produce an axis of march parallel with that of the rest of the army. The battalion commander strode out 10 paces in front of the centre of the first rank, a colour party of two ensigns and two NCOs took position behind him, and together the battalion commander and the colour party formed a perpendicular to the front of the battalion. The battalion then marched forward, preserving the right angle as accurately as possible. A number of Prussian officers were said to have used little set squares for this purpose, and the Duke of Bevern once said jokingly that he was surprised that nobody had thought of fixing a compass to a soldier's back. The colour parties of the neighbouring battalions in turn took their alignment from that of the regulating battalion.

'The colour party is considered the keystone of the battalion. Every soldier marching to its right, must feel the pressure of the man to his left; every soldier marching to its left, must feel the pressure of the man to his right' (Berenhorst, 1798–9, I, 236). In addition to the physical pressure towards the centre of each unit, the soldiers looked out of the corners of their eyes in the same direction, so as to keep a visual impression of the alignment. Well-schooled men and horses developed an instinct for regularity, and the Prince de Ligne had a mount which was capable of aligning itself without any assistance.

Absolute silence was enjoined, and the infantry were commanded to keep their muskets shouldered, and not, as we might have expected, pointing at the foe:

In advancing towards the enemy, it is with great difficulty that the officers can prevent the men (but more particularly when they are fired at) from taking their arms, without orders, off from their shoulders, and firing at too great a distance. How much more difficult must it be to prevent their firing, when

they have their arms in their hands already cocked, and their
fingers on the triggers? I won't say it is impossible though I
look upon it to be almost so. (Bland, 1727, 80)

Here we must address ourselves for the first time to one of the
crucial questions of military history, namely how far the prescribed
drills really corresponded to what went on in combat. Something
that approached the perfection of the peacetime training did occasionally occur on the battlefield. Thus, when the regiment of Bevern
reached the crest at Kolin (1757), the Prussians saw a column
advancing against them from the Austrian second line 'in excellent
order, with the soldiers closed up man to man just as on the drill
square' (Prittwitz, 1935, 131). Such a happening was considered
noteworthy because it was so rare.

There were powerful obstacles in the way of an orderly advance
by formed lines. Slight checks in the leading rank of the cavalry were
transmitted with increasing force to the rear, and were capable of
bringing the horses at the back to a complete stand (Mottin de la
Balme, 1776, 30). Among the infantry, the step was very easily lost
through the effect of casualties, or obstructions like stones, holes or a
ploughed field: 'the majors shout "Close up!" The troops accordingly
close up towards the centre, which gradually collapses until the men
there are eight ranks deep . . . nobody who has been in action would
dispute this fact' (Saxe [1732], 1877, 32). The mechanical regularity
broke down altogether when bodies of troops had to be moved at
anything faster than a slow walk:

> When he sees the enemy the commander of the advancing force
> knows very well what kind of formation he should take up,
> and he has no need of points of view in order to open the combat
> in parallel or oblique alignment, as his imagination prompts
> him for better or worse. If, however, he loses time by correcting
> irregularities, a punishment will almost invariably be visited
> on his head. (Berenhorst, 1798–9, I, 221. See also Lossow, 1826,
> 242)

At Krefeld (1758) many French officers cursed the Marquis de Saint-
Peru for the deliberation with which he moved the brigade of
Navarre and the Grenadiers de France from the right wing to support
the left. The troops marched in step to the beat of the drum, and
arrived in rank and file – and too late. Veterans recalled how in the

War of the Polish Succession the reinforcements were moved almost at a run, with the swiftest men in the lead (Mercoyrol de Beaulieu, 1915, 184).

Forms of action

THE INFANTRY BATTLE

Shock action

The officers will take all proper opportunites to inculcate in the men's minds a reliance on the bayonet; men of their bodily strength and even a coward may be their match in firing. But the bayonet in the hands of the valiant is irresistible.

(Lieutenant-General Burgoyne, General Orders, 20 June 1777; Hadden, 1884, 74)

There is not probably an instance of modern troops being engaged in close combat; our tactics, produced by the introduction of firearms, are opposed to such a mode of action; we are dependent on the dexterous use of our firelock.

(Dalrymple, 1782, 113)

The employment of cold steel by infantry (like an orderly advance in line) was not unknown in the Age of Reason, but the well-authenticated instances are much rarer than might be supposed, and they are associated with specific circumstances. Here is an explanation of sorts for the contradiction between the quotations entered above.

Soldiers of 'hot' nations and certain crack troops undoubtedly had the elemental courage that was required to press home attacks sword-in-hand, like the Turks at Belgrade (1717), the Scots at Prestonpans (1745), Falkirk and Culloden (1746), some of the Austrian grenadiers at Prague (1757) and the Hungarian infantry regiment of Haller at Kolin (1757).

Among 'cold' troops of the line the bayonet was most likely to find employment when the combat was for some sort of defended position. Surprise attacks against fortifications were almost invariably carried out at night, when musket fire would have betrayed the design. Thus, in General Wayne's successful *coup de main* against the

English garrison in Fort Stony Point (15/16 July 1779) the front of the American column

> led with unloaded arms, relying solely on the use of the bayonet. As they approached the works, a soldier insisted on loading his piece – all was now a profound silence – the officer commanding the platoon ordered him to keep on; the soldier observed that he did not understand attacking with his piece unloaded; he was ordered not to stop, at his peril; he still persisted, and the officer instantly dispatched him. (Heath, 1901, 193. See also Wolfe, 1768, 53)

Likewise troops were known to resort to the bayonet in a full-scale battle when the fighting was for a fieldwork or a defended house, where the combatants were jammed together and the normal relationships of space did not apply. An inexperienced Prussian soldier found himself in the first line of the advance guard which stormed the Russian fortifications on the Mühl-Berge at Kunersdorf (1759):

> This young grenadier was accustomed to the drill of arms on the square, but not to making real employment of the bayonet. He advanced boldly enough to the entrenchment, but he could not bring himself to put his bayonet to deadly use against the Russians who were standing before him. Whereupon an officer, who had noticed his indecision, dealt him a heavy blow on the shoulder and yelled: 'Get stuck in, lad, or somebody will stick one in you!' This produced such a marked effect that he at once plied his bayonet with a will. So he continued in all his later actions, and showed himself to be a consistently brave soldier. (Kriele, 1801, 171–2. See also David Holbrook's experience at Kennington, in Dann, 1980, 91)

The last well-established instances of genuine bayonet fighting relate to accidental clashes of bodies of infantry, when the troops collided in the fog on ran into one another at the top of a hill.

The Prince de Ligne drew on what he had seen and heard during his many years of service in the Austrian army, and he proclaimed that it was 'almost impossible to attack an enemy force in the open country without firing. If you try to do so your troops will be wiped out, it is as simple as that' (Ligne, 1795–1811, I, 47). Indeed, outside the eventualities described above, all the evidence suggests that the clash of steel among infantry was almost unknown. We must respect the authority of Puységur, who maintained that

> firearms are the most destructive category of weapon, and now more than ever. If you need convincing, just go to the hospital and you will see how few men have been wounded by cold steel as opposed to firearms. My argument is not advanced lightly. It is founded on knowledge. (Puységur, 1749, I, 227. See also Guibert [1772], 1804, I, 89; Warnery, 1785–91, IV, 287; Edward Wortley Montagu, in Colville, 1949, 167; Kennett, 1967, 116)

We are left with a number of actions, such as the Prussian triumph at Kesselsdorf (1745), the French victories at Madonne de l'Elme, Rocoux (1746), Laffeldt (1747) and Johannisberg (1762), as well as a number of Russian battles against the Turks, which are loosely described as having been won with the bayonet. In France, authorities like Mesnil-Durand and Joly de Maizeroy were inspired to declare that 'cold steel is made for the French nation' (Mesnil-Durand, 1755, heading of Chapter IV) and that the shock of infantry was a physical reality (see p. 199). Frederick himself misread what had happened at Kesselsdorf, and for a dozen years thereafter he persisted in a belief that his infantry could overthrow the enemy without having to fire.

What had been going on in these so-called victories of the bayonet? Many of them involved combats for houses or entrenchments, in which hand-to-hand action undoubtedly took place, as we have noted. Otherwise they were probably attacks that were pressed home with such determination that the defenders were presented with the sight of bristling moustaches, bared teeth and glistening bayonet points emerging through the smoke at terrifyingly close range. A very brave man might stand unmoved,

> but the kind of soldier who acts only under pressure will be frightened to see the enemy come so near, and he will often seek safety in flight without attempting to defend himself. The closer you approach the enemy the more fearsome you become, and a coward, who will fire at a brave man at one hundred paces, will not dare to so much as aim at him at close range. (Guibert [1772], 1804, I, 216)

The fire-fight

Most encounters of infantry against infantry developed as standing fire-fights. They were conducted at ranges of between 30 and 200 paces, and they endured until one side or the other lost heart and gave way. Where the combat was obstinate and prolonged, as at Klosterkamp in 1760, the evidence was clear to see: 'The battlefield was strewn with dead, but we did not notice a single enemy uniform on our ground, or a single French uniform on that of the enemy' (Besenval, 1827–8, 97. See also Saxe [1732], 1877, 22; Toulongeon and Hullin [1786], 1881, 335).

The details of the combat seldom corresponded to what was attainable on the drill square. In the world of the theorists the battalion put out a storm of bullets at a rate of 1,800 rounds a minute, and the firings of the individual components – divisions, platoons or ranks – succeeded one another like hammer blows. The reality was far different, as we might have expected from our review of columns and bayonet-fighting, and in this case the discrepancies have to do with the limitations of the individual soldier and his weapon, and the ways in which bodies of troops behave in combat.

The standard muzzle-loading, smooth-bore flintlock musket threw a leaden ball nearly three-quarters of an inch in diameter. The bullet left the muzzle at a velocity of about 510 paces a second, and at close range it had enough force to penetrate right through a pine post 5 inches thick. As regards penetration and accuracy at longer ranges, eighteenth-century Prussian muskets yielded the following results; the target was a pine board 6 inches thick and 100 feet (50 paces) wide, and 200 rounds were fired at each range:

Paces:	100	200	300	400	500	600
Hits:	92	64	64	42	26	19
Penetrations:	56	58	56	23	28	2

(Scharnhorst, 1813, 80–3)

It will be seen that the performance of these weapons was very erratic. Moreover the hits by no means corresponded to kills, for the Prince de Ligne once conducted a test against a comparable target which was painted with figures of Prussian soldiers, and he discovered that nearly one-quarter of the rounds that struck the target would have passed between heads and legs, leaving the soldiers totally unscathed, and that only one-ninth of the bullets would have hit the soldiers in vital parts (Ligne, 1795–1811, I, 49–50).

Backsights were never provided for ordinary muskets, and as a result the following adjustments in aim were recommended for different ranges:

Paces:	Aim:
150	At the knees
225–300	At the waist or chest
375	At the head
450	At the hat or 1 foot above the head

However the men rarely bothered to seat their musket butts firmly on the shoulder, and this practice and many others (see below) only served to augment the inaccuracy inherent in the musket.

Many veterans could tell of battalions or entire lines of battle which had fired without causing any perceptible casualties. In combat conditions the hits at 450 paces (300 yards) were negligible; there were a few losses at 300 paces (200 yards), some more at 150 paces (100 yards), and real execution at 75 paces (50 yards) and below. The English officer Nicholas Cresswell has a telling description of a skirmish on Staten Island on 22 June 1777:

> When they were about 100 yards from each other both parties fired, but I did not observe any fall. They still advanced to a distance of 40 yards or less, and fired again. I then saw a good number fall on both sides. Our people then rushed upon them with their bayonets and the others took to their heels; I heard one of them call out *murder!* lustily. (Cresswell, 1924, 241).

Unusually determined troops firing at close range must have delivered the heavy and accurate fire which took such a toll of the Prussian high command at Hochkirch (1758) in a matter of minutes. Frederick's horse was hit in the shoulder, and Major Haugwitz nearby took a bullet through his left arm; Field-Marshal Keith was plucked dead from his horse, and Prince Wilhelm of Brunswick was drilled through-and-through and fell lifeless from the saddle. One of the lowly subalterns received two bullets through his hat, and he observed that the majority of the hits on the other men were in the head and chest (Barsewisch, 1863, 75–7).

The most systematic investigation of the efficacy of musket fire was the one initiated by Frederick after the battles of Mollwitz and Chotusitz (1741 and 1742), where the Prussians had kept up a heavy fire without killing many Austrians. From the findings (reproduced in Jähns, 1889–91, III, 2, 425) Frederick recommended that the troops of all ranks must ensure that the butts of their muskets were held firmly against the shoulder, and that the barrels must be pointed at the ground eight or ten paces away, to compensate for the kick of the weapon and the natural tendency of the soldiers to fire into the air. It is likely that E. Mauvillon used the material which came to light on this occasion in order to write a passage which caused a considerable stir in military Europe:

> According to my sums, the Prussians fired 650,000 rounds of musketry during their advance at Chotusitz, and the enemy lost scarcely 2,500 dead and as many wounded. If you subtract the men who were killed or wounded by the sword, a mighty great number of rounds must have gone astray! (*Histoire de la dernière guerre de Bohème*, 3 vols, Amsterdam, 1756, I, 100–1. He discounts the effect of artillery, which was considered of little importance at that time.)

By Mauvillon's calculations, the ratio of rounds expended to deaths sustained by the enemy therefore amounts to about one in 260, which equates roughly with the one in 200 given for the English fire at Wandewash in India (1760), one in 300 for the American fire at Concord (1775), and one in 460 for Wellington's fire at Vittoria (1813). The lethality is diminished by the allowance that must be made for the contribution of the other weapons, but increased by the knowledge that about half the rounds nominally 'fired' were probably thrown away by the soldiers (Ligne, 1795–1811, I, 49).

An altogether higher rate of kills was achieved by riflemen who were shooting at carefully-selected targets. The thump and whistle of a musket shot was much less feared by troops standing in line than the crack and buzz that told you that jägers or American backwoodsmen were at work. In America, unlike the theatres of war in Europe, the life of an individual was sought 'with as much avidity as the obtaining of a victory over an army of thousands' (Anburey, 1969, I, 331).

In 1947 a pioneering study by Colonel S. L. A. Marshall (*Men against Fire*, reprinted Gloucester, Mass., 1978), established just how few men in the conditions of modern combat actually fire their weapons. From his study of the engagements in the Pacific and Normandy he discovered that the soldier was often an isolated individual, gripped by a paralysing inertia, and that 'out of an average of one hundred men along the line of fire during the period of an encounter, only fifteen men on the average would take any part with the weapon' (Marshall, 1978, 57).

The experience of combat in the eighteenth century was radically different. Ranged in close order, the soldiers at that period appear to have been in the grip of a compulsive urge to use their weapons at any price, as if they found relief in the physical exertions of loading and the stunning noise of the discharges. It did not matter to them where the bullets went. After the first couple of volleys the men neglected the usual procedures of loading (see p. 114). The ramrod was flung in and out of the barrel, without any attempt to push the powder, ball and wad firmly home, and sometimes the ramrod was not employed at all, the soldiers preferring to thump the butt on the ground so as to shake the load down the barrel.

The rate of fire in ideal conditions gave an altogether false idea of what was attained by a soldier who was burdened by his sixty cartridges, his rations and perhaps also some items of camp equipment:

> Bowed down under this load, the warrior goes *omnia secum portans* into battle. Now, how many rounds of rapid fire do you think he can loose off in a minute when he is in this condition? At least five a minute? That is certainly the norm for fire on the drill square, which conjures up visions of enemy corpses by the thousand. But, when we consider all the encumbering burden of the soldier, and especially the fact that he is *never trained on the drill square with his full load*, any more than he carries it on the way to the peacetime show camps, then, taking everything into due account, it would be optimistic to suppose that he fires as many as one or at the most two rounds in a minute. (Cogniazzo, 1779, 147)

Even at this low rate of fire twenty or thirty rounds were enough to make the barrel too hot to hold, and during prolonged fire-fights the inside of the barrel became so fouled with carbon that loading required a great deal of time and considerable effort. The occasions of misfires were numerous, and they all placed the soldiers in real danger, whether through the bursting of their weapons, or by leaving them defenceless in the face of the enemy.

Early in the morning, or in damp weather, the most common cause of malfunction was damp seeping into the firing mechanism. An English soldier reported after Culloden (1746) 'they [the Jacobites] thought it was such a bad day that our firelocks would not fire, but they were very much mistaken for scarce one in a regiment missed firing, for we kept them dry with our coat laps' (Linn, 1921, I, 24).

After a number of rounds (which varied according to the quality of the stone) the flint became blunt and failed to ignite the charge in the priming pan, which forced the soldier to stop and fit a replacement. Frequently the touch hole became blocked with fouling, and the priming charge literally 'flashed in the pan', without communicating with the main charge in the barrel. In the excitement and noise of action there was no guarantee that the soldier would notice that his musket had failed to fire, and in such a case he loaded round after round, until five, six or more charges were superimposed. If the first round now took fire, the barrel exploded like a bangalore torpedo. The barrel was also liable to burst when the muzzle was obstructed by dirt or snow, when a bullet happened to stick in the bore, or if the ramrod was left in the barrel after loading.

Ramrods were originally of beech or some other wood, and tipped with brass. These frail sticks frequently broke in the stress of loading, and the Prussians gained a clear tactical advantage when they introduced ramrods of iron, beginning with the regiment of Anhalt-Dessau as early as 1698. The English and other nations gradually followed suit in the course of the eighteenth century, but Colonel Hawley complained that the new rammers had vices of their own:

> The iron ramrods that the Foot are coming into are very ridiculous . . . for if they have not some alloy of steel they stand bent and cannot be returned. If they have the least too much steel they snap like glass; in wet weather or in a fog they rust and won't come out, as always by standing in the bell tents where arms always rust a little by the dew. (Hawley [1726], 1946, 93)

It is clear that the first round must have been a precious resource, for it was loaded at leisure before the action began, and it was fired from a clean weapon with a sharp flint. When a volley of such rounds was discharged at short range, it was capable of causing a massacre

like that at Fontenoy (1745), when 19 officers and 600 men of the
French and Swiss Guards were killed in an instant. Quincy was
adamant on this point: 'We must train the soldiers above all to hold
their fire, and to endure the fire of the enemy. In normal circumstances a battalion is beaten once it has opened fire, and the enemy
still has all its fire in reserve' (Quincy, 1726, VIII, 67). However,
one of his countrymen argued no less forcefully:

> Is it credible that, having sustained several volleys from the
> enemy, a battalion will be in any condition to open fire when
> it finally desires to do so? Will it be in any state to withstand a
> charge, or launch a charge of its own against a fresh and intact
> enemy? Can such conduct be imagined, let alone recommended
> by officers who have seen anything of war? (Bigot, 1761, I,
> 260. See also Santa Cruz, 1735–40, VI, 50–1)

As often as not the question was settled by the infantry opening fire
anyway. Where fresh and very well-trained troops were concerned,
the process was initiated by the battalion or platoon officers through
an almost automatic procedure. The French diplomat Valori
accompanied the Prussian army during the Silesian Wars, and he
noted how

> at Mollwitz they fired at a range of 800 or even 1,000 paces. At
> Hohenfriedeberg part of the left wing opened fire without
> seeing anything of the enemy – the spring was wound up, and
> platoons on the right and centre loosed off and the others
> followed in a mechanical way, though always in strict order of
> platoons. (Valori [1748], 1894, 308)

The Prussian infantry at Mollwitz had no conception that combat
could develop in any other way than the one they had learned on
the drill square. They kept step under a hail of bullets, and when
they were ordered to make ready to open fire 'the first rank knelt
down in regulation style and waiting patiently upon the word of
command. If any disorder now became manifest in the ranks, the
officers ordered the men to return their muskets to their shoulders'
(Archenholtz, 1974, 22–3. See also Berenhorst, 1845–7, I, 70–1). A
regular fire by volleys was kept up by the Austrian grenadiers at
Prague (1757). Strict fire discipline was also observed by the Prussian
regiment of Lestwitz in the counterattack on the village of Kleinburg
in the battle of Breslau (1757).

The regiment of Lestwitz had been heavily engaged at Prague less than seven months before, but it is notable that all the other instances cited are from armies which encountered their first experience of combat after an intensive period of peacetime training. Every reliable source indicates that in the later battles of the wars the regular volley firing, and especially the complicated firings by division, platoons or ranks, came to an end soon after the fire-fight had begun (Fermor's *Disposition* of 1736, Baiov, 1906, 55–6; Dalrymple, 1761, 51; Saint-Germain, 1779, 225; Wissel, 1784, xxxix; Toulongeon and Hullin [1786], 1881, 197, 355; Houlding, 1981, 354).

In battle conditions the platoon firings demanded altogether too much of the officers. They had to step three or so paces in front of the first rank, then turn left and look along the front of their platoons,

> whereupon every platoon officer finds the bullets streaking past his chest and back at a distance of between eight and ten inches . . . The soldiers in the platoons have to be extraordinarily attentive to the commands of their officer, and learn to recognise him by his voice so as not to be confused by the shouts of the neighbouring officers. If they turned to look at him they would have to take their eyes off the barrels of their muskets, which is not permitted.
>
> The officer commanding the second platoon must keep an eye on the seventh platoon, just as the one commanding the first platoon marks the eighth, because they must follow them in the order of the firings. If a cloud of smoke hangs between the platoons the view of the officers is blocked. (Berenhorst, 1798–9, I, 226–7. See also Bigot, 1761, I, 273)

The men were in a state of high agitation, and none more so than the unfortunates in the front rank, who were in danger of having their heads blown off by their comrades behind (see p. 246). Once the troops of the first rank had loaded, knelt down and fired, they were therefore under a powerful incentive not to stand up again. At the battles of Parma and Guastalla in 1734 a large part of both the French and Austrian infantry sank to its knees, and ended up crawling around on the battlefield and firing 'in the fashion of the Croats' (Guibert [1772], 1804, I, 102; Warnery, 1785–91, II, 210–11; Ligne, 1795–1811, XVIII, 70).

The Prussians found that in most of their battles they could hope at the very best to get off crude battalion salvoes, or mass discharges of the whole line of infantry, like the great volleys at Gross-Jägersdorf (1757). Far more frequently the conventional fire discipline was broken and the troops blazed away at will (*feu de billebaude*, *Placker-feuer*, *Bataillenfeuer*). Thus at Dettingen .(1743) the English infantry

> were under no command by way of Hyde Park firing, but the
> whole three ranks made a running fire of their own
> accord . . . with great judgment and skill, stooping all as low
> as they could, making almost every ball take place . . . the
> French fired in the same manner . . . without waiting for words
> of command, and Lord Stair did often say he had seen many a
> battle, and never saw the infantry engage in any other manner.
> (Quoted in Orr, 1972, 65. The description rings true, even if
> the deadliness of the fire is exaggerated)

Prussian and Hanoverian officers were embarrassed by this phenom-enon, which appeared to destroy the possibility of control even at the lowest level of command, but two at least of the French writers recognised the *feu de billebaude* as a reality, and proposed that it should be turned to positive use. General Chabot pointed out that individual fire permitted the soldiers to select their own targets, fire at their own best speed, and attend to misfires as they occurred, and he attributed the victories of 1734 to this way of fighting (Chabot, 1756, 5–20). Guibert regarded the *feu de billebaude* as the most effective of all, and he emphasised that it required only two commands, namely to signify when to start and when to stop. He had seen the regiment of Royal Deux-Ponts fight in this way at Vellinghausen (1761), when the appropriate signals were given by a ruffle of drums (Guibert [1772], 1804, I, 108).

The battle against cavalry

Versatility was the greatest single strength of infantry, and on campaign the foot soldiers enjoyed a number of advantages over the cavalry. Except in certain specific areas, like the plains of Silesia or Hungary, the theatres of war in Europe were composed of broken terrain which favoured the action of infantry. The infantrymen did not have horses which demanded to be watered and fed, they could be ready for action much sooner than cavalry, and they could operate with much greater freedom at night.

In open combat it was less easy to distinguish which party had the upper hand. The quantifiable superiority of the cavalry in weight and speed was counterbalanced by the fact that more infantrymen could be crammed into a given frontage: the cavalry were usually formed in two or three ranks, as opposed to the infantry's three or four, and a file of cavalry was at least 3 feet wide, whereas a file of infantry took up only 2 feet. Moreover the infantrymen had the capacity to inflict casualties on the horse before they suffered any losses themselves, and in close-quarter combat the foot-soldier had a weapon (musket and bayonet) about 6 feet long to present against a cavalryman whose sword measured only just over 3 feet.

These calculations do not allow for the fact that the cavalry were employed, if possible, not against unbroken infantry, but when the tactical situation favoured the mounted arm, as for example when the infantry presented a vulnerable flank, when they were depleted by casualties or when they were already in flight. There was also an important psychological dimension. The combat of infantry against infantry was usually a prolonged affair, and was ultimately broken off when one side or the other became disorganised and gave ground. In most actions the beaten troops were allowed to march away unpursued, for the victors were likely to be as exhausted as themselves. The relations in a contest against cavalry were different, for in this case a defeat could be followed by instant annihilation: 'Where do we find the kind of men who will stay calm at the terrible moment when they face the charge of a force of cavalry which happens to be well led? No other episode in warfare is more destructive, except the explosion of a mine' (Mottin de la Balme, 1776, 94).

No infantrymen could withstand cavalry without confidence in themselves and their weapons. Probably the crucial zone for their survival was between 50 paces, when musket fire became really effective, and a lower limit of about 30 paces when the soldiers might become subject to panic and began to open their formation (Turpin de Crissé, 1754, I, 204). However, success was nearly assured when you brought down enough horses in the leading rank to form a barrier against the advance of the cavalry coming up behind.

The remaining cavalry seldom reached the infantry at anything faster than a trot, and even at this late stage the horses might be disconcerted by a hedge of bayonets presented at their muzzles (in his peacetime training Santa Cruz used to show his troops how a horse could be turned aside by a man armed with nothing more than a stick (Santa Cruz, 1735–40, III, 68)). However, a potentially lethal gap could be opened up if a few men fell or turned, and wounded horses had a way of gathering furious strength and bursting through the ranks (Grandmaison, 1756, 194).

Well-disciplined troops might still be able to close up the gaps after a breakthrough, and turn about to fire at the cavalry. The 21st Royal North British Fusiliers accomplished this evolution at Dettingen (1743) and brought down large numbers of the French Gendarmerie. The third rank of the Prussian regiment of Bevern tried to do the same at Kolin (1757), but its fire had little effect and the troops were virtually wiped out. Lieutenant Prittwitz began to get up after a storm of horses had passed over him, but a veteran NCO shouted to him to lie down again. This was good advice, for a prone figure was out of reach of the cavalrymen's swords, and Prittwitz survived the day with cuts and bruises (Prittwitz, 1935, 139).

In the Napoleonic period the square was the classic formation which was adopted by foot soldiers against cavalry. In the Age of Reason, however, linear tactics were paramount, and the square was normally adopted only by isolated bodies of infantry, like the French units which so often had to fight for their lives against the swarming Austrian hussars during the War of the Austrian Succession. Squares were almost invulnerable as long as they possessed a reserve of fire, but the troops were in mortal danger if they were goaded into firing all their muskets at once.

In all of this we have assumed that the infantry were content to receive the attack of the cavalry. There were isolated but striking examples of the foot soldiers going over to the offensive, like the English infantry at Minden (1759) and the Prussian regiment of Anhalt-Bernburg at Liegnitz (1760). These apparently suicidal enterprises were more successful than might have been expected, 'for nothing upsets horses more than to see a mass of troops . . . coming resolutely at them' (Silva, 1778, 53).

Under shot and shell: the infantry as targets for artillery

The foot soldiers were rarely in a position to take direct action against their most formidable enemy, the artillery, which grew markedly in power in the 1750s (see p. 231). Lieutenant-Colonel Francis Downman gloated on the effect of his guns in an action on St Lucia in 1778:

I had a fine situation for galling the French army as they marched to the attack in columns. I had them charmingly, and while forming, and after being formed, and also in their retreat. I kept up as heavy a fire as I could on their flank which was presented to me the greatest part of the action. My shot in this situation swept them off by the dozens at a time, and Frenchmen's heads and trotters were as plenty and much cheaper than sheep's heads and trotters in Scotland. (Downman, 1898, 105)

The missiles on this occasion were solid shot, which represented the most versatile of the tools of the artillerymen. Weighing up to twelve pounds, the iron balls worked to devastating effect on the battlefields of the Age of Reason. They were capable of inflicting multiple casualties both at the first graze and the subsequent ricochets, thanks to their stored energy, and they could not be considered safe until they had rolled to a complete stop.

The heavier roundshot could be used effectively from about 900 paces downwards. For shorter-range work, at some 400 paces or less, the gunners might choose to employ canister fire, which turned the cannon into a giant shotgun, discharging a sheet metal can which burst open at the muzzle and scattered a shower of bullets or small shot. Canister was the tactical equivalent of machine gun fire, and in the Seven Years War it probably inflicted more casualties on the Prussian infantry than any other weapon. Colonel Eckart reported to Frederick about the experience of the regiment of Kalckstein at Kolin (1757): 'It was the enemy canister fire in particular which hit the second battalion, leaving not a single survivor among the lieutenants who commanded the platoons' (Duncker, 1876, 55).

Howitzers were stubby artillery pieces which threw explosive shells at high trajectory. They were encountered much less frequently than the conventional cannon, but they had a distinctive 'signature' what with the shell trailing its thin stream of smoke across the sky, spinning and fizzing after it had dumped itself on the ground, and finally exploding with a howl.

Scharnhorst once conducted a series of elaborate tests with canvas screens. He discovered that the 7-pound shell (Frederick's favourite) burst into about twenty-four splinters; the 10-pound shell of the Prussian battery howitzer produced a considerably greater blast, but no more effect from its splinters. He concluded that 'when a shell or bomb explodes on the surface of the earth, the splinters will hit a [continuous] six-foot high object only occasionally at a distance of forty to fifty feet, and at greater ranges they are almost totally ineffective' (Scharnhorst, 1813, 31). The most productive targets for howitzer fire were in fact not the infantrymen in the open field, but defended buildings (which were readily set on fire by the bursting shells) and the cavalry (whose horses might be thrown into panic).

The morale results of the various kinds of artillery fire counted for as much in their way as the physical damage. At first the missiles took their effect on the vegetation, as clods of earth were flung into the air and leaves and branches cascaded from the trees. Then a clattering ran out from the bayonets, and thuds told of the impact of shot upon horses and files of men, producing the most horrible sights, sounds and smells. Almost every soldier could tell of experiences like those of Lieutenant Hülsen at Zorndorf:

> My flank man's head was blown off, and his brains flew in my face. My spontoon was snatched out of my hand, and I received a canister ball on my gorget, smashing the enamelled medallion. I drew my sword, and the tassel of the sword knot was shot away. A ball went through the skirts of my coat, and another knocked my hat aside, stripping the knot from the band in the process. (Hülsen, 1890, 88–9)

Artillery struck from a distance, and killed impersonally, and recruits who came under artillery fire quickly lost the confidence they otherwise enjoyed in their first experience of action. Veterans respected the artillery for what it could do, but they knew when it was, and was not, really dangerous. They were aware, for example, that a cannon shot coming straight at you might be visible as a black dot, or be seen as a quivering in the air. The experience was inherently alarming, but at least it gave you a chance to get out of the way. At Dettingen (1743) an Englishman saw the Austrians 'dip their heads and look about them for they dodge the balls as a cock does the stick, they were so used to them' (Davis [1743], 1925, 37).

However, all troops found the ordeal near-intolerable, if they had to stand immobile in the open and at the mercy of these blind forces. Montbarey condemned the perverted sense of honour displayed at Minden (1759) by Lieutenant-General de Saint Pern who,

> having seen the bloody losses sustained by his poor grenadiers, nevertheless kept them exposed to fire throughout the battle,

instead of ordering them to sit on the ground, or descend a few
paces to the rear, where they would have been covered by the
crest of the hill on which they were standing. (Montbarey,
1826–7, I, 175)

Some kind of movement not only made the troops more difficult to
hit but did a little to assuage the acute demand for action. At Hochkirch (1758) Saldern successfully covered the Prussian retreat with
five battalions, which escaped largely unscathed by the intense fire
of the Austrian cannon and howitzers:

as soon as he saw the enemy cannon shot falling in one of the
regiments, he would immediately draw it off to the right or
the left, so that the balls fell too long or too short. Through this
useful expedient he accomplished most of the retreat in a zig-
zag movement . . . Saldern's eyes perpetually switched between
the enemy, the regiment in question, the surrounding terrain
and his destination. (Küster, 1793, 12–13).

The infantry had some guns of their own, in the shape of the
little regimental or battalion cannon which were served by artillery
detachments and borrowed foot soldiers. These pieces made an
encouraging noise and created at least the illusion that you were
hitting back at the enemy.

The infantry officer in battle

The colours served as rallying points, just as the drums might be
used to convey some basic orders, but the officer's authority and
power of control depended on his voice more than anything else:

Every officer must practice giving his words of command, even
to the smallest bodies, in the full extent of his voice, and in a
sharp tone. . . . The justness of execution, and the confidence
of the soldier, can only be in proportion to the firm, decided,
and proper manner in which every officer of every rank gives
his orders. (Dundas, 1788, 28)

Every unit was enclosed within a light cordon of officers and
NCOs. In armies like the Prussian, the lieutenant-colonel and the
major usually had their place at the head of the regiment or battalion,
and it was their particular responsibility to preserve the direction of
the march and the alignment of the front.

A second and slightly thicker line of individuals (captains and lieutenants) was positioned just in front of the first rank, or actually inside it, with the main purpose of regulating the fire (see p. 213). In this location an officer was 'in danger of being shot by his own men, among whom there might be untrained recruits or ill-intentioned characters . . . I served one campaign as captain of infantry, and I confess that I suffered frequent anxieties on this account' (Warnery, 1785–91, II, 54).

A final line of officers and NCOs extended across the rear of the battalion, and employed whatever means were necessary to keep the troops in action. 'Inner Leadership' was a concept unknown in the eighteenth century (and perhaps held in exaggerated regard in the later twentieth), and according to the universally accepted code of the Age of Reason superiors had the right and duty to kill any soldier who ran away, or even looked as if he might turn tail. The men could be directed from behind much more easily than from the front, and by dint of shouting commands, manhandling the troops into place, or pushing them forward with spontoons and halberds levelled across their backs, the officers and NCOs preserved the regularity of the line as best they could. Casualties in the first two ranks were replaced by men who were fed in from the third, and all the time the officers and NCOs sought to prevent the 'scandalous evil' of bunching (*Reglement für die sämmentliche-Kaiserlich-Königlich Infanterie*, Vienna, 1769, 229).

In the Austrian and Russian armies the rear was also the station of the lieutenant-colonel and the major. They were on horseback, and 'enjoying a higher position, they were able to see along the whole length of the battalion under their command, and remedy any of those sudden disorders which might arise in some part of the formation' (Vorontsov [1802], 1876, 474).

There was a sharp difference of opinion as to whether it was proper for the officers to take part in the combat with personal weapons. A number of English senior commanders insisted that 'no officer is supposed to fight himself, any more than to defend his head; his business is to see the men fight and do well; that's sufficient' (Cumberland, [1755], 1945, 99. See also An Old Officer, 1760, 180; Burgoyne's *General Orders*, 30 June 1777, Hadden, 1884, 74–5). A clear case of an officer forgetting his priorities occurred in the action at White Plains on 28 October 1776, when the advance of two English battalions on the far side of the Bronx stream came to a fatal halt, simply because the officer at the front stopped to fire against the Americans.

The opposing party argued that many officers carried light muskets (fusils) anyway for immediate self-defence, and that by arming all the officers and NCOs with long guns you could augment the firepower of a battalion by about fifty barrels (Fermor's *Disposition*, 1736, Baiov, 1906, 56; d'Espagnac, 1751, I, 281; Pictet, 1761, I, 24; Bonneville, 1762, II, 46; Dalrymple, 1782, 16; Vorontsov [1802], 1876, 474).

Officers were objects of interest to certain sharp-eyed people in the enemy army. The English lieutenant Thomas Anburey noted after the battle of Freeman's Farm in 1777:

> The officers who have been killed or wounded in the late action, are much greater in proportion than . . . the soldiers, which must be attributed to the great execution of the riflemen, who directed their fire against them in particular; in every interval of smoke, they are sure to take off some, as the riflemen had posted themselves in high trees. (Anburey, 1969, I, 429)

Frederick, who killed men at one remove by the scores of thousands, objected to the killing of individuals as murderous. In the Seven Years War he hauled one of his jägers out of a ditch where he had been lying in wait for a victim, and he was singularly reluctant to allow his gunners to knock down enemy officers.

Infantry officers were naturally delighted to survive a day of battle unscathed, but we are told that the experience of combat left them with feelings of frustration:

> In battle, an officer of the infantry can make not the slightest movement of his company or division on his own initiative . . . Whether in general actions or formal sieges, the individual officer is lost in the crowd of combatants, and he kills or is killed without any hope of sharing in the glory which is desired as greedily by every military man. (Warnery, 1785–91, III, 120; Lacuée de Cessac, 1785, 2)

The cavalry battle

The clash of steel

The chopping down of the infantry was a bloody kind of work which usually came, if it arrived at all, towards the end of an action.

Cavalrymen were trained and equipped in the first place to do battle with their fellows.

The basic unit of cavalry combat was relatively small, namely the squadron of between 130 and 160 officers and men (see p. 121). The combat formation was in two or three ranks. The Austrian regulations stipulated that

> when it is drawn up in line of battle, every squadron must have a first rank of thoroughly good and reliable men who are mounted on sound horses. The less good men and the recruits go to the second rank. The third rank, however, must have the most senior and steady men of all. (*Feld-Dienst Regulament.* Vienna, 1749, unpaginated)

All the authorities agreed that the first rank of horse bore the brunt of combat, and that it was of much greater relative importance than the first rank in the infantry. The rearward ranks acted as a reserve – supporting the first rank as necessary, or veering out on the flanks. They also compelled the first rank to keep straight on for the sake of physical survival, for if any horse checked the animal and its rider would be trampled under the hooves of the horses coming up behind. The files rode as close together as was possible, and in the Prussian service even the intervals between the squadrons were omitted, which produced walls of cavalry several hundred paces long.

By the middle of the eighteenth century a consensus was being reached on one of the most enduring debates about cavalry action, namely whether cold steel should be preferred to the use of firearms. The majority now favoured an unchecked charge of cavalry relying on shock and the sword. A force of cavalry which halted to fire with its pistols or carbines would be blinded by smoke and deafened by its own discharges, and it forfeited all the advantages of getting in its blow first:

> At a range of more than fifty paces a pistol shot and a well-thrown stone have just about the same effect. In a mêlée a discharged pistol is useless for parrying, and the only thing you can do is cast it away, for if you replace it in its holster and draw your sword you will receive a cut over your ear for your pains . . . .When a first rank opens fire with its forty carbines, there is frequently not a single hit. Can we be surprised? Not only is a carbine too heavy to be fired single-handed, but the

troopers usually fire at long range when the horses are galloping and the men are shaken about, and the target itself is moving so fast that it is quite impossible to take proper aim. (Berenhorst, 1798–9, II, 434–5; d'Authville, 1756, 309)

The use of firearms by cavalry was normally relegated to specific situations. One of these was when the men were doing dismounted service as sentries or foragers. Carbines and pistols proved to be useful or even essential against the wilder types of light cavalry, which would have evaded an organised charge but were easily deterred by fire (Cogniazzo, 1779, 78). Frederick was amused to see how a Prussian musician saved his own life simply by pointing his woodwind at a Cossack who was bent on his destruction.

Firearms were also admitted to be of service in the pursuit, when the quarry could not be reached with the sword. During the battle of Zorndorf (1758) an impudent Cossack emerged from a wood and skewered a Prussian Garde du Corps from behind with his lance.

'Your Majesty', said an officer from the suite of General Seydlitz, who was standing right next to the king, 'with your permission I shall catch the Cossack.'

'Go ahead, then.'

The officer darted away and succeeded in taking the Cossack unawares. The man saw no alternative but to seek safety in flight, and he came closer and closer to the king. The officer took aim with his pistol and shot him between the shoulder blades, and he fell instantly from his horse. (Anon., 1787–9, XI, 50–1)

We must imagine the officer holding his pistol in the conventional style, with his arm fully extended and the weapon tilted over to the right, so that the priming charge covered the touch hole.

This kind of work was a diversion from the real business of cavalry, which was delivering shocks in the open field. We must once again address ourselves to the problem of reconciling the image of combat in which everything appears orderly, clean and decisive, with what happened in reality, which is much more difficult to establish.

One of the accepted wisdoms about cavalry attacks was stated by Turpin de Crissé: 'We may suppose, indeed it has been demonstrated, that in a contest between two equal forces, the one which strikes first must drive the other back' (1754, I, 188). In the course of the century there was a movement of opinion in favour of beginning the advance at a considerable distance from the enemy, and building up by successive increases in speed to an all-out gallop. The cavalry started at a purposeful walk. The break into the trot accelerated the laden cavalry horse to very approximately 10 miles per hour and the gallop to about 25. The gallop was supposed to be kept up for about 180 paces, after which the horses were given their heads for the last few strides before the line crashed into the enemy.

Possibly only the Prussian cavalry at its best was capable of attcking in good order at anything like the prescribed velocity. At Minden (1759) Lord George Sackville led his cavalry onto the field at a slow trot, halting every now and then to adjust the dressing of his eighteen squadrons on their frontage of 1,950 paces. He explained that he had

> ever found the greatest difficulty in preserving intervals, or even the appearance of a line, without a considerable attention to their motions, and stopping the first appearance of irregularity. To attack with vigour and velocity, you must advance without hurry or confusion. (Mackesy, 1979, 198)

An attack at speed was only too liable to collapse into what the French called a *charge en fourrageurs* (glorified by the Marquis d'Argenson, Richelieu, 1918, 103; castigated by Guibert [1772], 1804, I, 158).

What happened next is generally described as 'shock'. Horses were heavy and relatively fast-moving objects, and something loosely approximating to shock accounts for episodes like the overthrow of the Saxon cavalry at Hohenfriedeberg (1745), and of the Austrian cavalry at Soor (1745) and Prague (1757). However it was noticed that the horses did not actually collide chest-to-chest like inanimate masses which were thrown together. Usually the rival squadrons clashed only briefly, or failed to engage at all, for one or the other force would sink into confusion and turn tail:

> When, however, the two squadrons are made up of men and mounts which are equally experienced in war and equally well trained, the charge proceeds as follows – the ranks run at each other, the horses seek the intervals of their own accord, the riders engage in hand-to-hand combat, and the forces are so completely intermingled that the two squadrons cross and emerge in the other's rear. In this mêlée the issue is decided by

the most agile of the horses and the most skilful of the troopers. (Guibert [1772], 1804, I, 164. See also Tempelhoff, 1783–1801, I, 68; Mirabeau and Mauvillon, 1788, 104; Ligne, 1795–1811, I, 23–5; Vorontsov (1802), 1876, X, 481)

The experience of the mêlée had much in common with that of aerial combat in the two World Wars, for the orientation of individuals was rapidly lost, friend and foe appeared and disappeared in an entirely arbitrary fashion, and the cavalrymen were in perpetual danger of being assailed from behind (Lojewsky, 1843, I, 181).

During all of this the cavalrymen had to contend with their own horses. These were irrational creatures which might take fright at a scrap of paper floating in the air, while ignoring a block of marble falling on their heads, 'from which we may guess how terrified they must be by the polished and shining metal of the weapons, the different kinds of explosions, the fire and smoke, the warlike yells, and the smells given out by wounds, spilled blood and corpses' (Mottin de la Balme, 1776, 104–5). In combat the rider could spare only one hand to manage his mount, and even this measure of control was lost when the reins were cut, as very frequently happened (see p. 119). Many a hero was borne away from the combat willy nilly, and it was all too easy for somebody who was less than a hero to absent himself from the scene as well:

Cavalry are everywhere treated better than the infantry, and rightly so, for the trooper of necessity follows different principles of conduct from those of the foot soldier. The performance of the cavalryman in combat depends almost entirely on his good will, for it is difficult to compel him to do his duty. When he does not wish to do that duty, his horse will offer him endless excuses to avoid it. The officer cannot keep him constantly in his view, and moreover the officer himself sometimes has his hands full with individual combat. (Warnery, 1785–91, II, 90–1)

Seydlitz was one of the very few cavalry leaders in the Age of Reason who gave swordmanship the prominence it was going to acquire in the nineteenth century. Most authorities were content to recommend that the sword should be held with the blade forming a straight line with the arm, the hilt covering one's face, and the point projecting straight ahead. This posture was the one best suited for delivering a blow with the point of the sword, which was universally admitted to be the most lethal stroke of all: 'a single thrust into the body with the point will kill a man, which frequently cannot be achieved with twenty cuts with the edge' (Grandmaison, 1756, 21).

The Hungarian hussar captain Jeney was virtually alone in advancing the virtues of the cutting edge over the point, and he maintained that dragoons should abandon their straight swords in favour of curved sabres like those of the hussars:

> I know that straight swords deal a more deadly blow, but they are not nearly as effective in combat. If you need convincing, I will explain the mechanism of the two kinds of weapon. When he is at a full gallop and a cavalryman attacks his enemy with the point, he will inevitably pierce him. But then he must stop his horse and break off his part in the action, so as to pull the sword out. During an equivalent amount of time a dragoon with a curved sabre will have wounded three or four enemy, without having to stop his horse or stop fighting. The enemy will not be mortally wounded, but at least they will be disabled, which is what we ought to look for in battle. (Jeney, 1759, 17)

The use of the edge also accorded with the instinctive reactions of the horseman, as Grandmaison was forced to concede (Grandmaison, 1756, 21).

The most detailed accounts of eighteenth-century mounted action come from the Prussian hussar Lojewsky, whose bloodthirsty memoirs are full of stories of mighty blows delivered with the edge of the sabre. At Grottkau in 1741

> my first blow hit the enemy officer and severed his arm. The hand and sword landed almost beside me, and the crippled man fell from his horse. . . . I made another powerful cut at the next enemy to present himself, and he fell with his skull split open. I shouted a warning to Captain Kladowsky. I dealt a third full-blooded blow, but I struck the carbine of an enemy hussar and the blade shattered. At that very instant an enemy split Kladowsky's face, and he sank from the saddle to the ground. (Lojewsky, 1843, I, 67)

The straight swords of the Prussian heavy cavalrymen were less suited for this kind of work. The Prince of Sachsen-Hildburghausen was surrounded by enemy troopers at Rossbach (1757), but he was merely belaboured with the flats of their swords and he was able to make good his escape. On the night after the battle an apothecary found that his back required only to be bathed with distilled water (Kalkreuth, 1840, III, 202).

It is significant that the great majority of wounds sustained in cavalry combat were painful but not particularly dangerous cuts to the sword arm. 'Prague was one battle where a genuine cavalry shock took place. Afterwards I showed my officers 150 Prussian and Austrian cavalrymen who were lodged in a barn; nearly all of them had been wounded in the right arm between the hand and elbow' (Warnery, 1785–91, IV, 83. See also Corvisier, 1964, 681).

The collapse of one side or other during the combat appears to have proceeded less from the losses sustained than from an infectious panic, and it was noted that the second rank was much more likely to give way than the first, which was fully engaged in swapping blows with the enemy (Puységur, 1749, I, 246; Turpin de Crissé, 1754, I, 179; Saint-Germain, 1779, 205). The defeated cavalrymen now drew on the remaining strength of their horses in order to make good their escape, which they usually accomplished without difficulty, since the victors were by now in disorder and (unless they were Prussians) they were seldom in condition to mount an immediate pursuit. An artilleryman commented bitterly:

> You must pardon me if I venture the opinion that the shock of cavalry is not as decisive as it seems to be. In the campaign of 1762 I witnessed a shock [at Reichenbach] which was delivered by the greater part of the Prussian cavalry against a still larger force of Austrian cavalry. It resulted in a few hundred wounded and prisoners on the two sides. Not a single dead man lay on the field of battle (Tempelhoff, 1783–1801, I, 63).

Special forms of cavalry action

The heavy cavalry had to keep a watchful eye on the movements of the enemy hussars and the other kinds of light horse. Turpin de Crissé, Grandmaison and Warnery all emphasised how dangerous those folk could be, for they were quick to exploit any sign of disorder in a running fight.

The curved sabre was the classic arm of the hussars, but the lance was carried by more exotic forms of life like Cossacks, Polish uhlans and Frederick's Bosniaken (who were dressed like wild men from the Balkans). In the Napoleonic period the lance became probably the most deadly of all the weapons that men put in the hands of the cavalry. It far outreached the bayonets of the infantry, and in cavalry actions it could disable an oncoming enemy horse just as readily as it could be jabbed into the small of the back of a fleeing rider. However the knack of wielding the lance was something which mostly escaped the Age of Reason. In 1741 the newly formed Prussian lancer regiment of Natzmer plunged boldly into two regiments of Austrian hussars in Silesia, but

> the lance was of no help to us in the press, in fact it acted to our disadvantage. Our uhlans found that they were skewering one another with these long weapons, stabbing the next man's horse, or sticking them in the ground in the general confusion and heaving themselves from the saddle. (Lojewsky, 1843, I, 66)

The Austrian hussars closed in from two sides and gave the Prussians a terrible beating.

When the survivors of the Natzmer regiment were reformed they became a regiment of conventional hussars. At Trautenau in 1778 the Austrian hussar regiments of Esterhazy and Wurmser repeated the same tactics at the expense of four squadrons of Bosniaken, who disappeared thereafter from the Prussian order of battle. Adrian Denisov, although a born Cossack, never used the lance again after an episode in 1789, when the head of his weapon stuck in the clothing of a Turk and could not be pulled free.

Whereas the combats of infantry against infantry had an attritional quality, the chance of success of horse against foot hung above all on the *coup d'oeil* of the cavalry commander. Cavalry could work to murderous effect against the infantry of a defeated army, or when an isolated body of enemy troops was caught at some disadvantage in the open field (see p. 216). The cavalrymen had to brave the inevitable losses from musketry, and control their mounts while the bullets screamed about them, but once the horse had reached the enemy line the animal could exert something like a sevenfold advantage in strength and weight over the individual infantryman (Joly de Maizeroy, 1773, 31; Mottin de la Balme, 1776, 63).

Cavalry fared least well when they attacked firm and disciplined infantry head-on. The details are illustrated by the experience of the French Gendarmerie and Carabiniers at Minden in 1759.

> They set off at a considerable distance at the gallop, and in a continuous line. To begin with the advance had the effect of squeezing the centre, and then the wings felt the pressure, especially on the right. The fire of the enemy infantry opened in the centre of their formation, and progressively extended towards their wings, and when we were only about fifteen paces away our horses tried to escape by throwing themselves to left and right. The force exerted by this phenomenal pressure became enormous. The men were no longer able to control their horses and the mass piled up so deeply that only eight or ten men at the most remained in the saddle in each squadron. These in turn were borne instantly away, and although some of them passed through the enemy ranks they were too few to cause any disorder. Only a few men were killed by the enemy fire, but many suffered contusions or broken or dislocated limbs, and a number were suffocated or trampled under the horses' hooves after falling from the saddle. (Mottin de la Balme, 1776, 105)

Old warriors like Santa Cruz and Frederick were much concerned to spare their cavalry a further ordeal: 'It is no way to inspire courage among your cavalrymen to force them to stand cold-bloodedly under prolonged cannonades, and see their relations, comrades and friends carried away by the shot' (Santa Cruz, 1735–40, VI, 35). Howitzer fire was particularly dreaded, for the shells searched out the cavalry in dead ground, and when they exploded in a tightly-packed regiment they were capable of killing eight or ten horses at a time and of terrifying many more. Few things in the annals of eighteenth-century combat are more impressive than the ability of disciplined cavalry to stand or manoeuvre under such an ordeal. The performance of the English Horse Guards at Dettingen (1743) was as striking in its way as that of the Prussian cavalry at Soor (1745) or of the Austrians at Lobositz (1756).

The cavalry officer

The officer of horse was under a constant pressure to exercise his own discretion:

> I allow that the strength of an army consists chiefly in its

infantry, but cavalry service requires more judgement and presence of mind on the part of the officer, and more speed, bearing and skill in manoeuvre and tactics than in the work of the infantry, which fights in a slower and more mechanical way, and whose success depends merely on its endurance and cohesion. (Warnery, 1785–91, III, 119–20)

Unfortunately the nature of cavalry combat was such that the officer might find himself caught up in the general onrush of the attack, and be unable to exercise any control. The usual position of most of the officers was in the first rank, or just in front of it, where they merely served to get in the way of the troopers in the mêlée. The Austrian field service regulations of 1749 laid down a much better scheme, whereby the senior captain (as squadron commander) nosed a little in front of the first rank, but a lieutenant was stationed in front of the squadron, and the rest of the officers were arranged across the rear.

The general of horse inevitably put his own life at risk when he led a wing of cavalry into battle (see p. 238), but he was not expected to take a personal part in the fighting. The Prussian general Zieten wore the ordinary sabre of the hussars, but he drew it only once in the course of the Seven Years War, and that was during a reconnaissance on 2 November 1760, the day before the battle of Torgau, when he was surrounded by the Austrians: 'He cut his way out in regulation style, and calmly replaced the bloody blade in its sheath. He never spoke of this affair, but even now you can clearly distinguish the bloodstain as a reddish-brown rust on the blade' (Fontane, 1906–7, I, 8).

THE BATTLE OF THE GUNS

The materiel and the personnel

So far the artillerymen have figured scarcely at all in our pages, for they have left virtually no record of their communal life in peacetime. A little more survives to tell us of their experiences in combat, but it still does not correspond to the greatly increased importance which the artillery acquired during the Age of Reason.

After the wars of the 1740s it was still possible to maintain that 'cannon fire does no great damage during a battle, and that it is a proverb among our military men that you have to be specifically foredoomed if you are to die of a cannon shot during a general action' (Mauvillon, E., 1756, II, 101).

From this level of insignificance the guns gained mightily in power with almost every campaign of the Seven Years War. On the eastern theatres the Prussian and Austrian armies went to war with trains of three or four hundred pieces each, while the Russian ordnance became more numerous still. Combats like Kolin (1757), Liegnitz (1760) and Torgau (1760) saw the attacking infantry massacred under the guns, and Frederick, much against his will, was forced to invest more and more heavily in his artillery.

In the campaigns in western Germany the new strength of artillery first impressed on the combatants at Bergen (13 April 1759), when the French threw back the assaults of the allied army under Prince Ferdinand of Brunswick. The main reason was that he was totally outgunned and had no means of driving the French from their positions (Mauvillon, J., 1794, II, 19). It was with a sense of real urgency that Ferdinand reinforced his artillery park, and on the day of Minden (1 August 1759) his guns achieved a clear superiority, beating down the artillery of the French and slaughtering their infantry and horse.

On both theatres the confrontations between the armies sometimes developed into cannonades which lasted for hours at a stretch. The Austrian bombardment in the Waldenburger-Gebirge, on 17 September 1760, was matched by the fire which the French directed at the redoubt at Amöneburg on 21 September 1762, when 'the surrounding ground was streaming with blood, and covered with dead or dying men' (Mauvillon, J., 1794, II, 253). By the end of the Seven Years War the relationship between the artillery and the other arms was seen to have fundamentally changed: 'Canister kills a six-footer as effectively as a man who measures five foot seven. Artillery does everything, and the infantry can no longer come to grips with cold steel' (Frederick, *Testament Politique*, [1768], Frederick, 1920, 146. See also Koch, 1765, ii–iii; Nockhern de Schorn, 1783, 194; Zimmermann, 1790, II, 109).

What had produced such a transformation? It was essentially a process of change which began in about the middle of the century and continued without a break into the Revolutionary period. Artillerymen had entered the Age of Reason in medieval guise. They worked by judgement, eye and experience. They recruited by word of mouth, and their democracy was reinforced by shared mysteries and the fact that much of the cruder work was delegated to inferior persons – the transport to civilian drivers, and the heavy labour on the guns to soldiers whom they borrowed from the infantry. Even a non-commissioned artilleryman like the celebrated Prussian bombardier Kretschmer might be a householder and a solid citizen in his own right. The feast of St Barbara was celebrated in due form, and the gunners continued to lay claim to ancient rights, like the bells of captured towns (for melting down into gun metal), or the straw, firewood and hunks of meat which the Austrian gunners collected from local fairs.

Much of this was swept aside by the blast of rationalism. In the 1750s the Austrian *Generaldirector* Prince Joseph Wenzel von Liechtenstein and the Russian Master General of the Ordnance Petr Ivanovich Shuvalov transformed the artillery in their respective countries into military professions, complete with training schools, testing grounds, annual camps, textbooks and a proper structure of ranks. Both men published comprehensive regulations in 1757. In France the militarisation of the gunners was a gradual process which began as far back as 1695. It was interrupted by an ill-conceived union with the engineers (1755–8), but the work was nearly completed by Jean-Baptiste de Gribeauval in the 1770s.

The nobility now began to make their way in some numbers to the regenerated French artillery corps. In contrast Frederick was unwilling to allow his artillery officers a full professional status, and the social standing of the Prussian gunners remained low. 'The officers of all the regiments in the other arms intermingle freely, and seek each other out with no distinction; something altogether extraordinary would be required to establish a connection between artillery officers and the officers of the other services' (Mirabeau and Mauvillon, 1788, 162).

Artillery 'systems' were another characteristic expression of the Age of Reason. They eliminated the wild diversity of the old ordnance, established the design of barrels and gun carriages on data which were deduced from practical experiments, and incorporated whatever technical improvements might be available in the way of manufacturing techniques (especially boring out the barrels from the solid), ammunition, sighting and elevating mechanisms, and harnessing for the horses. There was no radical change in design to compare with the rifled barrels or breech-loading mechanisms of the nineteenth century, but the many smaller improvements introduced during the eighteenth century brought a significant increase in the mobility, weight of fire and accuracy of the artillery of old Europe. The Austrian System of 1753 was a pioneering establishment of its kind, and it exercised a considerable influence on the work of Gribeauval, who after years of effort gained approval for his own system in 1776.

Field cannon became standardised in Britain, Austria, Prussia, Russia and Denmark on 3-pounders, 6-pounders and 12-pounders (so called after the weight of solid shot they fired), and in France and Spain on 4-pounders, 8-pounders and 12-pounders. These pieces fell into three categories: the lightest calibres (3- and 4-pounders) were attached to the infantry for close support; the medium guns (6- and 8-pounders) were grouped in batteries for longer-range work; the 12-pounder heavyweight was another battery piece, and a genuine battle-winner, representing the best that the age could bring together in firepower and mobility. Liechtenstein's 12-pounder was recognised as a masterpiece, and it was sedulously copied by Frederick in a 12-pounder he adopted for the Prussian artillery in the Seven Years War.

Heavier cannon still were occasionally discovered on the battlefield, but they made their principal contribution in sieges. Howitzers were short pieces which fired an explosive shell, and they were particularly well suited for use against cavalry, fieldworks and defended villages. Frederick persuaded himself that his heavy 10-pounder battery howitzer could carry 4,000 paces, and he became obsessed with the potential of the howitzer towards the end of his reign. NB howitzer shells were designated by 'stone weight', i.e. that of a stone shot of the same calibre.

The artillery in the field

The individual gun and its carriage weighed about a ton. It was transported to the battlefield by horses, and manhandled into its firing positions by unskilled labour drawn from the infantry. The medium and heavy pieces could be most effectively deployed in

> large and strong batteries which lay down a cross fire. They make a potentially decisive contribution to the offensive by overthrowing lengths of the enemy line and making gaps

therein. On the defensive they sweep extensive areas of ground, and beat and defend the approaches and avenues along which the enemy must advance. There is a second maxim which is no less important, namely to try to take up positions from where you may take the enemy in enfilade and in the rear, so that you take them under an oblique fire and torment them from every side. (Nockhern de Schorn, 1783, 196)

The best sites were not the summits of high hills, but on low eminences which commanded a wide field of fire and permitted the artillery to exercise the full grazing effect of its missiles.

From their ammunition chests or limbers the artillerymen selected the rounds which best answered the needs of the moment. The solid roundshot carried furthest, and it continued to wreak execution by ricochet and rolling long after it first hit the ground, which might extend its lethal range from the 600 or 800 paces of the first graze to as much as 2,300 paces (Scharnhorst, 1813, 5).

At close range the most devastating kind of artillery fire was canister (see p. 217), such as the French employed against the celebrated English column at Fontenoy (1745): 'There was not a single shot from those cannon which failed to produce a dreadful carnage, and the first two discharges threw the enemy into such disorder that they rapidly betook themselves to the rear' (quoted in Richelieu, 1918, 107).

The officers of the other arms did not always understand that the accuracy of the ordnance was affected by considerations as diverse as the unevenness of the ground on which the piece stood, the balance of the barrel on the carriage, the quality of the gunpowder, the fit of the shot in the bore, the temperature of the metal and the direction of the wind. Frederick was once dissatisfied with the performance of his artillery. He dismounted, adjusted the aim of a cannon, and hit his target at the first round:

'There you are,' said the king, 'you don't bother to aim properly, otherwise you would have hit.'

'You can't always rely on it' said a veteran gunner.

'Just let me show you!', riposted the king, and he aimed the cannon once again. They fired the gun, and this time the ball followed a totally different path. (Anon., 1788–9, IV, 17)

The initial rounds fired by the artillery in battle were ranging shots from the batteries of medium and heavy pieces. It usually took three discharges at least to find the range (Silva, 1778, 66–7), but the first truly effective rounds were a valuable asset, comparable with the first volley in infantry combat (see p. 211). The guns were clean and cool, and loaded and aimed by gunners who were out of reach of the enemy musketry. This was the kind of fire which laid low the ten leading battalions of Prussian infantry at Torgau (1760) at a range of 850 paces.

Such advantages, as well as a lot of precious ammunition, were thrown away if the gunners opened fire too early. Frederick warned his gunners that they would unfailingly come under heavy moral pressure from the officers of the infantry to do exactly that. He conceded that the gunners could hardly refuse if the officer in question happened to be a general: 'In that case the [artillery] officer must certainly obey, but he must fire as slowly as possible, and take every conceivable care with his aim, so that not every round goes for nothing' (*Instruction für meine Artillerie* [1782], Frederick, 1846–57, III, 392).

The gun detachments fired their pieces with a practised routine. Four professional gunners were usually sufficient to see to the tasks that required skill or careful timing – inserting the load, ramming down the barrel, adjusting the aim, and applying a burning linstock to the vent. The assistants from the infantry were put to work hauling the gun backwards or forwards, or traversing it under the directions of one of the professional gunners. The artillery officers commanded guns by ones, pairs or entire batteries of about six pieces each.

In emergency a field piece could be fired at least as fast as a musket, but the normal rate of fire was conditioned by the heating of the barrel, and how often it was considered necessary to have the piece swabbed out or re-laid after successive rounds, which produced a sustainable average of about two rounds a minute for the light and medium pieces, and one and a half for the 12-pounders and howitzers.

Both the speed of fire and the accuracy were liable to fall off once the gun detachment came under the fire of the enemy infantry. At worst the gunners took to their heels, but more often the experience reinforced the bond which bound them to their pieces and to each other, for the gun was a focus of loyalty still more potent than the colours of the infantry: 'The gunner stands firm, while the infantryman and the cavalryman love movement. This proceeds from the differing nature of their arms' (Schaumburg-Lippe, 1977–83, II, 148). The Austrian artillery had the good practice of assigning the gunners and their officers permanently to the same pieces throughout the campaign, while in Russia the attachment to the gun was cemented by a holy oath. The course of an entire battle could be influenced by a resolutely fought battery, like the guns of the Russian major Tyut-chev which were positioned on a hill at Gross-Jägersdorf (1757).

Guibert, du Theil and Frederick in his later instructions all condemned the penchant of the artillery for counterbattery fire, which the gunners saw as the highest demonstration of their skill. It also helped to win the artillerymen some friends among the other arms, like Lieutenant-General Saldern, who asked Bombardier Kret-schmer to turn his howitzer on an Austrian battery which was ravaging the Prussians at Liegnitz (1760). His first shell forced the Austrians temporarily from their guns, and enabled him to get off a second bomb undisturbed. This second round arched towards an Austrian ammunition cart, and 'when the shell reached the waggon the vehicle exploded, together with another which was standing next to it. Two gunners were blown into the air, and eight more were mutilated or killed. Now the enemy abandoned their battery altoge-ther' (Barsewisch, 1863, 115).

THE BATTLE OF THE GENERALS

Such moments decide the fate of a whole nation,
and it is then that the wisdom of the general must
shine forth.

(Turpin de Crissé, 1754, I, 385)

It was the duty of the commander in chief to betake himself to wherever gave him the best view of the battle as it developed. The centre might seem the most advantageous place, but the Spanish commander Gages was blamed for holding himself immobile there during the battle of Campo Santo (1743) when the critical action was being fought on the right. Frederick was a very hard rider, though commanders who were too old or too infirm for this kind of exertion could still have themselves carried about in chairs by porters, like Montecuccoli or Villars in olden times, or equip themselves with a little carriage, like Saxe at Fontenoy (1745) or Kutuzov at Borodino (1812).

The commander and the senior generals were by no means exempt from the physical dangers of the battlefield. Browne, Schwerin, Keith and Wolfe all went to the same Valhalla in the course of the Seven Years War, and there were many occasions when Frederick nearly joined them. However the Duc de Crillon spared the life of Old Fritz just before the battle of Rossbach (which was a bad mistake), and the Marquis de Lafayette showed the same consideration for the enemy generals Philipps and Arnold, when they wandered within rifle shot of the Americans in Virginia in 1781. James Johnston drew Lafayette's attention to this splendid opportunity, and

> immediately after, there was a bustle at the door occasioned by five riflemen in hunting shirts and moccasins who eagerly solicited permission to steal down to a point from which they felt sure they could pick off these officers. The marquis refused his sanction, declaring that he would meet the enemy openly in the field but would not authorise anything like assassination. (Dann, 1980, 406)

Concerning this kind of danger, Frederick explained that it was not the business of a commander to risk his life. It was, however, worse to be captured than to be killed, and worse still if the commander failed to give an example of personal courage when the need came: 'When a prince embarks on war, and is unwilling to share the consequent dangers, he has no right to expect anyone to be interested in what happens to him' (Catt, 1884, 31).

For the rest, the commander could best serve his army by clearing his mind and maintaining a certain detached serenity. 'On a day of battle, therefore, a general should do nothing. He will see all the more, he will preserve a more balanced judgement, and he will be better able to exploit situations to the disadvantage of his enemy during the course of the combat' (Saxe [1732], 1877, 135–8. See also Silva, 1778, 176). This striking statement corresponds to the realities of command in the eighteenth century. To keep himself informed of what was passing on the battlefield, and to convey the appropriate instructions, the commander was largely dependent on his aides-de-camp and staff officers (see p. 177). These fast-moving gentry spoke with the authority of the commander in chief when they transmitted his orders, and it was still more important for them to understand the sense of the instructions than to be word-perfect. However they were all too often defective in both regards. At Minden (1759) Lord Sackville searched in vain for Prince Ferdinand of Brunswick to find out what was meant by the orders he had received, and he explained to his court martial:

> The distinctness or indistinctness of two young aides-de-camp might have decided the fate of an army. . . . Entrusted with such a command as I bore . . . I determined to act on more certain grounds, having already experienced too much of the confusion of orders sent by aides-de-camp. (Mackesy, 1979, 197. See also Santa Cruz, 1735–40, V, 14)

Probably the most that a commander in chief could hope to do was to move reserves or other uncommitted forces. This appears to run counter to the histories of the wars, which are full of master-strokes which are traced directly to the intervention of the commander. Berenhorst writes that at Prague (1757) a vital gap in the Austrian line was discovered by Colonel Herzberg, who proceeded to roll up the Austrian right flank:

> Several officers of the regiment of Darmstadt told me of this deed of their colonel in the days immediately after the battle, and they added that no general had given the appropriate order. Nowhere have I found that the action was recognised by higher authority. Nowadays the printed accounts attribute the manoeuvre in question to the king, even though it was impossible for him to have issued any such order, because he was far away on the left flank. (Berenhorst, 1845–7, I, 102. See also Puységur, 1749, II, 79–80)

In reality, 'at the moment that the armies collide, he [the commander] is incapable of doing more than one of his generals. He cannot be everywhere, he cannot ordain everything that ought to happen, and it is impossible for him to foresee everything that might take place' (Saxon *Dienst-Reglement* (1753), Jähns, 1889–91, III, 2, 032). In so far as combat could be managed at all it was essentially the work of the subordinate generals. The infantry commanders in the centre conformed as best as they could to the briefings or dispositions they had received before the battle, but an altogether higher level of initiative and mental and physical energy was demanded of the lieutenant-generals and major-generals of the cavalry. Lucchese paid with his life when he brought the right wing of the Austrian cavalry down on Frederick at Leuthen (1757). Seydlitz saved the Prussians through his direct intervention at Zorndorf (1758), but in the following year he was disabled most painfully at the terrible battle of Kunersdorf. After the battle Lojewsky found him lying nearby on a bench:

> His hand had been shattered by a canister shot, and a surgeon was bandaging it up. Next to him was his sword, the hilt of which had been broken by the same ball. Seydlitz's wounded arm was shivering with pain, and his face wore an expression of acute torment while the surgeon picked the splinters of the broken hilt from his stricken hand. (Lojewsky, 1843, II, 272–3)

THE TURNING POINT

The contending forces

Morale and cohesion

If it was necessary to describe in the fewest possible words what determined the outcome of a battle, we should probably not go far wrong if we talked about the circumstances in which the action was given (considerations like numbers, surprise and the advantage of the ground), and the ability of one army to outlast the other once combat had been joined. The endurance was strongly influenced by moral forces:

> In the study of combat one must establish a clear distinction between what is inherently effective, by rendering the enemy physically incapable of doing you any more harm, and what produces the same result through fear, operating principally through moral force. Most of the actions in our modern wars are decided in the second fashion. (Schaumburg-Lippe, 1977–83, II, 146)

Those who had seen war knew that it was not accurate to describe such and such a person as cowardly or fearless, for they knew that during combat everybody was afraid to some extent (Turpin de Crissé, 1754, I, 391). Also courage was not an unchanging commodity which could be transported from one battle to the next. On this point Saxe took issue with the 'scientific' Folard:

He assumes that soldiers are always brave, without taking into account the fact that the courage of troops varies from day to day. . . . Good explanations are rare, for they lie in the hearts of men, and it is there that we must search them out. Nobody has yet expounded on this subject, which is nevertheless the most important, the most subtle and the most fundamental in the trade of war. (Saxe [1732], 1877, 6)

Saxe would probably have agreed that a sense of religion was at work deep inside the soldiers, and that it was given expression in some scarcely recognisable forms. Talismans, personal rituals (see p. 195) and the mechanical performance of engrained battle drills all had a religious, or at least a magical element. Twentieth-century analysis claims that about four-fifths of officers and men experience a heightened sense of religious awareness as the result of exposure to combat, and in the Seven Years War *Feldprediger* Küster found that the effect over a series of campaigns was cumulative. The French were notable for appearing impervious, but among troops like the Russians, the native Prussians and the Spanish the religious observances were strong and formal:

On the day before the battle of Piacenza (1746) all the churches were full of Spanish who were making their confessions and receiving communion. All the inns were full of Frenchmen, who were cursing, making a noise and breaking the windows. When battle was joined the Spanish marched in full daylight across a broad meadow which was swept by ten batteries. They braved the cannon fire with a steady courage which distinguished them markedly from the French. (Wolff, 1776, 51–2)

Among the external influences which made troops disciplined and 'brave', by far the most powerful was the leadership of the officers. Frederick declared with only a little exaggeration that 'the courage of the troops consists entirely in that of the officers: a brave colonel means a brave battalion' (*Règles de ce qu'on exige d'un bon commandeur de bataillon* [1773], Frederick, 1846–57, XXIX, 58. See also Griesheim, 1777, 59).

Many commanders had an understanding of positive leadership of the kind which is applauded at the present day. The Hereditary Prince of Brunswick explained:

The inclinations of the soldiers are such that they will never forsake the officers whom they love. They must be repaid in the same way. Go out and visit them in their tents. Go out to where the advance guards are fighting, and never leave them until you die at their side. (Ray, 1895, 231–2)

However, leadership by example had a way of losing its power in the stress of combat. This was clearly understood by military men in the eighteenth century, and they made no secret of the fact that they applied various degrees of force in order to make up the deficiency. The officer frequently became a driver rather than a leader, like Lieutenant Jakob von Lemcke, who tried to force his platoon to attack a Russian battery at Paltzig (1759):

The men, however, absolutely refused to advance, and stayed behind the trees and shot at the enemy from there. My sword ultimately became . . . completely bent from beating these disobedient fellows, and I still had experienced no success in getting them to move forward when a cannon shot came skipping along and shattered the instep of my left foot, whereupon I crashed instantly to the ground. (Lemcke, 1909, 36)

Lemcke's men at least stayed in the combat, but in countless other actions the soldiers ran for their lives. The disintegration might be checked by immediate and drastic action against an individual (Quincy, 1898–1901, II, 366–7). Things had gone too far for that in the regiment of Normandie, which began to turn about at Kolster-kamp (1760), and a collective effort was employed: 'All the generals of the staff, the aides-de-camp, the volunteers, in fact everybody who was at hand . . . hastened to this regiment, and formed a barrier which not only prevented it from running, but pushed it towards the enemy' (Besenval, 1827–8, I, 93–4). In extreme cases entire unbroken regiments were deployed in the rear of shaken troops, with orders to shoot the fugitives down.

All the time solitary soldiers or small groups stole away from the action whether or not their side was winning. It was well known how at Gross-Jägersdorf (1757) 'the baggage and the bushes and scrub nearby were packed with the [Russian] troops who had sidled away from the battle, and by probably still greater numbers of those who had avoided it altogether' (Weymarn, 1794, 98). At Torgau (1760) the flow became something of a mass resignation, which filled the woods with thousands of Austrian and Prussian soldiers, who peaceably awaited the outcome of the battle. The leaders did not always set the best of examples. At Prague (1757) large numbers of unwounded Prussian officers and NCOs were skulking behind a hill, and one of Frederick's aides-de-camp shared a ditch with Pierre, the notoriously cowardly servant of the Abbé des Prades.

It was a profitless exercise to try to route these people from their hiding places, but something might still be done to rally troops which were broken by outright enemy action. A great deal of detail has been preserved about an episode at the battle of Prague which opened as an almost unrelieved tactical disaster. It concerns the left wing of the Prussian infantry, which contained a large number of unwilling Catholic conscripts. These second-rate troops had been flung forward without the support of artillery or reserves, and they ran into a zone of boggy ground, a battery of Austrian 12-pounders and a line of advancing Austrian grenadiers. They broke under the ordeal. Field-Marshal Schwerin rode forward with a regimental colour in his hand, and was struck dead by a canister blast. (This was in any case a futile gesture, as Frederick discovered at Kolin and Kunersdorf, and old Blaise de Montluc could have told him from the sixteenth century). The surviving Prussian officers fared no better, shouting at the troops not to retreat another step.

General Henri de la Motte Fouqué now applied the experience he had acquired during years of sport in the fields and woods at Dessau. He galloped to the rear of the various battalions, which were bolting with greater or lesser velocity, and he called out to the officers: ' "Let them run! Over there," (pointing with his sword to the edge of the marshy meadow through which the troops had waded, which was five or six hundred paces to the rear), "over there! That's where we will bring them together again." This is an expression used by huntsmen at a shoot, when they wish to restore the lines of beaters and groups of guns. The fugitives were duly brought to a stand, and after the battalions were reformed they were led once more against the enemy' (Berenhorst, 1845–7, I, 103).

Many other agents were capable of influencing the soldier to the good. Some were at the command of the officers, and some were not. Regimental colours were an important symbol of cohesion and loyalty on the battlefield, and a well-timed invocation of military ceremonial was capable of producing the same effect. At Brandywine Creek (1777), after the Hessian grenadiers had crossed the ford, they halted at the foot of the hill below the Americans, under a warm fire, and with great deliberation changed their hats for their heavy brass caps, which they carry by a loop on a button at the hip, and then ascended the hill, from which the Americans were obliged to retire. (Heath, 1901, 117)

Battle-cries were a positive sound which served to alleviate the other noises of combat, which were all too often of a distressing or intimidating nature. The Russians had their deep 'Ura!' just as the Germans and Austrians gave vent to their characteristic 'Victoria!' The trumpets of the cavalry were capable of cutting through the din of combat, though the drums were easily confused with the cannon and musketry, and the woodwind of the regimental 'music' was deficient in power. On 25 August 1758 some of the Prussian music continued to play up splendidly until the rival infantry got to grips, but the regiment of Bevern found that its musicians exhausted their breath and resolution in the neighbourhood of Zorndorf village, and

now they abandoned us and removed themselves to safety. We may compare the conduct of these men in a battle with those swallows which disappear in autumn before the onset of harsh weather, and come back in fine condition in spring. Nobody knows in what corner of the world they hide themselves away in the meantime. (Prittwitz, 1935, 218)

Taken to some excess, alcohol proved to be calming, invigorating and comradely. It only became dangerous when the warriors were exhausted and came upon a store of unusually strong spirits. The Prince de Ligne saw how a keg of brandy poleaxed the officers of his regiment at Leuthen (1757), while at Zorndorf the Russian infantry broke open the army's supply of liquor and ended the day in a state of stupefaction and bestial rage.

The finest intoxicant of all was the sight or news of some success along the line of battle, and this experience was capable of energising troops who had seemingly passed the limit of their physical and moral resources. The capture of Lobositz village produced such an effect among the Prussians towards the end of the very long combat on 1 October 1756. At Gross-Jägersdorf, in the following year, a yell spread along the Russian line that some kind of victory had been attained on the left:

Wherever this shout came from, it produced some undoubtedly good effects. The Second Grenadier Regiment found new stores of courage and went out to attack the enemy once again. The Narva Regiment advanced with levelled bayonets under a constant fire, even though most of the officers were dead and wounded and it had thereby been reduced to such disorder that the ranks and files had disappeared. (Weymarn, 1794, 200–1)

The Prussian army in the Seven Years War offers perhaps our best example of how stress might be surmounted or at least mitigated by a large body over a long period of time. It survived as an effective and disciplined body, fighting against immensely superior odds, until it underwent a near-collapse towards the end of that struggle. A number of explanations may be advanced:

1   The army was backed by good administration in the form of regular issues of pay, rations and clothing. It is remarkable how on the march from Rossbach to Leuthen in 1757, which was a period of dire emergency for Frederick, the troops halted for a day at Torgau so as to fit themselves out with the annual issue of uniforms.

2   The system of 'cantonal' conscription made good the losses in personnel and provided every regiment with at least 3,000 recruits in the course of the war. The quality of the army was actually never better than at the end of 1757, by when many of the foreign mercenaries had died or run away and had been replaced by native soldiers. However the king continued to recruit heavily from among enemy deserters and prisoners, so as to supply himself with expendable cannon fodder.

3   Formal discipline was savagely maintained for most of the war. Frederick had only 5,000 troops under command at the end of the battle of Kunersdorf in 1759, yet on the next day men were being beaten if they were found without weapons.

4   Frederick reserved most of the best troops for the army under his direct command. The army of Prince Henry and the various detached corps were left with a higher proportion of the Silesian fusiliers, the regiments from East Prussia and the western provinces, and the rabble of the free corps.

5   Artillery was increasingly used as a substitute for infantry. Frederick built up a powerful reserve of howitzers and thick-barrelled 12-pounders as battery pieces, and in 1760 he assigned

ten light 12-pounders to every brigade of infantry for close-range fire support. The Austrian grenadiers ran into these weapons at Liegnitz (15 August) and were massacred.

6 Finally, a number of the symptoms of stress probably helped to alleviate the basic disease. The heavy desertion among the troops was very damaging, but it acted as a constant purge of the most unreliable elements, and it was a preferable alternative to mutiny. Many officers hoped for some kind of ultimate salvation through the royal brother Prince Henry, who was a cautious commander and an accessible individual. They made little secret of their dislike for spiky Old Fritz, but they meanwhile fought like lions in his cause.

Stress and disintegration

Casualties were often the most tangible sign that a unit was under stress in combat. In the Second World War men were lost by their hundreds of thousands at a time in the battles on the Eastern front. These, however, were engagements which lasted for weeks on end, and they were spread over great tracts of ground. One of the distinguishing features of the older battles was that they were extremely concentrated in both time and place. The issue was commonly decided between daybreak and noon, and the lines of battle of whole armies might be crammed into a space equivalent to the frontage of a couple of modern battalions. Experience showed that an eighteenth-century army could consider itself lucky to survive a day of battle with less than 25 per cent casualties.

It is impossible to establish exactly what proportions of casualties were inflicted by the various weapons. The most convincing evidence appears at first sight to come from records like those of the Invalides in Paris, which detail the admissions for 1762 as follows:

68.8%	wounded by	small arms
13.4%	,,	artillery
14.7%	,,	swords
2.4%	,,	bayonets

(Corvisier, 1964, 65)

However, these were by definition survivable wounds. The proportion of casualties inflicted by the sword is greatly exaggerated as a result, just as the effect of artillery is very much understated (see p. 265).

Again an unquantifiable number of these wounds was inflicted not by the enemy, but accidentally through one's own comrades. Bayonets were a notorious cause of accidental injury, and so were badly aimed bullets. An Austrian officer noted:

> The battle of Kolin in 1757 was the first and only action I have ever seen where our troops kept up an orderly and aimed fire in tightly-closed ranks, and yet many a brave lad fell dead of wounds inflicted from the back, without having turned tail to the enemy. . . . The surgeons were later ordered to inspect the battlefield, and it transpired that these mortal wounds had been delivered by men of the rearward ranks, who carelessly mishandled their muskets in the heat of the fire. (Cogniazzo, 1779, 31)

Storms of bullets and canister howled across the eighteenth-century battlefield, and at long range they pelted the combatants with lead and iron, inflicting contusions, knocking off hats, bending buckles and sword hilts, and lodging in the uniforms in quite astonishing quantities. Lieutenant Thomas Anburey wrote after the action at Ticonderoga on 12 July 1777:

> That soldiers have many hair-breadth escapes, I am sure was never more fully verified than in regard to Lord Balcarres, who commands the light infantry; he had nearly thirty balls shot through his jacket and trousers, and yet received only a small graze on his hip. (Anburey, 1969, I, 338–9)

The effect of missiles at short range made the certainty of being wounded part of a military career in the eighteenth century (Mercoyrol de Beaulieu, 1915, 4–5), and from the grisly details supplied by the necrologist von Pauli it is clear that individuals could be hit many times over in the course of a single action. Colonel Hermann von Wartensleben of the Prussian Carabiniers hewed into the Austrian cavalry at Mollwitz (1741) and made off with a standard:

> But he acquired this trophy at a very high price. The enemy were eager to bring him down and they made after him. His horse received two wounds, and both reins were severed. The Austrians then began to hack at his jerkin, and they ripped it

in several places. Now things became really dangerous for him. First of all an enemy bullet dealt him a very hard glancing blow on the right knee. Then a ball took him under the left arm and lodged near the spine, from where it later had to be cut out. Finally the most painful and serious wound of all was caused by a ball of deliberately cut lead, which he received in the neck under the chin. (Pauli, 1768, 283–4)

Wartensleben survived the day (unlike most of von Pauli's subjects), but he had to retire from the service as an invalid.

When a full-bore musket bullet penetrated with force, it frequently described an eccentric course as it skidded off the tissues inside the body, causing horrible damage on the way. Pellet wounds were disabling in the short term, but less lethal. Many Prussians were rendered temporarily *hors de combat* at Zorndorf and Kunersdorf, for the Russians were firing buckshot along with their musket balls. Likewise an English surgeon wrote from Boston in 1777 about a habit of the American rebels:

Their muskets were charged with old nails and angular pieces of iron, and from most of the men being wounded in the legs, I am inclined to believe it was their design, not wishing to kill the men, to leave them as burdens on us, to exhaust the provisions, as well as to intimidate the rest of the soldiery. (Moore, 1860, I, 101)

The locations of the wounds yield an important insight into the experience of the eighteenth-century battlefield. Corvisier has noted that the infantry were most frequently hit down the left side, and he concludes that 'the left side was the one which he most frequently presented to the enemy, whether he was engaged with the bayonet, or loading or aiming' (Corvisier, 1964, 681).

As we have seen, cavalry wounds were typically concentrated on the right wrist and forearm. The most inherently dangerous wounds were certainly those inflicted by the sword point in the chest or stomach, but from the anecdotal evidence most of the mortal or disabling blows were chops with the edge, which severed arms, split heads or sliced off ears and noses. Major-General Ludwig von Zastrow was hacked about by Chevert's cavalry at Lutterberg on 10 October 1758, and afterwards he presented

a terrible sight. . . . His nose has been cut off, and one sees the

two holes of his nostrils . . . his two lips are missing, and the
saliva pours from his mouth; there are six or seven light wounds,
the scars of which are terrible. (Westphalen, 1859–72, II, 502)

Injuries were of course a catastrophe for many individuals.
Unbearable pain was likely to supervene after the first numbing
shock had worn off, and the long-concealed fears of the family men
now came to the surface:

'If I die on this spot, what will happen to my wife and children?'
This is a lamentation I have heard a number of times from
married officers who have received a mortal wound. Now at
last they surrender to the force of nature, and utter what they
have so long concealed in the depths of their hearts. (Santa Cruz,
1735–40, I, xvi–xvii)

In some actions Frederick and other senior officers had two or
more horses killed under them in as many hours. For the private
trooper the loss of a horse brought separation from a beloved
companion, whose name had for years on end been entered with
that of its master on the regimental muster list. To our eyes few
sights on the battlefield could have been more distressing than to see
one of these innocent creatures which had been disembowelled by
the artillery, and was tripping up in its own intestines or was trailing
them along the ground. It must remain a matter of surmise whether
the sensibilities of the men of the eighteenth century had been to
some degree blunted by the almost daily experience of the slaughter
of animals in the farmyard and on the hunting field. Frederick was
one of the very few soldiers who displayed any squeamishness in
this respect.

It might appear absurd to ask how important casualties really
were to the course of a battle. The veteran Zanthier brooked no
uncertainty in the matter: 'What is it that destroys the courage of
troops in action, what makes them take to their heels? I will tell you
– it is the losses which they sustain' (Zanthier, 1778, 107). Another
commentator noted that the allies lost the battle of Fontenoy (1745)
because

it became impossible for broken corps [i.e. regiments], who had
lost their generals, most of their officers, and at least one-third
of their men, without being sustained, and cherished by fresh

leaders, as well as fresh corps, to support the repeated efforts of fresh troops. (Rolt, 1753, 403)

The effect of casualties was undeniably felt in a diversity of ways. When a man was struck down, the army was not only deprived of a unit of force, but his comrades were affected to a greater or lesser extent. While a corpse might become an occasion of macabre humour, the sight of a wounded man was 'an unpleasant sight for all soldiers, causing, as it does, reflection, and awakening in them timidity and even fear of the future' (Pausch, 1886, 143). It was standard procedure before combat to forbid soldiers to carry away the wounded, for without this precaution four or five men would take it on themselves to leave the ranks to bear each casualty to the regimental dressing station, and they were unlikely to return in a hurry.

Heavy casualties among regimental officers usually brought an end to platoon firing and any elaborate tactical manoeuvres, and the death or wounding of a general was dreaded as much for the moral effect as for any loss of real control. Field-Marshal Daun was only following established custom when he sought to conceal his wound at Torgau (1760):

It is possible that the nearest regiments might learn that you have been wounded, whether through the blood, or a change in the colour of your face. In that case you must give out that your wound is slight, and forbid the soldiers to spread the news, for fear of alarming the other regiments. (Santa Cruz, 1735–40, VI, 118)

Modern Soviet strategists have established that casualties influence the outcome of an operation not just through their absolute numbers, but through the rate at which they have been sustained. Thus a butcher's bill of 40 per cent in two days is far more dangerous to a formation that 70 per cent losses which are spread over two weeks. This principle has a direct application to the circumstances of eighteenth-century combat, which was extremely compact in every dimension (see p. 245), and where casualties of these orders could be suffered in a matter of minutes.

If casualties might be important in determining how a combat went, they were by no means uniquely so. At Mollwitz (1741), which was the first battle of Frederick's career, the victorious Prussians lost about 300 more men than the Austrians, 'which furnishes a clear proof that the men with the wooden ramrods [i.e. the Austrians] might have fired less frequently, but certainly fired more accurately and effectively' (Cogniazzo, 1788–91, II, 47). So it remained for the rest of Frederick's reign. Regardless of the outcome of the battles, the Prussians nearly always suffered heavier casualties than their enemies. The only exceptions were the great Prussian victories at Rossbach and Leuthen in 1757, and even there the relative casualties at the decisive stages could well have been evenly balanced. Commentators from Plutarch onwards remarked that many more casualties were inflicted during the pursuit than in the crisis of the combat, and the old truth was affirmed by the sight of the field at Rossbach, where 'the roads were littered with French breastplates and great cavalry boots . . . which they have cast away to facilitate their flight, and with lost hats. The sunken road at Marktwerben was full of mutilated Frenchmen' (Wiltsch, 1858, 183).

Some units in the Second World War were capable of fighting effectively after they had suffered 70 per cent casualties. Comparable losses were sustained by the Swiss battalion in the Piedmontese pay at Parma (1734) which stood firm under the command of a second lieutenant, who was the only surviving officer. For a unit to stay in combat in these conditions it was important for every man in authority to be prepared to take on a higher responsibility as soon as the need arose, and Colonel Semen Romanovich Vorontsov claims that one of the reasons for the fabled tenacity of the Russians was that this kind of understanding reached down through the ranks of the NCOs (Vorontsov [1802], 1876, 475).

The casualties in battle were far from being the only ingredient of what is loosely called 'stress'. The morale and efficiency of the combatants were simultaneously being undermined by other processes.

The more a unit was attached to its colours, the more it was likely to be affected by their loss. Some were literally lost, like the three standards of the English 3rd Dragoons which were trampled into the mud at Dettingen. Many became the target of enemy attacks, or were shot to pieces along with their bearers. At Fontenoy (1745) the bullets buzzed around the English flags like bees, for 'they were shooting at the standards like mad' (Hamilton, 1927, 96), and Warnery noted that in Frederick's wars 'the discharges of canister were aimed mostly at the colours, and I remember how in one hard-fought battle all the *Fahnenjunkers* of a battalion were killed or disabled before most of them had reached their sixteenth or seventeenth year' (Warnery, 1785–91, III, 478–9).

Once battle was joined, the ears were afflicted by a ceaseless battering. The musketry was compared with a rolling of drums, and at Freeman's Farm in 1777 the English lieutenant William Digby was stunned by 'such an explosion of fire which I never had any idea of before, and the heavy artillery joining in concert like great peals of thunder, assisted by the echoes of the woods, almost deafened us by the noise' (Digby, 1887, 273). Hunger was sharpened by overexcitement, and raging thirst was another unwelcome companion of battle – which in the Age of Reason was usually staged in high summer. In the last stages of the battle of Zorndorf (1758) the advance of the Prussians became a scramble to reach the stagnant waters near Zicher, muddy though they were and coloured with Russian blood.

As campaign followed campaign, the character and performance of the army as a whole underwent a progressive degradation. In the Seven Years War the first changes were already evident in 1758. Many of the best officers and soldiers had not survived the intense campaigning in 1757, which had been a year of many battles and very heavy losses:

> To this consideration we must add the mournful prospect of
> further campaigns, and the way of thinking of the new
> generation of commanders, all of which made it necessary to
> spare the troops. Now we had to proceed with due
> deliberation, whereas previously we had acted with speed and
> thrown caution to the winds. (Retzow, 1802, I, 444)

The critical year was 1761, at least for Frederick and his allies. The royal army was near disintegration, and in western Germany Prince Ferdinand of Brunswick saw 'with the utmost concern . . . a total relaxation of discipline in the army under my command . . . order and discipline being entirely banished, every kind of excess has been committed with impunity' (Savory, 1966, 309).

Among the individual arms of the service, the cavalry was nearly always the one which was least affected by the deterioration. It suffered many fewer casualties in proportion than the foot soldiers, and it was an attractive trade which continued to draw good recruits. Warnery comments that day by day the infantry lost more and more men to the large trains of artillery which are taken into the field by all the different arms. Exhaustion and siegework also account for many men. And so, the more the infantry is exposed to combat and campaigning, the more it degenerates instead of improving. (Warnery, 1785–91, II, 102–3. See also Frederick to von der Goltz, Frederick 1879–1939, XX 478)

When veteran regiments went into battle, they had to cope not just with the natural apprehensions of the day, but the memories of what they had endured in previous combats. This grisly legacy accumulated from battle to battle, and its influence may be clearly traced in the Seven Years War. We will follow one of these sequences over a number of campaigns, starting with the troops of the Prussian corps of Bevern in the midsummer of 1757. These men had been engaged in the bloody battle of Prague (6 May), and shortly afterwards they were ordered to open an offensive against a new Austrian army under Field-Marshal Daun:

> No troops could have marched off with less good grace than did our men on this occasion. . . . It was as if they were being led to the scaffold, for the resistance of the Austrians had taken them by surprise and made them anxious for the future . . . our strength and courage seemed to have drained away. (Warnery, 1788, 135)

The Prussians might have been consoled to know that the Austrian survivors of the battle of Prague had been just as badly shaken by the experience. A number of these men had escaped to Daun's army, and they happened to be posted on the right wing when it came under attack from the Prussians at Kolin on 18 June. The Austrians on this sector now gave way, quite possibly on account of the 'fresh memories' of what had happened to them at Prague (Cogniazzo, 1788–91, II, 355). The tide was ultimately turned in favour of the Austrians by new and untried troops.

In its turn, the battering which the Prussians sustained at Kolin had an adverse effect on the performance of the two regiments of Bevern and Prince Moritz at Zorndorf (1758). This battle, together with that of Gross-Jägersdorf (1757) showed that the Russians were tougher enemies still than the Austrians. In 1759 Frederick marched against the Russian position at Kunersdorf, and on the night before this disastrous battle the Prussian army was overcome by exhaustion and unease: 'The one unit unaffected by this grim frame of mind was the hussar regiment of Colonel Belling, which had been raised only the year before. The men did not share the mood of the other regiments, and found it quite incomprehensible' (Lojewsky, 1843, II, 255. See Atwood, 1980, 129 for a similar process among the Hessians in the American War of Independence).

The soldier is overcome by the collapse of body and will when his moral resources have at last been drained away. The Prussian *Feldprediger* Carl Daniel Küster was thus overtaken after he had survived the worst of the battle of Hochkirch (1758):

> All of a sudden I was overtaken by a fear which deprived me
> of all my courage, and a terror which set my limbs a-trembling.
> A little child could have pushed me over. . . . On the subject
> of this so-called 'cannon-fever' I have often talked with officers
> of all ranks, as well as with valiant private soldiers. They assure
> me with one voice that anyone who maintains he has gone
> through battle, and never experienced this appalling fear, must
> be accounted a braggart and a liar. But they all talked about
> something which I have often noted myself, namely that such
> a sensation is spread in such a way over the early, middle and
> final stages of the battle that the stronger men bear up the weaker
> ones, and that a general flight sets in only when this disabling
> fear affects the morale of the majority of the army, and the weak
> men carry the strong along with them. (Küster, 1791, 61–2)

Küster's 'cannon fever' clearly has much in common with the 'battleshock' which has been identified by twentieth-century commentators. They have also drawn attention to a 'curve of combat efficiency' which denotes the individual's response to the stress of combat over the long term. After his first experiences of action the soldier attains a 'plateau of maximum effort'. All the time, however, his resources are being depleted by the effort required to survive stressful experiences, and his period of greatest proficiency is succeeded by an accelerating degeneration which may produce the collapse of all his defences.

A man's passage along the curve is not predictable. In the fighting in Normandy in 1944 the *via dolorosa* was completed in about fifty days, while in the bitter actions in 1973 the Israelis found that it was accomplished in just thirty hours. Küster was a careful observer, and there is no reason to doubt his contention that the warrior could be overcome by the 'cannon fever' at any stage in the combats of the Seven Years War – in other words much more quickly than in the modern experience. This supposition is confirmed by episodes like the fate of the Russian Observation Corps at Kunersdorf, where it came under a converging and intense artillery fire at the beginning of the battle. When the Prussian infantry came storming in 'this impressive formation made no attempt to defend itself, but lay on the ground and let itself be massacred by bayonet thrusts, and all in honour of St Nicholas their patron' (Warnery, 1788, 312). Here is striking evidence of the intensity of eighteenth-century combat.

The decision

What causes one side to give way, and the other to push on to victory, cannot always be determined with final conviction. We have paused to consider aspects of combat like leadership, morale, casualties and stress, but these alone do not necessarily supply the answer.

Scientifically minded analysts attach great importance to superiority of numbers in determining the outcome of a battle, but this consideration is meaningless unless we have an exact knowledge of what numbers were brought to bear at a precise time and a particular location. Information of this kind is difficult to retrieve from eighteenth-century records. In the experience of the Prince de Ligne: 'I have never yet seen more than six battalions simultaneously in action . . . has there ever been a combat in which twenty battalions have genuinely come under really heavy fire?' (Ligne, 1795–1811, I, 255). Frederick the Great gained almost all of his victories when he was inferior in total force, which bears out an old maxim that battles were 'usually won only by a small number of men. The whole art is to know how to choose them, and to place them in a way which most effectively answers your plan and their potential' (Turpin de Crissé, 1754, I, 390, quoting Vegetius).

Chance must also be allowed a place, for there were occasions when the outcome of a battle hung by a thread. The Austrians won Kolin (1757) when they thought it had been lost, and they lost at Torgau (1760) when they thought they had safely won. Lastly the higher leadership had the power to set all other considerations at naught, as was the experience of the Prussian army inthe Seven Years War (Bonneville, 1762, I, 65; Warnery, 1785–91, II, 170–1).

The turning of the battle might take the form of a measured withdrawal of one of the armies, an uncontrollable melting away of the troops, or an outright flight. One man who openly admitted to turning tail was the North Carolina militiaman Garret Watts, who fought at Camden on 16 August 1780: 'The cause of that I cannot tell, except that everyone I saw was about to do the same. It was instantaneous. There was no effort to rally, no encouragement to fight. Officers and men joined in the flight' (Dann, 1980, 197). The contagious and mindless quality of the thing had also been noted by a Prussian officer who saw the troops of the advance guard recoil towards him at Zorndorf (1758) 'and crash like madmen into our ranks, throwing our men into such confusion that they began to fire as well, and inevitably inflicted more casualties on our own side than on the pursuing Russians' (Prittwitz, 1935, 219).

Turning points often passed undetected for a considerable time, for the course of a combat was notoriously difficult to read. Louis XV and his generals met on horseback at the height of the battle of Fontenoy (1745) and 'raised their voices so loudly that all those within earshot could hear every word that was being said' (Richelieu, 1918, 106). Frederick and his commanders argued publicly at an almost identical gathering which they formed at Lobositz (1756), when their soldiers were already winning their battle for them around Lobositz village.

Even a trained observer like the Russian staff officer Weymarn was never able to discover what had passed before his eyes at Gross-Jägersdorf (1757), where the ground was cut up by villages and woods and 'everything was in continual action and movement, and the air was veiled in smoke and mist and reverberating with the most frightful noise' (Weymarn, 1794, 187–8. See also Berenhorst, 1845–7, I, 72).

Combat in the Age of Reason was as concentrated and hard-fought as in almost any period of history, and yet it knew many episodes which suggest that the 'empty battlefield' was by no means an exclusive product of the nineteenth and twentieth centuries. Dust, smoke, crops, bushes or field fortifications might conceal the combatants from each other even when they were engaged at close range. There were times when the French at Fontenoy (1745) were visible only through the white paper stuck in their hats, just as the glint of sunlight on brass caps might be the only evidence of the Prussian grenadiers. Sometimes the landscape seemed to have been deserted altogether. The rival forces at Zorndorf (1758) amounted to about 80,000 men, and yet the Prussian Gardes du Corps traversed the middle of the field and saw no troops except twenty Russian cuirassiers and a regiment of Prussian infantry which was marching to the rear with a total lack of any apparent concern (Kalkreuth, 1840, IV, 146). No less curiously the Prussian regiment of Darmstadt passed through the centre of the Austrian position at the crisis of the battle of Prague (1757), and 'the action had fallen so quiet that it did not hear a single shot during its whole passage through the camp which had been abandoned by the enemy' (Berenhorst, 1845–7, I, 102). At Liegnitz (1760) the Austrian commanders Daun and Lacy remained unaware that their colleague Loudon was desperately engaged against Frederick only two or three miles from their own locations.

If, however, the officers had a clear sight of the enemy, they searched for the well-known signs of impending collapse, like confusion in the ranks and files, or a wavering in the colours and muskets. With luck, substantial parts of the enemy line might be seen to be breaking away. A group of Russian officers happened to have a good view of the troops at the far end of the Prussian right at Gross-Jägersdorf:

> for a time they held their ground and kept on firing. But once they saw that their comrades were running away they believed that it was high time for them to do the same. What an agreeable and entrancing spectacle it was! . . . To begin with their line recoiled a few paces, then a little more, then more again and gathering speed all the time. We could see all of this happening, but we were still torn between hope and fear and hardly dared to believe our eyes. 'Are they really pulling back?' somebody asked. 'Oh God, grant us victory!' Soon our cup of joy was overflowing. We saw that their whole line was in full retreat, and we cried out 'God be praised, we're winning, we're winning!' (Bolotov, 1870–3, I, 539)

It was now possible to move forward with some confidence, though you were well advised not to take prisoners until the victory was absolutely assured. At the battle of Long Island (1776) the Americans' 'fear of the Hessian troops was . . . indescribable; in contrast they offered the British much more opposition, but when they caught only a glimpse of a blue coat, they surrendered immediately, and begged on their knees for their lives' (Atwood, 1980, 68). If men like these were spared, they could consider themselves lucky. The victors had to be on their guard against 'resurrection men' who shammed dead and then fired into their back. No less reprehensibly the second battalion of the regiment of Alt-Kreytzen threw down its muskets at Zorndorf (1758), then took them up again when the Prussian cavalry came spurring to the rescue.

Outright and unjustified massacre was usually the work of the cavalry. The English 15th Light Dragoons gained an evil reputation in this respect in the Seven Years War in western Germany, and the mood of collective savagery which could overtake the horsemen was discovered by an officer of the Prussian hussars at Hohenfriedeberg in 1745. The Prusssian cavalry was waiting for the signal to attack, and

> during this short pause I heard some commotion and loud
> chatter among the hussars standing behind me. This was an
> infraction of our strict standards of discipline, and I asked an
> NCO what was happening.
> 'The lads are beside themselves with joy,' he answered.
> 'They have been ordered to give no quarter to the Saxons.'
> 'This is the first I have heard of any such order. Who gave
> it?'
> 'I cannot tell, but somebody certainly did.'
> I wanted to ask Major Seydlitz, but at that moment the
> trumpets sounded the charge. The dragoons were formed up
> beside and behind us, and the whole mass crashed into the
> enemy like a thunder cloud driven by a storm. I cannot recall
> having seen another battle in which we displayed more
> enthusiasm or burning anger. (Lojewsky, 1843, I, 178–9)

Prisoners were most likely to be accepted after passions had cooled, or if they gave in before they had inflicted appreciable casualties on the victors. This notion of exchange was still more clearly expressed in the ritual which concerned the surrender of officers. These gentlemen were expected to purchase their lives by yielding up a watch, an embroidered sash or a purse of coins. If the enemy soldier was high-minded and proud, as well as merciful, he handed the present back to the officer, who in this case was now under a moral obligation to report this noble conduct to the man's commander.

A vigorous pursuit was recognised as the necessary consummation of victory, and for this purpose the authorities recommended that the commander should send his reserves or his light cavalry pounding after the enemy. It is all the more remarkable that 'there is perhaps not as much as one battle in ten when a few battalions or sections of the line can mount a pursuit of a retreating enemy according to the prescribed rules' (Bigot, 1761, I, 294). The prudent Daun was only acting in character when he failed to exploit his successes at Kolin and Hochkirch, but some of the most conspicuous failures were on the part of those who spoke most eloquently in favour of the pursuit à outrance. Nothing much happened after the victories of Saxe at Rocoux and Laffeldt. Frederick did little after Chotustiz and Hohenfriedeberg, and it was only with the utmost difficulty that he got his army to undertake an effective pursuit after his great triumph at Leuthen. How do we account for such a pronounced gap between theory and practice?

The more tidy-minded generals might wish to stay on the field so as to bring their regiments to order and wait for the provision trains to catch up. Others might attach importance to political constraints, or obey their own sense of caution: 'A commander shows his greatest skill when he knows when to set proper limits on his victory. There is only a certain point to which it is permissible to press your advantages' (Gaigne, 1778, 6). He might also flatter himself that he was contributing more surely to the enemy's ultimate destruction, for he had read in Vegetius: 'The maxim of Scipio, that a golden bridge should be made for a flying enemy, has much been commended. For when they have free room to escape they think of nothing but how to save themselves by flight, and the confusion becoming general, great numbers are cut to pieces' (Vegetius, 1767, 164).

The other inhibiting factors relate directly to the experience of war. After Gross-Jägersdorf the Russian commander called the pursuit to a rapid halt, and one of his reasons was that the field was virtually covered with men who had broken away 'and were busied exclusively with killing off the wounded Prussians, and stripping and plundering the bodies of our men and the enemy alike' (Weymarn, 1794, 99). The dead soldiers lost their stockings, shoes, shirts and hair ribbons, and were left crouching naked in a way which reminded a Russian officer of sleeping infants. The image conjured up by the English bodies on the hillside at Prestonpans (1745) was that of grazing sheep (for the state of the field of Parma, 1734, see Goldoni, 1926, 144).

Aparaksin was only paying tribute to a universal instinct of the soldiers and camp followers, and the military authorities considered themselves fortunate if they could bring this hideous business under a measure of control. Santa Cruz commended the arrangements which had been instituted in the Spanish army to set aside share in the plunder for the officers, while the Austrians laid down that after the enemy had been seen out of sight

> the commanding general is to permit the taking of plunder in such a way that it does not take place all at once, but is carried out by relays of troops . . . with their respective officers and NCOs. (*Generals-Reglement*, Vienna 1769, 127)

The nerves of the victorious high command were still stretched to breaking point, and a single cannon shot or the mistaken report of a counterattack were capable of producing panic of the kind which broke out in the Spanish headquarters after Velletri (1744) or in Frederick's after Lobositz (1756). One of the first instincts of the commander was to reassure himself that he had really won, and while the enemy were already making good their escape he might throw himself into the ritual prescribed for the victorious general – clearing the field of equipment and weapons, and gathering the trophies of prisoners, artillery, trumpets, drums, standards and colours. He also had to arrange a *feu de joie*, and render suitable thanks to the Almighty through the Te Deum or public prayers.

Only the strongest-minded generals could make headway against the euphoria and lassitude which now engulfed the army. In the late afternoon of the battle of Prague (6 May 1757) the Prussian hussars were lying gorged and bloated in the captured Austrian camp. General Zieten galloped up and commanded them to launch a pursuit:

> This put Colonel Warnery in some embarrassment. He pointed to the countless knots of revellers, and the long rows of sleeping drunks. Zieten looked in the indicated direction. 'My God,' he said, 'is there anybody who is sober?' Warnery, who was a hot and fiery character, exclaimed 'Tomorrow I'll have the lads beaten within an inch of their lives!' 'No, Colonel

Warnery, don't do that,' answered Zieten softly. 'Let them enjoy their rest. They have had a hard enough time today.'
(Lojewsky, 1843, II, 61–2)

Finally a crowd was assembled from all the cavalry regiments of the army and was sent after the Austrians. The Prussians no longer had the heart to kill the enemy, and they were content to round up their defenceless prisoners like sheep.

After the battle

On the evening and night following the battle, peasant children might be revelling in their new playthings, like the caps of the Prussian grenadier battalion of Nimschöffky, which had been annihilated at Kolin. A few soldiers might be abroad, rummaging for fur hats or other items of clothing which could be cut up and put to good use. Others broke up waggons and musket stocks for firewood, or dragged the dead and wounded unthinkingly aside in order to make themselves space to sleep: 'It is not a question of being hard-hearted, unless you are an authentic villain. But you are so glad to have survived the day that you become a little insensitive' (Ligne, 1928, II, 7).

The next day brought a horrible awakening, for

the conflict once over, the mind returns to its proper sense of feeling, and deeply must its sensibility be wounded, when the eye glances over the field of slaughter . . . and the ear is continually pierced with the deep sighs and groans of the dying. (Anburey, 1969, 338)

The nose was simultaneously assailed by the abattoir reek of split-open bodies, the foxy stench of bloody hair, and the roast-pork smell of gunners who had been blown up by their ammunition waggons.

The spectacle of the ground was not without interest for officers who were capable of showing some professional detachment. After Zorndorf (1758) the bodies of the well-disciplined infantry lay in lines. Dead artillerymen were piled in heaps, and the scenes of cavalry action were shown by isolated corpses spread over a wide area (Kalkreuth, 1840, IV, 152). The retreat of the Russians could be traced by little wooden crosses, marking the graves of soldiers who had died along the way.

Indeed, 'the men under your command if they see their comrades left without burial, they believe with good reason that you will treat them in the same contemptuous way if they too come to die.' (Santa Cruz, 1735–40, VI, 182). The rebels outside Boston in 1775 were distressed to hear that the body of one of their comrades had been dug up and removed, probably for sale to some barber-surgeon.

The soldiers seldom had the opportunity to lay their friends to rest in the way they desired. For the great majority of the dead the last offices were performed by conscripted peasants and drivers, who dug great pits, brought up corpses by the cartload and tumbled and kicked them inside – officers and men, friend and foe terribly intermingled. On the field of White Plains (1776),

> some of the bodies had been so slightly buried that the dogs or pigs, or both, had dug them out of the ground. The skulls and other bones and hair were scattered about the place. Here were Hessian skulls as thick as a bombshell. Poor fellows! They were left unburied in a foreign land. (Martin, 1962, 134)

The survivors could laugh when the call now came to retrieve the body of some eminent individual. After Hochkirch (1758) 'although a corpse was buried as that of Field-Marshal Keith, it is very doubtful whether it really was him' (Kalkreuth, 1840, IV, 165). The Prince de Ligne knew for certain that the remains of a Prussian soldier were transported more than 400 miles to rest in an elaborate tomb at Namur, in place of the officer son of a wealthy Netherlandish family. Likewise the body of Frederick's court dancer Barbara Campanini received the ceremonial reinterment due to General Winterfeldt. One can only speculate as to who really dwells in the crypt of John Paul Jones at Annapolis, or who (Seddon the Poisoner perhaps?) is revered as Roger Casement in Dublin.

The victorious commander had meanwhile addressed himself to the more agreeable duty of announcing his triumph to his sovereign. The first notification was a verbal report or a hurriedly written note, entrusted to an officer who sped from the field on the day of battle. A couple of days after the action the commander dispatched a second officer, who bore a more detailed relation and was accompanied by the trophies of the battle. The royal court was alerted that he was on his way, and mounted trumpeters rode in front of his coach on the last stage of his progress. The colours were deposited at the sovereign's feet and afterwards hung up for display in one of the principal churches.

Santa Cruz wrote that just as the commander was well advised to spread the responsibility for battle before the actual event, to allow for the possibility of defeat, so he should now ensure that the officers he sent to the sovereign would give him all the credit for the victory. His warning was borne out by the conduct of Don Ferdinando La Torre, who was dispatched to Spain with the trophies taken at Campo Santo (1743). La Torre had arrived on the field only towards the end of the battle,

> but he was vain enough to arrogate to himself all the glory of
> that day, and he requested – and was granted – the title of
> Marqués de Campo Santo. . . . Most of the brave men who had
> genuinely distinguished themselves were left without reward,
> because the king was not told about them. (Power, 1784, I, Part
> 2, 250–1. NB the battle was actually indecisive).

Apart from an epidemic of disease in winter quarters, an uncontrolled flight was the most destructive single experience which an eighteenth-century army could undergo. The Austrian losses after Leuthen (1757) amounted to no less than 38,000 men, when we include the men who dropped on the way, and the stranded garrisons of Breslau and Schweidnitz. Parks of heavy artillery and carefully hoarded stocks of fodder were likewise abandoned by the French when they ran away before Prince Ferdinand of Brunswick, who took them by surprise in the early spring of 1758. The Prussians were never plunged into a disorganisation as prolonged as this, but the impact of defeat was capable of rendering their leader prostrated for days at a time. Old Fritz was in a state of total collapse when he reached the headquarters of Field-Marshal Keith after the battle of Kolin (1757):

> Only a few days before he had considered himself the conqueror
> of the world, but when he came back to us he presented a
> sorry sight, all bent over with distress and anxiety. He had been
> on the same horse for thirty-six hours, and although it was all
> too evident that he could scarcely stand from his exhaustion, he
> forced himself to put on a brave face. (Henckel von
> Donnersmarck, 1858, I, Part 2, 235–6)

The Age of Reason therefore held a well-managed retreat in

peculiar reverence: 'It is rightly regarded as the heroic pinnacle of the military art. It is an extraordinarily delicate manoeuvre, and the one best calculated to develop the prudence, ingenuity, courage and skill of a commander in chief' (Jeney, 1759, 137. See also Quincy, 1726, VIII, 10; Silva, 1778, 131).

As the battle had drawn to its close, the immediate responsibility of preventing the retreat from degenerating into something a good deal worse had probably fallen to a few middle or lower-ranking commanders. The infantry of the rearguard might hold off pursuing cavalry by platoon fire, and withdrawing by stages to the cover of ditches, hedges or other obstacles. At Lobositz (1756) the first Austrian disengagement was threatened by the infantry of the Prussian left, which came streaming down from the Lobosch Hill; they were presented by the sight of the orderly ranks of the regiment of Alt-Colloredo, which was literally marching backwards under the direction of Colonel Lacy. Saldern executed a comparable *tour de force* with his rearguard of infantry at Hochkirch (1758) (see p. 219). The contribution of cavalry was displayed by the squadrons of the Duc d'Armentières, who saved the French left wing at Krefeld (1758): 'This body of horse withdrew by slow bounds, periodically re-forming in line and halting the enemy by showing a bold front, even though it was shot up by cannon which were close enough to be firing canister' (Mopinot de la Chapotte, 1905, 193–4).

At Prague (1757) Fouqué had demonstrated an effective way of rallying infantry in the crisis of a battle (see p. 242). The same method could be used to reform the cavalry (Warnery, 1785–91, II, 282–3), or to consolidate an entire army which was in danger of disintegrating in disorder and panic. In all of these cases the troops could usefully be allowed to run until they were exhausted, or had reached the far side of a bridge, a pass or some other constriction where they could be reorganised out of immediate danger of enemy pursuit. In this way the river Oder helped to save the Prussian army after its near-catastrophic defeat at Kunersdorf (1759).

Now the commander had to discover the extent of his losses, which he did by calling for returns, regiment by regiment. It was a bad idea to put the whole army on parade, for then the gaps were only too evident.

The defeated general usually had an inkling how the news of his misfortune would be received. Loud recriminations were the order of the day in faction-ridden Paris and Versailles. Maria Theresa of

Austria was excessively loyal to her commanders in the field, and after giving way to floods of tears and prayers she was in the habit of sending messages of sympathy and support. Frederick was answerable to no other person, since he was king as well as commander, but he was merciless to generals who let him down.

The commander's powers of leadership were tested to the utmost when he addressed himself to the task of restoring the morale of a broken army. Frederick's instincts and experience inclined him to severity. In 1760 he put the regiment of Anhalt-Bernburg on its mettle by having it shamed after a discreditable episode during the siege of Dresden; the men were burning to recover their reputation, and five weeks later they purged their guilt by charging into the Austrian cavalry at Liegnitz. The shade of Santa Cruz gibbered its approval: 'If the offence concerns an entire regiment, you must reform it with certain marks of dishonour, or, better still, inflict some punishment which will endure for as long as it fails to recover its glory' (Santa Cruz, 1735–40, III, 71).

In some respects the general had an easier task when he came to the army as a new broom. When he arrived at the former command of the Duke of Cumberland in western Germany, after the reverses of 1757, Prince Ferdinand of Brunswick did good simply by touring the camp in full uniform, and increasing the rations of meat and spirits. Maurice de Saxe travelled to Bavaria in 1741 and found the French troops crouching behind their fortifications. He announced that he was about to take the offensive into Bohemia, and he ordered the entrenchments to be levelled and the brushwood entanglements to be burnt. Saxe hastened to the spot the first time that the main column came under attack, and he urged his men to charge in their old style. ' "This", said the marshal, "is how I restore the self-respect of my troops and win their confidence" ' (Ray, 1895, 20).

The battles, pursuits and rallyings left a trail of human wreckage, whose fate is a significant part of the eighteenth century's experience of war. During the actions the streams of wounded were carried to the regimental aid stations, where the surgeons and their assistants plied their trade. Their basic techniques were established in the first half of the sixteenth century, by surgeons like Hans von Gersdorf (*Feldbuch der Wundarzney*, 1513) and the humane and skilful Ambroise Paré. The medieval way of amputation had been a massive blow with an axe, followed by the application of a red-hot iron. Now a tourniquet was applied above the site, the limb was removed with a saw, the blood vessels were tied up, and flaps of skin were drawn over the stump. Enough patients survived this treatment to encourage the surgeons to devise some very modern-looking artificial limbs. Likewise new instruments were designed to enable bullets to be extracted with care, together with mortified flesh, splinters of bone and foreign matter (Guillermand, 1982–4, I, 322–4).

The sufferings were admittedly acute. The Prussian lieutenant Prittwitz had been wounded in the right leg at Kunersdorf (1759), but the worst ordeal awaited him far from the field at Stettin:

> The regimental surgeon set out his instruments, which were all of silver. To begin with he enlarged the wound in all directions, so as to gain better access to the bullet. This had lodged under the main tendon, though it had not damaged it. He now cut it through, crippling me in the process, and after sounding the wound he took his silver forceps and gripped the ball.
> However, the bullet had become so firmly lodged with the passage of time that he could not gain a grip, and the forceps slipped off the surface at every attempt, causing me dreadful pain. After seeing a couple of minutes of this useless activity the company surgeon took pity on my sorry condition. He handed the regimental surgeon his iron forceps, which were equipped with teeth, and suggested that the silver instruments should be laid aside. The iron forceps won a purchase, and the ball was removed from my wound. (Prittwitz, 1935, 303).

Many men were beyond all saving. Mopinot de la Chapotte wrote after the battle of Vellinghausen in 1761 'We had . . . fifteen hundred wounded in Soest. The chief surgeons have informed me that they can hope to save scarcely two men out of every hundred. These men had nearly all been wounded by canister' (Mopinot de la Chapotte, 1905, 332). In most countries the training and regulation of the surgeons and their assistants was scanty or non-existent (see p. 171), and the medical auxiliaries commonly escaped all control.

When a field hospital (see p. 170) was moved from one location to another, the wounded were simply piled into country carts or bread or ammunition waggons, and were frequently left without any attention on the way. On the march of the Prussian field hospital after the battle of Hochkirch (1758) the carts had to make frequent halts to enable the corpses to be removed and buried, which gave rise to heated arguments between decent soldiers and those who wished to help themselves to the dead men's shirts (Küster, 1791, 133).

Interrogation of prisoners, in the twentieth-century meaning of the term, was usually carried out only after small-scale actions (Wissel, 1784, 123–4) when the captives might have something of immediate operational interest to reveal. The other prisoners were merely asked for their name, rank and regiment, and escorted on their way.

In normal circumstances military captivity was accepted as a temporary condition and it was ended as soon as practicable by exchange or ransom. In the campaigns in western Germany 'it was something of a joke in the English and French armies to be taken prisoner. . . . You had supper with Prince Ferdinand of Brunswick and the next day you were back with your regiment' (Ligne, 1795–1805, I, 243). The arrangements were settled in documents called 'cartels' which were arranged between the belligerent powers. In the War of the Austrian Succession cartels were signed between France and Austria in 1742, and France and Britain in 1743. Corresponding cartels in the Seven Years War were those made by Prussia with the German Empire (1757) and France and Russia (1759), and between Britain and France on 6 February 1759 (the Convention of Sluys).

The rates were measured in cash or kind. Thus a field-marshal could be exchanged for another field-marshal in a straight swap, or for an equivalent number of soldiers (say 3,000) or officers and NCOs. Any imbalance could be made up by paying sums of money, ranging from about £2,500 for our field-marshal to the region of 8 shillings for the private soldier. Prisoners were meanwhile tended by their own medical staff, and their home government was responsible for compensating their captors for the cost of the prisoners' pay and upkeep.

Until their exchange or purchase was consummated, the officer prisoners were usually lodged in private houses and were free to wander about on parole. In the Seven Years War Prussian prisoners of the Austrians might be seen taking the air in the park at Schönbrunn, or strolling along the banks of the Danube at Krems. In Berlin the high-ranking Russian and French officers entranced the ladies through their wealth and splendid manners, and wherever they appeared in the Prussian dominions the allied officers gave a valued stimulus to local trade. As captors, the French military men were the most considerate of all, and French officers earned golden opinions among the English for the efforts they made to rescue their prisoners from the grips of savages in India and North America. It would have been churlish to insult such hosts by breaking your parole and escaping as a 'self-ransomed' prisoner.

In the Seven Years War the Austrians and French had an embarrassing surplus of their officers and men in Prussian captivity, and as the conflict wore on they became less and less interested in exchange or ransom. This is one of the reasons for a souring of relations which culminated in the Prussian general Fouqué being confined under close arrest in Carlstadt in Croatia. By way of retaliation Frederick had a number of Austrian senior officers evicted by force from their comfortable quarters in Magdeburg town and consigned to the citadel.

One of the more notorious lacunae in military historiography concerns the experiences of the rank and file in enemy captivity. In all periods the private soldiers have fared conspicuously worse than most of their officers. Enemy prisoners by the thousand were forcibly enlisted by the Prussians in the Seven Year War, or confined under dreadful conditions in the casemates of fortresses like Cüstrin, Schweidnitz and Magdeburg. The English, as we shall see, were going to behave just as badly towards the captive Americans in the War of Independence. Obviously there were places and circumstances in which the celebrated moderation of eighteenth-century warfare failed to take effect. We shall examine some of them in more detail in the next chapter.

7

On the wilder fringes

The European light troops

THE RISE OF LIGHT FORCES

In October 1745 Marshal Saxe congratulated Frederick of Prussia on his two recent victories in the open field at Hohenfriedeberg and Soor. At the same time he felt bound to add:

> It seems to me that in all periods there have been two basic methods of conducting war, and each has its own advantages. The Romans followed one way, and all the peoples of Asia and Africa have followed the other. The first procedure supposes exact discipline and gains permanent conquests. The second is carried out through raids, and passes in an instant. (Frederick, 1846–57, XVII, 301–2)

Saxe was influenced by one of the strongest movements in military affairs in the Age of Reason, comparable in a different dimension with the rise of field artillery. By the early 1770s Guibert estimated that the light troops amounted to about one-fifth of the forces of the French monarchy, and he maintained that they owed their importance to the fact that modern armies were too big, which produced overburdened and vulnerable lines of communication (Guibert [1772], 1804, I, 33).

These were long-term views. More immediately, the usefulness of light troops was proved during the war of the Austrian Succession 'by the torrent of the light and irregular troops of the Queen of Hungary [later the Empress Maria Theresa], who flooded over Bohemia, Bavaria and Alsace at a time when France had no comparable force . . . it was a kind of second army acting in support of the regular troops' (Grandmaison, 1756, 2; Ray, 1895, 19). In those campaigns the Austrian hussars, Croats and free corps destroyed the French convoys, hospitals, depots and foraging and marauding parties, and they probed and harried the main army. Saxe compared a force without light troops to a heavily armoured man who is pelted by schoolboys and has to retire in shame and confusion.

The French sought to reply in kind by forming bodies of light troops from deserters and other riff-raff. The most famous of these units was that of the Chasseurs de Fischer, raised by a French soldier who had distinguished himself at the siege of Prague in 1741. The French light troops did not compare with the Austrian originals, but they were good enough to gain a complete ascendancy in *la petite guerre* over the Hanoverians and their allies in the opening campaigns of the Seven Years War in western Germany, and for a time the enemy scarcely dared to venture a step outside the perimeter of their camps. Ferdinand of Brunswick was therefore compelled to raise light forces of his own, recruited from 'enemy officers who had turned spy and deserted, and former servants, cooks, clerks and so on' (Mauvillon, J., 1794, II, 283), which launched yet another generation of light troops onto the theatre of war. Gifted leaders like Scheither, Riedesel and Lückner transformed this unpromising material, and in their turn they drove their French counterparts onto the defensive.

By the second half of the eighteenth century, therefore, light troops had become an established feature of warfare. Their character and their modes of action were now explored by authorities of the calibre of Turpin de Crissé (1754) and Silva (1778), as well as in a library of specialised literature (Grandmaison, 1756; Jeney, 1759; Griesheim, 1777; Wissel, 1784, *et al.*).

Types of light troops

In the eighteenth century the great majority of light forces came to their trade through natural habits of life, or through an enterprising and semi-criminal turn of mind. Only gradually did the Age of Reason awaken to the possibility that it might be preferable to adapt regular troops to this kind of work.

The native hussars of Hungary were the fastest-moving and most famous of the light troops in this period, and Maria Theresa of

Austria was never more indebted to them than in the earliest years of her reign. This land produced the best light cavalry in Europe, 'through the skill of its horsemen, their strength of body and temperament, their ingenuity and boldness, and the quality and speed of their horses' (Grandmaison, 1756, 11). Eight regiments of regular hussars stood at the disposal of Maria Theresa in 1740, and together with flocks of volunteers they contributed powerfully to saving the monarchy from the French, Bavarians, Saxons and Prussians in 1741 and 1742, and then to carrying the war to the enemy.

The French built up a few hussar regiments of their own, which were recruited almost exclusively from foreign deserters and Hungarian refugees and renegades. Ladislac Ignac, Comte de Berchény, was the most renowned of the 'French' officers of hussars. The pinnacles of his long career were in 1758, when he was elevated to the marshalate and mounted one of the more effective pursuits of this age, which was following the battle of Lutterberg. Nevertheless we look in vain for the true hussar spirit. Berchény said in his retirement:

> I loved my hussars, and I urged them to spare themselves for
> the work of finishing off battles, meanwhile avoiding those
> terrible situations from which you can escape only by losing
> some of your men. 'Go forth!' I used to tell them. 'Keep on
> the move, and make a lot of noise and commotion, but for
> God's sake be sure you all come back!' I used to count them
> on their return, and not a single one was missing! (Ray, 1895,
> 207–8)

The native Prussians Winterfeldt, Natzmer, Seydlitz and Zieten worked wonders with the Prussian hussars, who were only two squadrons strong in 1740 and who were in every way inferior to Maria Theresa's Hungarians. Eight regiments of Prussian hussars took the field in the Seven Years War, and they fought as effectively in the line of battle as in the war of raids and ambushes. The Black Hussars gained a fearsome reputation, all decked up in their black uniform and their cap with its death's head emblem. An English officer described them as

> A nasty looking set of rascals, the picture you have in the shops
> in London is very like them though it does not represent their
> rags and dirt; they make no use of tents; at night or when they

rest they run their heads into some straw or any stubble and
the rest of their persons lies soaking in the rain. . . . They drink
more brandy than water and eat I believe more tobacco than
bread. (Mackesy, 1979, 28)

However, the Prussian hussars became fat and lazy after the Seven
Years War, und only three of their regiments operated to any effect
in the War of the Bavarian Succession (1778–9), when the Hungarians
regained the superiority.

The celebrated Cossacks were peculiar to Russia. They comprised
four main groups – the regular and well-disciplined Chuguevskii
Regiment, the spiritless Little Russian Cossacks of the Ukraine, the
wild Dnieper Cossacks, and the Don Cossacks, who provided the
main force. The most notorious of the Don Cossack leaders was
Krasnoshchekov (lit. 'Red Cheeks'), who arrived for the war with
Sweden in 1741 bearing a terrible reputation:

He is turned seventy, but has a great deal of desperate brutal
courage. He has knocked off several score of his prisoners'
heads, sometimes in cold blood, sometimes in drunken fits, but
always as he says, 'to keep his hand in', and has been wounded
all over his body, on which occasions he only makes use of
human fat by outward application, and inwardly also in a glass
of brandy. (Finch, 1892, 250)

The Cossacks were thorough and skilful plunderers, and they were
adept at wielding that difficult weapon, the lance (see p. 228). In
battle they employed the 'fish trap' tactics they had learned from the
Tartars, luring the enemy forward by a feigned retreat, then lashing
back in a devastating counterattack. Cossacks were masters of
reconnaissance, but they were very bad at reporting their findings to
their Russian masters.

Maria Theresa's Slavonic light infantrymen were known under
the generic name of 'Croats'. They were the product of the militarised societies of Christian refugees whom the Habsburgs first established along their borders with the Turks in the sixteenth century.
The Croats were hardly less renowned in their way than the Hungarian hussars, and they derived their military virtues from their hard
style of life, and from robust recreations like climbing hills and
jumping ditches. Lady Featherstonehaugh saw a typical band in the
camp of Ruremonde in 1748:

The men look scarcely human, the swarthiness of their complexions, their size, their whiskers, the roughness of their dress, without linen, and with bare arms and legs, two or three brace of pistols stuck into their belts, beside other arms, and their method of turning their heads and eyeballs all the same way to look at their general as they march, all this combined together, gives them a fierceness not to be described. (Chatterton, 1861, I, 23)

Altogether about 80,000 Croats saw service against Prussia in the Seven Years War. By then, however, their wild character had been modified by a process of reform which had first begun in 1744. The regularisation proceeded apace in the 1760s and 1770s, and some observers believed that the peculiar qualities of the Croats were weakened in the process: 'They lost the highwayman spirit, which depended on individual sturdiness, self-sufficiency, accurate and deadly shooting, and a delight in stripping the dead and wounded men where they fell' (Berenhorst, 1798–9, II, 108).

The German jägers, the French chasseurs and their counterparts in other lands were yet another category of light infantry whose skills came from their peacetime occupations, in this case as huntsmen or gamekeepers on the estates of the crown or the great landowners. The jägers were renowned for their skill in the use of the rifle, a weapon which took a long time to load, but had much greater range and accuracy than the smoothbore musket of the infantry of the line. Governments were willing to pay a premium for this kind of expertise, and thus the Hessian jäger corps in the War of Independence was 'by no means composed like the infantry of the lowest class of people. It is drawn from those employed in hunting and in the forests, in Germany a well-esteemed class, and forms by consequence what one calls a corps of distinction' (Lieutenant-General Martin Ernst von Schlieffen, quoted in Atwood, 1980, 133). The jäger corps of Hesse, Prussia, Austria and the other Germanic states were raised for the duration of hostilities, and disbanded thereafter. In Russia, on the other hand, a number of jäger companies remained in existence after the Seven Years War, and these became the cadres of six full battalions for the campaign against the Turks in 1774, and so provided a foundation which ultimately carried the Russian jägers to the huge establishment of forty battalions.

The jägers were a respectable body of men, but it is much more difficult to generalise about the hundreds of free corps, regiments, battalions or companies which sprang up in wartime and hung around the fringes of the armies. At one end of the scale we encounter the effective and disciplined Prussian free corps of Friedrich Wilhelm ('Green') Kleist, which operated in the Seven Years war like a miniature army.

> After he had won an action it was his habit to assemble the officers of his corps and point out the incidental mistakes which had been made, together with their causes and consequences, and teach them how they were to be avoided in similar eventualities in the future. (Griesheim, 1777, Introduction)

Conversely the ambitions of the Austrian Panduren-Corps von Trenck, which began its notorious life in 1741, rarely extended beyond rapine and plunder. In between, the careers of many of the other bodies read like pages from a picaresque novel, and they were raised or led by men as diverse as Cardinal Aquaviva (who attacked the Austrians outside Rome in 1744) and the failed professor Charles Guichard (see p. 168) who took over the Prussian free corps of du Verger. In general, however the reputation of the free troops was evil. Gaudi wrote of the typical Prussian version: 'They are neither drilled nor accustomed to discipline. They are supposed to prevent desertion from among the regular troops, but they themselves are so unreliable that they make off in droves' (quoted in Jany, 1903, I, Part 5, 13).

THE CHARACTER AND WORK OF THE LIGHT FORCES

The best kind of 'partisan' leader was a man who was fertile in projects and ruses. He combined a grasp of terrain and languages with a touch of wildness, for 'the partisan chief succeeds most frequently not in deliberate and well-concerted operations, but when he seizes an opportunity which comes his way through chance and good fortune' (Grandmaison, 1756, 34). He was above all a man capable of independent thought and action, and intolerant of the limitations which were observed by the officers of the line, who were guided from orders processed by a hierarchy of superiors. There was in fact no finer training for high command, a fact that was widely recognised in the military literature of the time (Turpin de Crissé, 1754, I, 312; Pauli, 1758–64, II, 146–7; Saint-Germain, 1779,

177–8; Lacuée de Cessac, 1785, 2–3; Warnery, 1785–91, II, 58; Ligne, 1795–1811, II, 162; Simcoe, 1844, Introduction). In 1763 Frederick ordered that officers from the heavy cavalry were to be sent every year to do spells of duty with the hussars, where they would learn some basic tactical principles. The skills of the celebrated Seydlitz had been honed by this experience, and in the Austrian camp the enterprising Loudon was also a product of the light forces.

For hard-pressed governments, one of the attractions of the light troops was that they could be raised so quickly and cheaply. There was seldom any shortage of recruits, 'for the common rabble prefer this kind of military service to all others, being attracted by the distinctive garb, and the freedom they hope to enjoy' (Griesheim, 1777, 23–4. See also Lojewsky, 1843, I, 35–6). Wissel reckoned that a body of light troops could give an effective account of itself after as little as eight or ten weeks of training (Wissel, 1784, xxxii).

The Croats and the Cossacks shared a number of characteristics. They were in the first place exceedingly literal-minded. Ordered to rummage through the Spanish and Neapolitan headquarters at Velletri in 1744, the Croats returned with sheets of blank paper, not imagining that their masters would be interested in anything which bore writing. In 1762 Frederick borrowed a force of 2,000 Cossacks from his new Russian allies, and decided to try them out by sending them to seize a detachment of Austrian cavalry. In his instructions he used the word 'horse' for cavalry, with the result that the Cossacks overran the Austrian position, let the astonished troopers go, and returned to the king with their animals.

These simple folk were also capable of showing an impulsive generosity. The Cossacks might burn down a village church, complete with its pastor and congregation, as happened at Ragnitz, and then do their best to save a wounded Prussian officer. A young mother in Pomerania feared the ultimate atrocities when a Cossack entered her house. His native ferocity melted at the sight of her young child. He took it in his arms, danced around the room with it, and then soothed it with a Ukrainian song:

Finally he took some roubles from his purse, gave them to the child's father, and indicated that he and his terrified wife should get themselves something useful with them. He extended his hands to the two parents, made the sign of the cross over the child in the fashion of his church, and departed wearing a peaceful and friendly expression. (Pauli, 1768, vi)

As native troops, the Croats and the Cossacks were valued as much for their loyalty as for their endurance. All too many of the Western light forces were notoriously lacking in such virtues. The men of the free corps had unlimited opportunities to desert, and some of them made a career of passing from one unit to another, collecting a bounty from each new master on the way. The physical character of the 'partisans' received just as little attention as their moral qualities, and

> the great consumption of manpower in the regiments of Grassin, de la Morlière and the Volontaires Bretons must be attributed to the large number of young men they enlist, who are still not old enough to endure fatigue. All of our hospitals were crammed with them during the last war. (Grandmaison, 1756, 16)

In the long term the light forces often proved to be expensive commodities, for they had to be recruited virtually afresh for every campaign.

The principal modes of action of the light forces were raids and ambushes, and secrecy and speed were vital to success in both. As they moved around the countryside the light troops were wary of putting themselves in situations where they might be taken off their guard, as in villages or isolated woods at night-time. Habitations were approached with caution, and when guides or provisions were required from a village, the leader was well advised to send a small party in advance to seize the burgomaster or mayor.

The best time to attack an enemy camp or garrisoned village was about one hour before daybreak, when most of the troops were still asleep, and you could still enjoy the cover of darkness if you found you had stirred up a hornets' nest. The enemy foot soldiers could be expected to react quickly,

> but the cavalryman must first saddle up his horse, attach the bridle, pack up his baggage, put on his sword belt, take up his weapons, mount horse and ride out of the camp . . . all of this takes more than a dozen minutes, even supposing that the trooper is well trained and extremely fast. (Warnery, 1785–91, III, 44)

'Field warfare is almost entirely based on ambushes . . . a well-designed ambush can frustrate the best-concerted enterprises of the enemy: it is a tactic with vast potential' (Turpin de Crissé, 1754, I, 299, 249–50). Almost every kind of terrain provided some kind of cover for ambush – if not rocks and trees, then hedges, walls, slight depressions in the ground, or growing crops (maize was the best of all). The neighbourhood of streams was a good location in hot weather, 'for the enemy soldiers will almost certainly flock to the water in disorder' (Santa Cruz, 1735–40, II, 191).

The security of the ambush demanded some attention. The chosen site was best approached by a roundabout route, and the hoofmarks and other spoor were to be wiped out with branches. An outer cordon of sentries gave notice of the approach of the enemy, guarded against desertion, and apprehended any peasants who might wander onto the scene. Before striking, the inner killing group bided its time until the enemy advance guard had passed, and meanwhile all the waiting troops observed the strictest precautions. 'The slightest thing can . . . betray an ambush. At night-time the fire of a pipe can be seen from a considerable distance, and besides, however few soldiers are smoking, there is a danger that the wind will carry the smoke and smell to the enemy patrol' (Turpin de Crissé, 1754, I, 253).

Attacks on convoys were a specialised and highly important form of ambush, for the trains of provisions, fodder, ammunition and other commodities might amount to thousands of vehicles at a time. The most spectacular episode of this kind was the monster ambush which the Austrians sprang at Domstadtl on 30 June 1758, which compelled Frederick to abandon the siege of Olmütz and withdraw his army from Moravia.

The site for the ambush of a convoy had to be selected with more than the usual care, so as to deny the enemy the space in which they might leaguer up their carts into a defensive *Wagenburg*. The attack was to be fast and clean, for it was important to derive the best advantage of your temporary local superiority over the escorting forces. These were almost invariably split into three elements – an advance guard, a rearguard, and flanking detachments. Some authorities considered that the attack on the centre of the convoy was especially important, 'for a convoy must be counted as lost, once it is split in the middle' (Zanthier, 1783, 129).

The attacking force rarely allowed itself the leisure to take the captured wagons away. Instead the convoy was destroyed on the spot. The horses were killed, hamstrung or turned loose. Bags of flour and grain were slit open, fodder was burnt, and waggons bearing gunpowder were blown up.

The light forces took prisoners less frequently than did the regular troops, and they could expect little mercy in their turn. Henri de Catt was present when an Asiatic auxiliary of the Russians was brought to Frederick's headquarters just before the battle of Zorndorf:

A general caught sight of this poor devil. He came up and proceeded to address him in terms which the man could not understand. Seeing an image hanging on his chest, the general reached out to touch it with his stick. The prisoner clasped his hands over the top, believing that the Prussians wished to deprive him of his patron saint. This put the general in a rage, and he beat him so violently on his hands that they swelled up and became black. The Kalmyk stood his ground, and held on to his ikon while fixing a mournful gaze on the general who was belabouring him so cruelly. The general was thereby provoked into raining blows on his face, which became entirely covered in blood. My gorge rose at this spectacle, and I informed the general that if they reproached these Kalmyks and Cossacks for their barbarities, I could think of other people who were more barbaric still. (Catt, 1884, 154. For the comparable treatment of jägers, see Salmon, 1752–3, I, 508)

The wider relations between regulars and light forces were extremely complex. Oddly enough, although the traditional light troops usually fought at the lowest possible tactical level, the cumulative effect of their many small actions was felt most powerfully at the highest strategic plane, for they made it difficult for enemy armies to stay in the field.

There was a still great deal of uncertainty as to how the light forces could best be employed at the middling level of war, in formal combat. There were undeniably some useful things that the light troops could do in a battle. The hussars might hasten ahead of the main body and seize important ground, like those of the Comte d'Estrées before the battle of Laffeldt in 1747, or the two regiments of Prussian hussars which occupied Neumarkt and the Pfaffendorfer-Berg on the eve of Leuthen. The various French free corps of infantry, and notably that of Grassin, were active on the battlefields in the Netherlands in the War of the Austrian Succession. The Grassins shot up the brigade of the Ingoldsby from the edge of the Bois de Barry at Fontenoy (1745), and in the following year they and the regiment of de la Morlière were the first troops to break into the village of Ans in the battle of Rocoux.

These, however, were exceptional cases, and the majority of the light troops remained impotent on the day of battle once the regular forces got to grips. With the advantage of hindsight, we can see that the future of light forces lay not in the hands of the native wild men, nor in those of the brigand-like free corps, but rather with the versatile regulars.

The regulars had already shown that they were capable of adapting to circumstances. Hedge-firing (*Heckenfeuer*) was a kind of controlled skirmishing by volleys, originally employed to drive away small but annoying parties of light troops. A Prussian noted how at Mollwitz (1741) the Austrian regulars replied to the volleys of the bluecoats with *Heckenfeuer* of this kind:

> The weapons that did us the most damage were their rifles, the use of which they had copied from the French. . . . We reproached them severely because they were shooting pieces of iron and bullets of hacked-about lead. Every Austrian company had six rifles, which they aimed mostly at our officers, who were stationed in front of the soldiers. (F. C. Geuder, in Meyer, 1902, 128)

At Lobositz in 1756 the Prussian infantry in their turn used skirmishing to drive the Croats from the Lobosch hill. We have already noted how the irregular *feu de billebaude* was the standard way of fighting of the line infantry, even though it was never sanctioned by the regulations (see p. 214).

As a matter of routine, the grenadiers and pickets or volunteers from the musketeers were employed on detached duties, away from the immediate support of the battle line. The utility of such detachments was shown towards the end of the battle of Krefeld (1758), when the French were pursued for several hundred paces by hussars.

> We left a large number of sharpshooters in the first hedges we encountered on our way. . . . These men concealed themselves with great care, and let the enemy come within close range

before they loosed off a well-timed volley which knocked over a number of men and horses. (Mercoyrol de Beaulieu, 1915, 186)

Mesnil-Durand, Joly de Maizeroy and Saxe were among the authorities who called for a closer working of regular and skirmishing tactics. Marshal Broglie did something to put this notion into practical effect when he assumed his command in western Germany in 1760. He upgraded the grenadiers, established a company of chasseurs in each battalion of the line, and, in one of his less happy inspirations, he dealt at blow at the existing bodies of light troops by recalling the veteran Fischer (see p. 269) to a staff appointment at headquarters.

Broglie and his fellows encountered much opposition from conservative circles, but in his officially approved Regulation of 1764 he was able to explain how regulars could be employed in skirmish order to prepare the way for columns of attack. The seeds had been sown. A light company was formed in every battalion of English infantry in 1771–2, by when military Europe was being conditioned to accept that regular troops could be used in ways that had once been the preserve of the Croats and the free corps.

War against the Turks

The regular forces of Austria and Russia had long known that combat against the Ottomans demanded different tactics, and even different items of equipment, from those employed against European armies.

The Turks brought into the field not just their regular troops – the Janissary infantry and the Spahi cavalry – but the hordes of irregulars who were their chief strength:

As is well known, the Turkish armies are superior to ours, two, three or more times over. Most of their men are personally courageous. They are also proud, and their principles inspire them with a hatred of Christians. From this it follows that all our battles and other encounters with them are invariably violent, and that, if they ever gain the upper hand, we will certainly lose a large number of men. (*Generals-Reglement*, Vienna, 1769, 47)

Death or slavery was the consequence of falling into the hands of the Turks, and these folk were never more dangerous than when they were able to catch a Christian force which happened to be without support. During the battle of Belgrade on 16 August 1717 Saxe was ordered to make his way to a couple of Austrian battalions which were standing on an isolated hill:

> At the moment I arrived behind the colours of Neipperg I saw the two battalions level their muskets, take aim and make a general discharge at a range of twenty paces at a mass of Turks which was coming to attack them. The volley and the ensuing mêlée were almost simultaneous. There was no time for the two battalions to flee, and all the men were cut down by the sword on a stretch of ground measuring thirty or forty paces deep. (Saxe [1732], 1877, 24–5)

The most tried and successful tactical formation for the Christians was an oblong phalanx made up of several battalions or regiments at a time. This formation had been adopted by the Emperor Charles V in 1532, and its enduring value was proved by the Russians at Kagul on 21 July 1770, and again by the Austrians at Mehadia on 23 August 1789.

The Austrian cavalry wore Cromwellian-type iron helmets as protection against the Turkish sabres and arrows, and among the other useful items of antiquated gear were the boar spears (*Schweinsfeder*), which the infantry could stick X-wise through baulks of wood to form obstacles called 'Spanish riders' or *chevaux de frise*:

> The drill with the Spanish riders looks difficult at first sight, but it is very easy to master. It takes little effort to learn the proper handling of the boar spears, and how to insert them smartly through the beams. They are then arranged in an orderly and speedy fashion around the front of our formation, and now we can use them as a stout rampart against the onrush of cavalry. (Cogniazzo, 1779, 68)

Colonial warfare

Campaigning outside Europe was dominated not by tactical considerations, but by the deadlines of the environment – swamps, jungles and deserts, poisonous insects and snakes, 'Yellow Jack' and other murderous diseases, and the annihilating heat.

The kind of fighting which approximated most closely to that on the Turkish borders was to be found in India, where the forces of the native princes, like those of the Ottomans, were undisciplined and conservative, burdened by heavy trains of artillery and baggage, and strong in cavalry but weak in effective infantry. The little European armies fought against them with astonishing confidence, and attained victories like Robert Clive's at Plassey in 1757, when 50,000 Indians were defeated by 784 English troops and 2,100 trained local auxiliaries. Frederick's friend Algarotti investigated this phenomenon, and he concluded that 'the superiority which we enjoy over the Asiatics is due mainly to the speed and skill with which we can change our ways, whether in military or civilian matters, and the facility we show in exploiting any good feature we happen to see in anything' (Algarotti, 1772, IV, 295).

The other extreme of colonial warfare was illustrated by the problems which the English faced in Jamaica in 1738. Governor Trelawney wrote to the Duke of Newcastle:

> The service here is not like that in Flanders or any part of Europe. Here the great difficulty is not to beat, but to see the enemy . . . in short, nothing can be done in strict conformity to usual military preparations, and according to a regular manner; bushfighting as they call it being a thing peculiar to itself. (Communicated by Jeremy Black)

This point was developed by William Smith, from his experience of the campaign against the Red Indian chief Pontiac in 1764:

> Let us suppose a person, who is entirely unacquainted with the nature of this service, to be put at the head of an expedition in America. We will further suppose that he had made the dispositions usual in Europe for a march, or to receive the enemy; and that he is then attacked by the savages. He cannot discover them, though from every tree, log or bush, he receives an incessant fire, and observes that few of their shots are lost. He will not hesitate to charge those invisible enemies, but he will charge in vain. For they are as cautious to avoid a close engagement, as indefatigable in harassing his troops; and notwithstanding all his endeavours, he will still find himself surrounded by a circle of fire, which, like an artificial horizon, follows him everywhere. (Smith, 1766, 44–5)

Men could fight effectively against such a foe only through radical changes in their training, equipment and tactics.

The experience of America

THE AMERICAN SOLDIER

The unsung military heroes of North America were the French Canadians, who were outnumbered by the order of twenty to one by the population of the English colonies, and yet contrived to maintain the balance for so long through their mobility and their skills with woodcraft and weapons.

A good deal more is known about the military effort of the English colonists in the French and Indian War of 1754–63, and more again from the experience of the War of Independence (1775–83). Writing about the Americans in 1775, Earl Percy emphasised that 'whoever looks upon them as an irregular mob, will be mistaken' (Percy, 1902, 52–3). The rebels had a great depth of practical experience from the French and Indian War, and Percy noted that during his retreat from Concord on 19 April many Americans pressed home their attacks with great determination.

The most immediate failings of the rebels came from their lack of acquaintance with regular warfare, and their unfamiliarity with the communal life of military men. There were many deaths from dysentery in 1775, for

> when at home, their female relations put them to wash their hands and faces, and keep themselves neat and clean, but being absent from such monitors, through an indolent heedless turn of mind, they have neglected the means of health, and have grown filthy and poisoned their constitution by nastiness.
> (Quoted in De Pauw, 1976, 177)

All of this was remedied with time.

As a volunteer with the rebel forces, the Marquis de Lafayette praised the hardiness and patience of the American private soldiers, and he found that they became more rapidly accustomed to active operations than did the European troops, since all the American battalions of the line were forced to do duty by turns in the outposts (Lafayette, 1837, I, 376. See also Closen, 1958, 49).

The Americans,

being yet in that stage of national growth, wherein the distinctions of birth and rank are scarcely known, consider the soldier and the officer in the same point of view, and often ask the latter, what his *trade* was in his own country, not being able to conceive that the occupation of soldier may be as fixed and permanent as any trade whatsoever. (Robin, 1783, 24)

The higher reaches of the military art were at first denied to these 'unprofessional' officers, but they embarked on a serious and successful programme of self-improvement. In December 1777 the Hessian captain Johann Ewald noted that it was common to find American officers in the possession of the standard texts of Santa Cruz, Frederick, Turpin de Crissé, Grandmaison, Jeney and Tielke, as well as excellent small handbooks recently published by their own countrymen. 'Upon finding these books, I have exhorted our gentlemen many times to read and emulate these people, who only two years before were hunters, lawyers, physicians, clergymen, tradesmen, innkeepers, shoemakers and tailors' (Ewald, 1979, 108).

The European encounter with the Americans

In the French and Indian War the officers from the Old World found much to displease them among their North American associates. The Marquis de Montcalm came to Canada as military commander in 1756, bringing what he called 'fresh views, fresh principles'. By his lights, the campaigns that the Canadians had been conducting so far had amounted to little more than raiding expeditions, and he suspected that the grand strategy of containing the English colonies, which was promoted by the Comte de la Galissonnière (Governor-General 1748–50), had been unduly influenced by local fur-trading interests.

In the same war the English regular officers were no less contemptuous of the amateurism of their American provincial allies. The Americans were unreliable on campaign, their camps smelt for miles around, and they lived by an elaborate network of personal loyalties and contractual obligations which the English newcomers found difficult to understand (Anderson, 1984, 168). The Americans on their side admired the professionalism and good order of the 'lobsters', and their courage in battle, but they resented the haughty manners of the English officers and the bad language and ungodliness of the English private soldiers.

For generations the Americans have been flattered by a statement of their Revolutionary drillmaster, the ex-Prussian 'lieutenant-general' Baron Friedrich von Steuben, who wrote to a friend in Germany: 'The genius of this nation is not in the least to be compared with that of the Prussians, Austrians or French. You say to your soldier: "Do this!" and then he does it. But I am obliged to say: "This is the reason you ought to do it", and then he does it.' The temptation is to conclude that the American rebel represented a new and elevated kind of being, a harbinger of a new age.

The superiority of the New World was by no means self-evident to Europeans who looked hard at the Americans. The iconoclastic historian Gilbert Bodinier has overthrown the old assumptions that the French officers went off to America burning with zeal for the rebel cause, and that they returned with a transforming vision which hastened the coming of the Revolution in France (Bodinier, 1983, *passim*). In fact, with the exception of individuals like Lafayette, the volunteers who travelled to America in the early years of the war did so out of boredom and the desire for experience and glory (in other words out of much the same motives which impelled Western military men to take service with the benighted Turks). Many of these first-comers were disillusioned by the way they were received by the Americans. They were succeeded by the officers who went out with the official French expeditionary corps under Rochambeau in 1780, and who can be counted as full-time professionals who were just doing a job. When their own Revolution came, the veterans of America were marginally less inclined to support the Republic than the officers who had stayed at home.

Most of the Hessians deplored the disloyalty of the rebel Americans to their lawful sovereign, and the wastefulness and materialism they encountered on the far side of the Atlantic. Both Hessians and French were revolted by the hypocrisy and idleness of the Virginians, who lived by the labour of Negro slaves.

In the province of Massachusetts, the great attraction for service in the French and Indian War had been the prospect of material reward. The men who survived the Crown Point expedition of 1756 collected an average of fifteen pounds, which was enough to buy at the very least fifteen acres of unbroken land, and so acted as a powerful incentive for young men who wished to settle down as householders.

In the War of Independence the promise of cash and grants of land continued to draw in 'the young, the inexperienced, the unemployed, the socially expendable' (Sellers [1974], 1976, 164) – in other words, men who did not differ in kind from the private soldier stock of Europe. Such at least is the evidence provided by formations like the Massachussetts Continental Line, and the Virginia Continental Line and Militia. There was little commitment among the American rank and file to the constitutional cause of Independence, and very few of our patriots chose to re-enlist for second or third engagements. After the war, when the Virginia veterans claimed their reward, they found that the best lands in Kentucky had been pre-empted by the established Virginia upper classes, who dominated the officer corps of their state.

It seemed to some Europeans that idealism was more conspicuously shown by the Americans who remained faithful to the crown. 'A large number of the Americans, the ones they call "Loyalists", were supporters of the English. They served them as spies and guides, and fought in their ranks with far more devotion than their compatriots showed in defending their liberty' (Chevalier Goislard de Villebresme, quoted in Bodinier, 1983, 352).

The specific point made by Steuben is contradicted by the reality of European armies. The relationship between officer and man was far from being as simple as that between master and slave. The idea of contract was by no means alien to the Old World, nor did European officers necessarily consider it below their dignity to explain the why's and wherefore's of training to their men. The Prince de Ligne knew that his soldiers were willing to exert themselves in hot weather, as long as he told them how useful this conditioning would be, while the Marqués de Santa Cruz went to some pains to convince his infantrymen that it was possible for them to withstand the onset of horse (see p. 215). A substantial minority, at the very least, of the Europeans would have agreed with Quincy that 'the more decently a man is treated, the more open he will be to feelings of honour, and the more inclined to do his duty' (Quincy, 1726, VIII, 78).

Did the American experience work any greater revolution in tactics than it did in relationships and values? The American backwoods riflemen were very good shots, and made a great nuisance of themselves, but the War of Independence was not won by eagle-eyed patriotic marksmen, picking off robotic regular soldiers and their effete officers. Their combats were usually long-drawn-out and indecisive when they were acting without the support of troops of the line, and the Hessian captain Max O'Reilly makes a telling observation about the skirmishing at Flatbush in August 1776:

> They have rifles, generally like the German, but of an extraordinary length, for forty hours they fired on us, and Donop's Jägers crept about through the fields like Croats on their bellies. More than two thousand shots, which they fired, had simply the effect of wounding twelve of our men and killed one Jäger (Atwood, 1980, 65)

The French victory at Ticonderoga in 1758 was the direct product of Montcalm's experience of campaigning in the Piedmontese Alps in 1747, and in 1781 the French expeditionary corps proceeded to fight for American independence on the best European principles. Regular tactics remained the ideal of Washington, Greene and the other 'Continental' officers, and the battle of Long Island in 1776 actually produced an episode when the Hessians threw out a screen of skirmishers and small knots of soldiers, and overcame a force of rebels which was fighting in close order in the Frederician style.

In both the French and Indian War and the War of Independence the English proved most willing to adapt to local conditions. For the expedition against Ticonderoga in 1758 the English commander, George Augustus Howe, ordered a drastic change in the appearance of the regiments. A Boston newspaper reported:

> You would laugh to see the droll figure we all cut; Regulars and Provincials are all ordered to cut the brims of their hats off. . . . The Regulars as well as the Provincials have left off their proper regimentals, that is, they have cut off their coats so as to scarcely reach to their waist: You would not distinguish us from common ploughmen. (Haarmann, 1977, 187)

On 6 April 1777 Lieutenant-General Burgoyne ordained the same measure for his command at Montreal.

A charge with cold steel was a perfectly valid tactic against riflemen who were engaged in the lengthy process of reloading, or against rebels in the open field. Thomas Sullivan of the 49th Foot wrote how at Bunker Hill (1775) 'our brave men ran through with their bayonets, such as them as had not time to run away' (Sullivan,

1967, 233. See also p. 307). However the basic methods of the English infantry of the line represented a compromise between European training and the demands of North America. The thin two-rank line was first adopted in the French and Indian War in 1759. It was the norm in the War of Independence, and it continued to influence English tactics for several years thereafter. Colonel David Dundas bemoaned that among the infantry of the line 'all idea of solidarity seems lost', while the ways of the light infantry seemed to be 'founded on a suppostion of the spirit and exertion of each individual, more than on the real feelings by which the multitude are actuated' (Dundas, 1788, 11, 14).

Dundas was heavily influenced by what he had seen of the peacetime manoeuvres of the Prussians, and he had forgotten that flexibility was one of the characteristics of European regular infantry in battle conditions. All the same he was right to point out that the methods which held good in North America could not be applied directly to combat in Europe, where the forces engaged were far larger than those in the New World and the soldiers had to move and stand in formations that were dense enough to defy the onslaught of heavy cavalry (see also Ewald, 1979, 340).

THE CRUEL WARS

The peculiar horrors of warfare in North America proceeded not from the scale of the fighting, but from the barbarous conduct of so many of the parties. *La petite guerre* was a cruel business wherever it was waged, and in North America it was the predominant mode of combat, if not the decisive one. The North American theatre added a ferocity of its own, from the struggle of brother-against-brother in the War of Independence and the grisly traditions of Indian fighting. Major Richard Rogers writes unfeelingly about having killed and scalped a Frenchman outside Fort Ticonderoga in 1755 (Rogers, 1883, 34), and four years later Ensign Malcom Fraser of the 63rd Foot learned with horror that a party of American Rangers had killed two Canadian boys in cold blood:

> I wish this story was not true, but I'm afraid there is little reason to doubt it, the wretches having boasted of it on their return . . . this barbarous action proceeds from that cowardice

and barbarity which seems so natural to a native of America, whether of Indian or American extraction. (Fraser, 1939, 142)

In the War of Independance the rebels and Loyalists waged an exceptionally cruel war in the southern states, and many further atrocities were laid to the account of the 'cowboys' who ranged from English-garrisoned New York, and General Benedict Arnold's expeditionary force in Connecticut in 1781. Both parties urged on the Indians to commit depredations at the expense of the other.

The coolness which the American officers showed to the English after the surrender of Yorktown (1781) was mild in comparison with these horrors, though it was still considered worthy of note by the French, who were accustomed to more polite proceedings. Strikingly, no cartel for the exchange of prisoners was ever concluded between the English and the Americans. The Americans treated the English prisoners well enough, in the physical sense, but the American captives of the English were cooped up in appalling conditions in prison hulks and overcrowded public buildings, from where bodies by the thousand were carried to unmarked graves or simply thrown into the mud of New York harbour. Colonel Ethan Allen witnessed the sufferings of his comrades in New York:

> I have gone into the churches, and seen sundry of the prisoners in the agonies of death, in consequence of very hunger, and others speechless and near death, biting pieces of chips [of wood]; others pleading for God's sake, for something to eat, and at the same time shivering with the cold. Hollow groans saluted my ears, and despair seemed to be imprinted on every one of their countenances. The filth of these churches (in consequence of the fluxes) was almost beyond description. The floors were covered with excrement, I had carefully sought to direct my steps so as to avoid it, but could not. (Allen, 1930, 80)

8

The march of the siege

The engineers

As it was understood in the Age of Reason, the science of military engineering had to do with the construction, defence and attack of fortresses. This occupation had undergone some profound changes since medieval times.

First of all, after gunpowder artillery had been perfected towards the end of the fifteenth century, Italian engineers had introduced Europe to a new kind of fortification. The high walls of the castles and towns now gave way to a defensive perimeter made of massive, low-lying banks of earth and masonry, cunningly arranged in geometrical patterns so that all the approaches could be swept by fire. The science received a further impetus from Sébastien Le Prestre de Vauban (1633–1707), who was chief engineer to Louis XIV. Vauban was the greatest of the fortress-builders, but he insisted that fortification did not exist for its own sake, but must be integrated into general schemes for state defence. Paradoxically enough, Vauban also showed how fortresses might be captured in a 'scientific' manner, by means of specialised and carefully sited batteries of artillery, and a systematic trench attack which was based on successive zig-zag saps (approach trenches) and continuous parallels (support lines).

No less importantly, in the long term, Vauban made the French military engineers into a fully professional corps, reinforced by rigorous training, a centralised bureaucracy, and a proper structure of rank and pay. The French engineering corps maintained its pre-eminence throughout the Age of Reason, at a time when the engineers of the German states still had to contend with the prejudice that classed them with hired functionaries like servants or musicians.

However, engineers of every country followed what was certainly the most dangerous of all military trades: 'In a single siege an engineer officer must risk his life more frequently, and expose himself to more danger than do many other officers in the entire course of a long war' (Mauvillion, J., 1794, II, 295–6). Such dangers had to be overcome without the support of the invigorating turmoil of a day of battle, from which Abbé Robin concluded that 'true bravery manifests itself chiefly in sieges' (Robin, 1783, 59).

When a fortress did not stand in immediate danger, it was occupied by relays of field regiments, or by low-grade garrison troops – who in Germany earned the nickname of *Mauerscheisser*, from the way they decorated the sloping walls of the ramparts. The typical fortress governor or commandant was an elderly officer, in whom mental activity counted for much more than physical dash.

The progress of the siege

Whether in the attack or on the defence, the task of the engineers was essentially to guide and direct the work of others. The artillerymen served the siege batteries and the guns on the ramparts, while the infantry executed the brute labour on the trenches, carried out assaults, and lined the parapets of the fortifications and siegeworks.

For the infantry, one of the most potentially dangerous operations was to establish a new trench parallel or lodgment. This was done in darkness, for the sake of secrecy, and the working parties strove to dig themselves sufficient cover before daylight arrived to reveal their activities. Mercoyrol de Beaulieu experienced an episode of this kind during the French siege of Maastricht in 1748. Fifteen hundred men were engaged in the operation, but for a time

> we could see one another only by the explosion of the mortar
> bombs, which was like a constant flicker of lightning. Then,
> in order to adorn the scene still further, and cause the blood to
> flow more freely, the enemy directed repeated discharges of
> firepots from twenty mortars against the covered way. The
> illumination increased with every second, and the enemy were
> able to aim their artillery against the works we had just begun,

and make effective use of their rampart pieces [ultra-heavy muskets]. As further entertainment they fired additional mortars which were charged with stones. Every now and again we heard the mournful cry of 'Stretcher bearer!' This invariably signified that some poor wounded soldier needed to be carried away, for the dead men were simply heaved over the rear of the works. (Mercoyrol de Beaulieu, 1915, 101–2)

Smaller teams of soldiers worked on the zig-zag approach saps, which were much narrower but inevitably attracted a great deal of enemy fire. They were encouraged in this work by large cash bounties, and in Vauban's experience they were so dominated by greed that it hardly mattered to them whether they lived or died.

The completed trenches were garrisoned by relays of infantry, in conditions which would have been familiar to veterans of the Great War:

During the cold nights, even when it is not raining, the officers commanding in the trenches make the soldiers walk up and down every so often, and beat their hands against their sides and stamp their feet on the ground. Without this precaution they will be incapable of using their muskets for a good six or seven minutes in the event of an alarm. (Santa Cruz, 1735–40, VIII, 289–90)

Here Santa Cruz was writing about the threats of sorties by the garrison. These counterattacks were most likely to arrive towards the end of cold or wet nights, or early on hot afternoons when the troops were comatose from the effects of heat, food and alcohol.

Artillery fire became a familiar enemy. James Thacher observed at Yorktown:

The bombshells from the besiegers and the besieged are incessantly crossing each other's path in the sky. They are clearly visible in the form of a black ball in the day, but in the night, they appear like a fiery meteor with a blazing tail, most beautifully brilliant, ascending majestically from the mortar to a certain altitude, and gradually descending to the spot where they are destined to execute their work of destruction. (Thacher, 1862, 284)

Siege and fortress artillery was usually of a much higher calibre than artillery for the field, and the shells in question were spherical mortar bombs of cast iron which measured up to 13 inches in diameter and made craters 'sufficient to bury an ox in' (Martin, 1962, 235).

The roundshot from the cannon arrived at low trajectory, and smashed through trench parapets, gun carriages and men. On a fort in the Delaware River in 1777 an American witnessed 'five artillerists belonging to one gun cut down by a single shot, and I saw men who were stooping to be protected by the works, but not stooping low enough, split like fish to be broiled . . . Our men were cut up like cornstalks' (Martin, 1962, 92). The massive bronze barrels of the cannon were virtually indestructible, but they were readily knocked backwards or sideways off their carriages by heavy roundshot, crushing everything in their way.

Vigilance was the best protection against fire from the fortress, and sentries were posted to warn the men to take shelter against the incoming rounds. The large mortar bombs were detected easily enough, though little notice could be given of cannon fire at short range (unless you happened to see the flash of the priming powder), or of bombs from the small 'cohorn' mortars.

The danger in sieges was omnipresent, but, except in the opening of a parallel or the storm of a breach, the infantry seldom encountered it in the overwhelmingly stressful form that could be experienced in pitched battles. For this reason siegework was universally recognised as the best means of conditioning raw troops to gunfire. Chevert remarked:

> Just watch how the battalions make their way into the trenches at the start of their first campaign. They proceed with all due caution, and keep themselves under cover by staying on the rearward side of the parapet. Twenty-four hours later you will see them leaping over the same works, and taking the shortest route back to camp. (Ray, 1895, 75–6. See also Moore, 1860, I, 112; Mercoyrol de Beaulieu, 1915, 31)

All the time the besiegers were hitting back with their own artillery. The French artillerymen concentrated their fire on the fortifications, for they were adept at clearing the parapets, dismounting the guns and knocking breaches in ramparts. Outside France the gunners and bombardiers were rarely so expert, and by accident or deliberate intent a large proportion of the shot and bombs landed in the interior of the fortress, or in other words among the civilian population of the town (at this period all-military fortifications were usually to be found only in remote places like frontier passes). The Prussians caused extensive damage in the fortress-city of Dresden in 1760, but the most complete devastation occurred in small towns of densely packed wooden houses, like Zittau, which was bombarded by the Austrians in 1757. Cüstrin received the same attention from the Russians in 1758, and the people could find no place of safety,

> being surrounded on all sides by burning houses. They tried to
> make their way along the streets, but further buildings
> collapsed from the sides, and fire balls rained down from above
> and smashed many folk on the spot. The air was resonating with
> the thundrous roar of the cannon and the frightful howling of
> the mortar bombs. (Ortmann, 1759, 417–18)

In the Age of Reason the citizens were usually spared the final ordeal of seeing their town stormed and sacked by the besiegers. This was a period of 'scientific' military engineering, and if the besiegers made a serious trench attack on the fortress, instead of merely throwing in shot and bombs at random, the progress of the rest of the siege could be predicted with reasonable confidence. Most importantly, it was recognised that once a breach had been effected in the main rampart, the besiegers had it in their power to storm into the town. However, neither party was willing to allow matters to come to this pass, for the principle of 'exchange' (see p. 287) now began to dominate their calculations.

Each side had something to offer the other: the attackers could give the defenders their lives or freedom, while the garrison could spare the besieger the heavy casualties and the breakdown of discipline which so often accompanied an assault. The outcome was a negotiated capitulation, which delivered the fortress to the attacker on more or less honourable terms. The most lenient kind of capitulation was one which contained safeguards for the citizens and allowed the defenders a 'free evacuation' with the honours of war.

Part III

The military experience in context and perspective

9

Land war and the experience of civilian society

The civilians as observers of the military condition

The most considered statements on the rights and wrongs of war proceeded from the jurists. Baron Charles de Montesquieu (*Lettres Persanes*, Paris, 1721) sought to equate the condition of warfare with civil law, and he made a declaration of hostilities the equivalent of passing a sentence of death on a criminal; the corollary was that the offending state, like the malefactor, must be considered deserving of such drastic punishment. Christian Wolff (*Institutiones Juris Naturae et Gentium*, 1750) looked more to the principles of natural law, and allowed states a greater measure of freedom. However the most readable and the most generally admirable product of our period was by the Swiss jurist Emerich de Vattel (*Droit des Gens, ou Principes de la Loi Naturelle Appliqués à la Conduite et aux Affaires des Nations et des Souveraines*, 1758). Vattel not only synthesised the views of earlier writers on the subject, but in Book Three he spoke with the authentic voice of the Age of Reason concerning the ways in which war ought to be conducted. Women, children, old people and private property were to be considered inviolable, and even a just war was to be waged with as much humanity as was compatible with attaining the object.

Simple patriotism was the dominant theme in the Prussian or pro-Prussian writings on the rights and wrongs of the Seven Years War. Thomas Abbt (*Vom Tode fürs Vaterland*, 1761) struck a chord of sentimental idealism, while Johann Wilhelm Gleim's 'Grenadier Songs' (first collection 1757 and 1758) were actually more blood-thirsty than the songs in the mouths of the genuine grenadiers.

Voltaire too had been a patriot at the time he celebrated the French victory at Fontenoy (*Poème de Fontenoy*, 1745), but he presented a most unfavourable picture of the military condition in his *Candide* (1759), and he and his fellow philosophers increasingly distanced themselves from the warlike values. Frederick complained:

> It pleases *messieurs les savants* to mock our profession, and Voltaire makes it a subject of ridicule. Our trade is bad, on account of the evils which it occasions, but it demands considerable talents if we are to be proficient in it. Voltaire is a rogue who understands nothing. (Catt, 1884, 111–12)

Benjamin West's celebrated painting of the death of Wolfe (exhibited 1771) was in every way a studio piece, and most of the officers depicted were on other parts of the field of Quebec when our hero was killed, and at least one was not in America at all. West was a native American, and the characteristically English response to the military life is better illustrated in Hogarth's painting of the chaotic *March of the Guards to Finchley* and in Smollett's novel *Roderick Random* (1748). Smollett's pages were solemnly perused by the Hessian colonel von Block when he was teaching himself English on the voyage to America in 1776.

The officer and soldier as individuals received a generally sympathetic treatment in the vignettes of military life which were presented by the playwrights of the period. *Le Deserteur* (1769) by Sedaine and Mercier has its counterparts in the Austrian Gottlieb Stephanie's *Die Werber* (1763, from George Farquhar's *The Recruiting Officer*, 1706) and *Die abgedankten Offiziers* (1770), and the more self-consciously highbrow *Minna von Barnhelm*, written in 1763 by Gotthold Ephraim Lessing, who was secretary to the fierce old Prussian general Tauentzien.

Military and civilian life was most closely integrated in the garrison towns (see p. 126). Thus the fortresses and other garrison localities in eastern France not only yielded a high number of recruits for the army, but engendered a characteristically sober and long-enduring bourgeoisie, accustomed to the military presence and capable of withstanding the rigours of a siege. With exceptions such as these, the relations between the French military and the French civilians appear to have been poor. Many officers considered themselves to be above the law and above normal conventions of behaviour. They beat up mayors and royal officials, and in 1739 a murderer like trooper Bellecoeur was saved from justice because his colonel prized him as 'an excellent dragoon, who has given no cause for complaint in the service' (Babeau, 1889–90, I, 250). Polite society responded in its own style. Lieutenant-General de Bombelles wrote in 1759:

> Nowadays the military men enjoy no consideration, either at court or in the society of the town. They seem to be regarded more as mercenaries, who are supported at the expense of the kingdom, than as citizens standing ready to sacrifice all that is most precious in the service of the fatherland. Things have gone so far that officers are ashamed to wear their uniform. . . . The status of the officer is demeaned, just as the condition of the soldiers is seen as the lowest of all. Troops are unfortunate wretches who are despised by the humblest working man. (Corvisier, 1964, 138)

This response was shared by civilians in most of the countries of Europe.

In Austria the Empress Maria Theresa succeeded only in part in winning over the old nobility to the military profession, and civilian values remained paramount in society and public life. An officer wrote:

> We are tormented by these terrible civilians, who in fact have nothing civil about them. . . . We are oppressed by trickery, injustice, overbearing authority and favouritism. If a quarrel rises in the town, then the civilians are always in the right – the officer is placed under arrest, the soldier is hauled before the provost, and the colonel is the object of a reprimand. (Ligne, 1795–1811, II, 177)

Frederick the Great virtually excluded civilians and the middle class from honour and consideration, and yet it was in Prussia that some of the happiest relations between officers and civilians were to be found. Away from Potsdam and Berlin celebrated commanders like Daniel von Lossow, Georg Friedrich von Manstein, Friedrich Christoph von Saldern and the highly cultivated Kurt Christoph von Schwerin all sought out the company of savants and other good conversationalists. Lieutenant-General Wilhelm Dietrich von Buddenbrock was an officer of the same stamp. He is described as

an outstanding friend of the civilians, and an officer who ensured that the soldiers protected the citizens [of Breslau] instead of harming them. He treated the men of learning like old companions, and he seasoned his conversation with stories that were calculated to sharpen the intelligence and elevate the sentiments of the hearer. (Pauli, 1758–64, I, 22)

Civilians as supporters and providers

Armies drew on the resources of civilian society for recruits, money and material.

Where at first sight the demand on manpower might seem to be the greatest, in countries like Prussia which had a formal system of conscription, the rigour of the principle was ameliorated by wide exceptions or the employment of foreigners. Probably no other state in Europe made demands as heavy as Hesse-Kassel, where the levy embraced one in nineteen of the civilian population (Atwood, 1980, 20). In neighbouring Württemberg the *Stände* (noble assemblies) were determined that their duchy would never be turned into a comparable reservoir of troops, and in 1770 they made their sovereign agree that 'No subject shall be compelled to serve against his free will. Should anyone desire to be released from the military condition, he must be allowed to go' (Jähns, 1889–91, III, 2, 231).

Military expenditure was just as prone to run out of control in the Age of Reason as in modern times. At the siege of Ochakov in 1788 a clerk in the office of Prince Potemkin calculated that a single bombardment, which was laid on as a kind of after-dinner entertainment, cost in the region of 125,000 roubles (Tsebrikov, 1895, 202–3). Ammunition, ordnance and other kinds of hardware were, however, among the least expenses of an army, since provisions, fodder and horses were cumulatively far more costly. It is hardly surprising that the Seven Years War left the French government with a debt of nearly two thousand million livres. The standing armies were much easier to sustain in peacetime, when the transport trains were disbanded and the regiments lived in their garrisons. The permanent military establishments accounted for about one-third of the state expenditure in Bavaria, one-half in Austria and at times up to three-quarters in Prussia, but these figures are much less alarming than they appear, since the governments did not have much else to spend their money on. Many responsibilities which are now run directly by the state, like education, justice, and medical and social care, were then managed from local or private resources.

It is difficult, perhaps impossible, to assess the overall balance of loss and gain. The military establishments clearly helped to mop up the surplus labour, and in Prussia the system of cantonal recruiting allowed native soldiers to go home on long periods of peacetime leave, which diminished the inroads on the truly productive workers. A closer examination however suggests that even in Prussia the military demands on manpower inflicted real economic damage:

> It is true that the presence of the garrisons helped to stabilise income in territories like East Prussia, Kurland and Prussian Pomerania, where there was little employment, but on the whole the comprehensive withdrawal of labour (which we can put at about 6 per cent of the population capable of work) had the effects of inhibiting the industrialisation of the Prussian territories, stunting the growth of the rural economy, and causing the landowners to burden the peasants with excessive demands on their labour and services. The only exceptions were offered by the Westphalian provinces and Upper Silesia. (Stutzer, 1978, 41)

Armies took labour and resources directly from the fields when it was a question of burying the dead of battle, lending a hand in siegework or carrying supplies and ammunition to the troops. A native wrote about the experiences of 1746–7 when

> the peasants of the Provençal mountains were each made to carry the 20-pounder cannon shot. In order to pass through the narrower passages they had to sling them fore and aft; a large number of the men suffered injuries from the pressure on the chest, and some died as a result. (Corvisier, 1964, 76)

Individuals and establishments were affected most unevenly by the great sums in cash and credit which went into circulation. In Prussia the annual demand for 500,000 yards of cloth (Zottmann, 1937, 35) set the textile industries at Bielefeld and Minden hard at work, just as there was ample occupation for the iron foundry at Malapane in Upper Silesia. In the Seven Years War the turnover of the arms contractors Splitgerber und Daum rose from 97,000 to 882,000 thaler, and yielded a clear profit of one million thaler in the period from 1759 to 1762 (Henderson, 1963, 13). In Berlin, just as in Paris, the contractors lived high off the hog. In both Prussia and France, however, the country nobility and all men on low or fixed incomes suffered in proportion. Frederick could not imagine what happened to the fortunes which the sovereigns spent on their wars: 'It is as if money dissipates in the air, like gunpowder after it is fired from a cannon' (Frederick, 1846–57, XXXIV, 98).

Prussia survived as well as it did by waging war largely at the expense of the neighbouring lands, which were forced to raise sizeable contributions in cash, fodder, cattle and recruits:

> All of these commodities were gathered in through measures of atrocious severity. Leading citizens were imprisoned and compelled to live on bread and water. In Güstrow in Mecklenburg the parish church served as a dungeon for the assorted recruits, who had to live there for weeks on end until they were taken off to the army. . . . They destroyed what they could not take away, and they went as far as to slash the mattresses of the poor inhabitants, throwing the feathers into the air to be carried away by the wind. (Archenholtz, 1840, I, 246)

States like Saxony and Mecklenburg therefore suffered a heavy outright loss, and had little to show in return.

All the active theatres of operations witnessed scenes of extensive devastation in the Seven Years War. In Westphalia a traveller saw

> the sad vestiges of what the ravaging flames had destroyed; or whole forests nearly reduced to ashes; of houses pillaged and half burnt; of towns entirely destroyed, and the wretched inhabitants, who watered with their tears the earth already drenched with human blood. (An American, 1773, 63–5. For conditions in Bohemia see Cogniazzo, 1788–91, II, 365)

The impact of the passing armies on a small society has probably never been investigated in greater detail than in the case of Cipières in the War of the Austrian Succession. The village in question was a community of 250 souls located in the Alpes Maritimes north of Antibes, and the study by Anthony Lewison shows how this little place helped to support no less than 30,000 soldiers between 1742 and 1747, providing billets, grain, hay and straw, transport in the form of mules and drivers, and labour for the Austrian siege of Antibes in January 1747. The village had already been reduced to near-starvation by a succession of bad harvests, and in order to satisfy its demanding guests the community had to go heavily into debt:

> Each army was in occupation under different conditions and each behaved differently towards the village. The Spaniards were there under licence of their ally and acted with decorum; the French army was there as of right, and cajoled with false promises backed by threats of punishment; the Austrians were invaders, who plundered and enforced obedience under pain of pillage and burning. (Lewison, 1987, 1)

At the behest of the Austrian general Browne the villagers had to fish for trout in the Loup, and go hunting for partridge, hare, deer and wild boar so as to provide delicacies for this great man and his fellow Irish officers.

One of the most remarkable and puzzling features of war in the Age of Reason was the extent to which sovereigns sought to justify their cause in foreign countries, and looked to their people not only for bodies, cash and kind, but for sympathy and moral support. Here it is legitimate to use the term 'public opinion' without any inhibitions, even if it runs counter to accepted notions about the divorce between rulers and ruled which is supposed to have obtained at that time.

In part, the opinion of the public was open to being manipulated:

> If the war is a defensive one, you show the people how important it is for them to bend their efforts to help you to sustain that war, so as to protect their hearths, their property, their lives, the honour of their families, and the crown of the prince who loves them as a father. (Santa Cruz, 1735–40, III, 3)

Offensive wars had to be presented with more care, and it might be necessary to persuade the people that the sovereign was forced to strike so as to forestall an impending invasion by the enemy (Santa Cruz, 1735–40, III, 4).

In the Seven Years War the belligerent powers put their case through covert and overt propaganda, as expressed through books, broadsheets, rude songs, forged documents and scurrilous stories. The rival parties in Germany produced two such measured assessments of Frederick as:

> The natural character of the Prussian monarch is such that he

has an extraordinary love for humanity. All his efforts are
devoted to promoting its welfare and happiness. (Anon., 1758,
93)

From the conformation of his nose one may read self-interest,
envy, displeasure and bad temper. Death and destruction glisten
in those wild, flashing eyes. His laughter has the scornful ring
of that of Hell, when it delights in the fall of a saint. (Quoted
in Cauer, 1883, 154)

Other manifestations of the public mood were spontaneous, as
was repeatedly to be observed among the English, or men of English
blood. Opinion moved in favour of the commitment of the British
army in Germany after the victory over the French at Krefeld in
1758, but sentiments changed towards the end of the Seven Years
War, when the people learned how badly the troops were suffering
in their cantonments at Paderborn. This change in mood contributed
towards Britain's withdrawal from the fight.

In the American War of Independence the battle for support was
at least as important as the military struggle. The individual leaders
of the rebellion were forced to sustain their credibility among their
own people, as well as to prevail against the English and Loyalist
publicists. In 1777, when Washington committed his army to action
on the Brandywine, he was thought to have 'made a sacrifice of his
own excellent judgment on the altar of public opinion' (Anderson,
1971, 38).

More striking, perhaps, was the agitation in Berlin, the capital
of well-disciplined Prussia, after the defeat at Paltzig in 1759: 'General
Dohna has been forced to give up the command, and he does not
dare show his nose here. The common people are inflamed against
him, and they threaten to tear him in pieces if he puts in an appearance. You can see how the war has sharpened men's tempers' (Lehndorff, 1910–13, I, 216–17).

The civilians as participants

Sieges carried the experience of war literally to the doorsteps of the
citizens of fortress towns. However the foreign occupation of towns
did not bring the kind of atrocities so commonly experienced in the
twentieth century, except in a milder form when the Prussians were

bent on raising contributions. The French officers proved to be considerate and agreeable guests in the quarters they occupied in enemy parts of Germany. In the East Prussian capital of Königsberg in 1758 the Russian soldiers spent the first night of their occupation waiting patiently on the streets, rather than burst into the houses, and the Russian officers soon won the hearts of the citizens by their liveliness and generosity:

> It became fashionable to drink punch. The Russian authorities held balls – invariably at their own cost – and the ladies were not conscripted, but invited by gallant, nimble and handsome aides-de-camp, who for a time included an officer named [Grigorii Grigorevich] Orlov, who later became so notorious. The [Prussian] nobility and bourgeoisie used to be on very bad terms, but they gradually came to accept one another in the course of these festivities. (Scheffner, 1823, 67)

It was in the countryside that invading troops were most prone to run out of control and once that had happened the verdict of the peasants became something to be feared. They turned into spies for the enemy, at the very least, and if they were provoked too far they might attack convoys and become a considerable embarrassment to the communications of the conqueror. Such considerations could not be ignored when the war was a contest between regular armies, and they became paramount when the invading force was seeking to pacify a conquered province.

Very characteristic of the period is the way the authorities obeyed their instinct to keep the more violent of the demonstrations of popular support under a modicum of restraint. The Austrian general Loudon reported from Moravia in 1758 how 'the peasants are all ready to take up arms and go out to fight the enemy. They desire only to be led. This could bring about a peasant war, which is scarcely desirable, but we must do what we can to sustain these good people in their zeal' (Buchberger, 1872, 386). The same response was shown among the rebel leaders in the American War of Independence, who feared that an all-out guerilla war would provoke unnecessary social and political division.

It is odd that in 1779, while revolution was prospering in America, a German general could maintain that successful rebellion was a thing of the past. He was influenced by the short-lived uprising of the Bohemian peasantry in 1775, which was put down in a matter of days by one regiment of Austrian horse and two of foot, and he found the explanation in the changed conditions of combat and society:

> In former times the outcome of an action depended almost invariably on the physical strength of the men, but nowadays it is a matter of their skill and speed. Then it was possible for anyone to take the field, but today only such men as are acquainted with firearms and trained in their use. Every peasant used to have a weapon to protect himself against violent neighbours. Now the soldiers are usually the only ones with arms, since the people are sufficiently protected by permanent militia forces. (Schertel von Burtenbach, 1779, 162–3)

The point about firearms was probably valid only for the more downbeaten peasantry of Central Europe. It does not apply even to a land as open and as well policed as the Austrian Netherlands, where a serious revolt was staged in 1789, and it carries still less conviction when we look at Scotland in the '45 or the prolonged resistance which the Corsicans offered to the regimes of the Genoese and the French. The American rebels were not only acquainted with firearms, but had the capacity to make revolutionary material out of the conservative demands which were characteristic of most rebellions of that period, and to establish an independent political authority and a standing army.

In Scotland after the '45 the English set about destroying a culture and a way of life. However, a much more developed and subtle way of counter-insurgency is set out in Book VII of the celebrated memoirs (first edn 1724–30) of Don Alvaro Navia Osorio, Marqués de Santa Cruz y Marcenado (1684–1732). Santa Cruz had acquired considerable experience of warfare against irregulars and peasants from his campaigns in Aragon, Catalonia and the kingdom of Valencia during the War of the Spanish Succession, and he was able to practise his skills against the Austrians in Sicily in 1718, and against the Moors in North Africa.

Santa Cruz bore the long term constantly in view, and he proceeded from the assumption that government and people must learn to live together. He was alive to the backward-looking nature of much revolt in the eighteenth century, and he advised the rulers to introduce new customs and laws only in cases of great necessity. They might also find it expedient to change governors and garrisons, if the complaints against them were found to be justified (1735–40 edn, VII, 13–15). All the same, conciliation had its limits, and the authorities were to be on their guard against indications of unrest like seditious writings, and they must pounce on the ringleaders before the intended revolt could break out (VII, 68, 85).

The regulars had to adopt suitable tactics, if they were faced with full-scale armed opposition. He recalled a prolonged action in the War of the Spanish Succession at the bridge of Trego, when seventeen Miquelets (Catalan light infantry) inflicted eighty casualties on a regiment of regulars, and he urged that

> whenever you attack the peasants, try to get to grips with the
> bayonet as soon as you can, for they are not used to this tactic,
> and as a general rule they have no bayonets. Also bear in mind
> that they are more effective in firefights than the troops, and
> that it is difficult for us to hit them, since they fight as individuals
> and hide behind trees or rocks. (VII, 160)

This runs counter to the experience of the Bohemian revolt, but it corresponds with Burgoyne's advice in America.

The movement of people in disaffected areas was to be controlled by the magistrates or military commanders, who would issue or deny the appropriate passports (VII, 203). It was particularly important to prevent arms, ammunition and provisions from reaching the rebels, and to this end Santa Cruz devoted Chapters 55 and 56 to various 'precautions to be taken, so as to force the enemy to abandon the countryside' (VII, 209).

Military and administrative action could never win over the people of a hostile province, and Chapter 62 is entitled 'Means of taming the spirits of the rebels, and of allaying the fear that they might be subjected to further punishment' (VII, 247). It was, for example, not a good idea to remind the local people of your victories (VII, 250), and, while you kept up all due military precautions, you must strive to win their 'friendship and trust' (VII, 253).

In the final stages,

> having beaten the rebels, and reduced them to a state of
> exhaustion and demoralisation, the time will be ripe for you
> to proclaim an amnesty. They will be only too glad to accept,
> for they will be fearful of being abandoned by their comrades,

and concerned that as their numbers melt away the diehards will find it more difficult to obtain mercy. (VII, 220)

Santa Cruz recalled the example of the French general D'Asfeld who landed with the Spanish army on the island of Majorca in 1716. He treated his prisoners well and released them to make their own way to the hills, where they persuaded the refugee people to return to the lowlands and submit to the rule of the House of Bourbon.

There is no reason to suppose that Briggs, Thompson, Trinquier or any other twentieth-century practitioners or specialists in counter-insurgency had ever heard of our old Spanish general, but it is remarkable how many of the teachings of Santa Cruz were being put into effect, item by item, more than two hundred years after he had committed them to paper.

10
The death of a memory

Time seemed to have stood still for German veterans of the Seven Years War, who found themselves in action two decades later as auxiliaries of the English in the War of Independence. A party of Hessians was once surrounded by the rebels, and they broke out yelling Frederick's old cry of *Allons! Allons!* A less happy precedent was called to mind by the German officers who were stranded with Burgoyne's army after the battle of Freeman's Farm (19 September 1777), and they told their chief that his situation was worse than that of the Saxons at Pirna in 1756 or the corps of Finck at Maxen in 1759. Following Burgoyne's surrender at Saratoga their one consolation was the sight of the American uniforms at close range, for 'various former Prussian officers were so delighted at the sight of blue coats that they recalled the battles of Soor, Prague, Kunersdorf etc' (quoted in Pettengill, 1864, 113).

Many of the Germans' comrades were no longer with them, for out of every fifteen soldiers who marched to war with Frederick in 1756, only about one was still with the colours at the end of 1762. The process was already far advanced when Count Lehndorff accompanied the coffin of old Field-Marshal Kalckstein to the crypt of the Potsdam Garrison Church in 1759:

> This occasion brought home to me what is the destiny of humankind. These field-marshals in their vaults took up no more space than the poorest workmen, and when the sexton showed me the coffins he gave each a kick in turn: 'That's the Duke of Holstein! Here we have Field-Marshal Keith! This is General Natzmer!' (Lehndorff, 1907, 405)

The Seven Years War was still a subject of everyday conversation

309

in the Berlin of the 1770s, but by 1802 the veteran Archenholtz testified that he knew of only two men – one was a distinguished general, and the other was the royal adjutant Berenhorst – who could speak with true authority on the wider issues of that great struggle. In that sense 'the generation which saw the Seven Years War has almost passed away. Among the few surviving warriors you could count on your fingers the ones who could write about anything but the most mundane events' (Review of Retzow's *Charakteristik*, in *Minerva*, August 1802).

Throughout the century the inarticulate witnesses of combat were released from the armies as a constant stream of time-served veterans, and they were joined by great floods of discharged soldiers at the close of every war. France demobilised at least 150,000 men after the War of the Spanish Succession, and 100,000 each at the end of the wars of 1735–5 and 1741–8.

The pensions or retainers paid to the officers were generally small, and these proud men might be reduced to conditions of great distress unless they were well set-up gentlemen in their own right. In 1772 the Bishop of Soissons reported the case of a retired lieutenant-colonel, a hero of the 1740s, who was left with 'just two coats, with which he dare not show himself in a house of the slightest distinction' (Tuetey, 1908, 24).

When they were released from the constraints of discipline many of the ex-soldiers returned to their old improvident ways and resorted to thievery or begging. Some of the more deserving sick and crippled were admitted by the military invalid houses, which on the continent had a generally evil reputation. However a number of the more intelligent and active soldiers, and still more of the NCOs, set themselves up in civilian life as traders or shopkeepers, or entered public service as customs officials, schoolteachers, postmasters or other minor functionaries. Their class became an important element in German society, and Lojewsky describes a typical example in his father, who was a retired sergeant of the Prussian Giant Grenadiers: 'he brought a strict, genuinely military sense of order into the smallest details; he showed a tireless activity, and an instinct for unconditional obedience' (Lojewsky, 1843, I, 12).

For many years the battlefields of the Age of Reason conveyed to the investigator a powerful sense of the scenes which had been enacted thereon. In some locations the legacy was physical. At Freeman's Farm 'not a season passes that cannon balls, grape shot, skillets, stone and iron tomahawks, short carbines used by the German jägers, and similar relics are not ploughed up by the husbandmen' (E. J. Lowell, in Pausch, 1886, 176). In Central Europe the landscapes were steeped in the memories of the Seven Years War. At Lobositz in 1773 Guibert was impressed by the military expertise of a peasant who showed him the ground on which Frederick and Field-Marshal Browne had fought their action seventeen years before. A fisherman called Mund had built a bridge for Frederick across the river Saale just before the battle of Rossbach, and he was only glad to be able to perform the same service for Blücher during the campaign of Leipzig in 1813. Twenty-three years later Zorndorf was still a location 'where we call Frederick constantly to mind, and the people love to hear and read about the old king and the battle of Zorndorf' (Kalisch, 1828, v).

Within another fifteen years time had completed its work of destruction. The blacksmith Johann Christian Bodenberg, who was the last man to have seen the battle of Rossbach, died in 1834 (Wiltsch, 1858, viii, 43). The Austrian officer G. Uhlig von Uhlenau was stationed at Kolin for two years in the 1830s, when he was still able to question eyewitnesses of the battle of 1757, but there was nobody left when he came to write his book on the subject in 1846 (Uhlig von Uhlenau, 1857, I, v, 53). For anybody who visits the dismal Polish village of Kunowice today there must be a hollow ring in the words of Thomas Abbt: 'How sacred to our descendants must be the fields of Zorndorf and Kunersdorf!' (*Vom Tode für Vaterland*, 1761). You do not need to be a Prussian in order to feel diminished by the experience.

The 1820s and the 1830s therefore emerge as the crucial decades for the handing-on of the living memory of the wars of the Age of Reason, and it is most fortunate that both Germany and the United States experienced a revival of interest in the old campaigns at that time. The historical record has been enriched thereby. The days of Old Fritz had not entirely slipped beyond recall when Hildebrandt compiled his collection of Frederician anecdotes (1829–35) and Varnhagen von Ense wrote his informative and scurrilous biography of the great cavalryman Seydlitz (1834). Varnhagen's next book (1836) was on Frederick's confidant Hans Carl von Winterfeldt. That general had been killed in 1757, yet Varnhagen was able to tap a source of living tradition in the stepson of Winterfeldt's secretary Glaser.

In North America

With Lafayette's visit to the United States in the 1820s and a
growing spirit of nationalism, the Revolution took on a
romantic aspect in the minds of Americans who had not been
through the conflict. The youngest veterans were in their
sixties, grandfathers with stories to tell, and the country was
wealthy and secure enough to show its gratitude . . . . The
last survivors of the Revolution were now cherished – their
memories and, to a lesser degree, their guidance, were sought.
(Dann, 1980, xvi; Kammen, 1977, 20).

The death of the last signatory of the Declaration of Independence,
Charles Carroll, occurred in 1832. It was seen as an event of great
symbolic importance, and in the same year Congress passed an act
giving an annual pension to every man who could furnish proof of
six months' armed service to the Revolution. Sworn statements now
came in by the thousand, and they continued to arrive until the late
1840s.

Meanwhile the heroes of the Age of Reason had gone to their
rest. Ferdinand of Brunswick died in 1792, and George Washington
followed him seven years later. Frederick of Prussia, the greatest of
them all, had preceded them in 1786. Near the close of his life he
had reviewed the Pomeranian regiments at Stargard. He was too
weak to progress down the line on horseback, and the regiments
were instead ordered to form column and march past the king. He
raised his hat to the colours of each battalion in turn, but in his mind
he was saluting a parade of ghosts.

11
Summary and conclusions

The 'Age of Reason' is a term which has been applied by historians to the period spanning the middle decades of the eighteenth century. In polite society it was an age of optimism and intellectual progress, for much which had been obscure was now being defined and elucidated through rational enquiry. In many countries the sovereigns and ministers were inspired by the ambition to regulate public affairs through 'Enlightened' reforms which were intended for the general good, even if their work often proved to be superficial. Warfare itself was limited and controlled by physical, political and ethical constraints. Large standing armies were another characteristic of the age, and they laid the foundations for a new military professionalism, though even here the transformation was incomplete, since the machinery of army and state encountered great difficulties in supplying, moving and directing these great masses of troops.

Individual nations or regions had pronounced military characteristics, resulting from geographical, political and social conditions, among which the most important were probably how far the political management was concentrated and sustained, and how much prestige was attached to being in the officer corps. This helps to account for the decline in the prowess of the Mediterranean states, and the military predominance of Prussia. Indeed, the more we look at other lands, the more we appreciate the fundamental soundness of the Prussian military institutions, and the more we understand why Frederick the Great was disinclined to tamper with a system which had served him so well.

The European nobility had long claimed peculiar rights to military leadership. The grandees maintained their privileged positions with effortless ease, and the officers from the lesser nobility, although they experienced a decline in their material conditions of life, were largely successful in fighting off the challenge from the middle class. True professional motivation was often deficient, and specialised military education was scanty or lacking altogether. The formative experiences of the officer were likely to be family tradition, the conditions of country life, and (for the more studious) extensive reading about military history and war. The rest was supplied by practical experience in the regiment.

Officer promotion was regulated by purchase, seniority or 'merit', and there was something to be said in defence of each of these principles. Ranks like major and lieutenant-colonel were essentially functional in character, and offered the less-privileged officers a path to further promotion. The ranks of captain and colonel were associated with old proprietorial privileges, and became a target for 'Enlightened' military reform with mostly unfortunate results.

The conduct of the officer class was strongly influenced by the dictates of honour, which were often eccentric and selfish in the ways they were expressed, but furnished the officers with a code of values independently of the state. The most effective style of man-management was a mixture of force, positive leadership and paternalism.

The eighteenth-century rank and file were not a mirror image of the rural working class, which undermines the generalisation that 'armies reflect society'. There was much justification for the severity of the discipline which was imposed on the soldiers, though in its more extreme forms it was disproportionate and demeaning. Regimental loyalties were strong, if not always developed to their full potential, and 'small unit cohesion' was most likely to be found among the grenadiers and other élite forces. The soldiers were far from being mindless machines, and the best officers appealed to their good will as well as conditioning them to formal discipline.

Peacetime armies remained little more than collections of individual regiments, and war was seen as a corrective to a process of otherwise inevitable decay. In the middle of the century, however, military relationships began to undergo a profound change. This period witnessed the emergence of the new professions of gunner, military engineer and staff officer, and, as we have seen, a drastic curtailment of the feudal privileges and responsibilities of the captains. Although no specific training was yet given for high command, the innate qualities in a senior officer were considered to be of less importance than *coup d'oeil* and other skills which could be developed through practice. Beneath their show of convention and formality, the leading armies of the eighteenth century experienced tensions that resulted from the end of a medieval military order.

In wartime Frederick of Prussia showed a style of personal leadership which it was impossible for others to follow. In Europe generally, the daily working of the military bureaucracy could not be counted as particularly 'Enlightened', but there was a wide appreciation of how useful it was to inform commanders in the field of the political dimensions of war, and to give them operational freedom. The failures in war management were those of individuals rather than of the system.

On campaign the armies became hard and *aguerri*, shedding the fatty degeneration accumulated in their peacetime life, but at the same time they were attacked by exhaustion, disease, marauding, desertion and a decline in formal discipline. Active operations called into being great supply trains and everything that went with them, as well as campaign managers in the shape of expert staff officers. The commander in chief nevertheless still had a great deal to do, and he bore the ultimate responsibility of deciding whether to give battle.

Plans of battle were conveyed to the armies through elaborately worked-up written 'dispositions', or by last-minute briefings on the field in the style of Frederick the Great or Marshal Saxe. Tactical principles were rigid and fundamentally simple, though they were difficult to apply in conditions of real combat. The fire discipline of the infantry was liable to break down altogether, and the charges of the walls of cavalry ended up as confused mêlées. Artillery – a 'blind' and nearly impersonal weapon – assumed more and more importance. For these reasons killing in battle was not so much mass murder by deliberate intent as a vast accumulation of lethal accidents.

The high command could exercise little control over the progress of the combat, which to a large extent became a contest between forces making for cohesion (religion, leadership, regimental loyalties, the inspiration of the moment), and those which threatened to precipitate confusion and flight (physical casualties, noise, hunger, thirst, 'stress' and the reawakened memories of bad experiences in earlier fights). It is probably true to say that in the course of a war the run-of-the-mill regiment had only one 'good' battle in it, and this was more likely to be its first than its last. Victory was seldom exploited by an effective pursuit, and the most important reasons were of a psychological nature.

Light forces of various kinds became an important feature of eighteenth-century campaigning. Most of them originated as game-keepers, marauders or ferocious men from the fringes of civilised Europe, but towards the end of our period a number of forward-looking officers began to explore how regular troops might be adapted for this work.

It is notable that many of the restraints usually associated with war in the eighteenth century did not apply to *la petite guerre*. They were still less in evidence in the campaigns against the Turks or in the fighting in North America.

The American Revolution was indeed revolutionary in some respects. Old Europe could show nothing to compare with the active intelligence of the self-taught American officers, who were thoroughly professional in the way they approached their task yet could by no means be counted as career soldiers in the European sense. Just as remarkable was the contrast with rebellion in Europe, which was usually inspired by conservative instincts, responding to the imposition of alien rule, the disturbance of religion or customs, or the violation of an unwritten consensus as to what could be rightly demanded in the way of food prices or labour. The American Revolution undoubtedly had its ritualistic and backward-looking aspects, but the rebels moved with notable speed to establish an independent political authority and a standing army.

However, the background and motivation of the rebel rank and file did not differ greatly from those of their counterparts in Europe. Nor did the virtues of American-style liberty appear self-evident to native Loyalists, or to most of the British, Hessians or French who travelled to the New World. There was a convergence in the ways of fighting, for the American forces strove to master the conventional linear tactics of Europe, while the British troops adapted themselves to the conditions of campaigning in North America.

Siege warfare in the Age of Reason was very dangerous for the relevant professionals – the military engineers – but was regarded as good conditioning for the ordinary troops. In some of its features it was the kind of eighteenth-century combat which corresponded most closely to the conditions of modern warfare.

Social relationships between the military and the civilians, like the verdicts passed on armies and war by the intellectual observers, were strongly influenced by time and place, which makes generalis-ations difficult. The military machines and warfare were stimulating to the economy in some respects, but extremely damaging in others. Strikingly, the sovereigns looked to civilian society not only for the physical means of carrying on war, but for the support offered by public opinion. The reason is by no means clear, though it probably has to do with the opportunities which existed at so many levels for obstructing the will of the ruler. Eighteenth-century political life was far removed from democracy, but to a greater extent than is usually recognised it was government with the consent of the governed.

We must finally return to the question posed at the beginning of this study, namely how far our knowledge of the present day equips us to understand the past.

In military life the correspondence appears to be greatest in the middle ranges of the experience. From what we are told about men who were accounted good officers in the eighteenth century we can be sure that they would most certainly make good officers today, which lends encouragement to the belief that enduring principles of leadership do in fact exist. It is, for example, as true as it ever was that 'the manner in which you behave towards the dead makes a great impression on the living' (Santa Cruz).

The continuity becomes more tenuous when we ascend into the higher spheres, where officers try to make sense of their trade and justify it in moral terms. The framework of reference has undergone great alterations, and the meanings of words like 'patriotism', 'honour' or 'courage', as they were understood in the Age of Reason, can be conveyed to a later century only through convoluted explanations.

Our review of the life and mentality of the old-time private soldier has probably detonated explosions of recognition inside anybody who has the slightest acquaintance with the military condition. Indeed, the well-tried maxims of man-management could hardly have remained effective over the centuries if they had not been working on the identical raw material. To that extent 'the essential soldier remains the same' (General Sir John Hackett). And yet some of the greatest changes in the experience of war have occurred where we might have expected them least, which is at the most fundamental levels of soldiering. Transformations in values, technology, organisation and recruiting all help to account for the difference.

The military professionals in the Age of Reason were typically hard old men of war in their thirties, with many campaigns and wickednesses behind them, and they were mentally and physically distinct in genus, if not order, from the young conscript of the period of mechanised warfare. While both sorts of warriors have encountered extremes of fear and stress, the occasions and the expressions have worn different guises. The old musketeer knew the comfort of the camp fire (and could never conceive that it would disappear from military life), and even when he was on campaign he was spared the sapping experience of physical danger for months on end; when, however, battle did arrive, it was likely to present itself in an overwhelmingly stressful form, and he had to face this ordeal without the support of his tent comrades, and in the knowledge that the slightest wound might condemn him to the most terrible and lingering death. Such considerations should inhibit us from generalising too boldly about the 'universal soldier', and transferring the lessons of the military experience from one age to another without due regard for the widest historical context.

The past remains a 'different country'. When, in our imagination, we travel through it, we are delighted when we encounter a landmark which we can recognise, but we must be prepared for a long journey through an alien landscape.

Appendix:
Principal wars and campaigns

The northern wars

THE GREAT NORTHERN WAR, 1700–21

This was a contest between Sweden and most of the rest of Northern Europe. Sweden's main offensive force was expended in the interior of Russia in the campaign of Poltava (1708–9), and over the following years the Swedes were evicted from the Gulf of Finland and their strategic bridgeheads on the southern shore of the Baltic. The Swedish King Charles XII was killed on an invasion of Norway on 29 November 1718. At the Peace of Nystadt in 1721 Sweden recognised the Russians in possession of the southern side of the Gulf of Finland.

THE FINNISH WARS

The conflict now narrowed to an argument between Russia and Sweden, which resulted in war in and near Finland in 1741–2 and 1788–90. The campaigns took the form of short overland advances, amphibious expeditions and flotilla actions. The borders changed little, apart from some small Russian gains in 1743.

The Turkish wars

In 1714 the Turks conquered southern Greece from Venice, but their advance in the Mediterranean was finally checked at Corfu in 1717. Hostilities opened on the Danube in 1716, and on this theatre the Austrians captured Belgrade in 1717 and retained it at the peace which was signed in the following year at Passarowitz.

The initiative against the Ottoman Empire was now taken by the Russians, who in successive wars fought their way down to the Black Sea and along its shores. The relevant wars are those of:

1736–40
1768–74 (following which the Russians annexed the Crimea in 1783)
1787–92

The Russian operations were characteristically offensive and fast-moving, and became the school of celebrated captains like Suvorov. The Austrians remained neutral in 1768–74, and joined in the other two wars only tardily and unwillingly. They lost Belgrade in 1739, and recaptured it only in 1789.

The contest between Habsburg and Bourbon in western and southern Europe

In the second half of the seventeenth century and the early decades of the eighteenth century the most important single theme in European politics was the rivalry between the two hegemonal powers of Austria and France. Among the smaller states the neighbours of France inclined to Austria, and those of the Austrians to France.

THE WAR OF THE SPANISH SUCCESSION, 1701–14

This very considerable war averted the dreaded union of France and Spain, but left the essence of the quarrel intact.

THE WAR OF THE POLISH SUCCESSION, 1733–5

The last of the dynastic conflicts in the old style, this war was precipitated by rival claims to the throne of Poland. The main success of the Austrian interest was in Poland itself, where Austria's Russian allies captured *Danzig* from the French party (30 June 1734). On the Rhine, however the fortress of *Philippsburg* fell to the French (18 July 1734), under the eyes of old Prince Eugene and his Austrian and German army of relief. In southern Europe the French and Spanish held the offensive. In 1734 the Spanish overran the kingdoms of Naples and Sicily, and in the north Italian plain the Austrians lost the closely fought battles of *Parma* (29 June) and *Guastalla* (19 September).

THE WAR OF THE AUSTRIAN SUCCESSION, 1740–8

The mould of European politics was broken when King Frederick II of Prussia invaded the Austrian province of Silesia (see below), and France, Spain, Bavaria and other states joined in what seemed to be the impending break-up of the Austrian patrimony.

Bohemia and Germany

1741

The French and Bavarians advanced almost unresisted down the Danube valley, but then turned north into Bohemia, where the city of *Prague* was taken by escalade (26 November). The allied change of direction saved Vienna and gave the Austrians a breathing space.

1742

The Austrians went over to the offensive and evicted the French from Bohemia; Prague was left under blockade, but the French garrison was able to break out (night of 16/17 December) and escape.

1743

The Austrians overran Bavaria early in the campaigning season. They now had the help of British, Hanoverians and German auxiliaries, and the combined 'Pragmatic Army' defeated the French at *Dettingen* on the river Main (27 June).

1744

The Austrians crossed the Rhine and threatened eastern France, but the Prussian attack on Bohemia (see below) forced them to retreat and abandon many of their recent gains in Germany.

1745

The Austrians once more conquered Bavaria, and a stalemate ensued on the Rhine.

Italy

Austria was able to detach Piedmont-Sardinia from the enemy alliance in 1742. The first major action was at *Campo Santo*, where the Austrians and Spanish fought indecisively (8 February 1743). In 1744 the Austrians sought to reconquer Naples from the Bourbons, but they were halted south of Rome at *Velletri*, where their *coup de main* on the enemy headquarters was beaten off (11 August). The war in northern Italy was renewed when the Republic of Genoa declared for the Bourbons in 1745. The Austrians beat the French and Spanish at *Piacenza* (16 June 1746), and in the following winter an Austro-Piedmontese army launched a brief invasion of Provence. Thereafter the Piedmontese maintained a defence along their Alpine border and crushingly defeated a French attack on the *Colle dell'Assietta* (19 July 1747).

The Low Countries

1744

The French invaded the Austrian Netherlands in the summer and reduced a number of frontier fortresses.

1745

Marshal Saxe invested *Tournai*. An Anglo-Dutch-Austrian army sought to break the siege, but was defeated at *Fontenoy* (11 May) – a large-scale and bloody battle which was typical of actions on the Netherlandish theatre. Tournai and several other fortresses now fell to the French.

1746

Marshal Saxe captured *Namur*, and at the very end of the campaigning season he overhauled and defeated the allies at *Rocoux* (11 October).

1747

The Duke of Cumberland sought to regain lost ground, but he was defeated at *Laffeldt* (2 July). After a difficult siege a separate French army stormed the Dutch fortress of *Bergen-op-Zoom* (16 September).

The wars in Central Europe

THE FIRST SILESIAN WAR, 1740–2

Frederick of Prussia invaded the rich but defenceless Austrian province of Silesia at the end of 1740. The Austrians launched a counter-offensive, but were defeated at *Mollwitz* (10 April 1741). Hostilities were renewed after a period of uneasy peace, and Frederick beat the Austrians at *Chotusitz* in Bohemia (17 May 1742). The subsequent peace confirmed Frederick as master of Silesia.

THE SECOND SILESIAN WAR, 1744–5

In 1744 Frederick carried the war deep into Bohemia, but he was forced to retreat by the Fabian strategy of the Austrians. The Austrians and Saxons took the initiative in 1745 but were defeated at Hohenfriedeberg (4 June). The Austrians lost a further battle in the border region at *Soor* (30 September), while Prince Leopold 'the Old Dessauer' beat the Saxons at *Kesselsdorf* (15 December). The Prussian offensive tactics appeared to be irresistible, and Frederick retained Silesia at the treaty of peace.

THE SEVEN YEARS WAR IN WESTERN GERMANY

Here the contest was between the French, who wished to conquer the electorate of Hanover, and defending forces made up of Hanoverians, German auxiliaries and (from 1759) the British.

1757

Marshal d'Estrées advanced the Army of the Lower Rhine and defeated the Duke of Cumberland at *Hastenbeck* (26 July). Cumberland was pushed back and forced to capitulate at Kloster-Zeven (8 September). Prince Ferdinand of Brunswick assumed command of the shattered allied army, repudiated the treaty of Kloster-Zeven and made ready for an offensive.

1758

In February and March Ferdinand undertook a six-week offensive which drove the French out of their winter quarters and across the Rhine. In the main campaigning season Clermont was defeated at *Krefeld* (23 June), but the French recovered their wits and Frederick in his turn was compelled to retreat across the river. Inside Hanover one of Ferdinand's detachments lost the little action of *Sandershausen* (9 October).

1759

Ferdinand advanced against the French base at Frankfurt, but Marshal Broglie repulsed him in a brilliantly controlled battle at *Bergen* (13 April). Ferdinand retreated in the face of the combined French armies, then turned and beat Contades at *Minden* (1 August), after which the French abandoned Hesse and Westphalia.

1760

This was a year of solid French progress. Broglie won an action at *Corbach* (10 July), and was able to reoccupy Hesse in spite of a French reverse at *Warburg* (31 July). Ferdinand sought to regain the initiative by transferring the theatre of war to the lower Rhine, but he was beaten off by Castries at *Klosterkamp* (16 October). Kassel and Hesse remained in the hands of the French.

1761

The most notable event of the campaign was a joint offensive by the two armies of Broglie and Soubise. By making a surprise night march Ferdinand defeated the combined force at *Vellinghausen* (15/16 July), but the season closed without a clear advantage to either side.

1762

Ferdinand took the offensive, despite his numerical inferiority, defeating the main French army at *Wilhelmsthal* (24 June) and cutting its communications through his further victory at the second battle of *Lutterberg* (23 July). Ferdinand was now able to recover the territory of Hesse, and the French lost *Kassel* on 1 November.

THE SEVEN YEARS WAR ON THE EASTERN THEATRES

1756

By the autumn of this year Maria Theresa of Austria was in the process of assembling a great anti-Prussian coalition. In a pre-emptive strike Frederick overran the electorate of Saxony. He narrowly defeated the Austrians in the little battle of *Lobositz* (1 October), just over the Bohemian border, and the isolated Saxon army was forced to surrender at *Pirna* (17 October).

1757

Frederick made an all-out invasion of Bohemia, and routed one of the Austrian armies at *Prague* (6 May). Field-Marshal Daun brought up a second army, and defeated Frederick at *Kolin* (18 June), which was the first time that Old Fritz had ever been beaten in the open field. Frederick retrieved his reputation by making a brilliant use of strategic interior lines, and in the space of a month he overcame a French and German army at *Rossbach* (5 November) and the Austrians at *Leuthen* (5 December). The Russians were not yet able to enter the main theatre of war, but at *Gross-Jägersdorf* (30 August) they defeated the Prussian forces in East Prussia.

1758

Frederick entered the Austrian province of Moravia, but he failed to take the fortress of Olmütz or bring the Austrians to battle. This was his last invasion of Austrian territory, and thereafter he was forced to fight north of the border hills. At the bloody and indecisive battle of *Zorndorf* (28 August) he learned what tough opponents the Russians could be, and in the late autumn the Austrians surprised and beat him in Saxony at *Hochkirch* (14 October).

1759

After a slow start to the campaign, Frederick marched against the Russians and sustained a very heavy defeat at *Kunersdorf* (12 August). He was rescued by 'the Miracle of the House of Brandenburg' – the failure of the victorious allies to exploit their success.

1760

Most of the season was spent in camping and marching in the hills around Dresden, the Saxon capital. However Frederick defeated the Austrians at *Liegnitz* (15 August) in Silesia, and he beat them again at *Torgau* (3 November) in Saxony, though at prohibitive cost.

1761

Frederick was now on the defensive. He held out against the Austrians and Russians in his entrenched camp at *Bunzelwitz*, but by the end of the year his army and state were near collapse.

1762

Frederick was delivered by the death of Empress Elizabeth of Russia. At *Burkersdorf* (21 July) he evicted the Austrians from their hilltop positions, which cleared the way for the reduction (9 October) of the important Silesian fortress of *Schweidnitz*. The war also turned to the advantage of the Prussians in Saxony, where Frederick's brother Prince Henry attacked and beat the *Reichsarmee* at *Freiberg* (29 October).

1763

Frederick retained Silesia at the Peace of Hubertusburg.

THE WAR OF THE BAVARIAN SUCCESSION, 1778–9

Frederick went to war to prevent the Austrians from annexing Bavaria. In the summer of 1778 the Prussians undertook a massive invasion of Bohemia. The western army, commanded by Prince Henry, ran out of supplies and resolution short of Prague. The eastern army, commanded by Frederick in person, was checked by Field-Marshal Lacy at the positions of Jaromiersch and Hohenelbe. Hostilities came to an end without any major action in the open field, but the outcome was a political victory for Frederick, since the Austrians renounced their designs on Bavaria.

North America

THE FRENCH AND INDIAN WAR, 1755–60

Until the middle of the century the contest between the French and British interests in North America was largely the affair of local forces, like the all-colonial expedition which wrested *Louisbourg* from the French in 1745. This conquest was exchanged for Madras in 1748. Regular forces began to arrive from Britain in 1755, but the English suffered a number of reverses before they won the upper hand. Major-General Braddock's expedition was ambushed and defeated on the Monongahela (9 July 1755), and an assault on *Fort Carillon* (Ticonderoga) was bloodily repulsed by the Marquis de Montcalm (8 July 1758). On the day of the battle at Carillon, however, a powerful British expeditionary force landed on Cape Breton Island and opened operations against *Louisbourg*, which fell on 26 July. In 1759 Canada came under concerted attack by the British. Montcalm was defeated and mortally wounded outside *Quebec* (13 September), and the fortress-city surrendered (15 September). In 1760 a three-pronged advance was directed against the last bastion of the French at *Montreal*, which capitulated on 8 September.

THE WAR OF AMERICAN INDEPENDENCE, 1775–83

1775

The American rebels set up a *de facto* government in 1774, but the first active hostilities were staged around Boston in 1775. A British expedition against the stores at *Concord* led to a running battle against the militia and minutemen (19 April), and on 17 June a further push from Boston evicted the rebels from the post on Breed's Hill (the so-called battle of '*Bunker Hill*'). A small rebel army invaded Canada and arrived outside *Quebec* in November.

1776

The British abandoned Boston on 17 March, but in the midsummer the rebels had to pull back their disintegrating force from Canada. The British general Howe went over to the offensive. He defeated the Americans at the battle of *Long Island* (27 August), and in November he pushed them from the lower Hudson and through New Jersey. After the main campaigning season had ended the Americans launched a damaging *coup de main* against the Hessian quarters at *Trenton* (26 December).

1777

The British attacked in two theatres. Howe kept up the pressure on George

Washington. He beat the Americans on *Brandywine Creek* (11 September), and after further manoeuvres he entered Philadelphia on 26 September. The Americans struck at a British detachment at *Germantown* (4 October), but were unable to repeat their earlier success at Trenton. Meanwhile a further British army under General Burgoyne was advancing south from Canada. Burgoyne captured *Fort Ticonderoga* (27 June), but he was repulsed from the American positions at *Freeman's Farm* (19 September) and his army was forced to surrender at *Saratoga* (17 October).

1778

The British evacuated Philadelphia, and in the course of their retreat they fought an indecisive action at *Monmouth Court House* (28 June). The British retained New York, and the stalemate on the northern theatre lasted until the end of the war. The French declared war on Britain, and Spain followed suit in 1779.

1779

The interest shifts to the South, where a force of Americans and French abandoned their siege of the main British base at *Savannah* after an unsuccessful storm (9 October).

1780

General Clinton captured *Charleston* from the Americans (12 May), then moved one third of the British force back to New York. General Cornwallis stayed in the South with the remainder. The new southern army of the Americans was defeated in its first battle (*Camden*, 16 August) though the rebel militia beat a force of Loyalists at *King's Mountain* (7 October). A full French expeditionary force under the Comte de Rochambeau had meanwhile disembarked on Rhode Island.

1781

Late in 1780 Cornwallis had opened a new campaign in the South by invading North Carolina. A Loyalist force was defeated at the *Cowpens* (17 January), but Cornwallis won a hard-fought action at *Guildford Court House* (15 March) and continued the offensive into Virginia. Against his better judgement Cornwallis now obeyed orders from Clinton and established a fortified base on the coast at *Yorktown*. Washington and Rochambeau moved down from the north and arrived outside Yorktown on 26 September, by when the French fleet had gained command of the sea. The allies opened a formal siege, and Yorktown surrendered on 19 October.

Bibliography

Abbreviation: *JSAHR* = *Journal of the Society for Army Historical Research*, London.

Algarotti, Count (1772), *Oeuvres du comte Algarotti*, 7 vols, Berlin.
Allen, E. (1930), *A Narrative of Colonel Ethan Allen's Captivity*, New York.
An American (1773), *The Memoirs of an American*, 2 vols, London.
Anburey, T. (1969), *Travels through the Interior Parts of America*, 2 vols, New York.
Anderson, E. (1971), *Personal Recollections of Captain Enoch Anderson*, New York.
Anderson, F. (1984), *A People's Army. Massachusetts Soldiers and Society in the Seven Years War*, Chapel Hill (N. Carolina).
André, J. (1903), *André's Journal*, 2 vols, Boston.
Andreu de Bilistein, C.-L. (1763), *Fragments militaires, pour servir de suite au Végèce françois ou institutions militaires pour la France*, Amsterdam.
Angell, I. (1899), *Diary of Colonel Israel Angell . . . 1778–1781*, Providence (Rhode Island).
Anon. (1758), *Abbildung derer Gemüthseigenschaften Friedrichs des Grossen*, Lippstadt.
Anon. (1787–9), *Anecdoten und Karakterzüge aus dem Leben Friedrichs des Zweiten*, 12 vols, Berlin.
Anon. (1788–9), *Beyträge zu den Anecdoten und Karakterzügen aus dem Leben Friedrichs des Zweiten*, 4 vols, Berlin.
Anon. (1881), 'Drei Jahre in Kadetten-Corps (1758–60)', *Jahrbücher für die deutsche Armee und Marine*, XXXIX, Berlin.
Anon. (1884), 'Erinnerungen an die letzte Campagne Friedrichs des Grossen', *Jahrbücher für die deutsche Armee und Marine*, LIII, Berlin.
Anon. (1928), 'The Battle of Minden – 1 August 1759', *JSAHR*, VII.
Archenholtz, J. W. (1840), *Geschichte des siebenjährigen Krieges in Deutschland*, 2 vols, Berlin.
Archenholtz, J. W. (1974), *Gemälde der preussischen Armee vor und in dem siebenjährigen Kriege*, Osnabrück.
Atwood, R. (1980), *The Hessians. Mercenaries from Hessen-Kassel in the American Revolution*, Cambridge.

d'Authville (1756), *Essai sur la cavalerie tant ancienne que moderne*, Paris.

Babeau, A. (1889–90), *La Vie militaire sous l'ancien régime*, 2 vols, Paris.

Baiov, A. (1906), *Russkaya Armiya v Tsarstvovanie Imperatritsy Anny Ioannovnyi*, 2 vols, St Petersburg.

Baldwin, J. (1906), *The Revolutionary Journal of Col. Jeduthan Baldwin 1775–1778*, Bangor (Maine).

Balisch, A. (1983–4), 'Infantry battlefield tactics in the seventeenth and eighteenth centuries on the European and Turkish theatres of war: the Austrian response to different conditions', *Studies in History and Politics*, III, Lennoxville (Quebec).

Barsewisch, C. F. (1863), *Mein Kriegs-Erlebnisse während des siebenjährigen Krieges 1757–1763*, Berlin.

Baurmeister, C. L. (1957), *Revolution in America. Confidential Letters and Journals 1776–1784 of Adjutant General Major Baurmeister of the Hessian Forces*, New Brunswick.

Belleval, L.–R. (1886), *Souvenirs d'un cheval-leger de la Garde du Roi*, Paris.

Berenhorst, G. H. (1798–9), *Betrachtungen über die Kriegskunst*, 3 vols, Leipzig.

Berenhorst, G. H. (1845–7), *Aus dem Nachlass von Georg Heinrich von Berenhorst*, 2 vols, Dessau.

Besenval, Baron (1827–8), *Mémoires du baron de Besenval*, 2 vols, Paris.

Bessel, F. W. (1778), *Entwurf eines Militair-Feld-Reglements*, Hanover.

Best, G. (1982), *Honour among Men and Nations. Transformations of an Idea*, Toronto.

Bigot (attr.) (1761), *Essai sur la tactique de l'infanterie*, 2 vols, Amsterdam.

Blanchard, C. (1881), *Guerre d'Amérique 1780–1783*, Paris.

Bland, H. (1727), *A Treatise of Military Discipline*, London.

Bodinier, G. (1983), *Les Officiers de l'Armée Royale combattants de la Guerre d'Indépendence des États-Unis de Yorktown à l'An II*, Vincennes.

Bolotov, A. T. (1870–3), *Zhizn*, 4 vols, St Petersburg.

Bonneville, Monsieur (1762), *Esprit des lois de la tactique et de différentes institutions militaires*, 2 vols, The Hague.

Bourcet, P. (1875), *Mémoire sur les reconnaissances militaires*, Paris.

Bourcet, P. (1888) (presented 1775), *Principes de la guerre de montagnes*, Paris.

Bräker, U. (1852), *Der arme Mann im Tockenburg*, Leipzig.

Brandes, A. J. (1774), *Abhandlung von Regeln und Grundsätzen des Krieges*, Hanover.

Brezé, Marquis (1779), *Réflexions sur les préjugés militaires*, Turin.

Broglie, V.–F. (1903), *Correspondence inédite de Victor-François Duc de Broglie avec le Prince Xavier de Saxe*, 4 vols, Paris.

Brown, T. (1862), *Memoirs of Tarleton Brown, a Captain in the Revolutionary Army*, New York.

Browne, OP. (1926), 'Letters of Captain Philip Browne – 1737 to 1746', *JSAHR*, V.

Browning, R. (1971), 'The financial management of the Seven Years War', *JSAHR*, XLIX.

Buchberger, K. (1872), 'Briefe Loudons', *Archiv für österreichische Geschichte*, XLVIII, Vienna.

Burney, C. [1775] (1959), *The Present State of Music in Germany, the Netherlands, and the United Provinces*, London.

Büttner, J. C. (1828), *Büttner, der Amerikaner*, Camenz.

Cameron, R. (1931), 'A prisoner of war in India, 1782–4', *JSAHR*, X.

Catt, H. (1884), *Unterhaltungen mit Friedrich dem Grossen. Memoiren und Tagebücher von Heinrich de Catt*, Leipzig.

Cauer, E. (1803), *Zur Geschichte und Charakteristik Friedrichs des Grossen*, Berlin.

Chabot, Mestre de Camp (attr.) (1756), *Réflexions critiques sur les différens systèmes de Folard*, The Hague.

Chatterton, G. (1861), *Memorials, Personal and Historical, of Admiral Lord Gambier, G.C.B.*, 2 vols, London.

Chaussinand-Nogaret, G. (1985), *The French Nobility in the Eighteenth Century. From Feudalism to Enlightenment*, Cambridge.

Chenevière, Monsieur de (1742), *Détails militaires*, Paris.

Choiseul, E. (1904), *Mémoires du duc de Choiseul*, Paris.

Clinton, H. (1954), *The American Rebellion. Sir Henry Clinton's Narrative of his Campaigns, 1775–1782*, New Haven (Connecticut).

Closen, L. (1958), *The Revolutionary Journal of Baron Ludwig von Closen 1780–1783*, Chapel Hill (N. Carolina)

Cogniazzo, J. (1779), *Freymüthige Beytrag zur Geschichte des östreichischen Militairdienstes*, Frankfurt and Leipzig.

Cogniazzo J. (1788–91), *Geständnisse eines oestreichischen Veterans*, 4 vols, Breslau.

Colville, C. (1948–9), 'Military memoirs of Lieut.-General the Hon. Charles Colville', *JSAHR*, XXVI–XXVII.

Corvisier, A. (1964), *L'Armée Française de la fin du XVIIᵉ Siècle au ministère de Choiseul. Le Soldat*, Paris.

Cresswell, N. (1924), *The Journal of Nicholas Cresswell 1774–1777*, New York.

Crillon, L. (1791), *Mémoires militaires de Louis de Berton des Balbes de Quiers, Duc de Crillon*, Paris.

Cumberland, Duke of (1945), 'Standing orders for the dragoons, circa 1755', *JSAHR*, XXIII.

Dalrymple, C. (1761), *A Military Essay*, London.

Dalrymple, W. (1782), *Tacticks*, Dublin.

Dann, J. C. (1980), *The Revolution Remembered. Eyewitness Accounts of the War for Independence*, Chicago.

Darut de Grandpré, F.-J. (1751), *L'Aimable Petit-Maître ou Mémoires militaires et galans*, Paris.

Darut de Grandpré, F. J. (1787), *Mémoires sur les moyens qu'il seroit facile d'employer, pour parvenir . . . à toute la perfection dont le militaire de France est susceptible*, 2 vols, Paris.

Davenport, R. (1968), ' "To Mr. Davenport" being letters of Major Richard Davenport (1719–1760) to his brother during service with the 4th Troop of Horse Guards and 10th Dragoons, 1742–1760', *JSAHR*, Special Publication no. 9.

Davies, S. [1743] (1925), 'The Battle of Dettingen', *JSAHR*, IV.

Denny, E. (1859), *Military Journal of Major Ebenezer Denny*, Philadelphia.

Digby, W. (1887), *The British Invasion from the North. The Campaigns of Generals*

Carleton and Burgoyne from Canada, 1776–1777, with the Journal of Lieut. William Digby, New York.

Dinter, E. (1985), *Hero or Coward. Pressures facing the Soldier in Battle*, London.

Dixon, M. (1976), *The Psychology of Military Incompetence*, London.

Döhla, J. K. (1912–13), 'Tagebuch eines Bayreuther Soldaten aus dem Nordamerikanischen Freiheitskrieg 1777–1783', *Archiv für Geschichte von Oberfranken*, XXV, Parts 1 and 2, Bayreuth.

Donkin, Major (1777), *Military Collections and Remarks*, New York.

Downman, F. (1898), *The Services of Lieut.-Colonel Francis Downman, R.A. in France, North America, and the West Indies between the Years 1758 and 1784*, Woolwich.

Dreyer, J. D. (1810), *Leben und Thaten eines preussischen Regiments-Tambours*, Breslau.

Duffy, C. J. (1974), *The Army of Frederick the Great*, Newton Abbot.

Duffy, C. J. (1975), *Fire and Stone. The Science of Fortress Warfare 1660–1860*, Newton Abbot.

Duffy, C. J. (1977), *The Army of Maria Theresa*, Newton Abbot.

Duffy, C. J. (1981), *Russia's Military Way to the West. Origins and Nature of Russian Military Power 1700–1800*, London.

Duffy, C. J. (1985a), *The Fortress in the Age of Vauban and Frederick the Great, 1660–1789*, London.

Duffy, C. J. (1985b), *Frederick the Great. A Military Life*, London.

Duncan, L. C. (1931), *Medical Men in the American Revolution*, Carlisle (Pa.).

Duncker, M. (1876), *Aus der Zeit Friedrichs des Grossen und Friedrich Wilhelms III*, Leipzig.

Dundas, D. (1788), *Principles of Military Movements*, London.

Dussauge, A. (1914), *Le Ministère de Belle-Isle. Krefeld et Lütterberg*, Paris.

Engelhardt, L. N. (1868), *Zapiski Lva Nikolaievicha Engelgardta 1766–1836*, Moscow.

d'Espagnac, S. d'A. (1747), *Journal historique de la dernière campagne du roi en 1746*, The Hague.

d'Espagnac, S. d'A. (1751), *Essai sur la science de la guerre*, 2 vols, The Hague.

d'Espagnac, S. d'A. (1755), *Essai sur les grandes operations de la guerre*, 4 vols, The Hague.

Esterhazy de Gallantha, J. (1747), *Regulament und unumänderlich-gebräuchliche Observations-Puncten*, Gavi.

Esterhazy, V. (1905), *Mémoires du Comte Valentin Esterhazy*, Paris.

Evelyn, W. G. (1879), *Memoirs and Letters of Captain W. Glanville Evelyn*, Oxford.

Ewald, J. (1979), *Diary of the American War. A Hessian Journal by Captain Johann Ewald*, New Haven (Connecticut).

Fann, W. F. (1977), 'On the infantryman's age in eighteenth century Prussia', *Military Affairs*, XLI, no. 4, Kansas.

Fanning, D. (1908), *Col. David Fanning's Narrative*, Toronto.

Fäsch, G. R. (1787), *Geschichte des Oesterreichischen Erbfolge-Kriegs*, 2 vols, Dresden.

Feltman, W. (1853), *A Journal of Lieut. William Feltman . . . 1781–82*, Philadelphia.

Fersen, A. (1929), *Lettres d'Axel de Fersen à son père pendant la Guerre de l'Indépendence d'Amérique*, Paris.

Fiedel, J. (?) (1784), *Zehn Briefe aus Oesterreich*, published 'on the Silesian borders'.

Feuquières, A. M. de Pas, Marquis de [1725] (1731), *Mémoires sur la guerre*, 4 vols, Paris.

Finch, E. (1892), dispatches in *Sbornik Imperatorskago Russkago Istoricheskago Obshchestva*, LXXX, St Petersburg.

Fithian, P. V. (1934), *Philip Vicker Fithian: Journal, 1775-1776*, Princeton (New Jersey).

Fleming, H. F. (1726), *Der Vollkommene Teutsche Soldat*, Leipzig.

Folard, J. (1727–30), *Histoire de Polybe*, 6 vols, Paris.

Fontane, T. (1906–7), *Wanderungen durch die Mark Brandenburg*, 4 vols, Stuttgart and Berlin.

Fraser, M. (1939), 'The capture of Quebec', *JSAHR*, XVIII.

Frederick the Great (1846-57), *Oeuvres de Frédéric le Grand*, 30 vols, Berlin.

Frederick the Great (1879–1939), *Politische Correspondenz Friedrichs des Grossen*, 36 vols, Berlin.

Frederick the Great (1920), *Die Politischen Testamente Friedrichs des Grossen*, Berlin.

Frey, S. R. (1981), *The British Soldier in America. A Social History of Military Life in the Revolutionary Period*, Austin (Texas).

Gaigne, K. (1778), *Militärisches Handbuch. Aus dem Französischen übersetzt*, Gotha.

Garve, C. (1798), *Fragmente zur Schilderung des Geistes, des Charakters, und der Regierung Friedrichs des Zweyten*, Breslau.

Generals-Reglement (1769), Vienna.

Gibson, J. E. (1937), *Dr. Bodo Otto and the Medical Background of the American Revolution*, Springfield and Baltimore.

Gilbert, A. N. (1979) 'Military recruitment in the eighteenth century', *JSAHR*, LVII.

Goldoni, C. (1926), *Memoirs of Carlo Goldoni*, London.

Gorani, G. (1944), *Mémoires de Gorani*, Paris.

Grandmaison, M. (1756), *La Petite Guerre, ou Traité du service des troupes légères en Campagna*, Paris.

Griesheim, C. (1777), *Pflichten des Leichten Reuters*, Warsaw.

Griffith, P. (1981), *Forward into Battle. Fighting Tactics from Waterloo to Vietnam*, Strettington.

Grimoard, Chevalier (1775), *Essai Théorique et pratique sur les batailles*, Paris.

Grosser Generalstab (German) (1901), 'Briefe preussischer Soldaten', *Urkundliche Beiträge und Forschungen zur Geschichte des preussischen Heeres*, I, Part 2, Berlin.

Gruber, I. D. (1978), 'British strategy: the theory and practice of eighteenth-century warfare', in D. Higginbotham (ed.), *Reconsiderations on the Revolutionary War. Selected Essays*, Westport.

Guibert, J. A. (1778), *Observations sur la constitution militaire et politique des armées de sa majesté prussienne*, Amsterdam.

Guibert, J. A. (1803), *Journal d'un voyage en Allemagne, fait en 1773*, 2 vols, Paris.

Guibert, J. A. [1772] (1804), *Essai général de tactique*, 2 vols, Paris.

Guignard, Chevalier (1725), *L'École de Mars*, 2 vols, Paris.

Guillermand, J. (ed.) (1982–4), *Histoire de la Médecine aux armées*, 2 vols, Paris.

Guy, A. J. (1985a), 'Minions of fortune. The regimental agents in early Georgian England, 1714–63', *Army Museum '85*, London.

Guy, A. J. (1985b), *Oeconomy and Discipline. Officership and Administration in the British Army 1714–63*, Manchester.

Haarman, A. W. (1977), 'Dress in North America, Seven Years War', *JSAHR*, LVI.

Hadden, J. M. (1884), *A Journal kept in Canada upon Burgoyne's Campaign*, New York.

Haller, F. L. (1787), *Vie de Robert-Scipion de Lentulus*, Geneva and Paris.

Hamilton, C. J. (1927), 'Letter', *JSAHR*, VI.

Hamilton, R. [1787] (1966), 'The duties of a regimental surgeon considered', *JSAHR*, XLIV.

Hanger, G. (1801), *The Life, Adventures, and Opinions of Col. George Hanger*, 2 vols, London.

Harrowby, Earl (1949), 'Fontenoy and other letters. From the Mss. of the Earl of Harrowby', *JSAHR*, XXVII.

Hartung, F. (1955) 'Der aufgeklärte Absolutismus', *Historische Zeitschrift*, CLXXX, Munich.

Hawley, H. [1726] (1946), 'General Hawley's chaos', *JSAHR*, XXVI.

Hayes, J. W. (1956), 'Lieutenant-Colonel and Major-Commandants of the Seven Year War', *JSAHR*, XXXVI.

Heath, W. (1901), *Memoirs of Major-General Heath*, New York.

Henckel von Donnersmarck, V. A. (1858), *Militärischer Nachlass des Königlich preussischen Generallieutenants . . . Henckel von Donnersmarck*, 2 vols, Leipzig.

Henderson, W. O. (1963), *Studies in the Economic Policy of Frederick the Great*, London.

d'Héricourt, N. (1748), *Élémens de l'art militaire*, 2 vols, The Hague.

Higginbotham, D. (ed.) (1978), *Reconsiderations on the Revolutionary War. Selected Essays*, Westport.

Hildebrandt, C. (1829–35), *Anekdoten und Charakterzüge aus dem Leben Friedrichs des Grossen*, 6 vols, Halberstadt and Leipzig.

Hoffman, R., and Albert, P. J. (1984), *Arms and Independence. The Military Character of the American Revolution*, Charlottesville (Va.).

Hoffmann, J. (1981), *Jakob Mauvillon*, Berlin.

Högger, G. L. (1956), 'Die Briefe des Georg Leonhard Högger von St. Gallen', *Neujahrsblatt des Feuerwerker Gesellschaft in Zürich*, CXXXXVII, Zürich.

Holmes, R. (1985), *Firing Line*, London.

Un Homme de Guerre (1739), *Sentiments d'un homme de guerre sur le nouveau système du Chevalier de Folard*, Paris.

Hoppe, musketeer (1983), 'A truthful account of the bloody Battle of Zorndof', trans. Lange, M., *Seven Years War Association Newsletter*, I, no. 5, Brown Deer (Wisc.).

Houlding, J. A. (1981), *Fit for Service. The Training of the British Army, 1715–1795*, Oxford.

Hoyer, J. (1797–1800), *Geschichte der Kriegskunst*, 2 vols, Göttingen.

Hughes, B. P. (1974), *Firepower. Weapons Effectiveness on the Battlefield, 1630–1850*, London.

Hughes, T. (1947), *A Journal by Thos. Hughes*, Cambridge.

Hülsen, C. W. (1890), *Unter Friedrich dem Grossen*, Berlin.

Jähns, M. (1889–91), *Geschichte der Kriegswissenschaften vornehmlich in Deutschland*, 3 vols, Munich and Leipzig.

Jany, C. (1903), 'Die Gefechtsausbildung der preussischen Infanterie vor 1806', *Urkundliche Beiträge und Forschungen zur Geschichte des preussischen Heeres*, I, Part 5, Berlin.

Jeney, Captain (1759), *Le Partisan, ou l'art de faire la petite guerre*, The Hague.

Jespersen, K. V. (1984), 'Claude-Louis, comte de Saint-Germain (1707–1778)', in International Commission of Military History, *Soldier-Statesmen of the Age of the Enlightenment*, Manhattan (Kansas).

Johnson, H. C. (1984), 'Frederick the Great: the end of the philosopher-king concept', in International Commission of Military History, *Soldier-Statesmen of the Age of the Enlightenment*, Manhattan (Kansas).

Johnson, S. (1801–10), *The Works of Samuel Johnson, LL.D.*, 12 vols, London.

Joly de Maizeroy, M. (1773), *La Tactique discutée, et réduite à ses véritables loix*, Paris.

Jones, C. C. (ed.) (1874), *The Siege of Savannah in 1779*, Albany (N.Y.)

Kalisch, C. G. (1828), *Erinnerungen an die Schlacht bei Zorndorf*, Berlin.

Kalkreuth, F. A. (1839–40), 'Kalkreuth zu seinen Leben und zu seiner Zeit . . . Erinnerungen des General-Feldmarschalls Grafen von Kalkreuth', *Minerva*, (1839) IV, (1840) II–IV, Dresden.

Kaltenborn, R. W. (1790–1), *Briefe eines altpreussischen Officiers, verschiedene Charakterzüge Friedrichs des Einzigen betreffend*, 2 vols, Hohenzollern.

Kammen, M. (1977), 'The American Revolution in national tradition', in R. M. Brown and D. E. Fehrenbacher, *Tradition, Conflict and Modernization, Perspectives on the American Revolution*, New York.

Keegan, J. (1976), *The Face of Battle*, London.

Keens-Soper, M. (1981–2), 'The practice of a states-system', *Studies in History and Politics*, II, Lennoxville (Quebec).

Keep, J. L. (1985), *Soldiers of the Tsar. Army and Society in Russia 1462–1874*, Oxford.

Kennett, L. (1967), *The French Armies in the Seven Years War. A Study in Military Organization and Administration*, Durham (N. Carolina).

Kennett, L. (1984), 'The Chevalier de Folard and the cult of antiquity', in International Commission of Military History, *Soldier-Statesmen of the Age of the Enlightenment*, Manhattan (Kansas).

Kirkwood, R. (1910), *The Journal and Order Book of Captain Robert Kirkwood*, New York.

Kling, C. (1902–12), *Geschichte der Bekleidung, Bewaffnung und Ausrüstung des Königlich preussischen Heeres*, 3 vols, Weimar.

Koch, J. B. (1765), *Artilleristen Hand-Buch*, Frankfurt and Leipzig.

Komlos, J. (1985), 'Stature and nutrition in the Habsburg monarchy: the standard of living and economic development in the eighteenth century', *The American Historical Review*, XC, no. 5

Königsdorfer, A. A. (1792), *Bemerkungen über das Geschütz*, Dresden.

Kopperman, P. E. (1982), 'The British high command and soldiers' wives in America, 1755–1783', *JSAHR*, LX.

Krafft, J. C. (1882), 'The journal of Lieutenant John Charles Philip von Krafft', *Collections of the New York Historical Society for the Year 1882*, New York.

Kriele, J. L. (1801), *Ausführliche und Zuverlässige Historisch-Militärische Beschreibung der Schlacht bei Kunersdorf*, Berlin.

Kunisch, J. (1973), 'Der kleine Krieg. Studien zum Heerwesen des Absolutismus', *Frankfurter Hist. Abhandlungen*, IV, Wiesbaden.

Kunisch, J. (1983), 'Feldmarschall Loudon oder das Soldatenglück', *Historische Zeitschrift*, CCXXXVI, Munich.

Küster, C. D. (1791), *Bruchstück seines Campagnelebens im siebenjährigen Kriege*, Berlin.

Küster, C. D. (1793), *Characterzüge des preussischen General-Lieutenants von Saldern*, Berlin.

Lacuée de Cessac, J. G. (1785), *Le Guide des officiers particuliers en campagne*, Paris.

Lafayette, J. (1837), *Memoirs and Correspondence of General Lafayette*, 3 vols, London.

Langeron, L. A. (1895), 'Russkaya Armiya v God Smerti Ekateriny II', *Russkaya Starima*, LXXXIII, St Petersburg.

Laukhard, F. C. (1930), *Magister F. Ch. Laukhards Leben und Schicksale*, 2 vols, Stuttgart.

Lehndorff, E. (1907), *Dreissig Jahre am Hofe Friedrichs des Grossen*, Gotha.

Lehndorff, E. (1910–13), *Nachträge*, 2 vols, Gotha.

Lemcke, J. F. (1909), 'Kriegs und Fridenbildern aus den Jahren 1754–1759', *Preussische Jahrbücher*, CXXXVIII, Berlin.

Lewison, A. (1987), 'Cipières. A Village in the War-Zone: 1742–1748', paper delivered to the Colloque Historique Régional, Mouans-Sartoux.

Ligne, C. J. (1795–1811), *Mêlanges militaires, littéraires et sentimentaires*, 34 vols, Dresden.

Ligne, C. J. (1923), *Mémoires et lettres du Prince de Ligne*, Paris.

Ligne, C. J. (1928), *Fragments de l'histoire de ma vie*, 2 vols, Paris.

Linn, E. (1921), 'The Battle of Culloden – 16 April 1746', *JSAHR*, I.

Lippe-Weissenfeld, E. (1866), *Militaria aus König Friedrichs des Grossen Zeit*, Berlin.

Lister, J. (1963), 'Jeremy Lister, 10th Regiment, 1770–1783', *JSAHR*, XLI.

Loen, Monsieur (1751), *Le Soldat ou le métier de la guerre considéré comme le métier d'honneur*, Frankfurt-am-Main.

Lojewsky, J. G. (1843), *Selbstbiographie des Husaren-Obersten von . . . ky*, 2 vols, Leipzig.

Lossow, L. M. (1826), *Denkwürdigkeiten zur Charakteristik der preussischen Armee unter dem grossen König Friedrich dem Zweiten*, Glogau.

Lynn, J. A. (1984), *The Bayonets of the Republic. Motivation and Tactics in the Army of Revolutionary France*, Urbana and Chicago.

MacIntire, J. (1763), *A Military Treatise on the Discipline of the Marine Forces*, London.

Mackenzie, F. (1926) *A British Fusilier in Revolutionary Boston. Being the Diary of Lieutenant Frederick Mackenzie*, Cambridge (Mass.).

Mackenzie, F. (1960), 'The voyage of the 23rd Foot to New York in 1773', *JSAHR*, XXXVIII.

Mackesy, P. (1979), *The Coward of Minden. The Affair of Lord George Sackville*, London.

McNeill, W. H. (1978), 'The American War of Independence in World Perspective', in D. Higginbotham (ed.), *Reconsiderations on the Revolutionary War. Selected Essays*, Westport.

McNeill, W. H. (1982), *The Pursuit of Power. Technology, Armed Force and Society since A.D. 1000*, Oxford.

Mamlock, G. L. (1907), *Friedrichs des Grossen Korrespondenz mit Ärzten*, Stuttgart.

Marshall, S. L. [1947] (1978), *Men against Fire*, Gloucester (Mass.).

Martin, J. P. (1962), *Private Yankee Doodle*, Boston.

Masson, C. F. (1859), *Mémoires secrets sur la Russie pendant les règnes de Catherine II et de Paul Ier*, Paris.

Mauvillon, E. (1756), *Histoire de la dernière guerre de Bohème*, 3 vols, Amsterdam.

Mauvillon, J. (1794), *Geschichte Ferdinands Herzogs von Braunschweig-Lüneburg*, 2 vols, Leipzig.

Mediger, W. (1952), *Moskaus Weg nach Europa*, Brunswick.

Mention, L. (n.d.), *L'Armée de l'ancien régime*, Paris.

Mercoyrol de Beaulieu, J. (1915), *Campagnes de Jacques Mercoyrol de Beaulieu Capitaine au Régiment de Picardie (1743–1763)*, Paris.

Mesnil-Durand, F. J. (1755), *Projet d'un ordre françois en tactique*, Paris.

Meyer, C. (1902), *Briefe aus der Zeit des Ersten schlesischen Krieges*, Leipzig.

Middleton, R. (1985), *The Bells of Victory. The Pitt-Newcastle Ministry and the Conduct of the Seven Years War*, Cambridge.

Mirabeau, H. G. and Mauvillon, J. (1788), *Système militaire de Prusse*, London.

Mitchell, B. (1974), *The Price of Independence. A Realistic View of the American Revolution*, New York.

Montbarey, Prince (1826–7), *Mémoires autographes de M. le Prince de Montbarey*, 3 vols, Paris.

Moore, F. (1860), *Diary of the American Revolution, from Newspapers and Original Documents*, 2 vols, New York.

Moore, J. (1780), *A View of Society and Manners in France, Switzerland, and Germany*, 2 vols, London.

Mopinot de la Chapotte, A. R. (1905), *Sous Louis le Bien Aimé*, Paris.

Mottin de la Balme, M. (1776), *Élémens de tactique pour la cavallerie*, Paris.

Muenchhausen, F. (1974), *At General Howe's Side 1776–1778*, Monmouth Beach (N.J.).

Müller, J. C. [1759] (1978), *Der wohl exercirte Preussische Soldat*, Osnabrück.

Murray, J. (1951), *Letters from America 1773 to 1780*, Manchester.

Nicolai, F. (1775), *Versuch eines Grundrisses zur Bildung des Officiers*, Ulm.

Nicolai, F. (1788–92), *Anekdoten von König Friedrich II von Preussen*, 6 vols, Berlin.

Nockhern de Schorn (1783), *Idées raisonnées sur un système général et suivi de toutes les connaissances militaires*, Nuremberg.

O'Cahill, Major Baron (1787), *Der Vollkommene Officier*, Frankenthal.

An Old Officer (1760), *Cautions and Advices to Officers of the Army*, London.

Orr, M. (1972), *Dettingen, 1743*, London.

Ortmann, A. D. (1759), *Patriotische Briefe*, Berlin and Potsdam.

Paret, P. (1978), 'The relationship between the revolutionary War and European military thought and practice in the second half of the eighteenth century', in D. Higginbotham (ed.), *Reconsiderations on the Revolutionary War. Selected Essays*, Westport.

Pauli, C. F. (1758–64), *Leben grosser Helden des gegenwärtigen Krieges*, 9 vols, Halle.

Pauli, C. F. (1768), *Denkmale berühmter Feld-Herren*, Halle.

Pausch, G. (1886), *Journal of Captain Pausch*, Albany (N.Y.).

De Pauw, L. G. [1974] (1976), 'Commentary', in *Military History of the American Revolution. Proceedings of the Sixth Military History Symposium USAF Academy 1974*, Washington, D.C.

Peckham, H. H. (1974), *The Toll of Independence. Engagements and Battle Casualties of the American Revolution*, Chicago.

Le Pelletier, L. A. (1896), *Mémoires de Louis-Auguste Le Pelletier . . . 1696–1769*, Paris.

Percy, H. (1902), *Letters of Hugh Earl Percy from Boston and New York, 1774–1776*, Boston.

Pettengill, R. W. (1964), *Letters from America, being Letters of Brunswick, Hessian, and Waldeck Officers with the British Armies during the Revolution*, Port Washington.

Phillips, T. R. (1940), *Roots of Strategy*, Harrisburg (Pa).

Pictet, G. (1761), *Essai sur la tactique de l'infanterie*, 2 vols, Amsterdam.

Pirscher, J. D. (1775), *Coup d'oeil militaire*, Berlin.

Porterie, Major de la (1754), *Institutions militaires pour la cavalerie et les dragons*, Paris.

Power, Chevalier (1784), *Tableau de la guerre de la pragmatique sanction en Allemagne et Italie*, 2 vols, Berne.

Preuss, J. D. (1832–4), *Urkundenbuch zu der Lebensgeschichte Friedrichs des Grossen*, 5 vols, Berlin.

Priestley, E. J. (1974), 'Army life, 1757', *JSAHR*, LII.

Prittwitz und Gaffron, C. W. (1935), *Unter der Fahne des Herzogs von Bevern*, Berlin.

Puységur, J. F. (1749), *Art de guerre par principes et par règles*, 2 vols, Paris.

Quimby, R. S. (1957), *The Background of Napoleonic Warfare. The Theory of Military Tactics in Eighteenth-Century France*, New York.

Quincy, Chevalier, Marquis (1726), *Histoire militaire du règne de Louis le Grand, roy de France*, 8 vols, Paris

Quincy, Chevalier, Marquis, (1898–1901), *Mémoires du Chevalier de Quincy*, 3 vols, Paris.

Qureille, Chevalier (1771), *Projet d'un établissement militaire*, Altona.

Mr R ***** (1759), *Mémoires d'un militaire*, Wesel.

Rathbun, J. (1911), *The Narrative of Jonathan Rathbun of the Capture of Fort Griswold . . . 1781*, New York.

Ray, Chevalier (1895), *Réflexiones et souvenirs du Chevalier de Ray*, Paris.

Reden, J. W. (1805–6), *Feldzüge der alliirten Armee in den Jahren 1757 bis 1762*, 3 vols, Hamburg.

Reglement für die sämmentliche-Kaiserlich-Königlich Infanterie (1769), Vienna.

Retzow, F. A. (1802), *Charakteristik der wichtigsten Ereignisse des Siebenjährigen Krieges*, 2 vols, Berlin.

Richelieu, A. (1886), 'Dokumenty i Bumagi', *Sbornik Imperatorskago Russkago Istoricheskago Obshchestva*, LIV, St Petersburg.

Richelieu, A. (1918), *Mémoires authentiques du Maréchal de Richelieu (1725–1757)*, Paris.

Risch, E. (1981), *Supplying Washington's Army*, Washington, D.C.

Robin, Abbé (1783), *New Travels through North America*, Philadelphia.

Rochambeau, J. B. (1809), *Mémoires de Rochambeau*, 2 vols, Paris.

Rogers, R. (1883), *Journals of Major Richard Rogers*, Albany (N.Y.).

Rohr, F. M. (trans. and ed.) (1756), *Des Herrn Grafen Turpin von Crissé . . . Versuche über die Kriegskunst*, 2 vols, Potsdam.

Rolt, R. (1753), *Memoirs of the Life of the Late Right Honourable John Lindesay, Earl of Craufurd and Lindesay*, London.

Le Rouge, G. L. (1760), *Le Parfait Aide-de-Camp*, Paris.

Rousset, C. (1868), *Le Comte de Gisors 1732–1758*, Paris.

Rumyantsev, P. A. (1953–9), *P. A. Rumyantsev. Dokumenty*, 3 vols, Moscow.

Saint-Germain, C. L. (1779), *Mémoires de M. le comte de Saint-Germain*, Amsterdam.

Salmon, Mr (1752–3), *The Universal Traveller*, 2 vols, London.

Santa Cruz y Marcenado, A. N. [1724–30] (1735–40), *Réflexions militaires et politiques*, 12 vols, The Hague.

Savigear, P. (1981–2), 'Intervention and the balance of power: an eighteenth century war of liberation' [on Corsica], *Studies in History and Politics*, II, Lennoxville (Quebec).

Savory, R. (1964), 'The Convention of Ecluse, 1759–62', *JSAHR*, XLII.

Savory, R. (1966), *His Britannic Majesty's Army in Germany during the Seven Years War*, Oxford.

Saxe, M. [1732] (1877), *Mes rêveries*, Paris.

Scharnhorst, G. (ed.) (1782–3), *Militair Bibliothek*, I and II, Hanover.

Scharnhorst, G. (ed.) (1785), *Bibliothek für Officiere*, I, Göttingen.

Scharnhorst, G. (1813), *Über die Wirkung des Feuergewehrs*, Berlin.

Schaumburg-Lippe, W. (1977–83), (ed. K. Ochwadt), *Wilhelm Graf zu Schaumburg-Lippe. Schriften und Briefe*, 3 vols, Frankfurt-am-Main.

Scheffner, J. G. (1823), *Mein Leben*, Leipzig.

Schertel von Burtenbach, A. E. (1779), *Betrachtungen und Erfahrungen über Verschiedene Militärische Gegenstände*, Nuremberg.

Seidl, C. (1821), *Beleuchtung manches Tadels Friedrichs des Grossen*, Liegnitz.

Sellers, J. R. [1974] (1976), 'The American soldier in the American Revolution', in *Military History of the American Revolution. Proceedings of the Sixth Military History Symposium USAF Academy 1974*, Washington, D.C.

Showalter, D. E. (1983–4), 'Tactics and recruitment in eighteenth century Prussia', *Studies in History and Politics*, III, Lennoxville (Quebec).

Silva, Marquis (1778), *Pensées sur la tactique, et la stratégique*, Turin.

Simcoe, J. G. (1844), *Simcoe's Military Journal. A History of a Partisan Corps called the Queen's Rangers*, New York.

Simes, T. (1768), *The Military Medley*, London.

Simes, T. (1780a), *The Regulator: or Instructions to Form the Officer and Complete the Soldier*, London.

Simes, T. (1780b), *A Treatise on the Military Science*, London.

Skalon, D. (1902–*c.*11), *Stoletie Voennago Ministerstva*, St Petersburg. (The total number of volumes and the final date of publication cannot be established.)

Smith, W. (1766), *An Historical account of the expedition against the Ohio Indians in the Year MDCCLXIV*, Philadelphia.

Sonnenfels, J. (1783–7), *Gesammte Schriften*, 10 vols, Vienna.

Sothen, O. (1787), *Versuch einer Abhandlung von der Militairischen Reiterey*, Göttingen.

Stein, F. (1885), *Geschichte des russischen Heeres*, Hanover.

Stevenson, R. (1775), *Military Instructions for Officers Detached in the Field*, Philadelphia.

Stone, D. (1983–4), 'Patriotism and professionalism in the Polish army in the eighteenth century', *Studies in History and Politics*, III, Lennoxville (Quebec).

Strandmann, G. (1882–4), 'Zapiski Gustava fon Shtrandmana 1742–1803', *Russkaya Starina*, XXXV, XLIII, St Petersburg.

Stutzer, D. (1978), 'Das preussische Heer and seine Finanzierung in zeitgenossischer Darstellung 1740–1790', *Militärgeschichtliche Mitteilungen*, XXIV, Freiburg.

Sullivan, T. (1967), 'The common British soldier – from the journal of Thomas Sullivan, 49th Regiment of Foot', *Maryland Historical Magazine*, LXII, no. 3, Baltimore.

Täge, Pastor (1864), 'K Istorii Semiletnei Voiny. Zapiski Pastora Tege', *Russkii Arkhiv*, II, Moscow.

Tarleton, C. (1787), *A History of the Campaigns of 1780 and 1781 in the Southern Provinces of North America*, London.

Tempelhoff, G. F. (trans, and ed. from H. Lloyd), (1783–1801) *Geschichte des siebenjährigen Krieges in Duetschland*, 6 vols, Berlin.

Thacher, J. (1862), *Military Journal of the American Revolution*, Hartford (Connecticut).

Thiébault, D. (1813), *Mes souvenirs de vingt ans de séjour à Berlin*, Paris.

Tillette de Mautort (1891), *Mémoires du Chevalier Tillette de Mautort*, Paris.

Toulongeon and Hullin, generals [1786] (1881), *Une mission militaire en Prusse, en 1786*, Paris.

Townsend, J. (1846), *Some Account of . . . the Battle of Brandywine*, Philadelphia.

Tsebrikov, R. M. (1895), 'Vokrug Ochakova 1788 God', *Russkaya Starina*, LXXXXIV, St Petersburg.

Tuetey, L. (1908), *Les Officers sous l'ancien régime. Nobles roturiers*, Paris.

Turpin de Crissé, L. (1754), *Essai sur l'art de la guerre*, 2 vols, Paris.

Tylden, G. (1969), 'The accoutrements of the British infantryman, 1640 to 1940', *JSAHR*, XLVII.

Uhlig von Uhlenau, G. (1857), *Bemerkungen an die Schlacht von Kolin*, 2 vols, Vienna.

Valentine, A. (1962), *Lord George Germain*, Oxford.

Valori, G. L. [1748] (1894), 'Observations sur le service militaire du roi de Prusse', ed. R. Koser, *Forschungen zur brandenburgischen und preussischen Geschichte*, VII, Leipzig, Munich and Berlin.

Vegetius [1767], 'De Re Militari', written c. 383–450 AD, trans. J. Clarke, printed in Phillips, 1940.

Vogel, H. (1739), *Kurtzer Bericht der Artillerie-Wissenschaft*, Zürich.

Vorontsov, S. R. (1870–95), *Arkhiv Knazya Vorontsova*, 40 vols, Moscow.

Vorontsov, S. R. [1774] (1871), 'Instruktsiya Rotnym Komandiram', *Voennyi Sbornik*, LXXII, St Petersburg.

Vorontsov, S. R. [1802] (1876), 'Zapiski S. R. Vorontsova o Russkom Voiske', in S. R. Vorontsov (1870–95), *Arkhiv Knazya Vorontsova*, 40 vols, Moscow, vol. X.

Warnery, C. E. (1785–91), *Des Herrn Generalmajor von Warnery sämtliche Schriften*, 9 vols, Hanover.

Warnery, C. E. (1788), *Campagnes de Frédéric II, roi de Prusse, de 1756 à 1762*, Amsterdam.

Wengen, F. (1890), *Karl Graf zu Wied. Königlich preussischer Generallieutenant*, Gotha.

Westphalen, C. H. (1859–72), *Geschichte der Feldzüge des Herzogs Ferdinand von Braunschweig-Lüneburg*, 5 vols, Berlin.

Weymarn, H. H. (1794), 'Ueber den ersten Feldzug des russischen Kriegsheeres gegen die Preussen im Jahr 1757', *Neue Nordische Miscellaneen*, Riga.

Wiltsch, J. E. (1858), *Die Schlacht von nicht bei Rossbach oder die Schlacht auf den Feldern von und bei Reichardtswerben*, Reichardtswereben.

Wimpffen de Bournebourg, F. (1804), *The Experienced Officer*, London.

Wissel, G. (1784), *Der Jäger im Felde*, Göttingen.

Witzleben, A. (1851), *Aus Alten Parolebüchern der Berliner Garnison zur Zeit Friedrichs des Grossen*, Berlin.

Wolfe, J. (1768), *General Wolfe's Instructions to Young Officers*, London.

Wolff, C. G. (1776), *Versuch über die Sittlichen Eigenschaften und Pflichten des Soldatenstandes*, Leipzig.

Yorke, P. (1913), *The Life and Correspondence of Philip Yorke Earl of Hardwicke*, Cambridge.

Zanthier, F. W. (1778), *Versuch über die Marsche der Armeen, die Lager, Schlachten und den Operations-Plan*, Dresden.

Zanthier, F. W. (1783), *Versuche über die Lehre von Detaschements*, Dresden.

Zedlitz, C. A. (1776), *Le Patriotisme considéré comme objet d'éducation dans les états monarchiques*, Berlin.

Zimmerman, J. G. (1790), *Fragmente über Friedrich den Grossen*, 3 vols, Leipzig.

Zottmann, A. (1937), *Die Wirthschaftspolitik Friedrichs des Grossen. Mit besonderer Berücksichtigung der Kriegswirtschaft*, Leipzig and Vienna.

Index

N.B. Thematic headings are grouped under 'Armies', and 'Warfare in the eighteenth century'